'The ongoing transformation of China is cultural and spatial as much as economic and political. This remarkable book brings all these dimensions together and integrates them into a coherent theoretical framework supported by empirical observation. A must-read for everybody interested in the scholarly analysis of China, as well as cutting edge contributions in cultural theory.'

Manuel Castells, Wallis Annenberg Chair of Communication Technology and Society, University of Southern California

'Scott Lash, Michael Keith and colleagues have an entirely original understanding of China which makes this book rare, relevant and new.'

Rem Koolhaas, Founding Partner, Office of Metropolitan Architecture / AMO

'Is there a China model? Is the economic development in China another version of neoliberalism or a socialist market economy? The authors of this book develop their argument that China is constructing its own version of capitalism by combining broad historical observations and sophisticated theoretical analysis. This is an inspiring intervention in the ongoing debate on China's past, present and future.'

Wang Hui, author of China's New Order, The Politics of Imagining Asia *and* The End of the Revolution

CHINA CONSTRUCTING CAPITALISM

The GDP of China has been growing at over ten per cent annually since 1978, but this has only come to widespread notice in the past decade.

The received wisdom about China has been largely of two types, both of which – more or less – understand China in the context of neoliberalism. The more business- or business studies-orientated literature seems to argue that if China does not adapt the rule of clear and distinct property and contract law – in short, of Western institutions – its economy will stall.

The second set of voices is more clearly from the left, arguing that the Chinese economy, and city, is neoliberal. For them, China does not diverge widely from the Anglo-American model that, from 2008, has brought the world economy to its knees.

China Constructing Capitalism takes issue with these analyses. The authors argue that it is not Western neoliberalism that is constructing the Chinese economy, but instead that China is constructing capitalism anew. The two central theses of their argument are:

- Economic life – neoliberal economic life is *individualised* and *disembedded*, while the China model is *relational* and *situated*.
- Urban change – China has created a form of 'local state capitalism', which stands in contrast to neoliberal versions of the city.

This book analyses China as a 'risk culture', examining, among other factors, Chinese firms and political ties, property development, migrant urbanisms and share-trading rooms. It scrutinises the ever-present shadow of the risk-averse (yet uncertainty-creating) state. *China Constructing Capitalism* is a must-read for social scientists, policy-makers and investors.

Michael Keith is Director of the Centre on Migration, Policy and Society and holds a personal chair in the Department of Anthropology at the University of Oxford.

Scott Lash is Professor of Sociology and Director of the Centre for Cultural Studies at Goldsmiths College, University of London.

Jakob Arnoldi is Professor at Aarhus University, School of Business and Social Sciences, Department of Business Administration. He is also affiliated with the Sino-Danish Center for Education and Research.

Tyler Rooker is Lecturer in Contemporary Chinese Studies at the University of Nottingham.

International library of sociology

Founded by Karl Mannheim
Editor: John Urry, *Lancaster University*

Recent publications in this series include:

Risk and Technological Culture
Towards a sociology of virulence
Joost Van Loon

Reconnecting Culture, Technology and Nature
Mike Michael

Advertising Myths
The strange half lives of images and commodities
Anne M. Cronin

Adorno on Popular Culture
Robert R. Witkin

Consuming the Caribbean
From arkwarks to zombies
Mimi Sheller

Between Sex and Power
Family in the world, 1900–2000
Goran Therborn

States of Knowledge
The co-production of social science and social order
Sheila Jasanoff

After Method
Mess in social science research
John Law

Brands
Logos of the global economy
Celia Lury

The Culture of Exception
Sociology facing the camp
Bülent Diken and Carsten Bagge Laustsen

Visual Worlds
John Hall, Blake Stimson and Lisa Tamiris Becker

Time, Innovation and Mobilities
Travel in technological cultures
Peter Frank Peters

Complexity and Social Movements
Multitudes acting at the edge of chaos
Ian Welsh and Graeme Chesters

Qualitative Complexity
Ecology, cognitive processes and the re-emergence of structures in post-humanist social theory
Chris Jenks and John Smith

Theories of the Information Society, 3rd Edition
Frank Webster

Crime and Punishment in Contemporary Culture
Claire Grant

Mediating Nature
Nils Lindahl Elliot

CHINA CONSTRUCTING CAPITALISM

Economic life and urban change

Michael Keith, Scott Lash, Jakob Arnoldi and Tyler Rooker

LONDON AND NEW YORK

First published 2014
by Routledge
2 Park Square, Milton Park, Abingdon, Oxon OX14 4RN

and by Routledge
711 Third Avenue, New York, NY 10017

Routledge is an imprint of the Taylor & Francis Group, an informa business

British Library Cataloguing in Publication Data
A catalogue record for this book is available from the British Library

Library of Congress Cataloging-in-Publication Data
Keith, Michael, 1960-
China constructing capitalism : economic life and urban change /
Michael Keith, Scott Lash, Jakob Arnoldi and Tyler Rooker. -- First Edition.
pages cm. -- (International library of sociology)
Includes bibliographical references and index.
ISBN 978-0-415-49705-3 (hardback) -- ISBN 978-0-415-49706-0 (pbk.)
-- ISBN 978-0-203-87739-5 (ebook) 1. China--Economic policy--
21st century. 2. Urban policy--China. I. Title.
HC427.95.K457 2013
330.951--dc23
2013007421

ISBN: 978-0-415-49705-3 (hbk)
ISBN: 978-0-415-49706-0 (pbk)
ISBN: 978-0-203-87739-5 (ebk)

Typeset in Bembo
by FiSH Books Ltd, Enfield
Printed by Bell & Bain Ltd, Glasgow

CONTENTS

LIST OF ILLUSTRATIONS

Figures

Tables

ACKNOWLEDGEMENTS AND DEDICATION

This volume represents the cumulative effort of the full team of authors over a long time. It has a biography of almost ten years, inspired by happenstance and serendipity as much as the attempt to synthesise scholarship from both China and the West and thinking from disciplines across the social sciences. There are consequently many debts incurred in the translating of a major research project into an academic monograph. One of the authors (Rooker) had been doing intensive research in China since the early 1990s. But in a sense the book started when another one of us (Lash) was asked to come to China by the architect Rem Koolhaas to work on a bid to write the conceptual masterplan for the 2010 Shanghai Expo. This was around Christmas 2002 when the Office for Metropolitan Architecture was about to build the controversial China Central Television (CCTV) building. Here we encountered Shanghai architect and now USC Dean Ma Qingyun. Both Koolhaas and Ma have fed our work with thoughts, arguments and ideas. By 2004, Lash, Keith and Arnoldi had joined to put together a proposal for research in China. And we are grateful that a Shanghai base for five years was subsequently supported by the UK Economic and Social Research Council (ESRC) World Economy and Finance Programme (WEF). We would like to thank the ESRC – and WEF Programme director John Driffill – for their very generous support of the project, which made this book possible. The project was entitled 'Risk Culture in China: An Economic Sociology'. Harrison White, whom we would also like to thank, inspired this proposal. The focus was further supported by the ESRC's funding of a small grant that developed some of the links between social relationality and economic externalities in an ESRC 'Rising Powers' research network that linked China colleagues with thinkers in Delhi, Mumbai and Bangalore, principally through the good offices of Ravi Sundaram and his colleagues at Sarai (in the Centre for the Study of Developing Societies in Delhi) but also through the committed and thoughtful contributions of Sandeep Kapur,

Will Davies and Li Shiqiao and other participants contributing to events in Beijing, Delhi and London including John Urry, Geoff Mulgan, Maliq Simone, Saskia Sassen and Martin Wolf. Tyler Rooker joined us early on as project Research Associate. He has been the motor of all of this research and has also joined us as co-author. In 2005, a Royal Society of the Arts trip to Guangdong with artists such as Jeremy Deller, brought us into contact with Jiang Jun and Doreen Heng Liu, who have had a fundamental impact on this book. Through Heng Liu, we came to engage with Shenzhen architects Liu Xiaodu and Meng Yan, and curator Ou Ning and with their collaboration gained a great deal from presenting urban strands of the work at successive architecture biennales in Hong Kong and Shenzhen. Jiang Jun, editor at the time of the hothouse journal *Urban China*, invariably gave generously of his time and contacts throughout and we have spent many days together in the urban spaces of Chongqing, Tianjin and Shenzhen. In 2003 Mike Featherstone of *Theory, Culture & Society* brokered an introduction to Wang Xioaming. Wang's Shanghai University Centre for Contemporary Cultural Studies provided research assistantship, an institutional base and a forum for intellectual exchange. Wang introduced us to the Shenzhen Academy of Social Sciences who we worked integrally with in our urban research in Shenzhen. Wang Xiaoming was also an entry for us to China's intellectual left, which had formed around the journal 读书。 Here we met and engaged with Wang Hui, Cui Zhiyuan and Huang Ping, all of whom gave generously of their time in sharing their ideas. As anyone can see in this book's text, Cui's thinking on property and his personal experience in Chongqing has been an inspiration. We read this as consistent with Wang's partly neo-Confucian understanding of Chinese modernity, which has greatly influenced the idea of 'relationality' in this book. We also want to thank colleagues at the ESRC Centre on Migration, Policy and Society and particularly Michele Drasdo for all their support.

In Shanghai, the tutelage, assistance and guidance of Wang Xiaoming was invaluable. But also his colleagues became both friends and supporters of the project. The help, solidarity and patience of Yi Yinjoing in supporting the research and all its problems ultimately made it possible. Further, Jolin, Xiao Shao, Zhu Shanjie and Yang Ge made life in Shanghai pleasurable and facilitated more than a few insights. Xu Xiaohong was a touchstone from overseas and David Nieh and Liu Yuyang provided invaluable inside views of the interplay of developers, planners and architects. Also much appreciation to Kitten Wang, Zeng Biao and Sam Sun. In addition the help of numerous others facilitated the multi-local nature of research: in Beijing – Zhu Shanjie, Gao Bingzhong, Michael Pettis, Kou Shuangxiang, Daping, Chen Yaling, Yu Laoshi; in Shenzhen – Le Zheng, Chen Chuzhang, Liu Xiaodu, Meng Yan, Wang Hui (Urbanus), Huang Weiwen; in Wenzhou – Xia Caiguo; and in Chongqing – *Urban China* team and UFIDA. Finally, the belief and ongoing support of Liu Xin and Nancy Chen was crucial to continuing the project to the end.

Jakob Arnoldi in particular would like to acknowledge financial support received from the Sino-Danish University Center, which furthered his personal contribution. He is furthermore grateful for help and assistance from Meng Sun and Si Liu. He would like to thank Joy Zhang, Chaohong Na and especially Xin Chen for invaluable input and thought-provoking discussions. Arnoldi owes special thanks to Anders Ryom Villadsen for collaboration and help and for generously letting him draw on data that was collected jointly. Finally, thanks are due to all the anonymous interviewees who generously took time to let themselves be interviewed.

Few co-authored books will have featured the level of intense intellectual exchange and co-working that *China Constructing Capitalism* has. In this sense we are all authors of the whole book. But inevitably some chapters are more closely the work of particular members of the team. Scott Lash was principally responsible for chapters on the synthesis of China and Western thought, for the risk biographies and much of the conclusion, Jakob Arnoldi for the chapters on economic institutions, financial development, and political ties. Michael Keith developed the work on property markets, migration and urban change. Tyler Rooker facilitated almost all of the fieldwork and conducted the two lengthy ethnographies in the trading room and through long-term placements in real estate companies. And finally as with all acknowledgements, if the debts and the contributions were plural the responsibility for any errors remains with the authors alone. The book is dedicated to the two children born during the project to Tyler Rooker and his wife Jasmine – Mia and Ryan – whose births were its greatest outcome, and whose patience will hopefully be rewarded.

INTRODUCTION

China versus neoliberalism

According to International Monetary Fund estimates, China's gross domestic product has grown at an average rate of 9.91% per annum from 1978 to 2012. The Organisation for Economic Co-operation and Development Economic Outlook in April 2013 forecasts that China will surpass the US in Gross Domestic Product (GDP) adjusted for purchasing power parity by 2017. Gross domestic product projections in the next decade have sharpened this focus. In this context thinking about China has been largely of two types, both that more or less understand China in the context of neoliberalism. The first of these is the more business- or business studies-orientated literature, for example, of Will Hutton (2008) or Yasheng Huang (2005, 2008). This literature seems to argue that if China does not adapt the rule of law, of clear and distinct property and contract law, in line with Western institutions, that its economy will stall. The second set of voices are more clearly from the political left – from more academic books in sociology, cultural and urban studies, such as Mike Davis (2006) in *Planet of the Slums*, David Harvey (2005) in his *Brief History of Neoliberalism* and Aihwa Ong (2006). These voices argue that the Chinese economy and city – and Davis and Harvey are urbanists – is indeed neoliberal. For them, however, this is not the solution, but, indeed, the problem. They argue that China does not diverge widely from the Anglo–American model that from 2008 has brought the world economy to its knees. It is understandable that these analysts should think this because in fact China's not-even-close to precedented 34-year long-wave of growth coincided with the end of the Cultural Revolution, the decline of Maoism and the rise of Deng Xiaoping. The rise of Deng in 1978 neatly coincided with the emergence of the Western neoliberalism of Margaret Thatcher and Ronald Reagan after their successful elections in 1979 and 1980, respectively. In the West, the rise of Thatcher and Reagan heralded the demise of social democracy, of some 30 years of social democratic hegemony – in China the demise of a Communist form of socialism.

This book takes issue with all of the above analysts. We argue that it is not Western neoliberalism that is constructing the Chinese economy but instead that China is constructing capitalism anew. We make this case via two central theses: one that addresses economic life and the other that is about urban change. The economic life thesis sets itself up against Western neoclassical economics. It looks not at the disembedded actor of neoclassical economics but instead at surrounding economic forms of life, at economic *cultures*. We can describe this thesis in terms of eight aspects that effectively constitute it as an ideal type of a sort of 'China model' that stands in contrast to a 'neoliberal model'. Here the neoliberal economic life is individualised and disembedded while the China model is *relational* and *situated*.

The eight aspects of this ideal type are as follows:

1 Economic actor or forms of economic life
2 Rationalism v empiricism
3 Not performativity
4 Encountering Weber
5 Confucianism and Daoism
6 Internal and external
7 Property
8 Risk

Economic life

Economic actor or forms of economic life?

The neoliberal model is rooted in neoclassical economics. The Chinese model stands opposed to neoclassical economics and its notion of the disembedded economic actor. This neoclassical model has been performative in constituting a sort of Western neoliberal economic culture. Whereas neoliberal economic culture features the disembedded actor, Chinese economic culture privileges not this disembedded goal-directed actor, but the web of economic life that surrounds economic action. Hence the subtitle of this book is not economic action but economic *life*.

Rationalism versus 'empiricism'

The neoclassical economic actor is a rational actor, and here we mean rational literally in the sense of rationalism. He/she thus takes a set of *a priori* rules to the marketplace. This is a Newtonian model, a sort of positivistic model in which time is reversible, and there is no path dependency. We saw this 'rationalism' in the all-at-once interventions, with privatisations, public spending cuts and opening of capital markets that have been so widespread from the 1980s. Here it is a question of taking a ready-made and disembedded model and applying it as a blueprint. We saw in the UK under the Thatcher government, and also in Chicago School all-at-once interventions in Russia, Chile and Argentina. China has preferred instead a gradualism, a step-by-step process based not on *a priori* rules, but a more empirical or better 'empiricist', *a posteriori* process of economic change.

Not performativity

Neoliberal economies have often operated through the performative intervention of economic theory in material economies. In China, although lip service is given to such theories, in day-to-day economic activity they are typically non-performative; Chicago School theory or Nobel Prize-winning theories of complex financial products and do not make the same sort of performative intervention.

Encountering Weber

Sociologists will know that Max Weber's notion of rational social action is consistent with the neoclassical economic actor. Weber's Protestant entrepreneur was similarly disembedded and transcendental in terms of material life. The Chinese model as Weber himself noted was based in an amalgam of, not transcendent assumptions of Protestantism but immanentist Daoism and Confucianism. These still underpin the Chinese model. But Weber's China that did not work at the turn of the nineteenth century seems to be eminently successful at the start of the twenty-first century.

Confucianism and Daoism

From Confucianism, the Chinese model takes not neoliberal individualism, but the more relational 'filiality', i.e. the framework of filial relations between teacher and student, father and son, etc. It also draws on a secularised form of Confucian rites and ceremonies. Rites are *li* (礼, 禮) and gifts are *liwu* (礼物, 禮物). *Wu* means thing: a gift hence is a 'ritual thing'. What this implies is that secularised economic life is not just commodity exchange but the superimposition of both gift and commodity exchange. Daoism will oppose to neoclassical economic action its *wu wei* of non-action. This *wu wei* does mean non-action in the sense of the goal-directed, the subject-verb-object of the rational actor. This actor comes to a situation purposively, with his aims and objectives already decided. In Mandarin this would not be *wu wei*, but *you wei* (有为). The *wu wei* points instead to a web of background activities. So, in Daoism, the *you wei* of the rational economic actor tends to dissipate and disintegrate onto this *wu wei*. Or the transcendental economic actor disintegrates onto the immanent flux and flow of the *wu wei*. This flux and flow instead constitutes a situation: a propensity that itself generates new emerging forms of economic action.

Internal and external

Neoclassical economics features the individual economic actor or economic exchange. The unintended consequences of such exchange are understood as 'externalities'. Neoliberalism suggests we solve the problem of 'social costs' through well-defined property rights that can internalise these externalities. Neo-Keynesians such as Paul Krugman or Joseph Stiglitz will understand them in terms of the necessity of social goods or public goods. But Krugman and Stiglitz still start from neoclassical assumptions, i.e. from the 'internal' of disembedded actor and exchange. In the Chinese model you start not from the internal of the economic actor or exchange but from the externalities themselves, from the forms of life (from the forms of social and natural life) that surround the exchange.

Property

Neoliberal, well-defined property rights are – almost in a Cartesian sense – 'clear and distinct'. Clear and distinct is who and what is included in ownership of such property and who and what is excluded. This involves a certain 'unbundling' of rights. But even in the Western tradition, property historically involves a 'bundle of rights' involving many claims on use, transfer and enforcement. In China a number of legal or quasi-legal persons have rights in the same unit of property (Cui 1998) and it is more common for property rights to be *ambiguous* as well as *plural*. The boundary between what (who) is internal and what (who) is external to a given unit of property thickens, complexifies, becomes semi-permeable and altogether less transparent. In this sense property is relational; a Moebius strip rather than a simple dichotomy of inside and outside. Unbundling individualises property: bundling makes property relational.

Risk

Non-relational risk in the Western ideal type is individualised. In the China model, as relational, risk is shared: especially between the generations of a family. Risk is also shared in long-term *guanxi*-like business relations. Western-model risk is based again on a disembedded goal-directed risk-taking social actor. What happens then if we substitute Daoist assumptions for our Christian and Cartesian prejudices? The classical actor of Western risk becomes always at the same time in a process of disintegration, of becoming multiple into the flux and flow of the *wu wei*. This is not the Western juxtaposition of disordered materiality and ordering transcendental actor. In the 'Daoist ethos' the actor is always involved in a process of becoming immanent and becoming multiple, hence not very much in control. In place of the Protestant Ethic's disordered matter, on the Daoist ethos, matter is always already incipiently ordered as the propensity of the *wu wei* in generating new actualities. In the West, as Harrison White (2002) has observed, markets themselves – even if they are complex metastable systems – offer entrepreneurs a space of relative security: otherwise they would not undertake the uncertainty of investment. In China, partly due to seemingly arbitrary state intervention, markets are not such a basis of relative security. Instead it is the relationality in the aforementioned web of activities, the partial gift exchange of *guanxi* relations that constitute such security.

China constructing capitalism is also China constructing urbanism. China constructing urbanism again stands in contrast to neoliberal versions of the city. Here we note six ideal-typical processes that generate a sense of the 'city as propensity'. These add up to what can be seen as a single phenomenon, what we call 'local state capitalism'. This local state capitalism thesis is about urban *change* and the six aspects are as follows:

1   Local-state private entrepreneurs – real estate
2   Complex property and experimental governance of relational markets
3   A step change in flows of capital and labour to the cities
4   Internal and external – governance autonomies below the level of the national
5   From *danwei* to *xiaoqu*
6   *Hukou*, migrants and new instituions of social control

Local state capitalism

Local-state private entrepreneurs – real estate

Of all the relationalities in contemporary China, the pivotal one may be between the local state and private sector entrepreneurs. This is complex too because often what look like local state firms are run as private firms, and what look like private companies have strong local state participation. Very often local government figures become private entrepreneurs. The relation between local government and private firms is typically long term, only quasi-contractual. It is a diffuse relation embracing commodity exchange and gift exchange. It involves *guanxi*: often the corruption it comprises is an extension of this *guanxi*.[1] It involves ties of not just contract but of affect. This local state–private firm relation is 'actual' at the same time as comprising – in its processual nature – an underlying virtuality.

The most central of the above relations is of municipal and district government with property (especially private-housing) developers. Municipal government gains significant revenues by selling land leaseholds and working through these developers. In this the national state holds on to the freehold but local government disposes of the leasehold. The developers then build gated purchase residential housing, or *xiaoqu*, typically a good distance from the city centre. Lower income workers are often displaced from the city centre and they relocate in this housing. Displacement can be unpleasant but the new flats may be twice or more the size of what they had in the city centre. Middle class migrants to the city also live in such *xiaoqu*, but in more expensive districts. Since 1997, mortgages have become ubiquitous. Local state government and party leaders are promoted on the basis of growth. They invest huge sums of money from these leasehold sales chiefly into infrastructure, such as urban rapid transit systems in cities such as Beijing and Shanghai. This suburban and ex-urban metro system carries such displaced workers from these far suburbs to jobs in the city. The local state typically overspends: it creates special purpose vehicles to promote city change. Local state debt is considerable, unquantified and frequently masked by local government.

Complex property and experimental governance of relational markets

Relational markets involve complex property relations. Local state capitalism emerges through experimental models at different scales of urban governance. State prerogatives and market freedoms revolve around different combinations of the rights associated with property ownership. Rural property is village property. It is collectively held and in this sense differs from urban state-owned property. This persists in some of the 'urban villages' (*chengzhongcun*), most strikingly in cities such as Shenzhen. In some cases property ownership, say, of commercial premises without a formal leasehold, persists year on year, often dependent on good relations with local district government. In some cases, a number of parties have claims on the same unit of property. For example, space in the art district in Shanghai, *Moganshan Lu*, is at the same time owned by an art gallery, a local-state-sector textile firm from which the gallery rents the property, by a Hong Kong property developer who is not yet allowed to build, by a combination of district council, municipal council and national state, and by residents who may have protested and for the moment cannot be moved out. All have some rights in this bit of property. Property involves bundles of rights linked to the different aspects of property rights (classically those of fungibility [exchange], use, development prerogatives and exclusion, but sometimes pluralised into many more individual rights). Western ideal typical property institutionalises clarity (and preferably singularity) of the bundles of rights in property, China pluralises the combinatory forms of property prerogatives between states and markets. In this plurality lies its complexity.

A step change in flows of capital and labour to the cities

Economic development and urbanisation are linked; the former realised through the latter. The integration of city dynamics and the imperatives of economic change raise analytical questions about both the trajectories of economic change and the sustainability of city form. More straightforwardly, the recent decades have witnessed massive flows of capital and labour to the cities as China's urban population is predicted to top 1 billion in the next 20 years and the country hosts a growing number of both megacities and medium-size urban agglomerations. By 2025, China is predicted to have 225 cities with one million people living in them (Europe has 35 today).

Internal and external – governance autonomies below the level of the national.

Economists often see urban space in terms of the externalities generated from economic activity, from economic exchanges. This is mostly a question of positive externalities. Social goods can be created by such positive externalities. These are side effects of, say, the clustering of a highly skilled labour force. These become the supply side of a labour market, a well-paid consumer market; they are a basis for the arts, etc. In Chinese urbanism this relation between internal and external is more complex. These configurations are particularly powerful at the level of the district where the power of new combinations of state and market mediate between global expertise in city building and local structures of autonomous governance; translating incalculable metropolitan uncertainty into calculable urban risks that can be managed in city growth models. This is the city as frame, the city as propensity.

From danwei *to* xiaoqu

This is about not just housing but urban life more generally. The *danwei* or work-unit was controller of all sorts of resource allocation. It allocated not just housing, but education, jobs, consumption goods, health, pensions, all of these aspects of urban life. *Danwei* buildings displaced, for example, alley-and-courtyard housing such as Beijing's *hutong* and Shanghai's *longtang*, and bungalow housing from the late 1950s. *Danwei* were the Communist form of housing. Alley-and-courtyard housing and bungalows were smaller one to three stories and located typically close to urban centres; *danwei* a bit taller, four to seven stories and located in the just surrounding districts, often near a middle ring road, while many of the *xiaoqu* are ten to 15 stories and are often located in the further suburbs, near outer ring roads. *Xiaoqu* mortgages pervaded very quickly from about 15 years ago. They have revived the filiality of the three-generational family and risk-sharing practices along the generations of this family.

Hukou, *migrants and new institutions of social control*

Central to what constitutes local state capitalism are the residual consequences of the *hukou* or residence permit. *Hukou* reflects location and type of work. Rural and urban *hukou* consequently differ significantly. There remains a great deal of difference between urban *hukou* in terms of quantity and quality of welfare resources. With the decline of the *danwei*, welfare–pensions, education and health service provision are often taken over by municipal government and you need, say, a Shanghai *hukou* to get full benefits. Migrants in principle are not eligible for this, yet their influx hugely contributes to the dynamism of local states. These migrants comprise not just the floating population of peasants that become factory workers, but also the armies of middle class incomers who come to universities and colleges in China's major cities and then stay on to work as engineers, traders and mid-level managers.

New 'social' models: the city as propensity

From the 1980s, such local state capitalism was a question of creating zones for private enterprise, for example, the Special Economic Zones (SEZs) developed from the 1980s onwards. More recently, more of a role for public investment and possibly social equality has begun to emerge in for example the local state investment in Shanghai Pudong in the nineties and in new social housing since 2011 and very recently Chongqing. The 'Chongqing Model' from 2007 has aimed to mitigate rural–urban disparities by extending Chongqing city *hukou* rights to large numbers of migrants, and in effect taxing property developers in constructing what is a *social* model. But it is an *urban* social model. In each case the introduction of new policies is on a local level that, if successful, is envisaged as spreading to others. Chongqing, following the Bo Xilai scandal[2], has of course now come very much more under central government control. Yet a Chongqing-like framework of urban–rural integration, development of a rental market and public investment for private sector growth is likely to be introduced more widely in future years. Chinese Communist Party leadership knows lower levels of growth are inevitable, and rebalancing towards consumption and increase of social welfare will be necessary.

Social theory: 'Chinese empiricism'

Now enter two very different kinds of thinkers – Michel Foucault (2008) and Adam Smith. Foucault's lectures from the late 1970s, and especially the *Birth of Biopolitics*, have become canonical for the understanding of neoliberalism.[3] Whereas for say, Davis and Harvey, neoliberalism is just an extension a radicalisation of classical Smithian liberalism, Foucault sees neoliberalism in fundamental violation of and in contradiction to the principles of liberalism. If neoliberalism in the form of, e.g. the Chicago School, is the villain of Foucault bio-politics, then liberalism and indeed Adam Smith are its hero. Smith is at the centre of the birth of bio-politics, which is also the birth of modernity. Foucault's Smith gives us, at the same time, Adam Ferguson and the emergence of civil society. Here Foucault is above all a *critical* theorist. Foucault was very much aware of Horkheimer and Adorno's (1997) *Dialectic of Enlightenment*, in which enlightenment itself was an opening, a critique of myth and the ancien regime. Here – and Georg Simmel's urbanism is of a piece with this – the initial moment of enlightenment was the positivity of markets, democracy and civil society. For Foucault, the birth of bio-politics is in part a sort of Scottish Enlightenment – Hume, Smith, Ferguson – operating against the old regime of Machiavellian and Westphalian 'sovereignty', and constituting instead a new bio-political regime of political economy and what Foucault calls 'population'. In this context we need to stress *political economy*: for the last chapter of Foucault's book is an homage to political economy, liberalism and Smith.

We think Foucault and Smith can can help us understand China. Here we want to take our distances also from the actor-network theory of Bruno Latour and Michel Callon. Callon's (1998) focus is on how economics and in particular neoliberal economic thinking are performative in the economy. He may be right in the context of Western economies, in which the disaster of financial markets may owe a lot to the interventions of, for example, complex financial products innovators, Nobel Prize winners Merton and Scholes (Mackenzie 2003). There have been such performative interventions of neoliberal (Chicago) economics notably in Russia, Argentina and Chile with mixed success. But there has not been the same kind of performative intervention in the Chinese economy. In fact, China's success may have been partly due to the absence of such performativity. Actor-network theory, in its focus on the micro-sociology of everyday life and the detail of say electronic share and bond trading, may have paid insufficient attention to the bigger picture of *political* economy. This book is very much in the tradition of such political economy. Actor-network work's focus is on the micro-level, while political economy entails a now unfashionable sort of macro-sociology. Actor-network sociology is in a very important sense apolitical. Its pervasion as almost the dominant paradigm of the past 15 years would seem to be indicative of sociology abandoning its critical project. This might be fine in an age of plenty. It may be a problem in an age of austerity. Moreover, we think a critical political economy can tell us a lot about China.

Foucault contrasted liberalism's *political* economy and Smithian bio-politics to neoliberalism's neoclassical economics. Here if liberalism[4] gave us the birth of a bio-political opening, neoliberalism signals a mode of bio-political domination. Political economy is vastly different from neoclassical economics. For one thing it is political, and Smith (2002) was perhaps first and foremost a political philosopher. His *Theory of the Moral Sentiments* preceded *The Wealth of Nations* (2008) by some 20 years, and even the latter is political in its address of the *Nationalökonomie*. Political economy could in this sense be a mode of critique while neoclassical economics bequeaths a mode of bio-political domination. This is where the benchmark work, *Adam Smith in Beijing* by the late Giovanni Arrighi (2009) makes its intervention. Arrighi's book has many flaws. It, for example, pays insufficient attention to exploitative labour regimes and phenomena of dispossession in China. But it is in our view a major contribution to both critical sociology and political economy. Arrighi's book, alongside Andre Gunder Frank's (1998) remarkably prescient *Re-Orient,* focused on the fact that China and India were economically far ahead of the West until the late-eighteenth century. Smith too was aware of this. If Karl Marx was the theorist of capital, then Arrighi's Adam Smith was the theorist of *markets.* Arrighi, close to Immanuel Wallerstein, was very much influenced by Fernand Braudel (1993), whose *Méditerranée* argued that Western economic space was for some three hundred years, 1500–1800, much more a question of markets than of capitalism. Smith understood how widespread markets were in the Song and Ming Dynasties, some half-millennium before their pervasion in the West. Smith's *Moral Sentiments* preceded Marx's (2005) *Capital* by 110 years. Marx himself understood the 'real subsumption' of labour by capital only with the advent of what he called *die grobe Industrie.* There was a lot of this large-scale industry about in Britain when Marx wrote *Capital.* In the age of Smith's *Moral Sentiments* – and even in *The Wealth of Nations* Smith talks about trade as much as production – there were mostly markets. Marx, looking at capitalist domination, wrote the critique of political economy. With Smith, and against both neoliberalism and capitalism, we can perhaps think instead of, not the critique of political economy and of a critical political economy.

Arrighi and Smith counterpose China's early proliferation of internal markets and peaceful economic growth to the very violent modernity of the West. For Arrighi, Western primitive accumulation of capital operated through raiding the Americas for precious metals to sell to China and India in exchange for crafted manufactured products. Arrighi contrasts the West's capitalist and industrial revolution to China's and Japan's 'industrious revolution'. The first was based on the domination of capital, the second on the predominance of (markets and) labour. The precedent for this, in contrast to extensive and land-intensive Western farming, is rice cultivation and labour-intensive farming, especially as during the Song Dynasty China's centre starts to move from the wheat-farming Yellow River to the rice-producing Yangzi. Intensive cultivation also meant sticking closely to budget and a degree of self-management. Even now, China is much more labour-intensive than the West. This labour-intensity is not just about armies of migrant workers, but also the sort of middle-salaried, very highly skilled armies of engineers and accountants and often nowadays English-speaking traders, university educated, who are a pivot of the contemporary Chinese economy.

China's modernity: questioning Max Weber

The question of Smithian markets is at the same time the question of Chinese modernity. Wang Hui has comprehensively captured this in his four-volume *The Rise of Modern Chinese Thought* (现代中国思想的兴起).[5] Here we see that in China the rise of the modern may be rather more a question of (Smithian) markets than (Marxo-Weberian) capitalism. The *Protestant Ethic* may have given us the rise of capitalism. But for Wang something like a neo-Confucian ethic gave rise to an alternative modernity of not capitalism but markets. At the turn of the last millennium, Song Dynasty modernity was not just a matter of markets, but also a proliferation of science and the arts and a more general liberal openness. This is a bit of a precursor to Adam Ferguson's civil society, but with its Confucian basis it is very different from civil society. With great respect to Weber's *Religion of China*, Chinese modernity is very *un*Weberian. For Weber, Confucianism and Daoism made modernity impossible in China: for Wang they have been a basis of China's modernity.[6]

Weber's (1991) theses in *Die Wirtschaftsethik der Weltreligionen* are very much of a piece with his action theory. The Protestant entrepreneur provided the frame for Weber's disembedded, rationally calculating social actor. From this viewpoint, the individual's action is at centre stage: the actor comes to a situation with his/her means and ends already decided in a kind of toolbox. This stands in contrast to the Wang Hui's implicitly neo-Confucian or Francois Jullien's (1999) neo-Daoist rendering of subjectivity in China. Perhaps it is not in spite of but because of the 'religion of China', because of the neo-Daoist and neo-Confucian currents in the Chinese habitus, that contemporary China has experienced such growth. Why dynamised growth in Nineteenth century Europe is radically different from growth's cultural dynamic in the twenty-first century global economy. Alongside the Weberian means-ends rational actor we see Daoism's *wu wei* (無為) of non-action. This *wu wei* means, not action in the Western, goal-directed sense of the disembedded rationally calculating actor, but instead something like a web of embedded *activities,* which are very situation dependent. It is not a mode of action that is taken from the outside of a situation, but a web of activities constituting a situation from which this action emerges. It is much less rationalist and much more 'empiricist' than Weber's instrumental- and value-rational action. It is already empiricist, in that what counts is less a set of rules than – like in the empiricism of English Common Law – the last time, the last instance or a string of instances. Weber's actor privileges the foreground: the Protestant entrepreneur working, not from Roman Catholic good deeds: but from faith alone, trying to prove that he will be saved through worldly success. Indeed Weber's actor has to disembed from the profane in order to have any chance of redemption in the sacred. Confucian- and neo-Confucian culture privileges not the foreground but instead a background whose lineage, as Wang notes, is 'rites and music', which are a set of surrounding actives again from which action emerges. These are embedded activities and not disembedded action. It should be noted that in the Confucian Rites and Ceremonies the *yili* (仪礼), the *li* of *yili*, means in the first instance as much 'gift' as rites. A gift is literally a *liwu* 礼物, a 'gift-thing'. An important aspect of Chinese economic life is that gift-giving and economic transactions are not as separated as they are in the West. In this Marcel Mauss's (2011) gift economy and commodity economy are much more one and the same thing: the economy, in other words, is somehow already cultural.

Weber's instrumentally rational social actor was quite similar to the assumptions of just-emerging marginalist, neoclassical economics. We are back to Foucault and the liberal/neoliberal juxtaposition, paralleling the juxtaposition of political econo-my versus neoclassical economics. To repeat, whereas classical political economy is empiricist, neoclassical economics is irreducibly rationalist. The empiricism of David Hume (2007) was Smith's most profound influence. In empiricism you start from one case and then onto the next until you discern a pattern and make an inductive judgement. Francis Bacon's (2000) understanding of the 'experiment' is the precursor of Hume's empiricism. This stands in contrast to the Newtonian assumptions of neoclassical economics. Empiricism can start from an embedded situation: rationalism starts from a disembedded actor: it starts from rules. The *wu wei* and salience of the context, of the background in Daoism and Confucianism seems closer to empiricism. At what point does this Smithian empiricism of liberalism turn into this rationalism as a precursor of neoliberalism? If we persist with Foucault (1975), the turning point was perhaps the rise of Benthamite utilitarianism and the Panopticon.

So our understanding of Chinanomics is Smithian liberalism and markets versus neoliberalism and capitalism: with Smith and Hume against rationalism. This book's authors and China are also with Smith on the non-separation of ethics and economic life. In Weber's action types you have the opposition of instrumentally rational and value-rational action, corresponding to the ultimate ends of the holy on the one hand and the selfish desire of the profane on the other. The original major debates on Smith's work were in Germany, in which scholars tried to reconcile what they saw as the polar opposition of *The Wealth of Nations* on the one hand and *Moral Sentiments* on the other. But more recent readings of Smith saw, and we want instead to think of, moral sentiments as an extension of economic activity, the moral sociality of the sentiments as a basis or a frame from which economic action can emerge (Haakonssen 2002).

At the centre of this is Smith's notion of the *imagination*. Smith's moral sentiments start from the same place as his *Wealth of Nations*, from the self-interested actor of desire, sensation and sentiments, feeling. For Smith we can only perceive our own feelings. We cannot perceive or sense the feelings of another. But what we can do is put ourselves in the other's place by means of our faculty of imagination and *imagine* the other's feelings. Smith here gives us a basis of a sociality, based on an empirical and social imaginary. Now this imagination comes straight from Hume's idea of the imagination. Immanuel Kant (1999) gives a brief account of this in his discussion of the schemata of the imagination in *Critique of Pure Reason*. The imagination mediates between, on the one hand, the perception of sense data and, on the other, the cognitive categories of the faculty of understanding.[7] Kant speaks of a number of schema of the imagination, and Kant often speaks of schema as representations that have a lot in common with images. The most important of these is the schema of cause. This schema – which lies between mere perception and full cognition – is the representation of a succession of events, one following the other with some kind of regularity. This schema intervenes analytically prior to the point at which the particulars of the event are subsumed by the universal of the concept or category. In the schema, empiricism and the imagination (or imaginary) give us representation without subsumption. Here we do not have the subsumption of particular by universal, but just the regular succession of particulars. This representation without subsumption seems (see Chapter 1) also to be prevalent in Chinese thought. It is also at stake in Smithian markets. If capitalism, fully fledged capitalism of *die große Industrie* gives us what Negri and Marx (1992) called 'real subsumption', then at stake here is non-subsumption. This is non-subsumption of 1) labour by capital and 2) particular sensations by the universal concept. But it can be also a morality or ethics of non-subsumption, in which our activities are not subsumed by Kant's abstract moral imperative, but instead engaged only in empirical relations, of teacher and student, of older and younger brother, of friends. In Smith morality or ethics is not an *a priori* condition of economic life as it is in for example Emile Durkheim. This moral *a priori* reappears in contemporary commentators on China's absence of 'soft institutions of capitalism'. Morality (or ethics) is instead an *a posteriori extension* of economic life.

China: risk and economy

As visible in the theses presented earlier in this introduction, this book is also about risk – both the risk and uncertainties facing the individuals making lives for themselves in this rapidly changing society and the risk and uncertainties facing companies operating in the Chinese markets. Hence, we are dealing with risk not so much in the sense of negative side effects of technology but instead in the sense of economic and financial risks as well as autobiographical risks; that is, the risks associated with choice of career, family and other decisions that may shape the course of one's life. That latter notion of risk may appear very individualistic as it contains an exaggerated sense of individual decision-making and control over the course of one's life. We argue throughout the book that these biographical risks are less socially atomised than one would think. Indeed they interlock with social and family networks. On the other hand, that does mean that these biographical risks are traditional. There clearly has occurred a transition from one risk regime to another. We describe in detail both how some public welfare regimes have broken down, particularly the *danwei*, and how Chinese entrepreneurs face a volatile economic market place where money is earned and lost. Newer generations navigate this uncertainty, influenced to some extent by cultural influx from overseas. They also navigate greater possibilities of mobility even though such mobility for many means giving up the social rights afforded by the *hukou* system, which in turns creates new social risks. Here, we wish not to engage in a discussion about whether Chinese culture (if one such homogenous entity at all exists) or any other culture for that matter has become more or less individualised. Indeed, we believe that the relationality described in this book is both more risk-filled *and* less individualistic than many Western countries and that this relational culture harbours different perceptions of risk.

The literature on risk perception provides support for many of our arguments. This body of research typically compares differences in risk perception with nationality or cultural values such as those derived from Hofstede's (1984) value survey. Several such studies find that respondents with Chinese citizenship have high levels of risk acceptance and assess risks relatively low (Nara 2008). This difference has been found to exist also when comparing with other East Asian countries (Zhai and Suzuki 2009). Furthermore, the cognitive framing mechanisms described by prospect theory – according to which potential losses are attributed more impact than potential gains – has in a study been found not to apply to people with a Chinese background (Brumagim and Wu 2005).

Slovic (1999) in a review points out that institutions can foster trust, but that such trust also is fragile. Informal institutions such as social networks may take their place, Slovic notes. This argument is elaborated by Weber and Hsee's cushion hypotheses (Weber and Hsee 1998a) that proposes that Chinese citizens have a higher acceptance level of economic risk because they can rely on support from extended family networks should the risk materialise as economic loss. Weber and Hsee use this to explain their finding that people with Chinese origin are highly averse to social risks because such risks potentially bereave them of their social network (Weber and Hsee 1998b). This is relational risk of course, a notion we will dwell on later in the book when we discuss filiality as a source of security.

In the various chapters of this book the theme of risk surfaces often. We generally do not necessarily find a high acceptance of economic risk but we find many cases of people trying to navigate economic and financial risks and taking risks. As just mentioned, we also encounter the importance of social and family relationships in connection to mitigating some of these risks. We also encounter another type of risk, namely what is sometimes termed political risk, that is, the possibility of arbitrary government interventions in the economic sphere. We will see that perhaps the only way of shielding oneself from such political risks is through social connections. Therefore, relationality reappears here. That also means that economic risk is an important prism for viewing the Chinese market because firms constantly attempt to reduce risk by engaging in social and political relations.

That thesis adheres with the thesis of social embeddedness of economic activities proposed by economic sociology. It is a thesis that stands in contrast to economics, even institutional economics that distinguishes between markets and hierarchies as proposed by Williamson (1983). The embeddedness thesis has gained considerable traction in recent years, not least in those scholarly fields that have looked at differences between various capitalist systems. It certainly applies to China, which arguably supports markets that are among the most socially and politically embedded of all. But exactly therein lies also a problem: the general applicability of the social embeddedness thesis means that we are reduced to distinguish Chinese markets from other markets by a difference in degree of embeddedness only. And we believe that there may also be differences in kind. Chapter Two is to a large extent devoted to this problem as in it we discuss different kinds of social capital derived from such social networks.

Embeddedness is, however, not the only insight which economic sociology offers when it comes to the understanding of risk and uncertainty in economic contexts. Indeed, the network theory of Harrison White provides one possibility for distinction in kind and not only in degree. White has demonstrated that firms reduce uncertainty through strategic actions based on constant and careful observations of the competitors, with each firm seeking to find protected market niches. Hence competition is really about niche finding and placement on a quality spectrum. White develops an elaborate network theory about three different forms of network orders or what he calls 'disciplines'. Any such order is part pecking order, part social structure and they are based on particular logics. One of the three disciplines is the type found in what White understands as 'production markets', in which as just described, firms seek out their place in a market profile largely defined by product quality. Firms occupy their respective positions on the market profile at the same time signalling to their 'competitors' their strategic intentions through information about volumes and revenues and general market gossip (White 2002: 31). White generally assumes that firms are orientated towards the greatest sources of uncertainty which can either be downstream (customers) or upstream (suppliers). But the real cause of uncertainty is that in any case firms cannot actually see downstream or upstream. White uses the metaphor of a one-way mirror and describes the market order as an 'interface', saying that firms from within the interface only see reflections of themselves (while suppliers or customers can see inside). Accordingly, firms position themselves on the market profile facing the direction where the most uncertainty is, be it either up or down stream but they do so based on observations (reflections in the one-way mirror) of their competitors' actions and signalling rather than on knowledge of the (other side of the) market *per se.*

White juxtaposes such interfaces with the two other types of the aforementioned disciplines, namely 'councils' and 'arenas'. As already indicated, all three disciplines are social structures that rest on valuation orderings, which again are social constructs and hence fundamentally cultural. And all three disciplines have emerged from social power struggles or 'control efforts' in White's parlance. Where interfaces rest on the valuation order quality, arenas rest on purity (a pure mutuality of interest) and councils on prestige (social alliances and personal commitments). An actor in an interface hence reduces uncertainty by committing to an identity (a place on the market profile) while the same actor in a council would commit to an alliance. Such an alliance of course also provides identity but the difference, according to White, is that identity in an interface is the focus while it in the other two disciplines is a by-product (White 1992: 38).

The talk about alliances and the contrast between alliances and quality order/ interfaces should make it clear why we find this theoretical framework particularly interesting in the context of Chinese capitalism. There, we find networked capitalism, often networks comprising alliances of both private entrepreneurs and government officials (we will see later an emphasis on local government officials). This suggests that Chinese markets embed into a different kind of discipline than White's ideal type Western markets. Yet the overall principle remains the same, namely reduction of uncertainty. And while dwelling on that topic, in interviews with Chinese entrepreneurs we see a deep concern not with the risk and uncertainty of the markets downstream or upstream but rather with the government – 'cross-stream' as it were. It seemingly is the main form of uncertainty – a source of uncertainty just as opaque, of course, as the market observed from an interface. Hence, Chinese firms and entrepreneurs seem not to reduce uncertainty by embedding into an interface but rather by entering into alliances, that is, council disciplines, with government. This however, to such an extent that our metaphor of cross-stream is strained. The involvement of government, especially local, is indeed so extensive that government may be said to be not so much across but simply down or upstream. That does not, however, take anything away from the proposition that market disciplines in the Chinese economy is not so much interfaces as they are councils.

The study of contemporary China

In the loosely grouped community of scholars who study contemporary China across disciplines, there is a plethora of theoretical models and empirical topics that run the gamut from China's exceptionalism to China as an empirical case study for universal theory. In this section of the introduction, the book discusses some of the more well-known scholars in Chinese studies in terms that underpin this chapter and the ones that follow. In our focus on economic life and urban change, there is significant overlap and insight gained from considering the debate over neoliberalism and varieties of capitalism in China, the *danwei* as *the* cornerstone to the city, the unfolding of *hukou* and migration, the rise of consumption and styles of life and unprecedented restructuring of the last 15 years in urban China. These five themes thicken the forms economic life and processes of urban change noted above, and individual themes are worked out throughout the rest of the book.

Neoliberalism and capitalism

Matching the interest of some parts of the academic world, the study of contemporary China is influenced by debates over neoliberalism. Of mainstream economic interest is certainly the debate over the Beijing Consensus (Ramo 2004), which is a direct response to the neoliberal Washington Consensus. In economic terms, this is a debate over privatisation, withdrawal of government from service provision, free trade and financial flows across country borders, and theoretical and policy focus on the neoclassical rational individual. When considering neoliberalism as a form of governmentality, the concepts of disciplining the individual self come to the fore. Rather than state administration or cadre pastoralism, it is a massive group of experts providing technical understandings that replace the state and facilitate economic neoliberalism. In the context of China, interest is in both the specific incarnations of neoliberalism and a China model that provides general lessons for economic development.

Yasheng Huang (2008) is a cheerleader for neoliberalism interpretation of China's development. His (2010) critique of the Beijing Consensus focuses not only on the insight that township and village enterprises refer to their location, rather than a (collective) type of property ownership, but on the assertion that these enterprises are private, regardless of the fact that their success and flourishing benefited local states both in taxation and in development. Guthrie's (2006) work can be viewed as a variant of this field of research in his views on normalizing rationality, the telos of legal systems and universal efficiency in China. His support for the neoliberalist interpretation of China's development is apparent in his rejection of *guanxi* relationships as out of place in a singular rational-legal system towards which he views China developing; and in his championing of a neoclassical economic actor in a universal, rational market economy, a model brought into China by multi-national corporations and aped by China through joint ventures (JV).

Another area of neoliberalism with which this book draws a sharper contrast is the 'varieties of capitalism' literature, in particular, the work to construct a 'Chinese' capitalism. In their monograph and a subsequent paper Redding and Witt (Redding and Witt 2007; Witt 2010) utilise the concept of a business system – a system of ways of doing things, embedded in institutions shaped by culture – to explicate the whole of Chinese capitalism, extending beyond mainland China and encompassing all 'ethnic' Chinese throughout Asia and beyond. With their yardstick of market-driven capitalism, Redding and Witt detail how essential Chineseness and Chinese instincts for business shape the three forms of state-owned, local corporate and private sector business system in China today. Much like Boisot and Child's (1996) infamous 'clan' or 'network' capitalism, this variety of capitalism literature is courageous in constructing a totalistic system of explanation. Yet in the process 'Chinese culture' becomes a holistic, traditional, meaning-making set of relations, structures and practices that has been in existence, unchanged, for millennia. While they divide business systems or capitalisms in China into state, hybrid or corporate and private, Redding and Witt do not afford the same treatment to culture. As such, theirs is more akin to a nineteenth-century armchair anthropologist's – for example Tylor or Frazer – conceptualisation. This serves their purposes well, as the state business system rests on authoritarian state descending not from Mao but from Confucius;[8] hybrid business systems are a clan form of capitalism dependent on ancient counties; and private systems arise from *guanxi* networks as 'ancient ways of thinking and behaving' (Redding and Witt 2007: 128) in a 'culture of dependence on the receipt of orders from above, and a reluctance to risk the taking of initiatives' (ibid.: 57) that result in the universal 'culturally Chinese economic system…[of] quintessentially "family businesses"' (ibid.: 71). On the whole, then, Redding and Witt offer an intriguing puzzle that is worth considering. They open a space for discussion; however, are overly schematic in their approach to culture and the economic lives and urban locations that have become the core of China's economy.

Attention to the issue of neoliberalism in general and China studies in particular is noted by both Nonini (2008) and Kipnis (2007). As Nonini (2008: 149) puts it, his issue is that neoliberalism in Chinese studies is '[a] term with so many meanings [that it] obviously has great utility, because most progressive scholars can agree that whatever neoliberalism is, they don't like it, and the ambiguity of the term allows discursive coalitions of the like-minded to form without the troublesome bother of having to clarify what it is they oppose or are critical of'. He uses four features of neoliberalism: the importance of markets, free trade, rational-selfish individuals and absence of state intervention, as the core with which to contrast China's blurring of public and private, suspicion of markets, building of large state-owned enterprises and relational definitions of self. Hence Nonini concludes there is an absence of neoliberalism in China. Kipnis (2007) similarly upbraids sloppy applications of the 'neoliberalism' discourse in contemporary research, a term which he prefers to define in economic terms as entrepreneurship, competition and market exchange, or in governmentality terms as the promotion of an autonomous citizen-subject (Kipnis 392–394). But his goal is to debunk the neo-holism evident in references to neoliberalism as a global system, both economic and governmental. In another piece that recapitulates neoliberalism in China, Wu (2010) points out that the coexistence of a market mechanism and state control in China's reform is contradictory. For Wu, the functional role of market society is to solve crises in capital accumulation; the state, as the originator of this process, has become a market actor though China's model is still neoliberal as markets dominate, and China's specific characteristics obfuscate the actually existing neoliberalism (ibid.: 629).

Finally, a provocative formulation of neoliberalism as calculations of an enterprising self, or calculative practices applied across diverse domains (beyond the economic), is given by Ong and Zhang (2008). For them, China is an instance of neoliberalism, though the continuing role of the state requires that China's neoliberalism be tempered by socialism at a distance – regulation and control by the state's authoritarian rule, while 'privatisation' goes beyond economic spheres to the realm of private self interests and care of the self. By contrast, Hsu (2007), in contemplating the meaning of market socialism with residents of Harbin, found that 'narratives are used by ordinary citizens to undermine and negotiate with state power, and to resist the reductive values of neoliberal capitalism' (185). She did not find a calculative regime being applied across multiple domains and to the selves of Harbiners. Instead, they, one of the urban populations hardest hit by the reform, emphasised social-structural conditions and a moral economy of status to make sense of changing world, shaping actions, institutions and transforming power.

Danwei

The *danwei*, the 'work unit', dominated China's cities as the crucial institution from the late 1950s, when over 90 per cent of the urban population belonged to either a state-owned or collective one (Bray 2005: 94), to the 1980s and 1990s when Deng's reforms began to be implemented and other institutions grew around *danwei*. The persistence of *danwei* forms of organisation throughout the 1990s and beyond has been documented (Francis 1996). Yet what concerns us here is the nature of *danwei* as a form of economic life and process of urban change. Thus the formulation of *danwei* simply as a total social institution is insufficient in revealing its relational nature as commensurate with the city yet in tension with the multiple local state bureaus and differently organised activities that constitute urban China. While *danwei* is discussed in this section, it actually underlies all forms of economic life and urban change as the fabric of the city.

Some of the earliest work on China cities following the return of Western social scientists to China with the rise of Deng Xiaoping and opening of China pays particular attention to *danwei* (Henderson and Cohen 1984; Whyte and Parish 1984; Walder 1986, 1989). These scholars recognised the all-encompassing totality of *danwei*, imagining them as self-enclosed and self-sufficient collections of people. They not only enclosed workers *cum* residents within guarded walls, but organised production and reproduction of work and life within the *danwei*. Within the confines of *danwei*, there was provision of both the means of production and the means of subsistence. As a total institution, the *danwei* was political, social and economic (Dittmer and Lü 1996), and the administrative hierarchy to which *danwei* were attached determined the importance of production activities and budget – and hence provision of housing, schools, hospitals, canteens – that a particular *danwei* provided (Bian 1994). It is possible to distinguish between state-owned and collective *danwei* in this sense, as state-owned *danwei* were tied to the central state through the administrative hierarchy, while collective *danwei* were run by departments of the local municipal government. However, the strong and total nature of *danwei* yields an image of China's cities as patchwork quilts; that is, rather than an integrated whole 'city' as a concentration of individuals, the city was a loosely-knit site for *danwei* more tied to state administrative structure than urban place (Bray 2005).

The reform of *danwei*, then, could not be more important for understanding economic life and urban change, both as the background from which new practices and configurations emerge, but, more importantly, as a total institutional legacy to which all of urban China can be traced. This is both an empirical and a theoretical specificity: the processual dynamic in China's cities is between local state-owned (i.e. not local-state-owned) *danwei* and the local state – the latter having only risen to prominence in the reform period as an entity different from the locale of state-planning production facilities (see Hsing 2010 for one instantiation). While earlier 'work unit socialism' (Womack 1991) combined Shue's (1988) locally isolated polity with Walder's (1986) clientalism and neo-traditionalism of authority relations, the reform of this system sees the growth of *danwei*-external economic life and a robust urban context. Spilling out of the *danwei*, the transformation in relations resulted from both decentralisation of authority structure and new relationalities of economic lives.

Hukou and migration

While *danwei* dominated the cities before reform, *hukou* – household registration – was a codified institution originating in the late 1950s classifying populations into job type (agricultural and non-agricultural) and location (hometown; urban or rural) (Cheng and Selden 1994; Chan and Zhang 1999). The *hukou* system effectively ended any population mobility in China from 1960 until its gradual reform in the 1980s, reinforcing insularity of place and place-based relationships. It is no coincidence that individual *hukou* in the city are in the hands of *danwei* rather than local government – as is the case in rural China – given the totality of *danwei* in the city.

Since *danwei* and *hukou* coincided in the city prior to reform, migration and changes to *danwei* organisation of labour and life are integrally related. While it has been shown that the majority of so-called migrants actually do not cross provincial boundaries (Rooker 2011), those that enter the city experience a dual form of outsideness – they are moving from rural to urban, and from one local place to another. The urban change brought about by the addition of migrants to the city reflects both local worker rootedness and migrant mobility, though it is the latter that has received the bulk of academic attention (Xiang 1999; Zhang 2001; Solinger 1999). The decline of the *danwei* 'public goods regime' in the 1980s and early 1990s was due less to the reform of *danwei* that to the externalities generated by migrants in the city (Solinger 1995).

A dual society – rural and urban China – now appeared in the city itself. Scholars have shown the decline of *gongren* – 'workers' – in empirical and ideological terms

(Pun 2005; Tomba 2011). Comparing three types of workers in terms of the determinants of urban labour-market stratification, Fan (2002) found that 'elite', those often college-educated and state-sponsored entrants to the city, have an advantage over both *hukou* 'natives' and 'outsiders', while natives are privileged over outsiders regardless of their individual attributes. Yet the rootedness of local workers, the former *gongren*, is not typically noted by scholars who do describe the radical change of transforming *gongren* into *xiagang* – that is, 'off their work posts', but not technically unemployed – in the late 1990s (Solinger 2002; Hsu 2007). Cai (2011) shows how the state handled this transformation differently according to the type of *danwei*, as state-owned ones were more strategic, larger and more likely to involve political risk of demonstrations and social instability, while collective ones were more scattered and disorganised hence not supported in the transformation process. Similarly, Liu (2007) shows how *xiagang* workers leveraged their positions in the *danwei* residential community to become apartment brokers, creating new social positions for themselves by engaging the new market for property.

More recent focus has been placed on the study of migration – the outsiders – by China studies scholars. When moving across provincial borders, migrants initially deploy social networks to work and take up residence in urban areas based on places of origin, sometimes forming enclaves such as the well-known Zhejiangcun in Beijing, constructed and occupied by migrants from Zhejiang Province (Ma and Xiang 1998; Zhang 2001). Yet extensive work done in Guangdong Province – the largest destination for China's rural migrants, and the heart of the global outsourcing of manufacturing – has shown that in the context of globalisation and China's liberal economic policies, a 'dormitory labour regime' has emerged, precluding enclave formation but heightening the use of place and kin networks for differential deployment in migrant work and life (Pun 2009; Pun and Smith 2007). Outside the factory, however, migrant workers continue to cluster in marginal areas within and astride urban developed areas underscore *chengzhongcun* (urban villages or villages within the city) as a significant site for the study of economic life and urban change in China (Zheng *et al.* 2009; Song *et al.* 2008). Lexicalisations, such as *nongmingong* ('peasant worker'), *dagongmei/zai* ('working little sister/brother'), reflect both the divergence from *gongren* non-sexed urban factory workers and the stabilisation of a new stratum of subjectivity (Pun 2005; Tomba 2011). Working as maids or in department stores, luxury hotels and even karaoke bars, urban employees continue to combine work and life but now in a context that has broken the link between the two to create a new urban context, defined as much by the legacies of *danwei* employment for life as by strangers-customers whose temporary or long-term relationship is defined by deference, configuration, distinction and defiance (Sun 2009; Hanser 2008; Otis 2007, 2009; Zheng 2007).

Consumption and style of life

Starting again from the *danwei*-era, urban consumption was *danwei* consumption, and the particular administrative level to which a *danwei* was attached determined the quantity and nature of consumption (Bian 1994). Within the *danwei*, particular individuals were given priority in consumption based on personal and professional relationships with managers (Walder 1986). Massified consumption (Lu 2000) in the *danwei* was about living, eating and working together in the *danwei* for life – neighbours and co-workers are there forever – and only a certain amount of goods was available to all, creating a similar lifestyle and consumption. Move to hyperbolic Shanghai in the late 2000s, where Giorgio Armani and Phillippe Patek share premises (owned and managed, by the way, by the Huangpu district SASAC via a restructured intermediary company) only somewhat distant (East Nanjing Road to the Science and Technology Museum via the underground) from knock-off markets of Gucci and LV handbags (see Lin 2011 for an overview of the latter). This contrast illustrates nicely Bray's (2005: 170) insight: 'Few realize, however, that in fact many of the new commercial retail outlets, business ventures, and service providers are either directly run by an 'old-fashioned' *danwei* or operated out of premises owned by *danwei*'. Yet the break – a consumer revolution – created new linkages and assemblages between economic life and urban change. This was an opportunity to refigure shopping and style of life in a new way, away from *danwei* and the Party.

Several scholars draw attention to the revolutionary nature of consumption in the 1980s and 1990s (Davis 2000; Croll 2006; Wu 1999). This is observed in the turn from 'massified' *danwei* consumption to mass consumption. Introduction of markets in place of *danwei* made the exercise of choice a possibility. But as consumption was no longer a *danwei*-level practice, actual purchase was determined by income and savings, thus inequality and distinction rose to new levels. Yet as Croll (2006) pointed out, it is often the perception, debate and representation of goods – goods as a means of social communication and agency – rather than buying and use that influenced everyday styles of life and activity.

Zhang (2001) noted that migrant entrepreneurs sought to define themselves as modern and cosmopolitan (more so than the poor local residents) through the purchase of leather jackets and consumer items; Pun (2005) berated herself for bringing fellow migrant workers to a coffee shop in the city where they were exposed to the distasteful stares of other patrons; Davis (2005) shows the care with which Shanghai residents, in their 40s and 50s, shop for and redecorate their homes to signal individuality and a realm outside work/party state – despite knowledge of growing inequality. Fast-food restaurants, also, have received considerable attention from Western scholars for their popularity in China's cities (Watson 2000; Yan 2000; Lozada 2000). And the migrants of the Pearl River Delta spend days on the factory floor discussing potential purchases of cosmetics and clothes while listening to romance-steeped pop music from Hong Kong (Pun 2005). These multiple examples, whose significance lies no doubt in the imagined space away from the *danwei* and party-state, shed light on the role of consumption and styles of life in urban China.

Finally, of particular importance in the realm of the consumer revolution and imagined lives is housing. Once part of welfare, housing has increasingly become a commodity, a form of wealth, and a basis for lifestyle and distinction. In advertising, the equivalence between private ownership of housing and an oasis is a frequent trope in urban China since the mid-1990s (Fraser 2000). This trend has only accelerated, with advertisements applying lifestyles and distinctions from the housing market to automobiles, vacations, personal beauty, health and clothing. But housing itself is a new space: residences are constructed in organisations outside of the *danwei*. These apartment complexes, called *xiaoqu* – which now are the general form of all residential housing in cities – come in a wide range of forms: from so-called 'gated communities' of villas to working-class former-*danwei* residences with ill-defined boundaries. This new urban form has spawned extensive interest from scholars, with '*xiaoqu* ethnographies' proliferating in recent years (Sun 2009; Fleischer 2010; Zhang 2010; Bray 2005, 2006; Tomba 2010; Read 2003, 2008). Again, the sudden salience of this new site for research should give one pause, but the role of *xiaoqu* housing in consumption and styles of life is unquestionably a crucial contemporary issue.

Restructuring

With the notable exception of Ji (1998), the process of *gaizhi*, or 'restructuring', often glossed as privatisation, has received comparatively little attention from China scholars. Starting with Jiang Zemin's announcement at the Fifteenth Party Conference in 1997, restructuring involved the so-classed 'grasping the large and releasing the small' (*zhuada fangxiao*) of state enterprises. This is also the point indicated by Naughton (2007) where 'reform without losers' became 'reform with losers'. Indeed, while smashing the iron rice bowl is sometimes applied to the entire reform process, the term is actually more applicable to the restructuring initiated in 1997 than to earlier reforms. Hughes (1998) pointed out the interesting fact that the 'socialist market economy' initiated restructuring, including sell-offs, bankruptcies and layoffs, without a social security net in place. It is also significant that Cai (2011) showed the difference between collective and state-owned *danwei* restructuring, as the central and local state prioritised assistance to state-owned *xiagang* workers, as they were more capable of initiating and organizing social instability.

The 'grasping' (*zhuada*) part of the restructuring process was the formation of China's version of business groups, known as *qiye jituan*, similar in some ways to the business groups of Japan, *keiretsu* and South Korea, *chaebol* (Keister 2001). The creation of the State-Owned Assets Supervision and Administration Commission (SASAC) in 2003 (Naughton 2003) signalled a major milestone in restructuring. Large, often stock market listed, business groups are the largest and most dominant enterprises in China, with some 73 appearing on the global Fortune 500 in 2012. What is often overlooked, however, is the fact that business groups are formed at every level of urban administrative hierarchy, from central state to province, municipality, city and district (as with the Huangpu district above). SASAC offices, then, are both national – as part of SASAC administration – and local, involving large and dominant enterprises in specific locations. The state-owned sector, although mediated by SASAC from direct attachment to government administrative bureaus and departments, remains an important part of both local and national economic leadership.

In his prescient work, Ji (1998) drew attention to restructuring as a process of '*de-danweiisation*'. Marking a fundamental change in state-society relations, the reform of urban industrial *danwei* had already taken the form of corporatisation that would separate state-owned enterprises from the state via property relations. Oi (2011) has recently reprised her concepts of 'corporatisation' and local governments as key decision-makers to explain the continuing process of enterprise reform in the mid-2000s (Oi and Han 2011). For Ji (1998), importance lies in modern enterprise system, an institution that converted state bureaus and factories into either joint stock or limited liability companies inserted as an intermediary between owners (then, administrative bureaus of state property, now SASACs). In addition, past social burdens of welfare, including housing, health care, and education, would be spun off to the local government. Yet, importantly, the local state retained control of the process, both in terms of timing and form of restructuring. Zeng and Tsai (2011) take a political economy perspective to show that the timing of restructuring – much of which was carried out in some form by 2003 – varied across regions. They explain the reason why cities with a preponderance of private enterprises were less likely to restructure local state-owned enterprises than those without, as cadre motivation rested not on restructuring *per se* but on evaluation criteria – cadres were judged on development of local areas, rather than degree of restructuring.

There is extensive literature on economic life and urban change in the contemporary study of China. This book makes a strategic intervention in terms of reformulating economic life in a way that is critical of neoclassical assumptions about economic individuals, based in part on relational markets and Chinese thought. It also interrogates the ubiquitous glossing of urban change as 'transition'. With the support of multidisciplinary works across the themes of neoliberalism, *danwei*, *hukou* and migration, consumption and styles of life and restructuring, the book claims these keywords of contemporary Chinese studies to explicate empirical research in the frame of a new model: local state capitalism in relational markets.

Overview

The book addresses the ways in which economic change in contemporary China is culturally mediated. Through a sustained and intense engagement with the realities of everyday life in rapidly growing cities such as Shanghai, Beijing, Shenzhen and Chongqing we develop an analysis that synthesises empirical evidence of the institutional imperatives of economic change, the logics of new market forms, an understanding of China's cultural traditions and the combinations of structures of governance and technologies of city building.

Max Weber's study of the religion of China was meant to be part of his series of the economic ethics of the world religions. This said, the China study was nearly all about religion and said not very much about the economy. That bifurcation has continued in more recent decades with books addressing either Chinese thought or Chinese economic life and urbanism. This book takes Chinese thought and culture very seriously. Thus Chapter One addresses Chinese thought in the light of concepts from cultural and social theory. It develops a concept largely via consideration of Confucianism and Daoism of a culture that is *relational* and *situated*. We contrast this with an ideal typical Western cultural paradigm that is individualised and disembedded. First we are talking about a relational culture, a set of religious and philosophical assumptions that are relational. The Confucian-Daoist immanentist and largely flow-based mentality thus contrasts with the Greco-Christian transcendental and analytic Western paradigm. Thus from Confucianism we draw on the filialty of social relations of father–son, teacher–student, etc. From Daoism there is an ethics that starts not from an individual and rules but an effectively intersubjective relation. This is very different from the normative, rule-following Western paradigm. The point is that it is never you and reason or you and God, but you are ever already situated in a relation, in a web of activities. It is also not you and some kind of Heideggerian 'world'. There is no abstract you to be 'thrown' into such a world. The situatedness is also at the same time Confucian and Daoist. From Confucianism come the Rites and Ceremonies, the Rites and Music. From Daoism the dimension of non-action, of the *wu wei*. These underpinnings are more or less secularised, but as a set of ongoing practices, as a set of background forms of life. As such they come to presume the primacy of the situation over the disembedded goal-directed actor. This means that you are embedded always already not just in a relation but a situation. In this, the background of the situation takes on primacy over the foreground of goal-directed action. There is a primacy of ongoing forms of life over subject-verb-object action. What this fosters is a mode of social and cultural activity that is in effect less 'rationalist' than empiricist, less *a priori* than *a posteriori*. You come to a situation not with the *a priori* rules of the economic or moral actor but you start out in the situation and work more or less in an inductive mode. Finally, in Daoism we see a much less dichotomous juxtaposing of virtual (or potential) and actual, of transcendental and empirical, of deep ontology and surface epistemology. In Daoism the actual, the analytic *you wei*, the clear and distinct form, is always already becoming virtual. Is already disintegrating onto the flow and flux of the *Dao*. Yet this flow and flux of the *Dao* is itself already becoming actual, becoming negentropic. Thus the situation is at the same time a *propensity*. The background forms of life are already actuality generators.

In Chapter Two we draw on research demonstrating that markets globally are not as disembedded from social life as conventional neoclassical economics assumes. Business studies, socio-economics and economic sociology are just three areas of scholarship that have highlighted global variations in trajectories and institutional forms of economic growth, comparison between capitalist systems commonly revealing as many differences as similarities. In the attempts to describe the rapidly changing models of economic development in China we address how economic agents mediate uncertainty. This in turn links our focus on cultural forms of change to emergent institutions, networks, social capital and culture. In China the state clearly retains a central role in the economy in a fashion that cannot be accounted for in terms of institutional voids. Land remains central to the economic power of government in the ongoing processes of 'opening up and reform'. In the transition from state socialism informal networks are clearly powerful, accounted for by the notion in China of *guanxi*. We theorise cultures of *guanxi* as relational social forms that mediate the process of change. *Guanxi* relations are too often characterised in terms of either impropriety or euphemistically in terms of community obligation. *Guanxi* is different from social capital we suggest principally through its sense of temporality. It involves the construction not just of bridging or bonding links between and within groups (respectively). It develops open-ended dyadic relations between parties, an orientation of linkage that is always about not just what happens today or tomorrow but is about mediating the uncertainties of the day after tomorrow. It is in this sense neither so distant from Western culture as to be incomprehensible nor so close as to be reducible to either social capital on one hand or corruption on the other. *Guanxi* and social capital are consequently not theoretically or straightforwardly commensurable one with the other. The open-ended nature of *guanxi* connections complements and reinforces the importance of informal institutions and a sense of network capitalism. The informal, the open-ended and the power of networks are all culturally mediated. So the emergent markets of contemporary China are culturally inflected, hybrid institutional forms that are characterised by internal diversity as much as by national framings. In this sense we caution against analysis that falls prey to a 'methodological nationalism' by attempting to describe China's social and economic changes as *singular*. Indeed we believe that the defining characteristic of China's model of social and economic change is the *diversity* of regimes of growth that function as experiments in modernisation. This process of experimentation draws its inspiration from the hierarchical structure of power in China's long history, the roots of early reforms in rural town and village enterprises and in the emergence of a system that in this volume we characterise as local state capitalism.

Land markets and property relations are central to the process of transition in China, particularly in the cities where the most recent phases of economic growth have been focused. In Chapter Three we highlight how the particular path dependencies of these property markets structure economic change. China is characterised by a distinction between rural and urban land rights. In the city, the state has retained the long-term right of ownership but use rights have been subjected to more standard models of market development. Consequently, the metropolis is characterised by something close to a leasehold property model with real estate markets increasingly developed in exchange and use rights that last for periods of 40, 50 or 70 years. The chapter makes two arguments. The first is that the separation of ownership rights from use rights defines the urban landscape in terms of its propensity for rapid development, attempting to secure both public interest and private gain. Disaggregated property rights develop models of real estate markets already introduced in other parts of south east Asia, and highlight the developmental links to the 'property states' growth models of Singapore and Hong Kong and the historical influence of 'red capped' enterprises that combined foreign direct investment and state interest in the early decades of modernisation. They also reflect the dilemmas of late-nineteenth-century capitalism that saw the hoarding and speculative holding of property in land banking as economically sub-optimal and sought to qualify the ownership rights of private property. Splitting user rights and ownership rights opens up the potential to sustain public interest in the scale and return of urban development while qualifying the tragedy of the commons through the continued public interest in both positive and negative externalities of change. However, the separation of property rights alone cannot prevent rent-seeking, oligopolistic and other forms of sub-optimal economic growth. The second claim made in the chapter is that in this institutional landscape the informal relations between the disciplines of city making – planning, architecture, construction and local governance – serve two discrete functions. These disciplines combine to make city development possible through the assembly of land, the determination of the possible scale and form of city change and the realisation of the development process. More counter-intuitively they generate productively rival measures of the value and worth of urban land whose combination demands appropriate systems of commensuration. The rationally planned city, the Ricardian optimal pricing of rental returns, the architectural utopia and the self-interest of city stakeholders are common – and commonly irreconcilable – features in the landscape of urban change globally. But the disaggregated distribution of bundles of property rights in metropolitan China generates geometries of interest that are reconciled through the mediating informal structures of expertise in systems of local state capitalism. The permeable boundaries of the state configure to a shape closer to a *Moebius strip,* a form with no clear boundaries between its inside and outside. The disciplines of city building consequently translate unknowable uncertainty into calculable risks within the process of city development through mapping and navigating this Moebius strip, facilitating the rapid and large-scale urban development China has become famous for in recent decades but set within frameworks that are structured by the strengths and weaknesses of the new socialist markets.

In Chapter Four we address 'local state capitalism'. We start with the fallacy at the heart of many analyses of post-Deng modernisation. The methodological nationalism that sees China as one nation state (with one economy) – equivalent to France or the UK or even the US – belies the enormity of China's geography and depth of its history. In terms of the spatial scale it is now commonly suggested that by 2025, 225 cities in China will have one million people living in them (Europe has 35 today). With a population of the order of 1.3 billion people the scale of analysis in today's China is continental in reach and yet increasingly diverse in its realisation. Importantly, this scale is not novel. The tension between the rule of the 'middle kingdom' and its territorial limits can be traced through several thousand years, the trajectories of tribute systems established by different dynasties and at the heart of Confucian systems of balance between local autonomy and centralised power. We draw on the work of China theorist Wang Hui and others who prefer the conceptual figure of, not necessarily the nation–state, but the 'civilisation state' to make sense of the variegated nature of economic change, jumping scales between the continental and the very local.

Modernisation has been both cautious and patterned. Crossing the river one stone at a time, from the first development of the SEZ onwards China's opening up has been characterised by a system of experimental attempts to draw selectively from both the lessons of Western economic growth and the potential for innovatory change. This system can be characterised by a combination of 'parallels', 'permeabilities' and 'particularities'. There are *parallels* between the transition model in China and other forms of post-socialist tradition. In particular, there is a sense in which the social and economic fabric of the Communist era becomes the material out of which modern China is shaped, a sense of building with the fragments of the past rather than an architecture of building anew on a *tabula rasa*. This sensibility creates a sense of path dependency to the social and economic life of contemporary China. The valorisation of social stability led by the Communist party leadership has led to a model of change that is incremental with traces of the past inscribed on the institutions of the present. However, there has also been a sense of *permeability* of today's China; developing a model of the market that draws on specific flows of Foreign Direct Investment, institutional imports of limited liability companies with traded stocks, western models of risks and derivatives in the financial services and European traditions of city building. But all of these technologies have been adapted to the particular forms of modernisation developed across China. In this sense we take the seemingly paradoxical notion of the 'socialist market' espoused by Deng seriously. As Adam Smith argued in both *The Wealth of Nations* and *The Theory of Moral Sentiments* the market is both an instrument of governance as well as a mechanism that determines the deployment of resources. New markets in China are in this way tools of governance that structure the scale relations across the civilisation state. The state is neither an increasingly ephemeral player in the state of perfect competition nor a shaper and regulator that makes sure the rules of the economic game are played fairly. It is instead a player in the market, in its constitution, its development and its future.

In this sense we understand China's modernisation in terms of *local state capitalism*. This local state capitalism plays out at different scales in the post-Deng era. At a national level the use of macro-economic fiscal tools has been used to prioritise sequentially different regions of China. First the SEZ, then the focus on the Pearl River Delta (particularly Shenzhen, Guangzhou, Hong Kong), then the Yangzi River Delta (Shanghai and parts of adjoining Jiangsu and Zhejiang provinces), then the Bohai ring (Tianjin, Beijing), then the massive fiscal stimulus following the 2008 global crisis that focused on the internal heartlands (particularly Sichuan and Chongqing). But equally the interplay of central control and local power plays both to longstanding concern about sustaining the integrity of the civilisation-state and the facility to develop experimental models of economic development through selective liberalisation of particular sectors of the economy. In the many articulations of local state capitalism in today's China the presence of the state within the market lends hierarchical order to the structure of market governance. To the extent that hierarchies can displace markets by reducing trans-action-costs and promoting strategic responses to new challenges, the local state capitalism model might be successful. To the extent that soft budget constraints promote sub-optimal allocations of resources, hierarchies are conventionally trumped by market efficiencies. To the extent that new economic institutions in China hybridise the separation of market and hierarchy, we may be dealing with new articulations of this traditional problem of economic organisation. In much of the rest of this volume we explore these articulations in the fields of the everyday lives of the new young professional middle class and the trading of stocks and shares by a diverse cross-section of urban society, the emergence of companies with sus-tained government ties, the deployment of new technologies of financial services and the accommodation of floating populations in the city.

Central to the way that local state capitalism works is the phenomenon of *relational markets*. We understand such relational markets in contradistinction to neoliberal, primarily individualist markets. Rural social change in China has long been understood in terms of ambivalent property rights. Here, analysts have spoken of the emergence of 'local state corporatism' through the reforming success of the Township and Village Enterprises. In a similar vein the analysis of property relations becomes central to our understanding of local state capitalism. We argue that the informality of economic institutions rests on the splitting of property rights in today's China. At their most basic in the separation of use rights and ownership rights this can actually become rapidly more complex. Legal theorists sometimes identify as many as ten to seventeen forms of property rights. The differential com-bination and bundling of these rights can be an important determinant of urban economic development.

Chapters One through Four proffer a cultural theory and social framework for understanding how China has and is constructing their particular mode of capitalism. Chapters Five through Ten draw on this to investigate particular modalities of economic life/urban change. Chapter Five is concerned with ties between firms and local and central government. It is based on the question of whether and how ties of firms to local government impact firm performance. We attempt to answer that question by a comprehensive analysis of half of all firms listed on the Shanghai and Shenzhen Stock Exchanges. We find that ties both to central and to local government aid performance. We, however, also find that there are differences in what level of ties between firm management and government officials can enhance performance. We analyse these findings using social capital and resource dependency theory and argue that the variations point to important differences in the roles of central and local government. Ties to central government may provide valuable information and some degree of protection. China's markets, similar to markets in many other emerging nations are indeed 'incomplete'. Markets are institutions as Oliver Williamson reminds us. And incomplete markets in a very important sense comprise 'institutional voids'. One of these voids is very limited information. Such information is valuable when taking long-term strategic decisions. Ties to local government may to some extent compensate for the void and provide such information. They may also provide access to vital resources (for example land), which are crucial for the day-to-day operations of the firm. Such control can be obtained by forging close alliances with local governments. We find that the importance of local government ties seem to be unaffected by degree of institutional development of the market while ties to central government have less effect the more developed (or less 'emerging') a market is.

Chapters Six and Seven demonstrate the consequences of this configuration of changing state power and new markets on individuals in Shanghai. In Chapter Six almost 18 months spent working in three real estate companies in Shanghai between 2007 and 2009 provides the ethnographic material to make sense of the real estate markets that set the pace of urban change. The formal corporate structure and the informal paths of both emergence from the local state and embeddedness within it structure the propensity to realise rapid urban transformation. The synthesis of foreign direct investment and access to the plans, design and intentions of the city that is yet to come demand an exercise that navigates the perils of the property development process between the Scylla of state demands and the Charybdis of financial returns within the cultural landscape of the socialist market. Chapter Seven draws on a year-long extended ethnography of a share trading room. Here we obtain a prism on the new rationalities that emerge in the connections between major policy changes and individual small investors. We witness the ebb and flow of *chao* and *tao* ('stir frying' and 'getting stuck') in the investment of private savings. In modern Shanghai rationality, uncertainty and market maturity relate to these new configurations of markets and publics.

Moving on from everyday cultures the book subjects further aspects of urban modernisation to empirical scrutiny. The system of local state capitalism fuses together formal and informal processes, hybridises states and markets, imports technologies of economic governance but sees them adapt, mutate and become part of a vernacular modern China. In the context of financial services, the industry's pricing models for creating, measuring and valuing derivatives have been imported and deployed performatively in a market that objectively lacks the physics and the arithmetic that might justify them. Yet this construction without belief cannot be seen as straightforwardly irrational, it instead represents one more example of crossing the river 'one stone at a time', implementing reforms gradually in a manner that reflects its own logic.

So Chapter Eight describes a synthesis of how new financial know-how at times can be instrumentally useful, serve as much as a tool of *a posteriori* justification as empirical prediction but still gathers a value consequently that structures financial risk. Here we explore particular aspects of the development of a foreign exchange (FX) derivatives market. Such a derivatives market can be expected to be dependent on the successful implementation of complex know-how and technologies, above all pricing models of these complex securities. The pricing models may even be performative, that is, influence the market so that they come to resemble the forecasts of the models. These models are, however, built on a series of assumptions about the underlying market, assumptions that by and large are not met in China. The pricing models do not show any signs of being performative in the Chinese setting. In some ways, the description in the chapter is one of a financial market that still is, if not dysfunctional, then still developing. But it is also a description of a market with functions based on premises other than those in the West and which exhibits no signs of coming to resemble Western markets in the near future. There is an ideological element to performativity because it only is if the theoretical assumptions embedded in the models are believed that they can be performative. The chapter suggests that exactly that belief is missing in China.

In Chapter Nine we look at China, in particular Shanghai as a 'risk culture'. This chapter is based on more than 100 one to two hour interviews with urban professionals, in which they reconstruct their life courses as 'risk biographies'. What we see is the experience of a vastly changed set of regimes of risk and security. We see a move from a regime of security in which the *danwei* was a basis of security in housing, health, education and welfare to one in which these security functions are taken on largely by the three-generational family. This is above all mediated through the rise and unusually quick spread of private housing unit ownership and mortgages from the mid- to late-1990s. At the same time people are thrown onto the labour market. Thus there is simultaneously a huge increase of both filiality and individualisation. The change in housing paradigm from *danwei* to *xiaoqu* establishes an individualisation and isolation of housing units in which often neighbours have little contact or knowledge of one another. At the same time there is a massive increase in filiality, in the sharing of risk over three generations. Thus the one-child policy fosters the three-generational unit of two sets of grandparents, their progeny, a married couple and the couple's child, with which often one of the pairs of grandparents will have moved in. A great number of these Shanghai residents come from elsewhere – in most cases originally came to Shanghai to study, especially from nearby Zhejiang and Jiangsu, two wealthy provinces with thriving private sectors. There is a risk-inclined ambition among these incomers, who provide a huge proportion of Shanghai's middle classes and in most cases they do not have a Shanghai *hukou*, and are not covered by Shanghai's comparatively generous welfare and security regime. We find a major disparity between them and more risk-adverse native Shanghaiese. We note an influence of Daoist cultural underpinnings. The Western, Greco-Christian paradigm underpins a cultural model of a risk-calculating individual facing a world of contingency and disorder. In the Daoist paradigm the risk-taking individual is already situated in these circumstances. Further, the circumstances themselves are seen less as random contingency but instead as imbued with an incipient ordering. The majority of these urban professionals work in commerce, trade and export. They in their considerable masses help constitute the highly skilled, yet not highly paid, Smithian labour-intensive market society that Arrighi describes. In their scaling up and scaling out such risk biographies impart a rhythm to Shanghai itself as an urban regime of risk and security. They impart an energy to Shanghai that itself takes on the shape of a force-field, a generative propensity constituting the city's global hypermodernity.

Chapter Ten focuses on the complementary dynamic of rapid urban change in China, the movement of people to the city from the countryside. In the 1970s, Manuel Castells defined as the challenge of reproduction of the city the (in)ability of the metropolis to accommodate new populations to service economic growth through the process of urbanisation. In China the scale of migration from the country to the city represents arguably the largest movement by humanity ever. The penultimate chapter of the book is based on life histories of several hundred migrants to Shenzhen, members of the floating population. The chapter argues that the combination of residual *hukou* (or local citizenship) and ambiguous property rights generates an urban system that appears economically sub-optimal but in effect works to adjust the fabric of the city to migrant flows. In Shenzhen, close to the Hong Kong border, the city has been structured by migration. The consequences of Shenzhen as an early Special Economic Zone has concentrated migrant 'handshake apartments' (*woshou fang*) in villages in the city (*chengzhongcun*). These villages in the city are paradoxical institutions. They are structured like single joint-stock companies that represent 'indigenous' village interests and ownership rights. Regulated informally in negotiations between municipal government and rational self-interest of the villagers, they have an economic functionality, internalising transaction costs. They also create flexible landscapes of residential informalities, regulation and development control. Their facilitating planning regimes, at their worst, may allow intense forms of labour exploitation. At their most flexible, they can be a basis for changing demands for skills and locational preference through their ability to accommodate rapid change.

1
CHINESE THOUGHT, CULTURAL THEORY

Emblem and efficacy

For the classical sociological theorisation of Chinese culture, we should perhaps turn less to Max Weber (1964) — than to Emile Durkheim, and Durkheim's eminent student, Marcel Granet. Granet, a younger contemporary of Marcel Mauss, featured a notion of the *emblem*, similar to Durkeim's totem, in his understanding of Chinese thought. Granet's emblem is a tool for classification, in the sense of Durkheim and Mauss's (1903) *Primitive Classifications*. Yet it diverges from these accounts in a way that Chinese culture, more generally, transgresses Durkheim's concepts. First, the Chinese emblem, unlike Durkheim's totem, straddles the sacred and profane. For us the relational is on this margin of sacred and profane. The individualism at the heart of the Western neoclassical subject is fundamentally connected with the dualist separation of sacred and profane. We see this in Weber's Protestantism and in Enlightenment secular thought. This is not the case in China. Indeed the thematic of Talcott Parsons (1967) *Structure of Social Action* and of Weber's (1988) *Religions-soziologie* was based on the contrast of transcendentalist Western, Judaeo-Christian tradition and the immanentist Daoism and Buddhism.

Granet's Chinese emblems are what Francois Jullien (2002) has understood as 'efficacious'. Emblems are symbols and Durkheim underscored the distinction between symbols, on the one hand, and images, on the other. *The Elementary Forms of the Religious Life* (1968: 78–9) was importantly a critique of English empiricist anthropology's understanding of tribal cultures in terms of not symbols but images. Images are sensible and derive from sense impressions, whereas symbols derive from collective representations, especially ritual. Granet's (1958: 180–81) emblems, however, are simultaneously images and symbols. Chinese culture and language consistently traverses and violates this boundary of symbol and image. As symbol-images, signs are much closer to the reality they represent. They are more 'motivated' by this reality than are symbols. As such, they are more immanent and less transcendental to this everyday reality. Their immanence is enunciated in the first lines of the *Dao de Jing. Dao ke dao fei chang dao. Ming ke ming fei chang ming.* Thus the *dao* that is explicit is not the genuine and enduring *dao*. Likewise the name that is explicit is not the genuine name. The point is that the explicit name is clear and distinct and separated from the process, the existence that it is. The real name and 'way' (*dao*) are implicit, is immanent.

Granet's *Pensée chinoise* straddles Durkheim/Mauss's *Classifications* on the one hand and Levi Strauss's *Pensée sauvage* on the other. Mauss's (2011) *Gift* is important here because Chinese relationality is a sort of gift giving, of symbolic exchange. Thus the relevance of Jullien's efficacy, which is neither utility nor even efficiency, but has to do with having an effect. Western culture characteristically works through non-emblematic symbols. Emblematic symbols are motivated by the profane in a way that purer symbols are not. Western religion in this context is non-efficacious: it is a separate realm that has its effects only in a very mediated way on the profane, through, for example, Christ. Chinese religion is immediately efficacious. For Durkheim, elementary religion or totemism does work through symbols immanent to the profane. In Durkheim, the sacred is about ritual and the profane is about utility. Chinese efficacy is not a question of utility. For Mauss too, the utilitarian exchange of the commodity develops out of the sacred and symbolic exchange of the gift. Indeed Marilyn Strathern (1992) in *The Gender of the Gift* effectively deconstructs Durkheim's binary of metaphysical ritual on the one hand and the 'physical' profane on the other, showing how both are constituted through gendered gift giving and exchange of useful labour.

The *Oxford English Dictionary* defines 'efficiency' very much along the lines of efficient cause. And something very much other than this is at stake in efficacy. At stake is something like effect without cause. This is partly due to the immanent role of the emblem in Chinese efficacy: where the cause is immanent to the effect. The emblem and efficacy override the distinction between gift and commodity. The very central complex of such emblems are for Granet (1989) the *Dao*, the *yin* and *yang*, number and the way time and space is experienced. These stand in contrast to Western, Greek notions of cause, substance, quantity and abstract, homogenous time and space. These latter are neither emblematic, nor efficacious. They are disembedded and abstracted from material relations of concrete economic life. By contrast, Granet insists the emblems are themselves 'real'. Western economic thought is somehow at the same time both disembedded and utilitarian. Chinese relational concrete economics is neither disembedded nor utilitarian. In place of the emblem then, we in the West have the Judaeo-Christian personal, hence individualised God and Aristotelian logic. Instead of efficacy we have efficiency on the one hand and a remote God on the other.

In China there is no parallel to Western philosophy's dogmatic system of thought. The ideas of the Chinese sages of the sixth and fifth century BCE Zhou Dynasty were incorporated into everyday life during the 224 BCE to 200 CE Han Dynasty. Instead of a system it is a question of identifying a 'master formula to be a central recipe' (Granet 1989: 19). These are *sages* and not philosophers, whose students are just as much disciples. These students do not become thinkers through dialogue and dialectic with their teachers, but instead through initiation and long training. At stake is not a doctrine or a discursive formation of any sort but 'recette d'action civilisatrice' (Granet 1989: 20). 'Civilization' is very important to relational exchange. Relational exchange in China is inscribed in a logic of lending stability and reproducing a given order of things. In the *Dao*, this extends from heaven to earth via man and the political order of the sovereign. At its heart is the social: the political order of the sovereign. Hence the thought of the sage – of Confucius, Mencius or Laozi – is efficacious in stabilising the social and political ordering. The point for us is that relational economics can provide an alternative mode of socio-political stability. Max Weber (1980: 503) understood the legal order of the *Rechtsstaat*, and as we will see (in Chapter Two) Harrison White has understood markets themselves as sources of stability, i.e. as providing conditions under which investors will invest. For Will Hutton (2008) the possible future failure of the Chinese economy would be due to the absence of such sources of 'soft power'. Our point, with David Wank (2001), is that there are alternative sources of such stability: in China's case the long-term relational connections between entrepreneurs and between entrepreneur and the local state.

According to the *Petit Robert*, the adjective '*efficace*' (efficacious) is that which produces an anticipated effect (qui produit l'effet qu'on en attend'). A medication can be efficace; so can an action. What is efficacious produces something that is actual rather than just the possibility of an effect. Thus theologians distinguish between 'sufficient' and efficacious grace. Efficacious grace gives us not just the possibility of good action but also the realisation of good actions. Efficacy is also the capacity to produce results with a minimum of expenditure. This dimension of realisation is at the heart of this. What is realised is also something that starts as virtual, as potential. So these emblems, these symbols of *la pensée chinoise* are virtuals more than actuals. This distinguishes efficacy from efficiency and utility. In efficiency there is efficient cause in which one 'appearance' produces an effect in another appearance. Yet emblems never quite appear. They never quite definitely and fully appear. Thus so many characters in Chinese are for Granet '*indéfini*' or polyvalent in meaning. Jullien (1993) understands this as 'blandness', in his *Eloge de la fadeur*. This blandness, this indéfini is neither virtual nor actual, neither potential not realised, but lies somewhere, in a state of more or less instability, more or less stability, between virtual and actual.

For Granet it is China, not as nation but as civilisation, that matters: the idea of 'recette d'action *civilisatrice*'. In this sense Chinese thought, unlike Greek thought, is not driven by the truths of epistemology or ontology but by this sort of efficacious, recipe-driven action. This is not just ethics or conduct in the Western sense. It is instead the agencement of people, things and emblems, in the whole of Chinese civilisation. Thus for Granet, civilisation *chinoise* is at the heart of *la pensée chinoise*. Hence the efficacy of thought, of the emblems, drives the general 'ordering (*aménagement*) of life: of social life, of the cosmos and of nature'. For

Granet, *yin* and *yang*, the *dao* and also number, time and space are emblems operating on all these levels.

Salient among Granet's emblems is the insignia. In China (Vandermeersch 1989) even in the Shang Dynasty (sixteenth to eleventh centuries BCE) there was a strong centralised state. Feudal fiefs emerge only subsequently. Unlike in the West and Japan with a pronounced intervening feudal moment, there was in China a direct transition from tribe and clan to centralised state. The tribes and clans (and later fiefs) had their insignias, their emblems: their ordering synthesised into the more complex emblem of the prince. For Granet, the more indefinite emblems are present at the same time in the appearances that we encounter. If clan emblems are at the very most particular level, the emblem of the fief, prince and later *yin* and *yang* and the *Dao* are increasingly universal. But their universalism is different from that of, say, the Christian God or Christ, or to the Greek thought of universal law and particular case. It is for Granet, not an abstract, but a concrete universal. This does not mean that there is no abstraction in Chinese culture. *Hanzi* characters become more and more abstract over time. The meaning radical too becomes less mimetic and more abstract over the centuries. Chinese medicine, engineering and science have made great advances. But this was rather separate from the thought of the sages and their generations of scholars, for whom such a universal is not abstract and transcendental but concrete and immanent. This mode of thought does not separate logos from religion. In China, a religion is always a 'teaching'. Thus Christianity is *jidujiao* or yesujiao (Christ-teaching, Jesus-teaching. In his classic essay, 'Violence and Metaphysics', Jacques Derrida (1967) traces Emmanuel Levinas's development from the 'Greek' ethos of Heidegger's and Husserl's phenomenology to the 'Judaism' of Levinas's ethics of the other. In concluding, Derrida argues that we are necessarily both Greek and Jew: that we are 'Jew–Greeks', 'Greek–Jews'. In China, however, we are neither Jew nor Greek. The concrete immanent and efficacious universals of Chinese thought/conduct, stand apart from both Athens and Jerusalem.

In China, language too is efficace. There is no separate order of discourse nor an abstract *langue à la* Saussure. There 'is no sign that that is given the simple value of a sign', instead all elements of language, 'vocables and graphics, rhythms and sentences, burst (*éclater*) with the efficacy proper to emblems' (Granet 1989: 24). There is also no separate realm that is emptied of language or signification in the Western sense. What language or signs describe is already itself full of signification. Roland Barthes saw Japan as the 'empire of signs': as the empire of clear and distinct signs. This is of a piece with Japanese minimalism in food and design. China, said Barthes (2012), had no signs. In place of a semiotics of clarity is an indistinct overlain amalgam of emblems. If the empire of signs is transcendental, to be without signs, is to live in a realm of immanence.

Granet's (1989: 21) Chinese 'efficace' is not just a power of ordering, but is also a force of animation: through an energetics in which the spiritual and the material are intertwined. Here language is 'solidary with all bodies of technics'. These technics 'situate individuals in a system of civilisation that forms (at once) a society and a universe' (Granet 1989: 31, 78). Thus Chinese, unlike Western language is not 'a symbolic system, specially organised to communicate ideas'. If Western ideas are formulated in defined concepts, emblems are not operative through definition, but instead through their very 'richness in affinities'. You know them through their efficacy: in the 'furtive singularities' they produce. Thus Chinese culture works not directly, but indirectly via a 'detour' (Jullien 2004). The sage does not define: he teaches not explicitly, but through example, through analogies. Thus there is an inseparability of real, symbolic and imaginary in Chinese thought. A language that works through pictographs is already not just symbolic but iconic, already populated by images. Language in the West is not efficace; it does not motivate. Chinese symbols are thus, not just emblems, but 'rubrics' and 'signals'. Signals are closer to the reality, more motivated than are icons while symbols. In Durkheim's *Elementary Forms* the sacred motivates and the profane regulates. Symbols in China are not so much Western tools for formulating concepts: they instead orient action.

Yet Granet's (1989: 27, 75) classification is supremely important: Chinese emblems also work as classifiers. There is something static and reproductive about Durkheim's and Pierre Bourdieu's idea of classification. Chinese classifications, by contrast, are nothing like empty genuses but instead full emblems. Their plenitude animates, imparts a rhythm to life, to society, nature and cosmos that 'brings time space, and number into an ensemble of concerted play'. There is neither abstract space of extension nor abstract time of succession. Chinese thought is not in pursuit of the general laws that will apply in all times and places. Instead times and spaces are solidary with each other. Time is full: it is an ensemble of eras, seasons and époques. It is heterogeneous. Sacred space, the space of the *mingtang* is square, with the knoll of the *mingtang* and the emperor or chief at the centre and sides of east, west, north and south. Here every space has a time: West is autumn, north winter, and east spring. Emblems are arranged in space. The chief's emblem is the red bull of the Zhou in the middle and the insignias of leading vassals are on the four corners. These embrace two rhythms: the punctuation of the ever-renewing cycle of the seasons, and the more overarching rhythm of the dynasties: of the centralised states and the cosmos (1989: 80–82).

Relationality has roots in the *Dao* and Confucianism. Such relationality is collective, with primacy of not the monad but the dyad: of a set of overlapping dyads. Its premise is long-termism and incompleteness. Thus Jullien (2004) underscores the Daoist ethos of *wu wei* and *wu ming*. The *wu wei* opposes not so much ongoing activity as goal-directed action. There is a parable of the celebrated archer who carried out the finest of archery until he started orienting himself to targets. This overlaps with Confucian ethics. Entry to the civil service was regulated by exams featuring knowledge of the Confucian Classics, the Great Learning (*daxue* 大学), the Doctrine of the Mean (*zhong yong* 中庸), especially the Analects (*lunyu* 论语) and the Mencius from the middle of the Han Dynasty, c. 200 BCE until the end of the nineteenth century.

Confucian ethics is a virtue ethics. It is neither a consequence ethics, in which the goodness of action is a question of the consequences it leads to, nor is it a rule-bound ethics, such as Kant's categorical imperative; nor is it a deontological ethics in which the goodness of an act lies in the character of the act itself. What counts in a virtue ethics is the character of the moral agents themselves. Thus instead of discourse between teacher and student there is exemplification, between master and disciple. The sage mixed the discoursing philosopher with the religious figure and the master craftsman. Thus sages train people and cultivate in them virtues.

Wilhelm Hennis (1987) understood in Max Weber's essays on '*Science as a Vocation*' and '*Politics as a Vocation*' in terms of a notion of *Personlichkeit*. At stake in China is not the personality of Weber's lone scientist or politician, but a far more situated ethics. What counts is the situational context. An action is determined as good by not a transcendental God, but instead the situational context. The idea is the perpetuation of the social fabric. There is a progressive de-linkage from notions of God or heaven (*tian*). A virtue ethics is a question not so much of the character of a given act but of a mode of conduct. It is though less self-propelling, and less ego-driven than conduct. It is instead more of a following, a lineage of the propensity of things in a given situation. To follow the propensity of things is to follow the *Dao*. The propensity of things and their flow is described in the *Yi Jing*, the *Classic of Changes*, in which each of the 64 graphemes is a combination of six figures, some of which are *yin* and others of which are *yang*. The mix of *yin* and *yang* underscores a combination of decline and flourishing: that there is a renewal at the bottom of a decline (Jullien 2001: 140–43).

What counts is less the individual than the dyad, of the five filial pieties: emperor-subject, etc. There are three main elements to Confucian ethics, the *yi*, the *li* and the *ren*. The *yi* signifies, in opposition to self-interest, righteousness and justice. In traditional Mandarin, the lower half of the character *yi* (義) is *wo* (我) or I. The *ren* (仁) brings in other people. The character has the people radical to the left and the radical for two (*er* 二) on the right. This is where the Confucian version of the Golden Rule comes in. Do not act vis-à-vis others in a way other than what you should wish for yourself. This again is relational and different from the individualist and rule-bound Kantian ethics. Kant said act as if the maxim according to which you act would be generalised universally through your will. Here, however, there is no general maxim and no individual actor, but a dyad, a relation. Benevolence is featured and harmony with other people. The *li* is usually translated as etiquette, rite or propriety – *liwu* is a gift, a gift-thing, indicating reciprocity.

Morality and solidarity: China's relational economy

This relationality is the subject of Jullien's (1996) treatment of Mencius and morality. Mencius wrote some 150 years after Confucius, in the middle of the fourth century BCE, a century before the rise of the Han Dynasty. This is the

Warring States period: there are many schools of philosophy in this period and considerable debate. At this point in time, Mozi is arguing for altruism while others argue for an ethics of self-interest. Argument and some notion of the truth are at stake. This is when China is at its closest to the West. Chinese thought is beginning to work in the register of not so much the sage as philosophy. Mencius is taking part in these arguments, but he is arguing in effect against argument. He is pitting the sage, sagesse, wisdom, against philosophy. He is looking back to a previous period of dynastic stability and to Confucius. He is saying that what counts is not truth but conduct. Central to Mencius's filial piety is the governing virtue of humaneness or *renyi* 仁義. *Renyi* is also righteousness. While Christian righteousness is a quality of the individual, renyi is a property of the relation. *Ren* itself means humane.

Mencius's ethical action is not guided by rules, but embedded in the facticity of the everyday. The point is to place yourself into the unfolding of a situation, into the propensity of things. Jean-François Lyotard (2003) has understood this as a 'practical empiricism'. Western notions of disembedded knowledge entails a notion of action based on means and ends, in which ends are set up as the ideal good. Chinese thought counterposes Laozi's non-action, Daoism's *wu wei* (無為). Here *wei* (為) also means cause, indicating a breaking with chains of cause and effect in understanding how we conduct our lives. In Chinese thought, the means are not thought of as being justified by the ends. Indeed there is often no notion really of legitimation at all. Instead the legitimation is carried in the action or conduct itself. This is what Jullien calls 'transformation'. Transformation or sagacity is to make your intervention upstream in the Daoist flow of things. As courtesan you intervene in the prince's thought before he has made up his mind. You let nature and your nature take their course. You do not launch a frontal attack on the thing – whether in war or in knowledge – but you detour around the thing(s) in the situation. You work not through argument but through purview, giving an ever-fuller view of the situation. You intervene before maturation of the situation where potential is at its greatest. You embrace the situation. This is efficacy. Efficacy is as Lyotard notes 'effect without cause'.[1] The effect comes not from the cause but the most efficacious unfolding comes instead from the way, from the *Dao*. The *Dao* and Chinese thought is a book of recipes to coordinate the fullness of the unfolding of the effects. Chinese thought consists less of rules or causes than recipes: as Lyotard notes, 'recipes for efficacy'.

We mentioned with Granet a sort of Chinese concrete universalist religious paradigm. Here on the surface is the tribal constellation of emblems. These open up onto a more immanent and more universalist levels of the fief and prince. At still more immanent levels are the totemic organisation of space in north, south, east and west and of time. At still deeper levels in Granet's framework are *yang* and *yin* and finally the *Dao*. In terms of Chinese time, there is, on the one hand, duration (*shijian*) and, on the other, the moment (*shihou*) (Jullien 1996, Ricoeur 2003). What you do not have is a sort of Western abstract temporal envelope that contains both. Again following from Granet, Jullien contrasts the Western idea of time with seasons in China, Western anticipation with Chinese availability, the Western 'deafening' intrusion of the event with Eastern quiet and constant transition, Western insouciance with Eastern care, time that passes with a time that is linked with domains and climates and the dramatisation of relations of time with silent continuation. Paul Ricoeur examined Aristotle's primacy of change in time, which we find in the succession of number and in the distinction of two instants separated by the interval. He points to Augustine's Neo-Platonic lived present, itself divided into the present-past, present-future and present-present, situated in a sort of 'tension between distension and intention'. Ricoeur recognises the distance between this Western time (the time of his own *Temps et récit*) and the permanent coming and going of Chinese time; the renewal without origin or conclusion where life is not between a beginning and end, where we do not live in a 'between'.[2] Without a creator God and an afterlife, beginning and end become less relevant. Time *de*-narratives: it escapes both Newtonian time and the existential drama of being and time. Time leaves the province of the subject in China: it addresses not the subject but the coming and going of time itself.

Justice should be about a certain recompense for virtue. Here Christians, noting that often the wicked and not the virtuous gain success in this world, posit another world. Jews orient towards a messianic age of justice as redemption or salvation. In China there is neither salvation nor redemption. Western transcendental religion in secular form bequeaths to us, on the one hand, a normative and regulating (indeed 'governing') 'ought', and on the other, an energising and factical 'is'. These presume a two-world cosmology of the intelligible and the sensible. Thus Kant's antinomy of practical reason leads him to posit the necessity of God, and the juxtaposition of this world that is experienced and another solely intelligible world that is not experienced. Here God has to mediate justice. For Mencius justice must be this-worldly and the long run reward of the virtuous prince. The efficacy of Granet's emblem is always this-worldly. Indeed efficacy is this-worldly and inefficacy always otherworldly, whether Platonist or Judaeo-Christian.

In modern Western morality there seem to be two basic directions. First, a sort of 'empiricism' may be encountered in say Adam Smith's moral sentiments, but also in Rousseau's assumptions that sentiments of 'pity' and 'compassion' are at the basis of morality. Rousseau's pity – like Smith's sentiments – starts from an 'inclination' or even an interest. The second direction is a morality – not of the sensible but of the rational and intelligible. Thus Kant looks – not at nature or the senses but at *a priori* obligation. Thus *The Critique of Practical Reason*, advocates 'pure practical reason' and not 'empirical reason', and now Kant juxtaposes the pure practical will with the empirical will. Chinese relational morality is not grounded in neither Rousseau's and Smith's empirical will nor in Kant's pure practical will. It is not grounded in an individual will at all. It is grounded instead in an intersubjectivity: in a dyad in which A and B are so implicated in one another that they cannot even quite be disentangled as individual subjects. Mencius, for his part, speaks of the prince whose feelings of pity make him protest about the slaughter of a cow, and who would risk his life to save a child who had fallen into a mineshaft. Here like Rousseau we see the empirical or sensible. Yet pity in Rousseau is the basis to ground morality. In Mencius it is just the empirical correlate of morality: of the intersubjective *ren* 仁 (Jullien 1996: 37–8). This ren is not empirical. But empirical pity is its outcome. As a virtue, it is a virtual and a 'generator' of empirical pity and (shame). This is the foundation of ethics and morality in China. So it is neither a transcendental foundation as in Kant's imperative, nor an empirical and actual foundation as in Rousseau's pity. But it is a virtual whose energy generates empirical pity. It is a virtual in the sense that virtue in *Daoism* – the *de* (德) of the *Dao de* (道德) is always invisible and virtual. The *ren* (仁) as humaneness and *renyi* as (仁義) righteousness or compassion signal a root of solidarity that is an original and natural human bond. For Mencius (and Confucianism) it fundamentally means human nature: it means humanity, not empirical humanity, but a non-sensible humanity as a virtue. Here virtue comes not from what we encounter but from our depths. This virtue of relational humanity is also in China a question of conscience. Conscience again is not sensible or experienced: conscience is *ben xin* (本心 or *liang xin* (良心). In *ben xin*, *xin* is heart or mind (psychology is *xinlixue* – 心理学). And *ben* is root. In this sense, relationality is between consciences asserts Mencius: between the roots of consciences. In the West we hear the 'voice of conscience', a voice that repeats the voice of God, in China conscience has no voice. There is no personal god as in Judaeo-Christianity, or Islam or the Zoroastrian tradition. There is instead a place: *tian* 天. There is talk of *tiandao* and *tiancheng*, the mandate of heaven. Instead of the voice of God there is the mandate of heaven. *Tian* is not a voice, but motivates and regulates the order of things. (Jullien 1996: 53–4). My conscience is virtuous by heaven's mandate. Whereas Rousseau founds morality in empirical nature, Chinese thought does so in an immanent nature. For Rousseau in the state of nature we are individuals, while for Chinese thought we are already bonded with one another. Economic connections are relational in China, and so is property: they are somehow shared and overlapping. They are immanent, that is not fully realised. As not fully realised, transactions and contract and property are fundamentally a question of process.

Myth to cosmology

This parting of East and West takes place, for Granet, at the transition from myth to cosmology. For Durkheim this was the transition from the immanent totemism, animism and myth to a more transcendental cosmological, less elementary form of religious life. This ran parallel to increased universalisation of political power from lineage, clan and tribe to more extended forms of political domination. For Weber, this was the shift from magic to the world religions. Granet's (1989: 110f) point is that in the West, in both Jerusalem and Athens, this shift was such that a transcendental cosmology was arraigned in opposition to myth. Thus we can understand Athens and the rise – via military solidarity of the various clans – of the more univeralist city and the corresponding counterpositioning, by Socrates and the other philosophers, of reason and enlightenment versus myth. In Jerusalem it was the transcendental Yahweh against the baalism of the twelve tribes. This was not just in Judaeo-Christianity, but also in Islam with the Muslim assumptions of a creator God, and indeed in Indo-European religion, and the shift from earth to sun in Zoroastrianism and Hinduism. In China, by contrast, cosmology was never arraigned against myth, but grew out of myth, was a prolongation of myth. The transcendental was less of height than depth, in the invisible immanence of the *Dao*. Thus the logic of divination, while rejected as magic elsewhere, was largely maintained. And it is thought/religion that is at stake here because Confucius's followers were as much disciples as a school. The sage incorporated both thought and religion, while being an advocate of neither philosophy nor church. The origins of *yin* and *yang* are in divinatory techniques as found in the annex to the I Ching (*Yi Jing* 易經). Here divination should be thought less as magic than as a sort of emblematic efficacy. *yin* and *yang* is less a refutation than a continuation of myth. *yin* and *yang* are already solidary. They stand not in opposition like holy and profane or thought and matter, but they implicate each other. And in their implication they, as a mediation of the *dao*, generate energy and impart a *rhythm* to the life of things that we encounter.

Yin and *yang* is far from being a first cause or a cause in our sense at all. *yin* and *yang* generate energy through their connection, through their connective solidarity. Thus, what is fundamental is not genus and particular, it is not indeed *genre* at all, which in French means both genus and gender, but it is instead *sex* (Granet 1989: 118). Thus we can understand the separation of sexes in face-to-face singing in certain rituals, and later the exaggeration of sexual difference through foot binding. *Yin* and *yang* generate through a complementarity and mutual implication that works more as harmony (*he* – 和) than contradiction. Contradiction is *maodun* (矛盾), meaning sword and shield, very different from the 'against-saying' in Latin-ate and Germanic (*Widerspruch*) languages. The emblem's efficacy works through a complementarity and mutual implication that is like the sexual connection. 'The *yin* and *yang* themselves unite and commune (*communier*) sexually'. Whereas Christian communion joins us with the body and blood of Christ, with the otherworldly, at stake here is a very this-worldly, though still immaterial, com-munion. The emblem that is for Granet also a means of classification, generates as it classifies. It classifies as *yin* and *yang* and generates as *yin-yang*. This emblem is concrete in Granet's China. It is a synthetic-concrete. So in Daoism we have the *yin* (陰) and *yang* (陽). The neutral electric pole, the moon, the female principle of the *yin* and the positive electric current, sun and male principle of the *yang*. These are not in contradiction but two aspects of the same reality of the *Dao*. Here cosmological time is grafted onto earthly time. Thus the time of the seasons is overlain by the time of the dynasties. And the cyclical seasons becomes the calendar time of the 'savants' and their '*notions astronomiques*'. These are the sages of the calendars, using the now solar (and not just seasonal) time. This is a step beyond myth towards cosmology, as the activity of *yin* and *yang* organises the calendar. It is the alternation of *yin* and *yang* that drive these rhythms: thus it drives mutations of animals, which are primarily the mutation of emblems, as sparrow hawks become wood pigeons. Thus in the transition of myth to the age of the sages the same mythic entities are given 'cosmological values'. These emblems are symbols and images, they are 'rubrics': they are 'signals', each connoting a different dimension of efficacy. In the West, rubrics normally serve for classification: in China they are '*rubriques efficaces*' (Granet 1989: 114).

Yet this emblem, as a synthetic concrete, is also an abstraction: it is less a Western transcendental abstraction, than an immanent, hence efficacious abstraction. In the West with the transition from magic, totemism and the tribal to what has been called the religio-metaphysical age, there is abstraction not just in language, with subject-predicate logic of the Greeks and the progressive abstraction of Chinese characters but also in number. But whereas in Greece the philosophers thought as much in terms of number as in linguistic formulations, in China notions of, for example, quantity, and the rationalisation of algebra and geometry were left to the surveyors, architects and musicians. The sages did not think in terms of quantity, and the distinction between the cardinal and ordinal. The sages, unlike Aristotle, do not understand the series of numbers as a framework for incipient time. Number instead again is an emblem. Even the category of the couple becomes the first of the 'numerical categories', the origins of the '*emblem numérique*'. And ' the signs of the decimal series give rise to a group of images', as a 'rubric' for 'concrete ensembles', which numbers locate in time and in space. There is a sort of geometric repartition and a numerical imparting of rhythm, of 'topographic indicators' and 'calendar signals'. In each case it is towards (Granet 1989: 128, 134–5) the classification of things. At stake is a 'vast system of correspondences', in which number goes beyond myth to 'connect things in cosmic proportions'. That is numbers are not 'abstract signs of quantity', but instead of 'value', of 'cosmic and social value'. The hierarchy of numbers attributes values of power to groups such as archers, officers, seigneurs, kings. They 'express the dignity, signal the importance of a group' (Granet 1989: 246). Numbers are signals of social value, indicators of cosmological roles.

For Granet (1989: 251) the power of the *Dao*, its efficacy, lies in its being 'a principle of order', in its being as one, a 'communing unity'. The *Dao* is '*rebelle* to all determination'. It is a '*puissance indefinie*'. The *Dao* 'renders sensible' the 'indefinite possibilities' that it confers'. The *Dao* is 'an indeterminate efficacy that is the principle of all (empirical) efficiency'. Unlike Western legitimation, virtue – the *Dao de* (道德) – is inscribed in 'the prince's efficacious authority'. The *Dao* is an (indefinite) efficacy that becomes singular (and thus determinate) in its realisation. The *Dao* and the other concrete-synthetic emblems classify, generate and regulate. In their classification they impart a hierarchy of values. Part of their generation is such singular determination, but part is also the distribution of such singularities in time and in space. Much of the *Dao* and its notion of the way, the path, go back to the age before history and myths of the Great Yu (*dayu*) and the Yellow Emperor (*huangdi*). In this narrative, Yu conquered the deluge of the Yellow River by building canals. He created order also by centralising the means of destruction on a regional scale. But the *Dao* also suggests Yu tracing the path of the river, the idea that he could '*parcourt* and *mettre en ordre*' (Ibid: 263). Here the circulation of the leader was at the same time efficacious classifying through 'delimiting bundles of realities', themselves consisting of 'names, emblems and insignia'. In 'rambling the earth, the sovereign, imitating the march of the sun, comes to be considered by *tian* itself as a son'. First the earlier principle of God (*shangdi*) and later the principle of Heaven (*huangtian*) was dominant. Thus Calendar masters define royal power, in which the chief institutes the five elements (*wu xing*) in order to distribute men and souls (*shen*). Here the king, as mediator between heaven (*tian*) and earth (*di*), prevents disorder: hence the *Wangdao* and the *Tiandao*.

The sovereign is to tour the 'four corners of the earth' to 'verify' the feudal insignias. The tour of the land and especially the south has been a trademark of a series of dynasties right up to Deng Xiaoping's in 1992. This connects to the *Dao* as a relational and virtual origin that brings about order through movement, through a way. Flow is present in a polity in which legitimation depends on preventing the deluge of rivers, in the movement of emperor or leader as master emblem, in uniting all the other emblems. This is a great part of the efficacy of Chinese culture, and of a capitalism that is unified at the highest level and intermediary levels by the state. The emperor is the *huangdi* (皇帝). Before the Han unification in 256 BCE it was *huang* or *di*, but the first Han emperor unified the two terms as his own. At the doors of the Forbidden City we see *huangtian shangdi* (皇天上帝). *Huangtian* is heaven and *shangdi* God. But the *huang* in *huangtian* is of course the imperial *huang* as is the *di* in *shangdi*: the heavens and God a bit less transcendent and the sovereign a bit more transcendent than in the West.

The sovereign, in his capacity as emblem, exercises efficacy in 'maintaining the order of civilization' (Granet's 1989: 275). Yet this is an order of civilisation 'with which the order of things is integral (*solidaire*)'. Granet's evocation of the order of things reminds us of the English title of Michel Foucault's *Les mots et les choses*, in which Foucault starts from Jorge Luis Borges's evocation of a Chinese thought in which words and things are, unlike Western modernity, not in separate realms but interlaced. Thus everything that is encountered in Chinese thought, and even in Chinese culture, is not just material, but also semantic, at the same time a sign. And these signs themselves are not in a separate Saussurean realm of the signifier but instead are efficacious as 'a mass of concrete signals'. Economic activity too is inscribed in a situation in which concrete entities connect to one another not as causal mechanism, but instead 'call to one another' in a relation of resonance. In which 'to concretely figure is also to describe and situate emblems'. It is to 'end finally in suggesting the possibility of mutations', where 'one appearance mutates into another...they can be signals of the emergence of a new concrete situation' that itself is an 'infinite ensemble of coherent manifestations' (Ibid: 273–4). Relationality, efficacy, immanence: three intertwined paradigms that structure the cultural logic of Chinese capitalism. Each stands in contrast to Max Weber's classical Protestant entrepreneur the ideal type for Western capitalism. In place of the individual there is instead a web of activities, of background activities, of forms of life that constitute the uniqueness of Chinese capitalism.

Civil society or forms of life?

Many commentators, both public intellectuals such as Will Hutton, and influential thinkers on the Chinese economy, such as Yasheng Huang, have argued that the problem with China is its lack of soft institutions of civil society. Our view, however, is that neither the Chinese economy nor any possible openings for Chinese democracy will emerge on any template that is close to Western ideas of 'civil society'. With Wang Hui (2008), we think that the political in China is inseparable from a neo-Confucian notion of rites. These rites as they more or less separate from the sacred – as formulated perhaps first by the third-century Confucian scholar Xunzi – come to take on the form of implicit practices, of social activities, of stock of knowledge, of what Wittgenstein called 'forms of life'. Both economic and political activities are embedded in these in China. Indeed it is possible any emerging rule of law and political democracy would itself be embedded somehow in these forms of life, these rites. Rights then will be less a matter of *civil society* than these rites themselves. Hence rights – as they emerge – will emerge in the context less of the institutions of civil society than in the context of rites. Hegel in *The Philosophy of Right* most systematically develops the notion of civil society. For Hegel civil society is, as we know, *bürgerliche Gesellschaft*. Its basis is property and contract law. One of the other main driving categories of *The Philosophy of Right* was *Sittlichkeit*. This is conceived in opposition to the abstraction of Kant's moral imperative, and is translated as 'ethical life'. This translation is not literal but it does work.[3] It points to an embedded and social – i.e. not individualistic – mode of not just ethics, but ethical *life*. Forms of ethical life. This is a question (not of law) but of custom, habit, everyday forms of social life. Indeed Hegel's *Sittlichkeit* is very close – and we can see this in the work of Charles Taylor (1971) – to Wittgenstein's forms of life. It is not to civil society but to such ethical life, secularised rites and forms of life that we need to look to in China.

To understand what might be a 'Chinese model', it may help to think in terms of Weber's types of social action. The two predominant forms of social action are, of course, zweck rational and wert rational action and the two residual types are traditional and affectual action. The paradigm for *Zweck*-rational or instrumentally rational and *wert*-rational or value-rational action are in the first case neoclassical economics and in the second Kant's categorical imperative. The first is about a rationality of means and the second about a rationality of ends. But both break with traditional and affectual action. Here, rational action, which is the basis of Western capitalism, is also the basis of civil society. The two types of Weberian rational action start from a refusal of both tradition and affect for a set of *a priori* principles: for *a priori* principles that disembed economic life from both tradition and affect. Economic life in China does not work this way. Instead of starting from an axiomatic, traditional action relies on previous cases. Traditional action is thus more empiricist than rationalist: it is more like English common law. Traditional action is less *a priori* than *a posteriori*. And there is something very *a posteriori* about economic life in China. It is also *affectual*,[4] in that it is based in long-term embedded relations between parties. This is the famous *guanxi* connection and, indeed, relationality is translated by *guanxihua*. Thus economic exchange in China is based not on the separation of gift and commodity exchange, instead the latter is rooted in the gift. Relationality is very different from the idea of network described in actor-network theory. The network starts from the individual (person or thing). Relationality starts from the relation and from the whole. Relationality is also very different from what Hardt and Negri (2000) call the 'multitudes'. These multitudes are understood as an aggregation of singularities. Again this starts from the individual. Relationality starts from the relation or dyad: while relationality in China starts from the relation, from the whole.

China has indeed veered from a model of the extreme *a priori* of the Great Leap Forward and the Cultural Revolution to that of the posteriori, to the sort of pragmatism invoked by Heilmann and Perry in *Mao's Hidden Hand*. Hence, the French Revolution and Russian Revolution against the Ancien Régime are two massive historical *a prioris*. Mao's revolution may have been less of one as he broke with the proletarian principles of Marxism and even Marxism-Leninism for the 'empiricism' of a peasant vanguard and the Long March. Benjamin Schwartz (1985; 2) in his *World of Thought in Ancient China* directs our attention to what Karl Jaspers (1994) called the 'Axial Age'. This Axial Age of 800–200 BCE produced civilisations, the world religions and what we know as reason. All – but one – of these Axial Age transformations was based in the rejection of things past. The Baal tradition was rejected for the personal God of Judaism, Homer for mathematics and logic in Greece, Zoroaster was pitched against tradition in Persia. The exception is the East Asian realm, which looked to the empirical and the past with its pictographic writing and final triumph of Confucianism.

Let us return to the Weberian ideal types. We previously discussed Weber's affectual action. All of Weber's ideal types of action work on the level of the actual, on the level of experience. They work through means-ends chains of causation by actual goals and ends and means. There is another literature in cultural theory today, influenced by the work of Gilles Deleuze (2009), which talks about, say, 'affective labour', but for which affect works in the level of the virtual; that is, on a level of what is not experienced and generates the actual. This level of something like potential or the potential is always present in Chinese thought. In China, however, the distinction between actual and virtual is much more tenuous than it is in the West. Life operates in an intermediate level, in a sort of permeable boundary region that overlaps the virtual and the actual, the potential and what is realised. This is characterised by Jullien (1999) in terms of 'propensity'. Such a propensity of things and people is not always being realised. It is often never realised. Yet it is as much on the surface as it is underlying, it is at the same time virtual and actual. This helps to understand forms of economic life in China. Jullien points to the *wu wei*, *wu ming* and *wu zhi* – the no action, no name, no property – of Daoism. Here the name that can be said, the actual name as it were, is not genuine or eternal name – *ming ke ming fei chang ming* (名德名非常名). Once it is said, it is realised and leaves the genuine realm of potential. As experienced, it can no longer be genuine or eternal.

The key to this is the *wu wei* (無為), the 'no-action'. This means no actual action, though potential activity is always going on: an economic activity that is empirical but at the same time always in potential. So in place of Weber's economic action as an actuals, we have the *wu wei*, of economic: not actual action, but quasi-potential *activity*. In simplified characters the *wu wei* is 无为. This *wei* here is not just action but cause: in everyday Mandarin you say *yinwei* or because (因为). So actual (as distinct from virtual) cause and action are very much the same, as they are in Western thought. Thus for Kant (1956) cognitive reason is caused and operates in the realm of necessity while moral reason is uncaused and operates in the realm of freedom. Indeed economic action by definition is 'caused' by need or necessity. At the centre of Daoism and Confucianism is a very different notion of cause that can be contrasted with wei. It is the *de*. Hence Laozi's *Daodejing* (*Dao de Jing*). The *de* (德) is often translated as virtue or goodness. As Graham (1989: 13) notes it has more to do with virtue in the sense of 'in virtue of', more to do with power or potential. Confucianism stresses the rites and music (*li hai yue*), the forms of life, whereas Daoism rejects these for retreat into the non-being (hence non-actual or non-experienced) of the *Dao*. Confucianism presumes a frame of civilisation, whereas Daoism rejects the trappings of civilisation. Confucius himself, who preceded any widespread Daoism, understood the *Dao* as it worked in the court life described by historians of the Zhou Dynasty. Confucius witnessed this *Dao* and political order to be unraveling in his own time of the Spring and Autumn Period.

The rites and ceremonies, the sacred-infused forms of life that Confucius described in the *Analects* featured the filial piety of ruler and ruled, husband and wife, master and student, older brother and younger brother. Its origins are in the very early centrality of ancestor worship in China – in the third millennium BC (Schwartz 1985: 68). Jaspers' 'Axial Age' is very much the same thing as Weber's (1988) age of the 'world religions'. Only Confucian civilisation, of the great Axial civilisations – Greek, Zoroastrian, Buddhist, Hindu and Judaic, was based on an order of the past. All the others are more *a priori*, started from a personal deity or an impersonal principle – constituted a break from the past, most clearly articulated by the Greeks counterposition of myth and reason or by the Jews in their rejection of Baal worship. Many of these civilisations were preceded by a past in which nature worship was more important than ancestor worship. For example, Baal worship is a mode of nature-worship. Here again we find classical sociology wanting. Durkheim's *Elementary Forms of Religious Life* focuses rather one-sidedly on totemism, on nature religion as *the* elementary form of religious life. Durkheim builds his sociological ontology and epistemology from such nature-worship elementary religion. This is for him the origin of society. In this, Durkheim argues against the British empiricist anthropologists who focus on ancestor worship. In China, where ancestor worship prevailed against nature worship. Here the sacred ancestors are an extension of the empirical family (Schwartz 1985: 20–28). So instead of the nature-worship dualism of sacred and profane, the ancestor-worship profane sort of slides into the sacred. Legitimation has to do less with a sacred core of 'beliefs', based around say God-the-Son or Buddhist non-being, than with justification through pointing to previous experience. This is a more empirical, traditional mode of legitimation. Ritual itself becomes more like Confucian rites and ceremonies, taking place on a sort of grey area that spans sacred and profane. For its part, everyday life becomes less purely utilitarian, but also governed by rites, by ceremonies and music.[5] Here music works through a logic of identity, of what Mary Douglas (1966) called 'group'. Music is etymologically connected to the graph meaning joy (Graham 1989: 11–14). The collective joy when music is played in the temple of the ancestors, the household or elsewhere provokes a solidarity, an identification with the ruler, the father, the teacher. And ceremonies are a question of Douglas's 'grid', of the distinctions, differences and variegations of activity, of the grid of convention in terms of how various categories should act in terms of one another.

Let us follow this thread through Wang Hui's theses in *The Rise of Modern Chinese Thought*. Wang disagrees with Weber's thesis that China was not modernising, but that a form of modernity was already developing in the context of Song Dynasty Neo-Confucianism. Wang is dealing with a sort of theory of 'Oriental Despotism' that reaches back from Wittfogel (1967) and Weber to Marx and Hegel. This addressed the 'static' nature of the ancient empires – Chinese, Indian, Egyptian and Persian. Aristotle even contrasted Greek and Persian culture in such a vein. In this context, Wang is concerned with the question of sovereignty. Already we can conceive of a notion of political action that is Western and purposive in contrast with what would be a Confucian notion of political forms of life. Wang (1997, 2009: 122–3) notes that for Confucius, politics is rites and music. This extends to Western notions of sovereignty, understanding the nation-state as an individual purposively rational actor, since the 1648 Peace of Westphalia. This is a very Hobbesian notion of sovereignty that is only echoed by that more-contemporary Hobbesian, Carl Schmitt. But what is assumed here is the European nation-state. In contrast Oriental Despotism assumes ancient imperial rule, what Wang calls a 'civilization-state' that stands in contrast to the modern nation-state. Wang's argument is that in China the civilisation-state and the nation-state very much overlap, and today they are in important respects the same. This is a different route to the modern. In this context sovereignty is also a question of some sort of exchange. Wang understands the post-Westphalia nation-state-sovereignty form of exchange as 'treaty' and the civilisational and imperial mode as 'tribute' (Wang 2011: 45–9). Tribute is ensconced in a political forms-of-life model: a sort of extension of rites and music. The assumptions of treaty are a sort of Hobbesian war of all against all, while those of tribute are asymmetric harmony. Treaty finds its homology in the property and contract law of civil society. Wang, writing of Tibet and China's ethnic minorities, speaks of a supra-systemic set of connections that couple today's Han nation to these minority areas. He looks to the work of Marcel Mauss for this. Rites are *li* (利), then gifts are *liwu* (礼物) or ritual things (Wang

2011: 65–7). In this sense the neo-tributary relations between the Han majority and the minorities in Mongolian and Tibetan and Islamic provinces are similar to a set of gift exchanges. Thus the politics of sovereignty as tribute involve the exchange of ritual things between political units. With the re-emergence of China and India perhaps a new global geo-politics of sovereignty is at stake. Perhaps in future the apposite units will not be the nation states on the European model, but supra-nations and continents like China, India, Brazil, the US and Europe itself. Perhaps something like neo-tribute or geo-political forms of life and indeed harmony will sit alongside Western Hobbesian assumptions. Indeed, in some sense empire was the rule and nation the exception. Europe was the odd one out, with the Carolingian Empire fragmenting into nation-states.

As importantly, a mode of governance based on the office, what Weber called patrimonial bureaucracy, fragmented into a set of feudal fealties in the West. In China, the logic went in the other direction. Feudal relations dominated under the Zhou Dynasty from 1046 BCE through the Spring and Autumn Periods and the Warring States. The principle of office decided more by merit in exams rather than family became important at the end of the Warring States with China's reunification under the Qin and Han Dynasties. Confucius himself was opposed to this and still believed in the possibilities of family and feudal order. But Mohist and especially Legalist thought was moving in the direction of power, office and ability (Balazs 1964: 144–5). Legalist thought dominated under the Qin, and Confucian principles were finally reconciled with the importance of law and the centrality of office against the feudalisms. We must understand such rites and music as much more – even when desacralised – than a question of rules of etiquette. They were endowed with meaning and an intensity of psychic-energy investment that paralleled such spiritual-energy investment in Durkheim's totemic sacred. This combined with the continued rites and music and filial piety provided the glue of a Chinese Empire that lasted from 221 BCE. Under this system, office holders could collect taxes and be moved from place to place every ten years or so. So we have a combination of filial piety, ancestor worship and a centralised proto-modern bureaucratically rational state. Thus, as Graham (1989: 267–9) notes, there was cohesion in China while feudal Europe fragmented.

Mohism, Daoism and Legalism contested the centrality of Confucian rites: Daoism for withdrawal and Mohism for Western-type logic, dialectic and utilitarianism. At the heart of Mohism was an analytic thinking that rejected Confucian and Daoist holism. Thus Schwartz (1985: 160) contrasts the 'yes-action', the *you wei* of Mozi to Daoism's but also Confucian *wu wei*. Mohism featured the virtues at the expense of rites and music. The virtues were also at the centre of the Greek polis. Alistair MacIntyre (1984) distinguishes the substantive nature of Aristotle's virtues from the empty proceduralism and assumptions of instrumental reason of modern politics. These virtues are circumscribed also by more or less ritual forms of life. The point is that in ancient Greece the core of virtues was the driver, while in China it was the peripheral forms of life. We need to note that other Axial religions sometimes also featured rites over virtues. Thus the importance of

Bahamian rites in the religion of India, to the point at which they supersede the sacred impersonal and abstract sacred of Buddhism. This triumph of rite-centred Hinduism over Buddhism bolstered the caste base of the Brahmins. (Weber 1958, Raju 1985). The rites are encoded in a sort of Brahmin legal power, which is rather the opposite of Chinese Legalism and an enemy of rational state bureaucracy. This would tend to promote what seems to be the chronic fragmentation of the Indian state. In ancient Judaism, the religious rites – as guaranteed by the Pharisees – became a basis for the law in the Old Testament of Leviticus. Thus Christianity fought against Pharisaic Law for the person of God in both Son and Father (Blumenberg 1985).

Even the core virtues are relational in Chinese thought. These are *ren* and *yi* (仁, 義). Ren originally meant a noble person, but has come to mean just a human being. On the right side of that graph is the graph for two or an intersubjectivity. *Ren* is often translated as benevolence. But the original intersubjectivity belies the individualist starting point of Christian benevolence. In Christianity you and God come first, or you and perhaps a generally poor, deserving public. *Ren* is always virtues in the context of an embedded relation of you and, say, your teachers and disciples. *Yi* is righteousness, but again this is not a Christian righteousness of a man in the eyes of God. It is more doing the right thing in these concrete relationships (Graham 1989: 19–22). While in Greece, Western modernity and Judaeo-Christianity at the core is the individual actor, in China it is the original intersubjectivity in *ren* (仁).

Sometimes we see these forms of life rendered as rites and music *li hai yue*, often just as ceremonies, again *li*. We recall that whereas Greek thought is focused on truth, in regard to which governing and the state are thought, Chinese thought is focused not just on the *Dao*, but on governing and on order in an intact and great China. The fragmentation into states, into say the idealised city-states of Greece and Geneva – is always understood as a bad thing. The way forward is to look back to the Zhou dynasty, to Xia-Shang-Zhou and the 'sage-kings' that governed. These are all dynasties. These dynasties ruled by on the one hand these sage-kings (*xianwang* 賢王) and on the other 'tyrants'. For Confucius and Mencius only sage-kings, and never tyrants, could bring stability. The sages, much more than Western philosophers, all wanted primarily to be political actors. (Lloyd and Sivin 2002: 47–8) Whereas tyrants would rule by force, sage-kings would use something like soft power. There was dispute as to what constituted this soft power. Daoism advocated withdrawal, yet Confucianism significantly incorporated Daoism's *wu wei*. These schools of thought, with the exception of the Mohists, who were thought to be based in the trades, featured thinkers who were drawn from the class of gentlemen: the knightly class. Hence the rites and ceremonies of the nobles were class-related. At the birth of Christianity the Pharisees, with their focus on law and convention, were drawn from the priestly, though not knightly class. Jesus of Nazareth and his followers were tradesmen – fishermen, carpenters – and were anti-Pharisaic.

The sage-kings were knight-scholars, who attained sage status, wanting to find princes that would support sages, and seeing themselves as potential sage-kings.

During the Warring States period, ex-Zhou dynasty feudal dukes gave themselves the title of king (*wang*). Music here – which merged with the rites – worked as the unifying force of soft power through the joy and intensity of sound or poetic experience. With Confucius himself operating in the Spring and Autumn Period, about 500 BCE, there is not a great distinction between man's inner space and his outer practices and *ren* (Graham 1989: 108). They are seen in terms of noble virtues. The rites and music are also closely connected to heaven and at one with the sacred. Two hundred years later with Mencius, there is a separation and the virtues are now very much inner virtues, more separated from the rites. Now *ren* becomes more actually benevolence and less the embedded practices of nobility: it joins a set of inner cardinal virtues. Even later towards the end of the Warring States Period with Xunzi, about 260 BCE, also a Confucian, there is a return to the centrality of the rites yet this time conceived not as a sacred, but very much more as convention (Graham 1989: 255–60). The relations between schools are complex. Xunzi himself was the teacher of leading Legalist sage, Han Fei. Whereas Confucianism was largely based in the east in today's Shandong province, the first emperor from the Qin came from the northwest from near today's Xi'an. If Mencius (372–289) had a positive view of human nature, Legalism's focus was on punishment and force (Balzas 1964: 204-11). Thus law came to be separated from ceremony and Confucian books were burnt. The law is impersonal and rulers need to rule according to it. This is not to do with human rights though nobles are not privileged under the law. Law primarily regulates relations between rulers, and ministers and other office holders. Later Mao Zedong was an admirer of Legalism. Legalism is the father of Weberian legal-rational bureaucracy. Legalism holds sway only under the Qin. The previous Zhou Empire as well as Xia and Shang were based on feudal relations, on the granting of independent fiefs and vassalage. For this reason, the Qin Shi Huang Di (秦始皇帝) held that none of the their kings were true emperors and that there were no true empires. Thus Qin Shi Huang Di means literally the First Emperor. He destroyed the vassalage system and installed thirty-six commanderies through the country that were imperatively coordinated under bureaucratic rules. Legalism became predominant under the Qin at about 350 BCE, under the minister Shang Yang. Later, after the establishment of the Dynasty in 221 BCE, the ideas of Han Fei (student of Xunzi) were incorporated. The Qin, whose capital was Xianyang near present-day Xi'an (Shaanxi), were militarily without parallel. They defeated the other major warring states – Yan, Zhao, Qi, Han, Chu and Wei and established their dominion as far as present-day Fuzhou and Guangzhou and even Hanoi. The elements of legal-rational bureaucracy were that the Qin was based on office and not fief and that no one was above the law. Military power was valued above all, and Confucian etiquette, rites and legitimation on grounds of tradition were rejected. There was standardisation of money, language and measures. There was a centralisation of the 'means of destruction' as all weapons of former warring states were melted down into material for statues dedicated to the glory of Qin and the First Emperor (Collins

1998: 148–55). Rule was based not on ideology or etiquette, but on strict rules of reward and punishment (commonly execution).

The Mohists had for long promoted the idea of ministerial careers for the best qualified. But by the time of Xunzi (312–230 BCE) the principle of bureaucratic office power, as distinct from Zhou feudalism was widely accepted. The question was what would the education be that prepared these office holders? For Xunzi it was education in, not the law, nor a utilitarian Mohist education, nor world-abnegating education of Zhuangzi and the Daoists. It was instead a knowledge of the now secular rites themselves. Xunzi had, again learning from Mohists, accepted the importance of reason, of argument. Thus he made his points much less with reference to tradition, to the Zhou, or with reference to Heavens *Dao*. *Xunzi* accepts the necessity of laws and accepts a utilitarian dimension to human action. But it is only the rites, the rites and music that will provide the glue to his sought-for cohesion. Thus the sage will educate office-holders and office-holders educate the people in these rites, these conventions. Examinations will be based on, not utilitarian knowledge, but knowing the rites (Hansen 1992: 317–18).

Xunzi's arguments with the Mohists is that self-interested action will lead to disorder, not order. Ceremonies and music, are necessary for order. Utilitarian principles will not work because unlimited human desire will lead to excess competition and hence disorder. Ceremonies will lead to order partly through modulating these drives towards something like a mean. Thus funeral services modulate mourning to within an acceptable range after the death of a loved one, and music will help contain the excesses of joy. Xunzi proposed, in place of what he saw as the Mohist winner-takes-all mentality, a certain measured apportioning *fen* (分) of consumption resources as conducive to political order. Convention, or desacralised rites can regulate such apportioning to help make possible political order on a continental and civilisational scale (Schwartz 1985: 312 f.).

In the religions of the Axial Age, the World Religions, there is a move from the particularism of both ancestor worship and totemic nature worship to a certain universal, a single universal. This can be a singular personal God as in the Abrahamic religions or a space of non-being, of 'a will-less' void such as in Buddhism and Daoism. This impersonal yet (unlike the immanence of ancestor and nature worship) transcendental sacred cannot even be called a 'principle' like logical principles in Aristotle. The Way Dao is not a principle. There was a historical shift from a personal god to a heavenly notion of the sacred. In the Shang Dynasty (approximately 1600–1046 BCE) a personal God, the high god, *shangdi* (上帝) predominated, while in early centuries of the Zhou Dynasty (1046–c. 750 BCE) not a personal God but instead heaven, *tian* was supreme. Not *shangdi* but *tian* dominated during Confucius's Spring and Autumn Period (Granet 1975: 64–74). Later, during the Warring States, Daoism became a force in debate with Confucianism. For Daoism, similar to Buddhism, the sacred or the Dao is seen as in the realm of non-being. This will-less non-being is endorsed as opposed to Confucian rites and ceremonies. For Confucianism, the Dao is imbricated in forms of life. The Dao of

Heaven provides the impetus for the Dao of politics and man. In the *dao de Jing* the Dao gives rise to the energy of *yin* and *yang* and to heaven and earth. Daoism became a force after Confucianism during the Warring States. It is likely that the fragments of the Dao De Jing only date from the fourth century. The *Analects*, by contrast, were compiled from the beginning of the fifth century, from very soon after the death of Confucius, from the very beginning of the Warring States Period. The contrast of Confucianism and Daoism became most apparent during the middle of the Warring States, when Zhuangzi and leading Confucian, Mencius, were near contemporaries (Hansen 1992: 185 f.). In early Warring States, just after the death of Confucius, Mozi and Mohism had their influence.

The major intervention of Daoism began in mid Warring States, with the appearance of the Dao De Jing and the presence of Zhuangzi. The Dao De Jing saw the Dao as the basis or both heaven and earth. Dao began as a word for way in a rather empirical sense when the character first appeared as a bone inscription about 1500 BCE. It later enters the realm of non-being. Confucius in in the *Analects* spoke about the Dao, the way, under the Zhou dynasty. The Dao De Jing is structured in two parts, one on the Dao and the other on the *de* (德). Here the Dao is the driver of the *de*. The *de* is a morality and a 'potency'. The *de* mediates the Dao as it drives *yin* and *yang*. The *de* is a generating force prior to the energy, the *qi* (氣) of *yin* and *yang*, and to the Dao of heaven and earth, of *tian* and *di*. All of these are energisers of the 'myriad of things' (*shi* -事), the very material things (Zhang 1992: 14–15).

In the *Analects* the Dao has taken on aspects of the sacred. There is a Dao of heaven for example. Later neo-Confucianism incorporated elements of Daoism and Buddhism. Dominant Confucianism incorporated *yin* and *yang* and a large measure of the *wu wei* – indeed in many respects *rujiao* stood in a grey zone between the Daoist (and Buddhist) *wu wei* and the Mohist and Legalist *you wei*. If the Dao is non-being and sacred to the extent that it in the realm of the invisible, then the Dao of Heaven, which is for Confucianism the original Daois now a realm of being. Yet *tian* is unlike the personal God. *Shangdi* is not *a* being. It sometimes is spoken of as acting like a substantive, but it is more a space, a place. This Dao of heaven works more in the potential activity of the *de* (which is also an ought of morality and virtue) rather than the actual action of the wei (Schwartz 1985: 81–2).

But the Confucian Dao of Heaven only has a meaning in connection to man, to the human relational intersubjective rites and music and virtues. This Heaven is in effect an adverbial timing and spacing that is at the same time these relational forms of life. God not a noun, not a proper noun, who created the world: not a Subject that operates through verbs to create objects. It is instead a sacred that always was. (Graham 1989: 195–8). Such a sacred is not transcendent, but situated in already existing forms of life. Thus we have a culture of not civil society but *Sittlichkeit*, not of Weberian purposive or goal-directed action, but of situated activity, looking for possibilities in the propensity of things. We have not positivist action but phenomenological forms of life, we have even the sacred as not subject-verb–object of god created the world but as a 'there', not a 'there is', but a 'there'. We have a culture of what in Heidegger is not the present at hand or *vorhanden*, but instead the ready-to-hand (*zuhanden*), of not text but context, of not sphere but atmosphere, not explicit individuality but implicit relationality. Not economic action but forms of economic life, and finally not the *a priori* economic actor but the *a posteriori* consequences (and context) of such economic action.

2

CONNECTIONS, NETWORKS, CULTURE

The institutions of Chinese capitalism

Social embeddedness

We have so far described economic life in China as relational and contextual and also dwelled on the differences between such a view of economic *life* as opposed to economic theories of economic *action* – theories which to no small degree have been instrumental in the reforms and changes of market economies in the West. But an extensive body of work within economic sociology and the scholarly field loosely dubbed socio-economics has with considerable success demonstrated that Western markets are not quite as detached from social life or as based on rationality as an *apriority* in the way economic theory posits. We believe it worthwhile to draw on some of these concepts for our analysis both because they shed light on economic life in its embedded and contextual sense and also because several of these theories have already been applied to China and the Chinese economy. The following three characteristics are major features of these theories, stand in marked contrast to mainstream economic theory and should also make it clear why we find socio-economics applicable to the study of Chinese capitalism.

- *Social embeddedness.* While standard economic theory posits economic activity as largely disembedded from the social sphere and structured by formal institutions based on *ex ante* and codified 'rules of the game', socio-economics and economic sociology instead posit markets as embedded in social networks.
- *Informal, not (only) formal, institutions.* Rather than focusing on the *ex ante* rules of formal institutions, these theoretical traditions have developed theoretical notions of institutions that place much more emphasis on informal institutions based on cultural and cognitive schemata. Such institutions are therefore not based on *ex ante* rules, but rather on cultural frames. That is to say that such theories still see institutions as based on 'rules of the game' but the definition

of such rules has been dramatically changed. They are here conceptualised as among other things cognitive schemata (i.e. thought) and seen to emerge through, if not 'forms of life' (see previous chapter) then at least through (routinised) social action in a reflexive sense á la Garfinkel. We are dealing with reflexively reproduced meaning rather than *ex ante* formal codes.

• *Varieties of capitalism.* The socio-economic approach has also rendered it visible that capitalism can take different forms and that market efficiency hinges on more than just enforcement of formal legal rules.

Based on these notions, we in this chapter describe some of the general distinctive characteristics of the Chinese economy and the institutional rules of the game (in the just outlined sense), which shape these characteristics as seen through the lenses of socio-economics. In particular, we try to describe how the Chinese economy is embedded in political and social life and culture more generally. Drawing on socio-economics, we ask not *if* the Chinese economy is socially or culturally embedded or if it is more embedded compared to other economies, but *how* it is embedded. We draw on conceptual as well as empirical work on the Chinese economy. While drawing on insights from comparative studies of varieties of capitalism, our emphasis on embeddedness means that we do not adopt pure varieties of capitalism style of analysis which would tend to compare China with other national economies and perhaps even fit China into a fixed typology based on different configurations of ownership, labour markets and political regulation. We find such analysis potentially incapable of capturing in depth both the distinctiveness, diversity and transformative speed of an economy such as the Chinese, and we are wary of coarse-grained generalisations and comparisons that in the worst cases verge on the meaningless (see also Kristensen 2005: 386–7 for some critical reflections on this matter). An example of such generalisation could be when otherwise knowledgeable observers such as Fligstein and Zhang (2010) finds similarities between the economic architectures of China and France. We find that little insight into either economy is gleaned from this.

After emerging

In the spring of 2011, Jim O'Neill, the economic analyst who first coined the term BRIC, added four more countries (Mexico, Indonesia, Turkey and South Korea) to a group that originally comprised Brazil, Russia, India and China. At the same time, O'Neill remarked that the description 'emerging market' no longer applied to any of these countries (*The Guardian* 2011). Above all, China, by several measures the second largest economy in the world had long since grown out of this category. Several of the current main characteristics of the Chinese economy (not least the involvement of the state), have in some academic quarters (notably neoclassical economics) been seen as mere irregularities, which would be ironed out as the Chinese economy matures. But the persistence of these characteristics beyond the point where China is seen as an emerging economy raises questions about whether these traits are mere irregularities. Indeed, such questions have long since been debated by scholars working within the broadly defined field of socio-economics and researching the Chinese economy (Guthrie 1999; Walder 1993; Wank 2001). While there is a large deviation in the conclusions that have been reached, there is general agreement about some of the dominant traits of the Chinese economy, of which the involvement of central and local governments and the importance of social connections (*guanxi*) are the arguably most mentioned. The disagreement, on the other hand, is primarily on whether these will remain important traits as China's economy develops further. Whether these traits will be causes of continuing competitiveness and growth or if they will become liabilities for the Chinese economy in the long term (see Fligstein and Zhang 2010; Keister and Zhang 2009 for comprehensive reviews). Reflections such as the one above regarding the label 'emerging market' help remind us that even if the particularities of the Chinese economy are not sustainable, they have existed long enough that the Chinese economy has developed considerably under contin-uous influence of these traits, which in turn make their immediate dissolution seem unlikely no matter their long-term sustainability.

While standard neoclassical economics and some related scholarly fields, such as contingency theory in organisation science, assume that economic markets posit a range of universal characteristics, in the last 20 years a host of literature that subscribes to the contrary has appeared. Work on varieties of capitalism (Hall and Soskice 2001), business systems (Whitley 1994, 1999) and economic sociology (Fligstein 2001) has demonstrated that economies are differently structured and governed across and also in some cases within nation states; that they follow mutually different historical trajectories; and that they each over the years have undergone fundamental changes. These differences apply to how economic activities are organised (that is, what organisational forms firms take); how firms are owned and controlled; how firms are connected to suppliers, customers and competitors; what rationales drive managers and the strategies they follow; and how labour markets, legal institutions and other institutions, which are a major part of firms' environment, are structured.

It is therefore no surprise that most of the work on economic organisation in China draws on this type of research and falls within the field of socio-economics. What defines this field, apart from a suspicion of the universalist claims of neoclassical economics, is a general focus on institutions, networks, social capital and culture. Economic markets are seen as being in constant states of disequi-librium, which lead to high uncertainty (Thévenot 2001b; White 1981, 1988, 2002; Whitley 1994). Agents in such markets are in Whitley's (1994: 4) words neither 'atomistic price takers' nor 'omnipotent price makers'. What characterises economic action in such markets is that:

- Agents monitor and interpret each other in constant efforts to seek out individual niches in order to avoid direct competition and also seek to establish alliances with similar aims (White 1981, 1988).
- Agents bring into the market various resources such as social capital, which they use to reduce uncertainty (Adler and Kwon 2002; Granovetter 1985a; Podolny 2001).

- As described in detail above, all actions, decisions, and strategies are dependent on conventions, cognitive schemata and concepts (most of which ultimately are culturally based) that help to reduce uncertainty. As a consequence, what is 'rational' varies according to cultural and institutional context and there is much isomorphic imitation within any market (Fligstein 2001; Powell and Dimaggio 1991;Thévenot 2000, 2001).

In summation, compared with mainstream economics, socio-economics is more concerned with how economic agents negotiate perpetual uncertainty. Socio-economics does not subscribe to universalist assumptions about market equilibrium or rational profit seeking. Rather, what is 'rational' is seen to depend on social and institutional context and is hence much more complex and pluralistic – and ultimately grounded on meaning. Markets are not seen as simply sustained by a few formal market institutions such a property rights and contractual law – which by implication also would mean that markets are disembedded from the social sphere. On the contrary, socio-economics takes markets to be socially and culturally embedded and therefore a variety of (also informal) institutions sustain economic exchange.

It should then also be clear why we see socio-economics as a logical starting point for analysis of developing Chinese markets based on propositions such as those outlined in Chapter One regarding relationality and propensity. Rather than seeing relationality as an indicator of an emerging or imperfect market, socio-economics offer a conceptual toolbox for analysing how relationality might reduce uncertainty or otherwise function as a basis for informal institutions. From the viewpoint of socio-economics, no market is completely disembedded, governed only by formal and *ex ante* rules of exchange. Socio-economics, in other words, denies us the possibility of simply defining the difference between the Chinese economy and any given 'Western' ideal type through difference in degree of embeddedness (with less embeddedness being seen as more 'effective'). Any difference must instead lie in the type and form of political and institutional embeddedness. An indication that such differences exist may be that findings of socio-economic studies of Western economies may not in fact apply to China. For example, it has been argued that the celebrated finding of economic sociology and network analysis that so-called 'weak ties' benefit labour market participants (Granovetter 1985b) does not hold true in China where it instead are the strong ties which are beneficial (Bian 1997). In a similar vein it is often discussed whether *guanxi* is different from other forms of social connections broadly conceived of as social capital (Dahles 2007; Fan 2002; Gold *et al.* 2002; Lovett *et al.* 1999).

Hybrid organisations and (local) government control

One can argue that China since the late 1970s has deregulated or privatised its economy. This in the sense that private entrepreneurship has been allowed, that many state-owned enterprises (SOE) and town and village enterprises (TVE) have

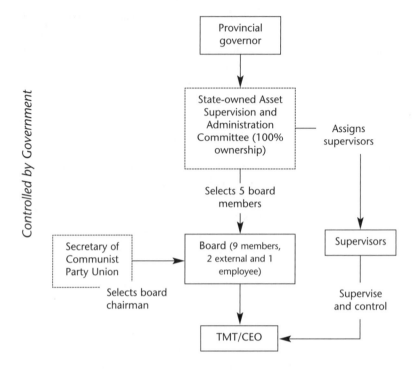

FIGURE 2.1 An example of how different government and party agencies exert control over a local government-controlled business group

Source: We are indebted to Professor Na Pengjie for providing us with this information and illustration.

been sold and dismantled, and that a good part of its labour force has lost its 'iron rice bowl', the security of state employment, housing and benefits (see Introduction and Chapters Three, Four and Nine). But, in spite of this, the Chinese government has remained in control of the economy. For example, many of the shares of listed companies are held by asset management companies that in turn are controlled by the government, be it central, provincial or local. The by far biggest and most important of these is SASAC, but similar government-owned asset management companies (in effect local SASACs) can be found in provincial, regional, municipal and district levels also. In the case of SASAC, which currently controls more than 120 of the biggest companies in China, this has resulted in a (state) ownership concentration (Wang *et al.* 2012). Many of these listed private companies are part of business groups (described in more detail later in this chapter), the parent company of which often is owned by state-controlled asset management companies (and in several cases in turn by SASAC). Various government organisations, as well as the communist party unions, can appoint board members of the business groups and in this and other ways exert considerable influence over the companies in the business groups. One example of this is illustrated by Figure 2.1. From a corporate governance perspective, questions over control of Chinese companies are therefore often extremely complicated and opaque matters, often resulting in the companies needing to be placed on a public–private continuum rather than being categorised as either public or private (Nee *et al.* 2007; Walder 2010). According to data developed following a method of the Chinese Securities Regulatory Committee for determining who is the ultimate controller of companies, a little less than 10 per cent of the listed companies in China are controlled by central government and approximately 18 per cent are controlled by local government. Some corporate governance scholars question this, arguing that government control via business groups *de facto* exceeds these numbers (personal communication). And of course, these figures are based on formal types of ownership (largely shareholding) and say nothing about the multiple – but informal – ways government exerts influence over the private sector.

These more informal linkages and ties between companies and government have been documented by many of the socio-economic scholars working on the Chinese economy. It has for example been emphasised that business–government hybrids not only exist based solely on ownership but also due to particular organisational forms. Victor Nee for example talks of close inter-organisational relationships between collective enterprises and local government, not only based on property rights but more generally on alignment of interests between these parties, which gives rise to what he calls neo-localism. Such a regime is dominated by 'cadre entrepreneurs' (Nee 1992: 14) who can reduce the transaction costs and uncertainties (due to the weak institutional framework of the Chinese economy) by means of their connections to local government as well as to the private sector. Nee's account is but one of a series of theories that all centre on the economic activities that happen in-between what in Western parlance would be public and private sectors. Oi (1995) has, mainly, in the context of rural areas and TVEs documented similar alliance making between government and entrepreneurs. Walder (1995, 1993) has described a regime of 'local corporatism' where government control over economic enterprises has been decentralised not only from central to local governments but also to sub-branches of local government. The result is mutual competition between local government branches and strong incentives for economic performance as the relatively small sub-local government branches do not possess great financial volume, which again means relative hard budget constraints for the enterprises even though they enjoy (nominally) government protection. Walder argues that these companies are facing neither hard nor soft budget constraints but rather flexible constraints in that they can bargain for funds. But if they are performing poorly, this reduces their bargaining power – hence an incentive for performance is created (Walder 1993).

While there is general agreement on the alliances between local government and businesses, the question of what creates the efficiency (if any) of such alliances is a contested one. For Nee and a school of neo-institutional theorists, the performative edge of such hybrids lies solely in the reduction of transaction costs in an uncertain environment with weak institutional frameworks. But according to this school of thought, formal market institutions, above all ownership rights and contract law, will with time be strengthened and the links to government will become liabilities rather than assets. Indeed, Nee finds empirical evidence that this is already happening with state- or party-controlled companies performing poorer relative to privately controlled companies. Hence, Nee *et al.* state that:

> China's success is built on the gradual liberalization of product and labour markets, increasing openness to foreign trade, investment in infrastructure and institutional reforms such as property reforms and privatization which provide individual actors with sufficient security for planning, investing and economic risk taking. The beneficial effect of the state results from its capacity to construct and maintain institutional environments that provide positive incentives to entrepreneurs and managers at the firm level to invest in economic growth.
>
> (Nee *et al.* 2007: 44).

Such reasoning is opposed by other work including the local corporatism thesis proposed by Walder (Guthrie 1999; Wank 2001). In fact, discussion of this matter has been a mainstay in the field of Chinese management studies for at least two decades now (see Keister and Zhang 2009 for a review). According to the former school of thought, China certainly is undergoing rapid changes, yet institutional path dependency, continuing political control, cultural influences and generally the weight of history will influence the developmental trajectory to such a degree that Chinese markets, while changing, will remain distinctly Chinese.

The future role of government in China and how that role will shape economic markets in China has as indicated been, and continues to be, a major point of discussion. These discussions regarding the shape, efficiency and robustness of the Chinese economy have been prolonged by very mixed and conflicting empirical results (Fligstein and Zhang 2010). Inherent methodological difficulties (what for example constitutes a tie between a private business and government official body?) and also simply the size and diversity of the country, has made it difficult to arrive at conclusive evidence. But as mentioned earlier, it is not only China but also other countries such as the other BRIC countries that have developed markedly in the last decades. These countries, and China not the least, have now developed to an extent where they cannot necessarily be described as emerging markets any longer. The label 'emerging market' has above all been used with reference to institutional voids, that is, the lack of efficient formal institutions such as law. Under such circumstances the state often gets to play an important role mitigating the increased transactions costs associated with such voids. To be sure, China's markets still exhibit institutional voids, but the form of state capitalism that has crystallised can be said to if not rest precisely on the creation of formal institutions, then at least help fill the voids. SASAC and other state-owned asset management companies today constitute highly important institutions. These institutions have their roots in the four state-owned asset management companies created to hold the bad debt of poorly performing state-owned banks, but that institutional form has since then become an important tool for the Chinese government to hold and control stocks in private companies. This is arguably the best example of an institution of state capitalism, which seems to perform efficiently (Wang *et al.* 2012) yet which at the same time is a far cry from the prescribed view of efficient market institutions.

How the Chinese market institutions will develop in the future is obviously anybody's guess, but based on the development of the last 30 years coupled with the scholarly analyses reviewed above at least the following points can be made:

- The current level of both central and local government control remains substantial even if taking into account only formal control through ownership.
- The current forms of state capitalism cannot be explained simply by institutional voids (see above). For example, SASAC is a direct product of economic modernisation – not a patchwork solution to lack of modernisation.
- Economic development continues. This development continues to rest on policies, which grant regions considerable autonomy and encourage regions to innovate policy-wise (with successful innovations later being implemented nationwide) at the same time as regions are competing fiercely with each other to create growth and tax revenues. An overall tendency is hence to promote regional experiments and autonomy.

An important element of this developmental trajectory has arguably been land and property development, especially in the first decade of the twenty-first century, which was dominated by a property boom (see Hsing 2010). As local governments are controllers and leasers of land, this has created a sizeable source of revenue for local governments and means that property developers have needed to maintain close ties to local governments and have become major players in defining economic change at the local level.

The diversity across regions has arguably been downplayed in the literature so far. The decentralisation and devolution of economic control has meant a development of rather different business regimes across regions and cities in China (Krug and Hendriscke 2008). Moreover, because the government apparatus is multi-layered, there may also very well exist different types of institutions within regional business regimes (Krug and Hendriscke 2008). Hence China's economy is an institutional bricolage in two dimensions, both within regions and across regions. Another aspect of this bricolage is arguably that the various business regimes are in experimental states. A central argument of much of this book is indeed that the Chinese economy can be conceived of as a series of experiments, conducted by central and certainly local governments who are adopting various strategies to various problems under varying political, economic and social constraints and seeking to exploit the various types and quantities of resources. This fact, and the subsequential fact that no one is likely totally to withdraw from a large-scale experiment (experiments in China are often local without being small scale) in the middle of the process, is a strong argument for why central and above all local governments will remain major players in China's continuing economic development. At the same time, some of these experiments may also be juggernauts on course to economic disaster – some highly leveraged property developments and infrastructure projects undertaken by local government are such prominent possibilities.

Finally, we would like to note that much of the literature on the Chinese economy has focused on the institutions, which are currently being created as part of the reform process while the history and the historically and culturally grounded institutions that have coordinated economic activities in earlier periods have largely been ignored. Having said that, it must be granted that historical path dependency is a complicated topic. This is both because the Communist revolution to some extent tried to eradicate some of these informal institutions (for example, patriarchal networks) and because the Communist rule till 1978 created new institutions that have been carried into the market-reform period (rural cooperatives, the precursor to TVEs, being one example). For the same reason the 'new' market reforms arguably in some respects should not be seen as the ushering in of the entirely new but rather as the re-emergence (and in the case of pre-1978 Communist rule institutions, reconfiguration) of the old. And finally, although many of these institutions have been ignored, there is one major exemption namely social networks (*guanxi*), a subject to which we now turn.

Social networks

So far, most of this chapter has based its analysis on ownership and corporate control and the changes in formal institutions in China. But another topic begs attention, namely the importance of social networks, *guanxi*, which is a topic, which has received a lot of attention both in trade and scholarly literature on Chinese business (Keister and Zhang 2009). At the same time, social networks have played a major conceptual role within socio-economics in the West. In the West, network theories such as those of Granovetter (1985a, 1985b) and White (1981, 1988, 1992, 2002) have been at the forefront of the conceptualisation of economic activities as embedded in social networks. Moreover, network theory has played a central role in the development and application of theories of social capital to economic life (Adler and Kwon 2002; Lin 2001; Moran 2005; Perera and Weisinger 2007; Rost 2010).

Networks feature just as prominently if not more so in the socio-economic literature on China a) because any emerging market normally is seen, due to weak institutional structures, as rendering coordination through personal connections and relations of personal trust more important, and b) because of the cultural importance of *guanxi* in Chinese culture and business (Chen and Chen 2004). In several theories, for example the work by Boisot and Child (1996) described in detail later in this chapter, these two perspectives are combined in an argument that *guanxi* networks essentially fill out the institutional voids of Chinese markets as these networks can facilitate expectation building and trust between transactions parties in otherwise uncertain conditions (see also Xin and Pearce 1996). *Guanxi* ties are thus held to reduce transactions costs by helping facilitate trust and reduce uncertainty.

Guanxi – a system of social connections developed and maintained through exchanges of gifts and favours – is deeply rooted in Chinese culture (Gold *et al.* 2002). At least three main features characterise *guanxi*. First, *guanxi* are dyadic relations between individuals who through such personal ties are bounded by an implicit psychological contract to follow the social norms of *guanxi* such as maintaining a long-term relationship, mutual commitment, loyalty and obligation. A quality *guanxi* is also characterised by the mutual trust and feeling developed between the two parties through numerous interactions following the self-disclosure, dynamic reciprocity and long-term equity principles (Chen and Chen 2004: 306). Second, *guanxi* is fundamentally relational (see Chapter One). It may signify a network consisting of more than two people or may be a dyadic relationship between Ego and Alter. It may, however, also be a relation between an individual and an organisation (Park and Luo 2001). It may be a relation between people with unequal social status – hence there may a strong element of clientelism or patronage in *guanxi* relations (Fan 2002). Third, *guanxi* also has a strong affective element (Gold *et al.* 2002: 7–8; Kipnis 2002), and in that respect it may be distinct from social networks in its Western, more instrumental sense. *Guanxi* is for the same reason not easily acquired, but deeply rooted in mutual personal affection. The affective element means that *guanxi* relations take time to establish and that they at least within the family sphere are based on rituals, which enforce mutual if not affection then at least respect (Kipnis 2002) and crucially also deference if the ties in question are vertical elements in hierarchical structures. But the affective element of *guanxi* also extends beyond the family and is also important in business relations (Kriz and Kealing 2010), which among other things means that *guanxi* ties build on, and create, deep trust. That does not mean that *guanxi* relations cannot also be strategic and used instrumentally, but they at least also involve a deep-rooted sense of mutual commitment and expectations of loyalty. *Guanxi* involves the exchange of both 'things and feelings' (Chen and Chen 2004: 309).

Guanxi ties of course constitute networks and actors can utilise the *guanxi* ties of those to whom the actor has ties, hence exploiting the network's *guanxi* rather than the *guanxi* only of the dyadic alter (Fan 2002). Nevertheless it has been argued that *guanxi* in essence is *dyadic*. It does not constitute group membership but rather denotes sets of dyadic relations, which in many instances are based on Confucian cultural scripts, for example the relations between father and son, wife and husband, etc. (Chen and Chen 2004). This is one reason why Chinese culture may ultimately be termed relational rather than, say, collective. Hence, in the case of family, *guanxi* constitutes not so much networks based on scripts concerning family (group) loyalty as a culturally scripted tie between two persons occupying different positions in a family hierarchy.

As mentioned, *guanxi* is widely held to play important roles in many spheres of society including business. It is frequently observed that *guanxi* relations can exist between government officials and private entrepreneurs, and hence *guanxi* ties can facilitate the hybrid economy described above (Nee 1992). There is an ongoing discussion about the implications of *guanxi* in terms of its legitimacy in economic markets. It is for example discussed whether exchanges of favours is a catalyst for corruption (Gamble 2007: 277–8; Lovett *et al.* 1999). A similar discussion concerns economic efficiency as there have been several attempts to establish empirically whether *guanxi* ties actually benefit company earnings (e.g. Luo and Chen 1997). The results of these studies have generally been somewhat contradictory and inconclusive (Dahles 2007 and see Chapter Five for a detailed review of literature on this), perhaps not surprisingly, given the complexities involved when attempting to create quantifiable measures of *guanxi* between not only individual actors but also whole organisations with very diverse environments. This topic is dealt with in Chapter Five where we also present our own empirical data on this subject.

The importance of networks in Chinese business extends beyond personal ties. Perhaps the best example of this is the already-mentioned business groups. These business groups were for a large part if not set up then strongly encouraged by the Chinese government during the privatisation of SOEs in the mid-1980s (Keister 2007). The Chinese government studied business groups in other Asian countries, not least the Korean *chaebols*, and decided to emulate these organisations. Business networks primarily consist of vertically linked companies controlled by one core company (Keister 2001: 339).

The benefits of business groups are by and large due to the uncertainties of the Chinese markets, which make internal transactions in the group beneficial. Companies may choose to pay a premium on, for example, supplies if this means that they can buy supplies from people and firms with which they have well-developed either organisational, business or social ties, and by so doing reducing uncertainty/ transaction costs related to delivery and quality of said supplies (Keister 2001). Hence, they often will choose suppliers within the business group. However, Keister also finds that internal business group transactions increasingly have become unprofitable as the Chinese markets have developed and formal institutions have been strengthened (Keister 2007). Then again, she concedes that in spite of this development, the government's continuing involvement means that the Chinese economy may still exhibit 'pre-reform' features (Keister 2009: 20), so networks today remain abundant as well as important. It is also important to note that even though these business groups today constitute formal organisational structures, they to a large extent spring from *guanxi* networks. When business executives under the auspices of the government worked towards establishing the groups, they drew on existing *guanxi* networks when selecting partners. On this basis, Dahles (2007) suggests that business groups are socially and culturally embedded in *guanxi* networks.

Theoretical implications of networks

So far we have seen how *guanxi* ties may facilitate trust and hence reduce uncertainty in markets characterised by institutional voids and therefore potentially high uncertainty as there is little by way of formal institutions to ensure transparency and sanctioning of breaches of trust. We have also seen how such networks can become organisational when they gel into business groups. Finally, it has been indicated that *guanxi* ties can span boundaries between market and government. In a now classic article, Boisot and Child developed a theoretical description of Chinese markets evolving into what they call network capitalism. Where Western markets have undergone a process of institutional change and modernisation, which Boisot and Child describe as a development of fiefs to bureaucracies to markets, China's developmental path has so far been one from fiefs to clan-like networks. Modernisation in the West, they argue, led first to a codification and hence a dissemination of information. Codification here means the formalisation and de-contextualisation of rights and information, two examples being property rights and accounting standards. On the back of this development, bureaucracies could be created – precisely because such forms of organisation rely on formal and context independent procedures. But this development also set off a large-scale diffusion of, in the context of the economy, transactional relevant information. The simple reason for this is that context-independent information with applicability across cultural and social contexts has widespread relevance and is easy to transmit and impart. This in turn leads to a decentralisation of central bureaucratic power into market structures, that is, a decentralisation of economic decision-making from central bureaucracies to private firms. Hence Western markets rest on formal rights, standards and procedures, which create information that is relevant across social contexts and easily diffused.

Boisot and Child argue that while modernisation certainly is happening in China, leading to and sustaining high-growth rates, the Chinese modernisation process is not evolving around clarified property rights in the neoclassical sense or other forms of codification. Rather, economic coordination happens through social ties between primarily local government and the private sectors, supported and legitimised by personal relationships rather than formal rights. The reform process has entailed decentralisation as economic decision-making has been moved from central bureaucracies to private companies. But in the absence of codified information and formal market institutions, private entrepreneurs instead rely on personal connection with local government:

> In this way, local agencies of the state fill many of the roles that in other business systems are played by private intermediary institutions. The isolation of firms in this sector from supporting institutions, at least those within the local economy, is therefore relatively low. The localised nature of state-dependency for firms in this sector supports the development of their personal interorganisational connections, which are of greater importance than appears to be the norm for this type of business system, as described by Whitley.
>
> (Boisot and Child 1996: 611)

According to Boisot and Child, the Chinese modernisation process is consequently one of decentralisation without codification. And precisely because decentralisation happens without codification, this modernisation process is stuck in the 'iron law of fiefs' (Boisot and Child 1996: 604): With more decentralisation there is an increased need for institutional support, which in this context means social networks. It should, however, also be mentioned that the absence of codification does constitute a limit to how decentralised markets can become. Indeed, they will often remain relatively local as they rely on local personal ties. It is worth noting that Boisot and Child's theory arguably is flawed by not paying attention to the early bureaucracies of ancient China just as their notion of modernisation has a distinctively Western-centric ring to it. However, the insights from Chapter One in this book concerning early forms of modernisation and bureaucratisation in China only adds to the argument which is central for us: Chinese bureaucratisation is not based on codification, that is, *ex ante* rules and standards as described earlier, but on 'rites and music' (see Chapter One). Accordingly, the marketisation now happening occurs without the support of such codified information.

David Wank, based on his empirical study of entrepreneurs in Xiamen, develops a theoretical framework labelled Institutional Commodification. The commodification in question is that of the vast variety of goods and resources held by the State and the Party. These resources have been commodified through a transformation of 'institutionalised social relations of control over these vast resources' (Wank, 2001: 29). For Wank, the economic reforms have entailed a reconfiguration of communist networks into hybrid (semi-private) and clientelist networks where private operators draw on connections to government actors to secure access to the now commoditised resources. The transition has led to the creation of clientelist networks where private operators draw on connections to government actors to secure access to the commoditised resources. They do so for strategic purposes, and the ties are characterised by social unevenness and power relations, but the networks and ties that are constituted rely on an institutional base of (personal) trust (Wank, 2001: 31).

These two complementary theoretical accounts, Wank and Boisot and Child, first both highlight the cross-sector, public–private relationships, which form the hybrid character of the markets described above. Second, they explain why hybrid forms of ownership and social ties may remain pivotal also during the later stages of economic modernisation. For both Wank and Boisot and Child, the networks are both substitutes and obstacles for the development of decentralised private markets and formal market institutions. As such, these theories clearly choose sides in the continuing debate about the role of networks in the face of economic modernisation.

Such theoretical accounts that emphasise *guanxi* also revoke the question if such networked capitalism really is that different from Western capitalism. In spite of the somewhat mixed results of empirical analyses of effects of *guanxi*, there is little doubt that *guanxi* connections constitute a resource in China. As such, *guanxi* is comparable to social capital, which is a theoretical concept that has gained much currency also in Western economic sociology and management theory. Yet with this comparison the distinctiveness of network capitalism is denigrated. Connections seemingly matter everywhere, so what, if anything, lends *guanxi* in China its distinctive nature and value?

Social capital, we should first note, refers to any type of social relation that may constitute a resource. That is, social capital as a concept does not refer to a specific type of social relation but to a resource: it covers any type of relation that constitutes a resource in a given societal setting. It follows that some social ties may constitute social capital in one context but not in another. *Guanxi* therefore cannot be compared to or contrasted with social capital but should be seen theoretically (given that *guanxi* is a resource) as one such contextually defined form of social capital. Second, while social capital hence is an open-ended concept, the social capital literature generally harbours descriptions of, and distinctions between, primarily two types of social ties that both constitute resources and hence both may be seen as social capital. These are most often named bridging and bonding ties (Adler and Kwon 2002: 24; Moran 2005). The former is often associated with the work of Granovetter (1985a) and Burt (2004), the latter with Coleman (1988) and Putnam (2000). In broad terms, these two different kinds of ties bring two different kinds of benefit for agents who possess such ties and hence belong to networks. Bridging ties bridge structural holes, that is, bridging ties are (from the viewpoint of ego) ties into a cluster of nodes that do not otherwise have ties to ego or to other participants in ego's network. For that reason, bridging ties tend to provide non-redundant information as Ego has no other similar sources (Burt 2004). Before Burt developed this notion of structural holes, Granovetter had already shown that ties that provide non-redundant information tend to be weak ties, in the sense that they are not established by or maintained through kinship or close friendship. Indeed, strong ties to family and close friends tend to generate more redundancy as these will be mutually acquainted and have similar acquaintances. But if strong ties are not providers of non-redundant information, they are, on the other hand, providers of other resources such as trust and social cohesion. This is obviously also a resource and hence also a form of social capital. This is the type of social capital emphasised by Coleman and Putnam. Bonding ties tend to be more intensive and based on mutually recognised norms. As such, they often lead to socially closed clusters of agents. Such networks, resting on mutually shared norms and reciprocity and mutual obligation, can in Coleman and Putnam's view secure social cohesion and a strong civil society. Such networks can, however, also develop into clientelism and corruption.

To sum up, the theoretical distinction is between open (with structural holes) networks of weak ties versus closed networks with more intensive or strong ties governed by shared norms, which form relatively cohesive groups. Rather surprisingly, some scholars, including Boisot and Child, tend to characterise *guanxi* ties as belonging to the former type (Boisot and Child 1996; Wang 2007). But as seen above, bridging ties constitute loose couplings between actors, loose here meaning ties without strong norms of reciprocity and mutual obligation. Such ties can provide information because they can span social and also geographical distances. As described above, *guanxi* ties are, however, characterised by a strong affective element, which is not ephemeral, but established through sustained social interaction, gift giving, etc. Moreover, *guanxi* networks are guided by mutual commitments and observance of norms and hierarchical structures. And finally, the *guanxi* ties described in the theoretical account of network capitalism are not (or rather cannot be) geographically dispersed as the uncodified information is useless outside of context. Although there are no theoretical grounds for postulating a direct correlation between, say, geographical distances, variance of social milieu and structural holes, some correlation between at least the latter two can be assumed. On the basis of this, we hold that *guanxi* cannot be described as weak ties. This may lead to the assumption that *guanxi* consists of strong ties. That assumption is of course seconded by the work of Bian (1997, also mentioned above) who shows how strong ties matter when applying for jobs in China, simply because it is not information (gained from weak ties or networks with structural holes) but favours – the exchange of which hinges on expectations of returns and hence norms of mutual commitment – which are exchanged in the networks (see also the discussion of Bian in Guthrie 2002). However, while *guanxi* ties can be directly compared to strong ties, they may at least not be similar to the bonding form of social capital. That is to say that *guanxi* ties are strong ties without a bonding effect. The reason is *guanxi*'s dyadic character, which means that it arguably creates not group solidarity but rather reciprocal commitments between dyads. Conflating strong normative dyadic bonds with bonding forms of social capital may therefore be a mistake. *Guanxi* in this sense might be said to constitute a third form of social capital, which constitutes resources for individual actors but not communities. Another formulation of the same point would simply be to say that *guanxi* is a dyadic form of bonding ties.

Culture and institutions: the foundation of network capitalism

Given the sweeping reforms that China has undergone, why are such social patterns of network formation not quickly eroded by modernisation? And how are such networks linked with the relational culture we described in Chapter One? Starting with the latter question we find some obvious linkages between accounts of network capitalism and the modes of thoughts, which were analysed in Chapter One. We see first of all some obvious parallels between network or *guanxi* ties and relationality, but on a deeper level we also find the importance of context and the absence of distinction between figure and ground – which results in less abstraction – to be important explanations for why (social) context matters relatively more and for why (abstract) codification (or disembedding) has not occurred to a full extent. Moreover, we have in Chapter One described relational culture as being dyadic, something that resonates with the *guanxi* networks described in the review here. These dyadic networks rest on a relational ethic. We saw in Chapter One that efficacy foregrounds the particular rather than the general. It rests on no abstract principles or distinctions between figure and ground, profane and sacred, etc. Similarly, the dyadic is social without an abstract other or abstract rights derived from such a projected other, collectivist yet also particular, and individualist yet rooted in respect for singular others. *Guanxi* ties, we have argued earlier in this chapter, are neither bridging ties nor bonding ties. Not being bonding means precisely that they are social yet particular. A relational culture is collectivist yet not necessarily generating solidarity with any abstract other – only with the dyadic other or family and only through ties, which also have an instrumental side to them. We have for the same reason talked of a civilisation without civil society.

Moving to the former question, if the existence of such a lack of abstraction is accepted as a reason for the institutional forms found currently in China, it can only be described and explained by deeply rooted schemata of meaning and modes of thought. We hence hold some deep-lying meaning schemata, which create comparable lesser distinctions between actual events and causal and social context; less of a distinction between sign and signifier, etc., to exert great influence on Chinese culture and through this on Chinese institutions, which for the same reason so far have been relatively more relational as well as contextual. Institutional theory, above all the branch of institutional theory developed by organisation theorists, provides one account of why there is a marked degree of cultural path dependency even in a phase of radical transformation. Institutions can, drawing on this tradition of scholarship, be loosely defined as 'rules of the game' or humanly devised constraints (North 1990: 4), which govern and structure human action. Such rules may be either informal (e.g. cultural norms) or formal (e.g. legal code). Institutional theorists have in various contexts studied how institutional changes rarely happen uninfluenced by cultural and social context. In that sense, what is 'rational' is a culturally negotiated concept and highly contextual. Institutional theorists draw on phenomenology and symbolic interactionism to describe how culturally grounded cognitive schemata and culturally grounded frames define what is taken for granted and what is meaningful (Powell and Dimaggio 1991: 8–28; Scott 2008). Such taken for granted frames form the basis of routinised professional practices, which has the consequence that mutually distinct and sometimes conflicting frames of understanding can develop across professions. None of this means that changes cannot occur, but it does sometimes mean that changes only occur on the surface while older cultural grounded practices remain underneath, decoupled from the high aspirations of institutional reforms (Drori *et al.* 2003: 15). In Chapter Eight we provide examples of such decouplings in the Chinese financial system, but the same argument extends to all spheres of the economy and beyond.

While the definition of institutions in this theoretical framework comprises much more than formal institutions, the basic premise of institutional theory still holds when it comes to economic markets: institutions reduce uncertainty and hence transactions costs. A definition of institutions as rules of the game that go beyond formal *ex ante* codes shows that while the formal or legal institutional framework remains relatively weak in China, informal institutions such as networks step into this void and assume similar roles – albeit arguably, following Boisot and Child, in a more local and contextualised mode. It may be argued that a weakness of this broad take on institutions is that the distinction between culture and institutions becomes fluent (Redding 2008), yet it also makes it possible to grasp the impact of culture on institutions and economic action without reducing everything to culture. The basic premise is that culture acts as a reservoir of meaning (knowledge and norms), which may form building blocks for institutions. Like many authors working with institutions, we here take point of departure in phenomenology with its focus on different meaning schemata that structure any actual perception of the world. Or put differently, the web of meaning that is culture not only contains a stock of knowledge (Berger and Luckman 1991) with which actors make sense of the world, but also structures how new knowledge is being created. This insight is embedded in the phenomenological tradition from which Berger and Luckman hail. The stock of knowledge differs across time as well as cultures, and hence things are perceived differently across cultures. Culture constitutes a web of meaning, which in the most general sense constitutes the schemata, or 'rules of the game' also for the generation of new meaning. Culture is hence prior to, or more basic than, institutions. Or as Redding puts it, meaning is the sediment at the bottom; whole intuitions are at the surface (2008: 266). By the same token (Redding 2008: 260–62), a key task for socio-economics is to relate institutions to culture.

Linking culture with institutions does not reduce agents to cultural dopes. The focus on phenomenology in new institutional theory leaves much space for individual action – one reason being that we are dealing not with culture as Parsonian norms but culture as a set of cognitive schema and classifications, which is a difference with wide-ranging implication (Powell and Dimaggio 1991: 19–26). Agents, while not being cultural dopes, are culturally formed and are constantly subjected to various control efforts. In Harrison White's network theory, control efforts both presuppose and generate new ties (White 1992: 67). Each tie in turn generates and is supported by stories and meaning. As ties stem from control efforts, 'stories come from and become a medium for control efforts: that is the core' (1992: 68). White in other words conceives of networks as social structures, which are formed in a recursive relationship with individual actors striving for control. Similar to Gidden's structuration theory or Bourdieu's relational praxeology, for White neither identity (action) nor control (structure) are *a priori* determinants. Nevertheless, meaning comes to play a prominent role in these recursive mechanisms as meaning (stories) come to frame configurations of ties (White, 1992: 87). Actors seeking control have their strategies for control framed by meaning stemming from previous ties.

Conclusion: market reforms and social networks

Having described in the above sections a) the path dependency of institutional developments; b) how networks may reduce transaction costs; c) how a relational culture is linked with networked economic practices and d) how control efforts are ingrained in all social tie formations, we put forward the following propositions: if market reforms in China (for sure at an initial stage, but we argue that much of the following also applies to later stages of reform) has meant a decentralisation of state decision power over, and interventions into, economic affairs, and if that decentralisation occurred without there being formal economic institutions in place, then it seems inevitable that the economic transaction structures that were created by the reforms would happen within social networks including local and regional government. There were resources to be exploited and hence incentives for entrepreneurial activity. But there were also immense uncertainties, and existing power (control) structures, with party officials remaining in the centre of the web, continued to exist precisely because the market reforms entailed decentralisation of political power rather than privatisation. Moreover, there were (and are) cultural norms and cognitive schemata prescribing networks as the means to navigate both uncertainty and power. As a result, *guanxi* relations with officials were a logical choice of strategic resource for doing business. Echoing David Wank's descriptions of commodified communism, Krug and Hendriscke argue:

> It was rather the way economic agents overcame institutional uncertainty (which weighed more than relational uncertainty of the Williamson transaction cost type) by devising new forms of corporate governance, networking and collaboration with local government agencies. The resulting new organisational forms aimed at a 'loose coupling' of ownership rights and resources as a more flexible way of exploiting new business opportunities.
>
> (Krug and Hendriscke 2008: 84)

As markets have developed and formal institutions have been created, the importance of *guanxi* networks may have diminished. However, good connections are always a resource, also in developed economies, and hence *guanxi* will remain social capital (albeit less pivotal) also in the time to come. At the same time, we suggest that the real crux when it comes to importance of political connections is the continuing control of governments (especially local) over key resources. As long as this control is maintained, new exchange structures will continue to evolve along a historical path of government–private relations.

3

RELATIONAL PROPERTY AND URBAN TEMPORALITY

China's urbanism in the city of experts

China's urbanism and emergent markets

There is a received common sense about the nature of China constructing capitalism. It appeals to the iconic landscapes of Shanghai and Beijing and the GDP growth rates both before and after the credit crunch that have dwarfed those in most countries in Europe and the US. In all of these narratives, *the city* in China exemplifies a speed of transformation that confounds reportage; facts on the ground change faster than the time it takes to report them. The city also realises the extraordinary scale of economic growth and demographic concentration; a movement of labour and capital that is arguably unparalleled in scale in the history of humanity. By early 2013 speculation focused on whether real estate had become a bubble market. The total value of property sales in 2009 – US$644 billion – were alleged to equal one-eighth of the total GDP for the year (Ramzy 2010). Sales taxes, loan restrictions and purchase restrictions were introduced in 2009 and 2010, the China Academy of Social Sciences argued that fiscal controls introduced had taken effect but that it remained unsure whether this would produce a 'soft landing' or a dramatic collapse as 'property sales have slumped by more than half across the nation prompting developers such as China Vanke, China Overseas Land and Investment and Longfor Properties to cut prices by 20 to 40 per cent to improve cash flow' (Li 2011).

How should we understand the emergent real estate market at the heart of urban change? The transformation from the control and allocation of housing by work based *danwei* systems of organisation in the post-war Communist years to more complex patterns of ownership, use and development rights, ways of dwelling in the city and modes of organising firms, companies and foreign investment has paralleled city growth (Zhu 2000; 2004). The future metropolis is consequently an outcome of both demographic and political change. It stages the cumulative outcome of the attempts of the technocrats of urban change – the planners, architects and local government officials – to map and control urban form on the one hand and the aggregated efforts of individuals and companies, civil society and property developers to translate their aspirations into places to live and spaces to work in the rapidly growing city on the other. And when the pace of change is so rapid and the scale of metropolitan growth so unprecedented globally, factors of temporality and scale reframe what it might mean to be metropolitan.

In this chapter we focus on the changing city through the lens of new property markets that have appeared in China since the 'reform and opening up' of 1978 and more particularly since the land use rights reforms of 1988 that structured the emergent urban real estate economy. If the former marked the moment that China began to open up to the global economy it was the latter that fundamentally marked the emergence of new urban market forms. In this chapter we suggest that the institutional architectures of these new markets are contingent. They reflect path dependencies of historical and geographical variation. The new markets are based on ambiguous and plural property rights rather than the clear and singular consolidation of bundles of rights advocated in certain articulations of neoclassical economics. The sustained combination of public and private interest in land and property markets reflect entanglement or hybrid combinations of state, public, sectarian and private interests. To this extent the invocation of Deng Xiaoping to create 'socialist markets' (or a socialist market economy) needs to be taken seriously in considering the new concentrations of growth in the cities of China. In China the culture of the economy reflects both the particular private/state hybrids of city markets that have evolved since land sales expanded after 1988 and the traditional networked interpenetration of economy and society that predates 1948 and post-dates the reforms and can be traced 'from the soil' as landmark scholar Fei Xiaotong first outlined in 1947 (Fei 1992 [1948]).

Primary research in Shanghai, Shenzhen and Beijing and ethnographic engage-ment with three real estate companies in Shanghai suggest that the strengths and weaknesses of China's opening up and reform are closely linked to this pluralisation of market forms and the working through of their ambiguous and plural property rights (Guthrie 1997; Ho 2001; Wank 1995). The standard analysis of market-based post-socialist transition argues that market efficiencies eliminate the inefficient allocation of resources promoted in socialised models of production and distri-bution – 'soft budget constraints (SBC)' – through the clarification of transaction costs. One way of analysing property markets in China would be to characterise their reform as partial and incomplete – some transaction costs have been intro-duced but others have remained in the tangle of state influence and private interest and are economically suboptimal (Huang 2008). But another way – that we prefer to suggest in this chapter – is that local states become the sites of pluralised experiments in urban change tied to the reform of city property rights (Oi 1995). Some are more successful than others. And so consequently growth models in one part of China compare with development models in other parts of China.

In the real estate markets of China, negotiating and promoting urban futures brings together incommensurable forms of expertise to address the 'problem of the city'. Expertise serves to predict and manage the future – investment strategies, architectural design and development planning are all mediated through social networks (*guanxi*). These forms of expertise translate unknowable uncertainty into knowable risk – not through calculable market optimal pricing alone but through effective combination. In one sense this is similar to the phenomenon that Thrift has described in the economic sociology of the West as 'knowing capitalism' – the production of social knowledges of the way the economy works that comes as much in the West from the private sector's reflexivity as from academic theorisation (Thrift 2005). It also relates to what Arrighi (2009) has characterised as Adam Smith's synthesis of governance and market making in a *political* economy.

The chapter argues that the emergent combinations of property rights in today's China are both the determining features of the market form and the drivers of a mode of urbanism that frames a particular understanding of 'futures present' in the city. The ways in which risk, uncertainty and market calculation are managed in the cities of twenty-first century China reflect particular combinations of knowledge and worth. Knowledges generate a calculus of future potential of urban form that is articulated by the work of *city experts* – architects, planners, local government officials. These experts bring to bear on urban terrain competing and sometimes incommensurable measures of the value and worth of both the parts of the present city and the potential form of the future metropolis or the good city (Boltanski and Thévenot 2006, Chapter 4). Their operation captures both *what works* and what does not work in the real estate markets of China. More particularly it opens up an understanding of how development is driven through combinations of institutional forms, cultures of governance and individual actions in a configuration that we argue in this volume in general and the following chapter in particular can best be described through the conceptualisation of *local state capitalism* rather than the teleological evolution of emergent markets that replicate a Western model. The chapter draws on both extended interviews with over 100 architects, planners, developers and local government officials in Shanghai, Beijing, Chongqing, Shenzhen and Tianjin between 2007 and 2011. It also draws on the engaged ethnographic placement in three real estate companies in Shanghai between 2007 and 2009.

Three matters are at stake when analysing the turbulent landscape of property markets that structure China's emergent urbanisms. The *first* is a historical inquiry into the movement from a Maoist past towards a present that may or may not be accurately described by the vernacular description of the socialist markets of the early twenty-first century. The *second* is a more normative argument about how these new forms of exchange – 'emergent markets' – should work both in China and across the world. The *third* is a necessarily more speculative exercise that considers the causal significance of those market formations that are particular to contemporary China and addresses their significance. In this context there is an analytical task to *describe* the nature of the markets in land and property that is logically distinguished from the task of *explaining* the causal consequences of these market formations. And in the expanding field of urban studies of China there is considerable and growing literature on both how we make sense of the contemporary city (Chan 2010; Chan and Zhang 1999; Wu 2002a) and how we might accurately describe the nature of the land economy (Haila 2009; Wu and Yeh 2007).

In the first part of the chapter we argue that the path dependency of emergent markets structures the emergent forms of urban China. An attention to the bundles of rights tied up in property and real estate makes visible the path dependencies of metropolitan change in today's China, the consequence of the reform process and the ongoing source of institutional ambivalence of the different rights linked to a single property. Markets are consequently dependent less on finite transactions between specific interests and more on ongoing relations between parties. This sense of relational market governance creates both unstable uncertainty and calculable risk. In the second part of the chapter we consider the different forms of expertise that measure the value of land in terms of its aesthetic value (architecture), market price (commodified real estate), functional relation to the city as a whole (development control and land use planning) and situation within governmental imperatives (local government). These forms of expertise emanate from incommensurable measures of land value and the worth of parcels of real estate. Mediating between these incommensurable forms of expertise demands particular norms of governance to facilitate development and generate manageable measures of risk. In Western models of city change the primacy of any single expertise is contingent, priced and realised in financial values of transaction sales and hope values. In the cities of China, relational governance provides the medium through which the commensuration of these measures of spatial worth lend city change particular temporalities – the pace of rapid urban transformation and the reason for development stagnation.

Part 1: 'Making markets': property rights and urban form

Routing urban change: path dependency and market formation

The city in Mao's China was viewed with a degree of suspicion, a bourgeois and consumerist site in a developmental model that privileged rural agrarian economic growth. Over time as the *danwei* organised urban life as a patchwork quilt of city spaces (Bray 2005), city residents became a relatively privileged group in Chinese society. However, the growth of cities was curtailed. After a period of productivity immediately after 1948 private property in the city was finally abolished in 1955 and urban populations barely grew over the next 30 years (Naughton 2007, 114–119). Over time, the city population was protected by the 'iron rice bowl' that guaranteed the fundamentals of urban life through the 'the five pieces of clothes' (Cui 2011): employment for life (the iron rice bowl), welfare for life, allocated *danwei* housing, and free educational and health facilities (provided by *danwei*). Not all *danwei* had these in the city, only the biggest ones; the collectives in the city provided its members with very few of these clothes.

But in the period of time since Deng's reform and opening up, economic development and hyper-rapid metropolitan change have gone hand in hand. McKinsey predicted that by 2025, 225 cities in China will have one million people living in them (Europe has 35 today). Three hundred and fifty million people will be added to China's urban population – more than the population of today's US and by 2030 1 billion people may live in China's cities. In comparison, from a population of just below a million in the 1801 census London took 140 years to reach its peak population of 8.7 million and for much of that time was the largest city in the world. In contrast the sheer speed of urban growth in China is extraordinary. Shenzhen grew from a population of 300,000 to a metropolitan region of between 10 and 17 million in just thirty years and even Shanghai's formally registered '*hukou* population' grew from 10 to 14 million between the reform and opening up of 1978 and 2007.

In 1980 the first wave of Special Economic Zones (SEZs) were concentrated at a distance from Beijing; in Shantou, Shenzhen and Zhuhai in Guandong, Xiamen in Fujian and (later) the entire island province of Hainan. Shortly afterwards the second wave of open cities in 1984 focused on 14 coastal cities including Dalian, Qinhuang*dao*, Tianjin, Yantai, Qing*dao*, Lianyungang, Nantong, Shanghai, Ningbo, Wenzhou, Fuzhou, Guangzhou, Zhanjiang and Beihai. The record of these experiments was mixed (Yeh 2000) but allowed for novel market institutional arrangements to evolve. These experiments drew on alternative and proximate models of economic development and generated rapid economic change. But to characterise the experiments as the dichotomous displacement of socialist control with capitalist markets would be both descriptively inaccurate and conceptually simplistic. The modernisation of the opening up in China consciously avoided the sort of transition seen in Russia and Eastern Europe from the mid-1980s.

Inspired by Demsetz's (1967) landmark intervention a long-standing literature in the sociology of property rights has identified how the particular configurations of property rights structure five (or more) dimensions of property (Alchian 1961; Alchian and Demsetz 1973, Carruthers and Ariovich 2004): the objects of property (what can be owned), the subjects of property (who can own), the uses of property (what can be done with it), the enforcement of rights (how property rules are maintained) and the transfer of property (how property moves between different owners). The legal philosopher, Tony Honoré, identifies 11 separate characteristics that may be present in property, and argues that there is no definitive characteristic, nor any case of 'absolute' property (Honoré 1987). Each of these at different times and different places has been subject to varying regimes of governance and commodification in the emergence and reform of the cities of today's China. Although post-1978 reforms are geographically uneven they have shared a sense in which some of the rights most closely associated with notions of ownership have been redistributed.

What remains of greater dispute is the extent to which optimal economic development rests on securing clear and unambiguous property rights that clarify (and potentially price) the responsibility and the unintended costs of development.

In neoclassical economics this was historically understood in terms of the problem of externalities (following Pigou); in development economics a longstanding debate questions whether or not the clarification of property rights is a prerequisite for successful economic development (De Soto 2000; Mitchell 2002, 2005). But as we shall see, the China model is characterised by what Peter Ho (2001) has described as a form of '*deliberate institutional ambiguity*'. In the context of 1990s rural reforms he argued that such ambiguity was economically functional for rural economic growth where 'institutional indeterminacy is the 'lubricant' on which the system runs: the ambiguity of legal rules allows the land tenure system to function at the *current* [stress in original] stage of economic reforms' (Ho 2001, 400). Whether or not similar uncertainty has helped or hindered either the pace of urban change or the efficiency of the economic model in China is more contentious (Read 2008; Zhu 2002; Zhang 2000).

Li (1998) suggested that in the first ten years after the Land Management Law reformed urban property rights in 1988 it is possible to 'calculate that the average annual growth rate of the revenue generated from the urban land and real estate markets (in both the private and public sectors) amounts to 32 per cent per year …This can be compared with the national GNP average annual growth rate (on nominal terms) since 1988, which is 18.27 per cent. A further breakdown of the revenue from urban land and real estate markets shows that the average annual growth rates for incomes generated from the market transfer of land use rights, from the sale of commodity real estate and the rental activities are 35.4, 29.7 and 48 per cent, respectively. They all exceed the national GNP average growth rate' (Li 1999, 195).

The centrality of land economy to both city change and GDP in China consequently demands an examination of the historical paths through which the particular property markets of urban China reconfigure both our understanding of the bundle of rights that defines the notion of property and the market formations that structure the metropolis. In this context, there is a geographical trace that links the emergent property markets in China to their most dramatic exemplification in the Special Economic Zone in the city of Shenzhen in the early 1980s, a path that links to the experiments in land markets in colonial Hong Kong and the central formations of liberal government. This historical path dependency is helpful in writing a history not only of the present realities of urban property rights, but also in making strange and contingent the seemingly familiar or taken-for-granted nature of property relations in the metropolis of the West.

The geographical dissemination of land reforms and property rights in urban China is interesting. For Li (1999) there was no official 'launch' of urban land use rights reform in China. In April 1987 (predating the normal start date of 'opening up'), the State Council proposed a new policy for the transferability of land use rights in the free market. The SEZ Office was delegated to test the idea in four areas of the nation: Tianjin, Shanghai, Guangzhou and Shenzhen (Li 1999, 194). The geographical spillover of an experimental model in the Shenzhen special economic zone demonstrates some interesting institutional similarities. It also resonates with efforts to qualify the monopolisation of land rights that were prominent in the West at the height of industrial expansion that can be traced to both colonial experiments with land and property reform and nineteenth-century concerns around the monopolisation or accumulation of land as a factor of production (Tang 1994, 1998, 2008a and b, 2009; Tang and Chung 2002).

Specifically, the land markets of both Hong Kong and Singapore owe their genealogy in large part to the combination of colonial rule and nineteenth-century debates around the reconciliation of capitalist growth, private property and general wellbeing that focused on the productivity of land ownership. In both sites the present 'natural' appearance of a capitalist property market belies particular histories of market formation where the state, far from retreating from interference in the market, continues to play a central and controlling role. Haila has characterised their status as 'property states' (Haila 2000), economic growth models that rely fundamentally on state control of the property market to drive the engine of development. Near-state monopolisation of land ownership (in Hong Kong) or expropriation (in Singapore) have generated dynamic property-driven city growth in these exemplars of 'tiger economy' capitalism, led by major oligopolistic real estate companies that have effectively been licensed by the state to use land under limited regimes of property rights. In separate dimensions of 'property rights' land *use* is fungible, but state prerogative remains. In each case, state control of some of the rights associated with property ownership has been deployed strategically in the service of generating economic growth.

In Hong Kong, after the Opium War and the slow demise of the East India Company the state owned almost all of the land. Developing a model originating in England, the Hong Kong government sold formal titles to land that was qualified as leasehold on a limited basis through auctions to private developers. The emergence of an oligopolistic market with five to eight major players in the real estate sector has been sustained to the present. Many of the early real estate interests in Hong Kong remain active inside and beyond the boundaries of Hong Kong to this day. Lai (1998) has characterised the leasehold system in Hong Kong as a system in which the government allocates land as a private commodity through the market mechanism, arguing that this is a form of neither collective nor common ownership, neither 'public' nor 'private'. In the 'high land price policy' of Hong Kong the state becomes a powerful rent-seeker through limiting the supply of land over time (Forrest and Lee 2004; Fung and Forrest 2002). Land revenues become central to municipal fiscal policy but scarcity is sustained (and high density encouraged) as part of municipal government revenue planning. In Hong Kong, the value of land sales were at their peak in the early 1990s when they constituted one-third of total public revenues (Lee 1999), while the price of land accounted frequently for up to 75 per cent of the price of private property. In these 'property states' the right to transfer land is time limited, the rights to earn income and transfer are regulated and the right to enforce property rights is guaranteed by the rule of law. Consequently, the market is structured in such a way that not all property rights are subject to the process of commodification. The archaeology of the urban fabric reflects this socio-legal configuration in both the trends in sales and ownership of dwellings and the architecture of what urbanist Li Shiqiao describes as the logic of maximum density (Li 2005) that takes in Hong Kong the city as a *tabula rasa* on which returns are safeguarded through scale, density and height of development, generating the iconic landscapes of central and mid-levels.

As scholars such as Chan (1999) and Li (1997 a and b, 1999 a and b) have demonstrated the land use rights model in urban China was first experimented with in the Shenzhen special economic zone and three other cities after 1987. It is not the case that we are asserting that the specific path dependencies of China's property market moves straightforwardly from Hong Kong a few miles north to Shenzhen and thence outwards across the Pearl River Delta and to the rest of China, although in one interview in 2008 a senior researcher in Shenzhen Academy of Social Science asserted precisely this process of geographical dissemination. The reality is much more complex, the speed of change and variation in the working of property markets more diverse in the period after the 1988 reforms.

However, Shenzhen represents the site that funnelled massive Hong Kong investment, the largest source of Foreign Direct Investment (FDI) in China, including the separation of 'the right to use' from 'the right to possess' (from Hong Kong's Land Leasing System (*tudi pizu zhi*) to Shenzhen's Land Transfer System [*tudi churang zhi*]), the separation of the management of assets from the ownership of assets (from Hong Kong's 'Window Company' to Shenzhen's 'Red-Capped' Enterprises). Red-Capped Enterprise formerly referred to those Hong Kong-based companies under direct or indirect control of the Communist Party of China (Chan 1999) including the enterprises such as China Merchants Bureau (tracing back to the Qing dynasty and operating first in Shanghai) and China Resources. Since 1980s, it also referred to those companies with governmental background. We return in Chapter 4 to a similar experimental company model that links the city of Tianjin to London's Docklands in the 1980s.

The routes followed by the reform and opening up process and the historical and geographical contingencies of market formation are important. Much of the initial experimentation in the early opening up period drew on expertise and capital that was routed through Hong Kong. Hamilton (2006, 140–44) has argued for the particular influence of the Hong Kong model on the path dependencies of China's reforms. For most of the opening up period the largest sources of FDI has been from Chinese transnational links to Hong Kong, Taiwan (Lin 2007; Ng 2004; Tseng 2009) and Singapore (Willis and Yeoh 2000, 2002). In part this is because of the location of SEZs – close to HK, Taiwan and SE Asia – so shared language – Cantonese and Hakka. Some of the most well-known residential property developers in China – including Vanke, the largest, and Shui On – the developer of Shanghai's prestigious Xintiandi – have origins in Hong Kong. The cultural links between Hong Kong and Shanghai are also long-term, historical and cultural (Lee 2008) and the expansion of some real estate companies from Shenzhen to Shanghai drew on such links.

The experiments in Hong Kong in the late-nineteenth century colonial period were themselves also reflective of the debate in the evolution of nineteenth century liberal government that frequently saw land banking and land holding as speculative and non-productive activity that should be discouraged in productive capitalism. In a critique that emerged more from Parliamentary Whigs than the conventional left, unproductive land ownership and rent seeking was a central focus of critical Liberal policy debates throughout this period. The nuances of the critical land debates of the nineteenth century, their fundamental questioning of specific property rights, are at times forgotten and the twentieth century's crude juxtaposition of 'capitalist' valorisation of property rights and 'socialist' collective ownership obscure their continued relevance today. Positions that saw the responsibility of government serving as the enforcer, which guaranteed land productivity rather than speculation, developed in ways as mainstream as William Gladstone's concerns with land reform when four times Prime Minister of the UK in the late-nineteenth century, and as populist as the American Henry George's land tax movement. In Henry George's land tax model speculation is prevented by taxing annually the full value of land, incentivising productive use and discouraging speculative land holding. George's ideas were taken up in many different parts of the globe, including by Sun Yat Sen, father of the nation of China (*guofu*) and first President in 1912 after the overthrow of the Qing Dynasty, and whose ideas are said to have influenced the land economy development model in Singapore in particular (Haila 2000).

It is through this historical geography that we can see the roots and the routes through which property markets emerge in today's China. The analysis here highlights both the familial links between Shenzhen, Hong Kong, Guangzhou, Tianjin and Shanghai and the contingency of property rights models. They also highlight the symbolic centrality of the Pearl River Delta appropriation and adaptation of the Shenzhen model in driving forwards metropolitan change in the 1990s in particular.

This trajectory also emerges from a very basic distinction in post-revolutionary China between 'urban land' that is owned by the metropolis and rural land rights that are collectively owned (Naughton 2007 118–120). Much of the Anglophone China studies literature in the post-war era has focused more on rural change than the city, following the agrarian emphasis of the Maoist model. Only more recently has the city become more of a focus as demographic transition has urbanised. If we start with the understanding that these city property rights are plural rather than singular then the ways in which the juxtaposition of politics and jurisprudence, economics and society are subject to multiple configurations – from the SEZ experiments onwards – it becomes a fascinating driver of both the patterns of urban change in China and the ways in which we might understand the dynamics of the cities of the twenty-first century globally. Interests in property might be variously ambiguous or clear, multiple or singular (Ho 2001; Zhu 2002). Reforms consequently relate to matters of clarity, plurality, efficient allocation of resources and collective interest.

If we unpick the historical trajectories through which real estate markets emerge, we can identify four contours around which the linked processes of urban growth, property rights reforms and market formation emerges in China. The first is the sense of *path dependency* of the property market, where historical configurations of property rights are articulated in the built form alongside current practice which is itself being changed by mutating property rights regimes. The second contour emerges from an understanding that what is at stake in real estate driven urban change in post-1978 China brings particularly *hybrid forms of state and market*. Unpicking the particular codes and practices of any specific regime of urban transformation rests in part on an understanding of the particular moment of mutation of this hybrid form. Third, the pace of change, the imperative to respond quickly to the planning, design, marketing and purchasing of real estate places a premium on those forms of knowledge and expertise that can understand these hybrids, calculate the risk involved in investment and construction, make sense of the futures of the city present in the contemporary, focusing particularly on disciplines such as architecture, planning and design alongside profiles of actuarial return that comprehend metropolitan speed and *urban temporalities of the contemporary city*. The temporalities of urban change lead us to make sense of the emergent markets through the ethnographic lens of these forms of disciplinary expertise that bring together alternative ways of evaluating, and calculating the potential to create new urban forms. Fourth, in situations where the legal obligations of the developer, the owner and the purchaser are commonly in flux then the responsibility for the unintended consequences of urban change becomes more important; the classical economics of *the externality* defines a territory in which uncertainty is subject to jurisprudential change and risk is calculated through the particular regimes of worth that shape the urban environment at any one moment in time.

Institutional configuration in urban China

A significant body of urban scholarship has emerged in recent years to make sense of the dynamics of urban change in contemporary China, linking the descriptive challenge on the forms of market that are emerging in the city to the normative challenges of preferred institutional configuration. In this chapter, we draw in particular on the work of three leading contemporary urban scholars of China – Fulong Wu, Anne Haila and You-Tien Hsing – to make descriptive sense of this patterning of the contemporary real estate market in China and on the work of the critical legal theorist Cui Zhiyuan to understand the alternative urbanisms that are made possible by the particular path through which markets have emerged at the heart of urban change in the transitions in China since 1978.

From Wu's work we take a sense of the importance of scaling reform changes and identifying the traces of past regimes of urban governmentality in contemporary urban form. From Haila, we draw a sense of the contested normative nature of property markets – both in China and globally – and the perils of ignoring the path dependencies that generate any particular city setting. And from Hsing we derive both a powerful description of the local dynamics of metropolitan change and a foregrounding of both the spatialisation of state power and the temporalities of the politics of city transformation. Perhaps most importantly, Cui's work suggests a sense of how the externalities of city change that emerge from the unintended consequences of urban China property regimes provide a boundary object of the different imperatives to rule, to calculate, to engineer, to plan, to design and to engineer urban form.

As one of the most extensively published urban scholars in China, Fulong Wu and colleagues have developed a longstanding research interest in the trends in real estate market development (passim Wu 2002a and b, Wu and Yeh 2007, Xu *et al.* 2009). Wu has described how new market mechanisms are grafted on to old state institutions rather than displacing them, the significance and structuring of FDI (particularly from Hong Kong and Taiwan) in mainland China real estate and the 'power persistence' of local government in emergent markets (2002a, 154–6). Wu and his colleagues distinguish between *denationalisation* and *destatisation* in the development of urban land markets (Xu *et al*, 2009, 892), with the state frequently reasserting state power. The juxtaposition between state and market in Wu's work is at the heart of an argument that 'the production of the built environment is more than an object of state regulation. If the creation of market institutions is facilitated by the state, better regulation is the result' (2009, 893). Consequently (2009, 900), 'because the state itself is becoming an actor, property rights in urban and rural land are in a dramatic process of commodification without due regulatory constraint…This absence has created negative externality which should be eliminated through regulation'. Wu's work also highlights the significance of land expropriations (through local government zoning rural land as urban) and the growing significance of illegal transactions.

The analytical emphasis in this perspective is on the need for more effective state regulation, the rehierarchisation of some state regulatory functions as central government tries to control the excesses of some municipalities described as an upwards rescaling of state power, distinguishing between spontaneous (commonly illegal) urban developments and prestigious local state-led renovation and regeneration programmes linked to multi-centred urban structures in context of general urban sprawl. Interestingly in Wu's work, the deep focus on the detail of real estate markets speaks to an urban studies debate about city form but tends to capture the state and its bureaucrats through a sense of singularity of purpose. This could be inflected productively through a more Foucauldian understanding of the plural governmentalities of state power and the contradictory impulses subsumed within the institution of the state at both central and local levels. Consequently, the state's rationality speaks clearly through Wu's work but the messy compromises of development that interest us here (and its resistance) is less of a focus.

Anne Haila, in a series of articles (Haila 1999 a and b; Haila *et al.* 2006; Haila 2008, 2009) has criticised both scholars on urban China and scholars inside China itself for adopting too readily a naïve realistic understanding of what the market is, how it should work and the sorts of reforms advocated. She has strongly criticised the manner in which the 'institutionalist' school of land economy and its putatively normative description of how markets should work is both advocated by external experts on China modernisation and some contemporary Chinese scholars of land economy and urbanism. By contrast, for Haila the particular realisations of the property market in Hong Kong and its translation through Shenzhen and Shanghai into a model of rapid city change in mainland China naturalises market forms that are contingent. By normalising a specific Western market form, disguising the plural and complex forms of actually existing markets, China scholars – Haila argues – ignore or mask contingent decisions about property rights and the contradictory rhetorics of Coasian markets that seek to price unintended consequences of development (externalities) and state imperatives. In contradistinction to the cognitive certainties of the institutionalists' arguments she suggests that the common law tradition of precedent and political contest allows for a more nuanced definition of both how the real estate market already works in many parts of the world and how it might work in an emergent real estate arena in China. For Haila, the market as an institution of governance potentially accommodates both (cognitive) utility maximising market rationalities and proper state prerogatives that act in the interests of the public good. Importantly, Haila's work involves both a contentious (and contested) description of what the emergent market is in China (Haila 2008 and 2009) as well as a powerful but controversial normative argument about what the market should be. In making sense of the speed, the scale and the future of China's urbanisms it is important to retain simultaneously consideration of and distinction between the descriptive and normative elements of these arguments.

In a series of articles and an important monograph You-Tien Hsing's work focuses on the territorialisation of power through the work of 'socialist land masters' in the great urban transformation of contemporary China. For Hsing (2010) land has moved to the centre of local politics in post-Mao China. It now shapes the restructuring of Chinese state power and radically influences state society relations. The 'urbanisation of the local state' leads to three types of distributional politics: a politics of resistance calling for land and property rights; non-confrontational politics of economic rights between land-owning village collectives and urban government at the urban fringe; and, third, the politics of the landless, the 50 million or more displaced peasants captured by a politics of deterritorialisation. In this theoretical framing, the city is mapped through alternative forms of civic territoriality. For Hsing, a former student of Manuel Castells – 'it is the dialectical "urbanization of the local state" – more so than the linear concept of "state led "urbanisation" – that characterises the relationship between the local state and the urban process in China today' (Hsing 2010, 7) and 'urban land-use planning has replaced economic planning as the main vehicle of state intervention in the political economy' (Hsing 2010, 9).

Her work generates a typology of three kinds of place and dominant power relations:

1   Inner city municipal government and state agencies that occupy and control premium land parcels.

2 At the urban fringe a contest between urban and rural governments competing for control of land conversion.
3 At the rural fringe (urban places in rural fringe) a struggle between township governments and rural villagers.

Hsing foregrounds two questions she suggests should be the heart of urban studies in China: how does state and society shape and become shaped by the great urban transformation and how does space play a role in these contested processes. But equally interesting in Hsing's work – though less explicitly examined – the contrasting temporalities of the city define the politics that emerge from this suggested focus. In the inner city the land battle is between the socialist past and the present market economy. On the urban edge it is a grab in the present for a bet on the future. At the rural fringe the low status of rural elites mean that uncertainty structures the attempt to squeeze as much as possible out of the present.

All of these powerful theorists share a sense of the city in China that is made into a political and economic subject by regimes of power. Such perspectives are helpful but only go so far in understanding the emergence of markets in the city and cities structured by markets. While some of these traditions of critical scholarship in urban studies destabilise a naturalistic understanding of the market that emerges through post-socialist transition, it makes less clear the sense in which markets assume particularly hybrid forms structured by both the cognitivist logics of economics and the institutional settlement of law and legal regulation of new property rights. In this sense if the work of urban studies directs us towards a sense of the city's subjection to regimes of power, the focus of Tsinghua and Cornell legal theorist Cui Zhiyuan in a forthcoming monograph effectively turns jurisprudential discourse back on the economic. Cui reverses the discursive play of Nobel laureate Ronald Coase, who argued in the 1950s and 60s that unintended consequences of growth, the externalities of urban change, could be internalised through pricing, clear and singular property rights. In Coase's school of 'law and economics' market mechanisms displace legal deliberation of Pigouvian externalities of change. In the wake of the financial crisis of 2008 where many Western financial institutions were seen as 'too big to fail' Cui argues for a rethinking of conventional Coasian logic. Considering the ethical basis of regulatory exception in an analysis of the interplay of Soft Budget Constraints, externality and property rights leads to Cui's central contention '…That the dilemma of Soft Budget Constraints (SBC) sheds new light on the legal doctrines of *competitive injury* and of *damnum absque iniuria*' – the ineradicable conflict among different holders of property rights and the infliction of economic harm without full compensation. The identifying of the institutional dilemmas of limited liability, central banking and bankruptcy reorganisation amounts for Cui to identifying the existence of vertical conflicts over property rights. Cui argues that conventional 'institutional' analysis of SBC is qualified by the policy constraints that are present in Western economies in the actions of central banks, in the institution of bankruptcy and the working of systems of limited liability (Cui, forthcoming), all of which implicitly socialise specific externalities. In these circumstances, Cui implies where and when externalities should be socialised and where privatised is more contingent than neoclassical economics sometimes suggests.

As Buiter (2009) claims, solvency is 'a private good that has been provided publicly and socially inefficiently by the state' because unlike the 'hard' budget constraints of true markets where you are responsible for your own debt, 'soft budgets' disperse the responsibility for debt and the consequences of failure. However, in its Coasian form this leads to an argument that 'hard budget constraint' is conceptually equivalent to well-defined property rights in the sense of 'internalizing externalities'. (Cui, forthcoming).

Cui's focus on limited liability, central banking and bankruptcy is tied to an American empirical field and speaks powerfully to the aftermath of the 2008 financial meltdown where the universal appearance of institutions 'too big to fail' mocked the rhetorical critiques of socialised SBC. But the power of Cui's arguments also speak to the contingency of costing externalities, not merely the historical accidents by which Coasian principles were adopted in some arenas but not others but also the arbitrary assignment of externalities through jurisprudential regimes that legalise some costed externalities and make temporally invisible others (such as bankruptcy, central bank prerogative and the winding up and restarting of some corporations through manipulation of bankruptcy law).

The problem of externalities returns not as the utilitarian exceptionalism of Pigou but as a product of particular historical realisations of the market and the arena of political contest and ethical settlement. Such thinking has particular power when making visible the calculus of risk and uncertainty that maps the future city at times of rapid urban change, where public interest in both development and sustainability is mediated by market driven self interest and publically regulated schemes of architecture, planning and local government. Again an understanding of how the hybridisation of state and market emerges to structure risk and uncertainty, separating internal costs from external consequences in the shaping of the contemporary city in China, becomes a matter of evidence based investigation of forms and norms of future thinking and empirical specificity of real estate markets as much as a matter of 'market completion'. How externalities of urban change are accommodated consequently depends on the particular models of metropolitan governance that structure China's growth, which reconcile the resource-optimising logics of economics and the ethical challenges of legal theory.

Effectively what Cui's argument begins to unpack is whether in the calculus of new economic development we might begin to understand the tension between two caricatures of the emergent market. The two sketches narrate the commons and the tragedy of the commons in different ways. In the first ideal type, the city landscape is characterised by a marketplace of unambiguous regulations (clear property rights and predictable legal regulation) where externalities in the short, medium and long term are costed and rendered visible by transaction costs between different parts of the market architecture. The commons are safeguarded by the pricing of externalities of development, ecological damage and diseconomies of urban life. In an alternative model, the separation of socialised land ownership from marketised leasehold exchange divides the costs and benefits of externalities ambiguously between private and public interests. Contingent institutions may socialise or privatise the externalities but contingent institutional form also allows flexible urban development. The commons are figured as the ongoing relational outcome of the city that is yet to come, the responsibility of both state and market, at worst nobody's responsibility; at best everybody's. These alternative market formations intimate two different kinds of urban politics of the role of the local state in real estate markets. The state form of the city in the former model is principally an arbiter of interests, in the latter it is an actor and architect of the future metropolis. In the rest of the chapter we suggest that the emergent model in urban China is much closer to the second rather than the first ideal type. Wu and Hsing's descriptive power in their taxonomisation of China's urban change could be supplemented by the consequent significance of the commensuration of deliberative (political) processes and technocratic city building disciplines in models of city development.

Emergent markets in the cities of China are characterised by ambiguous property rights, opaque legal processes and path dependencies emanating from the reform and opening up process where ongoing (frequently long-term) *guanxi* relations between stakeholders qualify impersonal relations between market players. Yet it is inadequate to caricature such configuration as immature or *a priori* as inefficient. Indeed its relative (in)efficiency will depend on the balance between whether or not the transaction costs of the arbiter model and the efficient costing of externalities outweigh the bureaucratic (hierarchical) costs of the state actor model and the facility to adapt to the 'unknown unknowns' of city change. In other words, the urban problem in China reconfigures both the longstanding tension between markets and hierarchies in cost allocation and the more interesting contingency of a future calculus of ecological, economic and social externalities that may or may not be reducible from (incalculable) uncertainty to (calculable and costed) risk. As we suggested in the introduction to the book, the sense of '*a posteriori*' governance offers a pretext for state prerogative and a limited license for market freedoms although it offers no guarantee that the balance between these forces will be optimal.

Property rights and the future calculus

China's expanding role in world markets in the last three decades has in some quarters been interpreted as symptomatic of globalisation and market completion, in others as marking an alternative to a dominant Western model – rhetorically an alternative to neoliberalism, resting on innovatively hybrid public–private arrangements and ambiguous property rights (Ramo 2004; Davies 2011). The diversity of local forms of property regulation is considerable and various experiments in shared land ownership demonstrate how the boundary between the private and the public can be blurred, without suspending market mechanisms, as Cui observes in the controversial urban development mode of Chongqing (Cui 2011;

Frenkiel 2010). Market competition between state-owned and privately owned enterprises challenge the neoliberal commitment to privatisation, or 'accumulation by dispossession', instead focusing on increasing levels of competition in the marketplace (Arrighi 2009: 359). One argument that is made for the competitive advantage of this version of the China model is precisely that it does not pretend to be able to privatise, quantify and explicate all risks, but involves instead a system of property rights in which the inter-penetration of the public and the private are acknowledged as foundational. Many of the most innovative reforms in China's modernisation have been those that do not formalise or privatise, but leave rights and responsibilities ambiguous and socio-economic in nature. As a case of this, Arrighi focuses historically on the creation of Township and Village Enterprises (TVE), arguing that this 'may well turn out to have played as crucial a role in the Chinese economic ascent as vertically integrated bureaucratically managed corporations did in the US ascent a century earlier' (Arrighi 2009: 363). As Ho (2001) claims, deliberate ambiguity worked in the TVE system as a 'lubricant'. For Ho ambiguous property rights may be objectively inefficient while still allowing room for (and even incentivising) negotiated and pragmatic settlement between parties that will sustain relations over longer periods of time. It is via models such as this that Arrighi (2009) argued that China was developing a non-capitalist system of market liberalism, which potentially exploits capital, rather than labour.

In these instances, the ambiguity of calculation and of property rights becomes a virtue. Externalities become accounted for through abandoning the pursuit of complete transparency, actuarial pricing, commensurability and framing of the economic. They are instead subject to alternative means of calculation and valuation that depend on different registers of value and worth. Externalities are not converted into items of property (as in systems of securitisation, emissions trading, road taxing, privatisation), but nor are they simply the problem of the state. The precedent for this approach to property and markets may lie in the tradition of 'revolutionary' or 'socialist' liberalism, as Cui acknowledges (White 2009). Focused on the pursuit of what Meade termed 'agathopia' ('good place') or Wright terms 'real utopias', liberals and 'civic republicans' offer a normative critique of property relations in terms of the public and democratic freedoms that they facilitate (Meade 1989, Wright 2010). The creation of 'social property' becomes a means of constraining both capital and the state. Of equal significance, this arena of ambiguity creates a contest between different ways of seeing the future city and an imperative to create institutional forms that can respond to the regimes of value and worth that are articulated very differently by alternative and commonly incommensurable disciplines of future thinking and city building.

Part 2: Future thinking and the city of experts in China

In this chapter we are making a case that both the architecture of the new markets and the nature of urban change are the cumulative outcome of different regimes of urban expertise coupled with alternative (and contingent) articulations and resolutions of the problem of property rights. Property rights are bundled, path dependent articulations of market form. To build on the theorisations of Hsing and Wu we need to consider how the reform process works alongside the structures of power to shape processes of emergent urbanism in China. We might consider the deliberative processes of city change through synthesising description of market form and analysis of the exercise of interest within these institutional arrangements. *Market formation* focuses attention on the particular configurations of property rights in the city. The *exercise of interest* depends on the relative power of financial interests, architecture, planning, local government, and demographic analysis to shape the metropolis through regimes of particular forms of expertise; to answer the perennial question 'in whose image is the city fashioned?'

In making sense of the reshaping of the urban we know that planners structure preferred future cities, architects design specific elements of urban fabric, real estate players buy and sell, legal imperatives regulate and the market's invisible hand and the rules (or lack of rules) of state power are ultimately simultaneously realised in the built form of the metropolitan stage. The city landscape produced is both the crucible of the urban dramas of street life and the organising frame of residence and workplace. Each of these *disciplines of future thinking* – architecture, planning, marketing, law and economics – subsume both technocratic practices and ethical or normative presuppositions. Each of the disciplines has its own system of rational organisation of the value of city territory: metrication, cadastration and valuation of property. Each measures the cartography of the city through its own lens of worth. A focus on property rights brings some of the discursive discontinuities between these disciplines to the foreground. The rational city is implicit in the planner's purpose, the good and the beautiful city at the heart of architectural doctrine. The Ricardian imperatives of spatial preference (that stress how rental value declines with distance from preferred locations) structure the utility-optimising logics of economics and the spatial economy (Fujita *et al.* 2001). However, they are mediated by the rule of law and the imperatives of spatial configuration determined by particular political struggles over power and the prerogative to shape the built form of the city.

This disciplinary plurality suggests a babel of technocratic forms of expertise that brings to bear competing and irreconcilable imperatives into the shaping of city form. Many metropolitan development offices in major cities across the world will testify to the difficulties of translating between these disciplines. And one way of narrating urban transformation and restructuring would suggest that mechanisms of price combine with mechanisms of regulation to produce contingent compromises between what experts thinks city form should look like and markets will deliver in the real world. But an alternative perspective that draws on contemporary economic sociology might suggest that what emerges from bringing together incommensurable regimes of value and worth can be a form of 'productive friction' (Stark 2009) that valorises the recombinant articulations of cultures and objects in a manner characteristic of the demands of twenty-first century economic change. Indeed David Stark has argued that such productive friction is the most effective way to optimise the more contemporary forms of 'network capitalism' where classification is less important than 'search'. We need to move from the diversity of organisations to the organisation of diversity, from the unreflexive taken for granted to the a sense of reflexive cognition, from a sense of shared understandings to coordination through misunderstanding and from single ethnographies to broader understanding of situations and risks (Stark 2009, 166–200). These 'broader understandings of risk' structure how we think about the future when acting in the present. And in the urbanisms of China, deliberative risk cultures of the present are realised through both discursively contested settlements of property rights and plural temporalities of the rapidly transforming city.

Coasian configurations

The tension between law and economics structures the market unevenly geographically and historically. The extent to which state sanctioned legal interests (eminent domain, compulsory purchase, public amenity) trump market forces is contentious across the cities of the world (Sanyal 2005). Whereas A. C. Pigou in his book *Wealth and Welfare* (1912) defined 'externalities' that needed to be mediated by public intervention through systems of regulation or taxation, Coase and his followers stressed the logical minimalisation of transaction costs through the structure of the firm that generated a potential to optimise resource allocation through a Schumpeterian representation of oligopolistic competition. For Coase, clear property rights minimise transaction costs and maximise the potential for market rational outcomes. But these property rights relate not only to ownership, they relate to the 'fruits' of the property, the control of its use and products as well as the right to sell or exchange. Clear property rights bring these together. The institutional focus on property rights in some land economy texts consequently conflates the normative and the descriptive, characterising the market both in terms of the way it does operate and the way it should, a subject of intense debate in both economic theory and in theorisations of property and real estate.

In the context of real estate markets the contested legacy of Coase plays differently in the US and the UK. The European model of metropolitan regulation and the Japanese equivalent all realise these tensions distinctively (Beatley 2000; Benfield *et al.* 2001; Calthorpe 1993; Calthorpe *et al.* 2001; Haussermann and Haila 2004; LeGalés 2002). Coase's influence has been more influential in rolling back state interference in some places (such as the US retreat from anti-trust regulation) than in others (as in French and German real estate markets). The variation in 'real market' realisation is massive between one governance regime and another (Sanyal 2005). The obligations of the state to mediate negative externalities and maximise positive externalities consequently varies historically and geographically and is subject to developments in the regulation and structuring of markets in the future. Any evolution from the socialist economy to something else – however described – is not straightforwardly teleological; the forms of real estate markets that might emerge are contested. And the arguments of scholars such as Cui and Haila in their different ways share an argument that if we take seriously the matter of property rights and its different anthropological realisations then we must also revisit some of the assertions that are at the heart of what is taken for granted in the doctrines of law and economics and the imperatives of the new institutionalists that emerged from it. They also imply that in so far as these contests between different forms of valuing the city make visible alternative contests between different urbanisms they might be economically productive. In terms of Demsetz's or Honoré's classifications of property as a bundle of rights (Demsetz 1967; Honoré 1987), in China the bundle is not always coeval. Three different rights in particular do not all come together: rights of income, rights to management and rights to disposal accrue differently between interests and may be held separately – a sense of the interest in the land's future, an emergent urbanism, may consequently be dispersed rather than singular.

The issue of speed

The second dimension of our argument suggests that how we come to think about risk cultures and the future problematises the classical academic separation between the diachronic and the synchronic in social analysis, the dynamic and the static in economic theory. This is the case because each 'discipline of future thinking' (in this case architecture, planning, local government) subsumes alternative and frequently contested notions of the temporal. In architectural practice the present form is displaced by a future structure, the sense of the city becoming something different is categorised by both a technocratic practice and an aesthetic sensibility. Hence for Li Shiqiao the architectural aesthetic takes its organising principle from a notion of proportion, with all its humanistic associations: 'Despite the modernist propaganda in the twentieth century, the city of the machine has always been moderated by the city of humanistic proportions'. (Shiqiao 2009, 644) But the city in China – taking its developmental lead from Hong Kong – at times surrenders to the logic of 'maximum density', a surrender that can be both socially liberating and politically challenging in some of the realisations of Hong Kong urbanism but engenders a specific sense of density and the built form that is premised upon both the opportunity to maximise value and a sense of the city as growing entity. The urbanism of maximum density has both different propensities and different disadvantages to it. And in the ethnographic work that informs this book the interviews and engagements with architects working in contemporary China stressed the institutional power of some of these senses of a city that is evolving, not merely an architectural sensibility but also a contingent sense of transformation of the spatial through reconfiguration of the urban. In architectural discourse the density is itself qualified by the size of the plot addressed in any one structural change, the floor area ratios of a single piece of the metropolis.

The city of becoming draws our attention back to thinking about speed more generally, on the pace of change evinced in the cities of China. A sense of the potentiality of the urban is rendered unproblematic within a certain register of

Cartesian space. On a Cartesian grid of the metropolis, Ricardian rent theory intimates a cartography of monetary value and consequently the logical structure of the metropolis that follows. But in a city of becoming that is structured as much by the temporal sense of flux as the spatial sense of organisation this might be less so. Former colonial cities such as Mumbai are notoriously constrained in the twenty-first century by British zoning rules, premised on the densities appropriate for the nineteenth century Garden City rather than the twenty-first century mega-city (Glaeser 2010). Zoning works synchronically, identifying optimal spatial form at one moment in time. Flux works always on the move and privileges flexibility, what is appropriate for the twentieth century might be less so in the twenty-first, not a problem in the city of reinvention but more difficult in the city of proportion and valorised historical form.

Understanding the temporalities of the different technocratic rationalities of the metropolis is important. To the extent that they are calculable we might consider that they can be reduced to a Knightian sense, a translation of uncertainty into measurable risk. So, for example the rates of return, rental values, changes in spatial preference and hope values associated with real estate all imply a certain Euclidian sense of the temporal. But to the extent that notions of quantum (densification of land development) are balanced against a humanistic sense of proportion in measuring the city, to the extent that economic and social processes outstrip rational deliberative judgement and the extent that the city itself becomes 'unknowable', a different sense of risk emerges that is subject to the plural temp-oralities of the urban. To the extent that the accelerators of city speed distort this calculus they generate more 'unknown unknowns' rather than calculable risks; the risks of Ulrich Beck rather than the risks of Frank Knight. Speed and twenty-first century urbanism consequently are tied together, a linkage illuminated by two scholars in particular that have attempted to develop a vocabulary of the flux that results.

Firstly, for Paul Virilio – former Architecture Professor at the Ecole Speciale d'architecture – 'to neglect the spatial temporal sphere would imply a total mis-reading of the world's future metropolitisation, would strip all objects and signs of their very meaning' (James 2011, Virilio 1999). The sense that land, territory and place have within them a potential *to become* as well as a state of *being* is not for Virilio a mystificatory notion. Virilio's contribution is useful because it provides a register of voice in which the cultural and the economic are inflected. Econo-mically a language of hope value, fluctuating locational advantage and transport-related reconfigurations of locational preference act cognitively on the monetised system of spatial preferences. But, culturally, a sense of predisposition, future potential, dwelling possibilities, architectural futures and utopian inclinations are mediated by the specificity of place. Speed and scale find convergence in the planning, design and fruition of Chinas' property – apartment complexes, trans-portation networks, five star hotels and office towers. As we see below, both a sense of the city always on the move at accelerated speed and a sense of competing forms of expertise that understand these city futures is at the heart of some of the ethnographic engagements with planners, architects and real estate companies in today's China.

For China the etymology of the notion of the plan is significant. 'Plan' of course is a word invoked by Mao – the planned economy. In Chinese, there are two words: *jihua* (planning from pre-reform) and *guihua* (urban planning) (Naughton 2007a). The temporality of the plan appears slightly differently in each term – in the former, the organisation of socialist optima; in the latter, the aspiration to build the good city. Speed disrupts the temporal logic of the plan. The simultaneous presence of past regimes and future values means that the city's urban landscape always contains a mixture of planning logics, yesterday's compromises and tomorrow's ideals. The land use development plans spatialises the form of the city against the known criteria of optimal land use at one moment in time. Technological change and the logics of city transformation undermine these optima. The discipline of land use development zoning rests in part on the facility to reconcile the pace of changing imperatives with the time taken to draft professionally, legitimise politically and confirm legally relevant planning frameworks that structure decision-making about spatial distribution inside the city. If the speed of urban change significantly outstrips the temporal rhythm of the planning cycle then the disciplinary hold of urban planning is significantly reframed.

Immanence and propensity

From a completely different perspective the China scholar Francois Jullien (1995) in his work *'The Propensity of Things'* has written an entire monograph that considers the Mandarin word '*shi*' (势). In a work that has become increasingly influential outside China, Jullien reads through this singular term a range of interdisciplinary scholarship on the strategy of war, the ethics of design and the aesthetics of script and painting. Throughout, Jullien emphasises that the term does not translate into a Western register easily because of the ways in which future potential and present disposition are both captured by the term. The pace of change from 'what is' to what 'might be' is captured by always considering the contemporary moment and the potential future as simultaneously present. In contrast to a genre of urbanism that focuses on the ghosts of the past that are to be found in the landscapes of today, Jullien directs us towards the presence of the future in the configurations of right now – a strong sense of propensity. In Jullien's work this refers to a sensibility of speech, aesthetic objects of design and the landscape configuration that frequently determines the outcome of the battle before the conflict has begun. In the context of the contests over city form we might read Jullien as speaking to an understanding of the city landscape as a field of potential that is always configured simultaneously by both what is and what might be.

Significantly, Jullien argues that the Chinese cultural construction of future things considers *disposition*, *propensity*, *potentiality* and – most significantly – *relationality* as a construction of the possibilities that emerge from the configuration of objects. In one sense a logical extension of some thinking around 'materialities' in the social sciences, in another a precursor of Latour's and Appadurai's notions of the agency and life path of objects, Jullien is of interest for urbanists studying China because the configuration of built form and political power, both an architecture of fabric and an architecture of the spaces between fabrics, can always be considered in terms of potentiality; a valorisation of becoming and *what might be* rather than an objectification of *being*, what is and what has been determined. This plays into how we might think about the discursive discontinuities between the architectural aesthetics and the technocratic functionality of the rational geometry or the economic imperatives of spatial preference. It finds its urban studies equivalent in Maliq Simone's (2004) stress on both the 'city yet to come' and his associated construction of 'people as infrastructure', an activation of the network society as agency.

Qin made a similar argument (2011) in developing a critique of the finite definitions of interest and cognitive rationalisations of decision-making that structure much of the discipline of international relations. Qin argues that such finite framing does not explain either what does happen in China or what should happen, that conceptually what is needed for the China context is a concept of 'relational governance':

> I agree that rule-based governance is extremely important to make actors' expectations converge, to encourage institutional cooperation, to maintain order, and to enable governance to be workable and effective, because individual rationalit – the premise of rule-based governance – is human. At the same time, I argue that *relational governance* is perhaps equally important in our world today. The reason is also clear: relationality, the premise of relational governance, is human too. The unconsciously exclusive emphasis on rule-based governance, as the existing international relations (IR) literature on global and regional governance has shown, might neglect social contexts, relational processes, and human practices, thus missing significant factors in this area of intellectual exploration and practical exercise of governance.
>
> (Qin 2011, 119)

From Jullien we might think more carefully about alternative constructions of risk and the juxtaposition of risk and uncertainty (after Frank Knight). Ulrich Beck's influential sociology claims that contemporary societies move from order to uncertainty in defining the risk society. In economic sociology, Harrison White claims that markets organise from uncertainty to order and valorises elements of the information flows that result. In the Western market model configurations of state and market we consequently find a contrast between the *insurable* and the *uninsurable* unknowns, the contrast between *market completion* and *path dependency*. Institutions are historically dependent on where they came from, contextually dependent on the contradictory normative models of where they are heading to. This poses empirical and theoretical questions, regarding institutions and multiple valuation frameworks made commensurable (or not), a problem that preoccupies the sociologists of convention and commensuration (Espeland and Stevens 1998; Boltanski and Thévenot 2006). These latter approaches are critical for understanding not only the limits of the calculable (as both welfare economists and Callon are concerned with), but also how neoclassical, formal calculation and rationalist governance coexists with rival conventions of valuation and informal calculation.

The problem of commensuration of rival spheres of value, and techniques of valuation, is germane to the development economics of Sen (1999, 2009) and Nussbaum (2003), for whom the politics of wellbeing need not be underpinned by a single idea or measure of value, but furthered by the collection of a basket of multiple, incommensurable indices. But this expert policy discourse necessarily depends on the aggregative statistical capacity of state agencies. By contrast, ethnography and intensive interviewing works collaboratively with urban professionals and advocates to uncover the ways in which rival values and techniques of valuation coexist, at the border of the 'economic' and the 'social', and of the 'private' and the 'public'.

Externalities appear very different in the cities of the China from in the West. The contingencies generated by ambiguous property rights are central to this difference. For historical reasons through articulations of the 'socialist market economy' in China that are path dependent on the development of new real estate markets, multiple valuation systems coexist, in ways that resist a clear privileging of neoclassical-style calculation, or a reduction of social values to economic costs as we explore further in both extended ethnography in real estate companies later in this volume and through ethnographic collaborations with architects and planners.

City futures tamed by experts

In the penultimate section of this chapter we exemplify the ways in which these forms of competing expertise structure the emergent markets of real estate in contemporary China.

Architects: building big

In a famous essay 'Bigness or the problem of large' the architect Rem Koolhaas (cited in Rajchman 1994) argued that the architects of the modern needed to scale up, to understand size, the movement from small and medium to large and extra large (Koolhaas 1995), a nostrum most clearly realised in his engagement with major projects in the Pearl River Delta and Beijing (see Figures 3.1, 3.2 and 3.3) in the last decade: 'Bigness, through its very independence of context, is the one architecture that can survive, even exploit, the now-global condition of the *tabula rasa*: it does not take its inspiration from givens too often squeezed for the last drop of meaning; it gravitates opportunistically to locations of maximum infrastructural promise; it is, finally, its own *raison d'etre*. In spite of its size, it is modest' (Koolhaas in Rajchman 1994).

FIGURE 3.1 China Central Television (CCTV) building caricature, 798 Gallery, Beijing. Koolhaas has become influential in the ways he has both interpreted China's new urbanisms in the light of his own theories – most notably in his celebration of hyper-growth in the Pearl River Delta in the collection 'Great Leap Forward' and his own interventions in urban space – most notably the gigantic asymmetrical China Central Television (CCTV) building colloquially known as the '*kuzi*' (trousers) because of the way it strands astride the Beijing skyline.

Source: Photo by Michael Keith.

China's cities grew big, fast. The very term 'Shenzhen speed' has a particular resonance in China. It allegedly originated from the construction of a whole floor of the prestige development of Guomao tower in three days in the city, although as Cartier (2002) has highlighted there is a need to be suspicious of some elements of this 'zone fever' and the iconography of Shenzhen speed at times outstrips its reality. In this changing landscape, iconic modern architecture plays multi-media metonymy when the distinctive parts come to signify an uncertain and rapidly changing whole. Shanghai is commonly invoked through images of the Andreu-designed airport at Pudong, the Maglev train from the airport and the self-representation of its own growth (Keith 2007; Wasserstrom 2009). The SOM Jin Mao Tower in Shanghai's waterfront business district of Pudong in design deliberately mimics a pagoda, ignorant of the fact that as Leo Ou Fan Lee

FIGURE 3.2 China Central Television building Beijing, designed by OMA, Ole Scheeren and Rem Koolhaas

Source: Rem Koolhaas owns the architecture company OMA, one of his principal partners was Ole Scheeren. Photo by Michael Keith.

FIGURE 3.3 'Can I wake up from this dream?' Beijing 798, representation of Beijing's new China Central Television building

Source: Photo by Michael Keith.

describes, the pagoda is meant culturally to atone for doing wrong. So the height of the Jin Mao Tower – with its Hyatt Hotel starting on the fiftieth floor – must pay penance to quite large number of sins (see Figure 3.4).

The view from the Bund, silhouetting the Pearl Tower has become an icon of a global generic urbanism captured in the advertising shorthand of the Financial Times (see Figures 3.5 and 3.6).

FIGURE 3.4 Views inside Shanghai's Jin Mao Tower

Source: Photos by Michael Keith.

FIGURE 3.5 Financial Times advertisement: 'The generic city'. The Financial Times' generic urbanism – capturing (*inter alia*) New York, London, Tokyo, Paris, Kuala Lumpur and Shanghai in a singular generic global urbanism.
Source: The Financial Times Limited © All Rights Reserved.

FIGURE 3.6 The 'real view' from the Bund to Pudong
Source: Photo by Michael Keith (2009).

Shanghai's population – as covered by its eighteen districts and one county – was placed at almost 17 million based on data from the 2000 China census. Again the estimates are only rough guides, 2004 figures calculate a population of nearer 14 million but the sheer scale of these districts is formidable. Populations of 1.77

million in Pudong New District or three quarters of a million in Minhang make them larger than all but the most sizeable European cities. The 2007 Shanghai statistical yearbook estimates the population as 18.15 million. And below the level of the city, the level of most land allocation and sales, and above that of the street is the district of governance, which in Shanghai and most other cities is arguably the most significant in structuring real estate market governance and the most powerful planning and construction bureaux.

In transcribed interviews with major architects working in Shanghai the importance of ongoing relationships developed with main officials that need to move fast to secure their reputation comes out of the material repeatedly. One architect practicing in a part of the city known for architectural quality, stressed the distinction between formal and informal protocols of securing architectural excellence. At times – as with Qingpu District (population approximately 0.5 million) – a deputy mayor with architectural qualifications will be seen to pursue open competitions and a particular focus on the quality of development, but more commonly the pressure on officials is to deliver high-profile urban-change projects on a short-time scale (Interview Liu Yuyang Architectural practice), enhancing the political imperative for rapid delivery, diminishing the propensity to articulate architectural quality. But in each case, what remains clear is the sense of the blurred boundary lines between public interest, client relationships, today's contracts and tomorrow's relationship. In an inspiring early interview in 2006 with architectural theorist and founder of the practice MADASPAM in Shanghai, Ma Qingyun suggests 'you have to understand there is no such thing as public space in China – the notion of a separation of the civic realm from the state does not make sense conceptually'. Ma goes on to describe how he has been influenced by his own teacher – Koolhaas at Harvard – to think of the city as always in flux. He outlined a project that he wanted to develop for the Shanghai Expo in 2010 that would occupy a site on the Bund with a countdown until the day after the Expo. Never realised on the site, its essence was its ephemerality: the notion that the architect should eschew the monumental, that the imperatives of urbanism were always to 'melt what is solid', to privilege the city of flux over the urbanism of stasis. For Ma this juxtaposition defined China's metropolitan dynamic in contrast to the staid cities of European social democracy and American capitalism; it flourished in Shanghai but had implications that were epochal.

Architects: building small and the construction of social need and the Tulou project

By most measures of asset size, competitiveness, development scale and profits, Vanke is one of the largest real estate companies in contemporary China. In 2002 it was the largest real estate company in China by market capitalisation and in the first quarter of 2008, before the downturn, it reported RMB 718.1 million quarterly profit (approximately US$103.7 million) on official revenue of RMB 6.06 billion turnover. While the largest concentration of business reflects the company's Pearl River Delta roots, it has a presence in most of China's major cities. The chairperson of Vanke – Wang Shi – had both a certain cult status as a heroic entrepreneur and was famous inside and outside the corporate world for his commercial success and Richard Branson-style stunts, such as climbing Mount Everest, a reputation that was slightly tarnished when he questioned the levels of contributions that might be expected from his employees to the general disaster funds after the 2008 Sichuan earthquake.

In many ways the company represents a typical example of the new China. Its corporate history is shrouded in a degree of mystique and rumour but some elements are clear. Wang Shi was born in 1951 in Liuzhou, in Guangxi Province. His biography covers his role as a trader in the Pearl River Delta at the height of the Cold War and, subsequently, operating partly out of Hong Kong as an individual that set up first the trade exhibition centre in the early days of Shenzhen and had early connections to the Hong Kong/mainland company China Resources. Much of the capital generated by the company was raised first in Hong Kong. Vanke exemplifies the trend for real estate corporates to emerge both with a familiarity with the institutional workings of the Hong Kong property market and from the particular market institutions in Hong Kong that from early investment in real estate projects give the company one leg in mainland China and one leg in Hong Kong.

The architectural partnership Urbanus have an office in Beijing but operate mostly out of Shenzhen offices in the Overseas Chinese Town (OCT) (a national, listed property development company) cultural industries zone of Nanshan District. Urbanus are mostly US trained with a large portfolio of work in the Pearl River Delta that includes several commissions from Vanke, including their Shenzhen corporate headquarters. So when in the 2005–7 period a debate developed about how to house the most excluded in the rapidly growing metropolis of Shenzhen that avoided the exploitation of migrants commonly seen in some of the *woshou fang* (handshake apartments) Wang Shi challenged Urbanus to design a form of social housing that could be financially sustainable, humanely homely and yet be premised on the rental returns that were no greater than might be paid in the *chengzhongcun* (villages in the city).

In repeat interviews with members of Urbanus team in September, December 2008, March 2009 and April 2011 the Urbanus team described the evolving outcome of this challenge. The architectural form Urbanus turned to was a traditional Hakka design of the *Tulou*, adapted to provide 40m² apartments (for five people) (see Figures 3.7 and 3.8). In early discussions with municipalities the intention was to develop several Tulou sites in Shenzhen. But the developments met with resistance. Those controlling migrant rental housing through *woshou fang* were not interested, those controlling land in other parts of the city were not keen on the location of extra housing for *wailai renkou* (floating population). Largely through resistance to the new developments a single site was eventually chosen, intended as a demonstration project, premised on a rate of return on capital that would cover investment in 20 years. The resulting scheme – architecturally lauded in the US and China was a strikingly beautiful development on a less-than-desirable landlocked site at the intersection of major roadways in Guangzhou. And although the site was designed for migrant populations it has become increasingly popular – possibly because of its design. In 2008 the Smithsonian's Cooper-Hewitt National Design museum in New York showed the Tulou design in a major exhibition. For museum director Paul Warwick Thompson, 'the Tulou project…will unveil a world few people in the West have witnessed and spotlight a paradigm for future living that may well hold clues to the new direction of affordable housing in other emerging economies'.

By mid 2009 a large number of the residents in Guangzhou's Tulou included former university students, start-up cultural entrepreneurs and a young population that sometimes occupied the development at the densities imagined but other times rented out the apartment spaces at a lower occupancy than was originally imagined. Architecturally successful, the site demonstrates the perennial pheno-menon of unintended consequences, arguably a concentration of multi-media and cultural industries start ups on a residential base that has become well known among those just graduating from university; not exactly a form of gentrification China style, but clearly not the residential alternative to the *chengzhongcun* villages in the city residential concentration of the *wailai renkou*.

On Tulou, the rate of return on capital is factored into the financial viability of the project based on the calculable rents permitted and the plausible equivalents in low-quality migrant housing. In this sense it is premised on a Knightian sense of risk that reduces the unknown to the calculable. But in another sense the development's utility rests on the uncertain imperatives of social reproduction, the potential demand for subsidised housing and the putative and contested role of developers and states in China to provide the needed housing for migrant populations in the future Shenzhen. A low-cost, high-density urban form was created that (with the major contingency of land value held constant) would generate an investment return and accommodation for residents at rental levels lower than those found in some of the least desirable migrant housing. But equally importantly, Wang Shi's challenge has been met, the prestige of Vanke and Urbanus was enhanced and a challenging new intervention in the fabric of the city embossed.

Planners

Planning practices have spun off directly from the university sector, a rapidly growing array of companies that look both in one direction inwards towards teaching practice in the academy and outwards to a hands on engagement with city building. We interviewed on repeat occasions several planning practices where academics – partly driven by the low salary levels of universities in China – were simultaneously inside and outside the academy, working in the public (and private) domains of city change. In September 2006, we interviewed two members of a planning company spin off from Tongji University Planning Department in Shanghai. The academy in China is replete with large numbers of such institutions, 'jumping into the sea of commerce' from the academy; they became increasingly

FIGURE 3.7 Guangzhou Tulou 'social housing' development
Source: Designers URBANUS Architects. Photo by Michael Keith.

common from the 1980s onwards. Tongji 5, Tongji7, a host of companies reframes academic collegiality, recasts the relationship between the academy and the market as rival firms from within a single academic department ostensibly bid against each other in the competition to masterplan Shanghai's future. Heyhoe (2009, 103) references a People's Daily article on 3 November 1967, arguing that Mao's ideas about knowledge arises from practice and should be refined through further practice directly impacting on Tongji: 'A second model of that period illustrated how a major national university, Tongji in Shanghai, reorganised itself as part of a commune attached to a local architectural firm. Teaching and research were patterned around urban and rural construction tasks in an integrative way'.

The phone rings and one of the interviewees takes the call that informs him that he has been awarded the contract for a role in the first stage masterplan of the 2010 Shanghai World Expo. In January 2007 – four months later – we re-interview the same planner and he explains how this masterplan has now been researched, drafted and approved by the city government. In contrast one of the authors of this book was simultaneously involved at first hand in setting up the approval process for the master-planning requirements for London's 2012 bid for the Olympic Games. Negotiations with the London Boroughs covered by the bid started in late 2002, a process is provisionally agreed by 15 May 2004 when Tony Blair announced government support for the bid itself. Just ahead of the 15 November 2004 bid submission – over 12 months later – an outline masterplan goes before a five borough planning committee convened at London's City Hall, although significant details around funding, the burial of overhead cables and the main issues around transport infra-structure are to wait until July 2008 before being processed and approved (Olympic

FIGURE 3.8 Images of Guangzhou Tulou 'social housing' development
Source: Photos by Michael Keith.

Development Agency Planning Committee minutes, 22 July 2008) – five years later. Globally, in the world of development control the London process was seen as relatively rapid, in contrast to New York, that designed their bid around a yet-to-be-approved new Olympic Stadium in Manhattan's West Side but where approval was denied just days before the US bid, forcing organisers to scramble and come up with plan B, a less desirable Queens location for the stadium.

Some interesting characteristics emerged from discussions with some of these spin offs that relate closely to Jullien's notion of the *relational*. There was a sense of networked relations that were always ongoing and never finite in a city, which had both the most rigid set of five-year plans (endorsed at municipal level), alongside a set of empowered districts with a facility to produce rapid change at the level below that of the metropolis as a whole. Dating back to its nineteenth century Germanic highs, the logic of the land use plan rests on the possibility that it is possible both to know the city (a question of epistemology), to model it (a question of design) and to institute zoning controls and regulatory policy (a question of institutional politics) anticipating ahead (and more rapidly) than the dynamics of economic change. If the technocratic shaping of the city through the plan moves more rapidly than the economic fundamentals the former can optimise the latter. If it cannot do so quickly enough, if the diachronic pace of urban change outstrips the ability to institutionalise even the most flexible synchronic snapshot, this logic breaks down. In this sense, development control practice in Shanghai appeared paradoxical, at one moment fine details of mass, density and height were fixed; at others the imperative for the development planning approval driven through the grey interface of *xiaoqu* (gated community) estate builders and local bureaucracy and approval procedures, a paradox amplified further in the 18 months experience of real estate company ethnography described later in this volume.

A further fascinating example can be seen in the 'One City, Nine Towns' plan to suburbanise some of the urban growth pressures in Shanghai in the early 2000s. Nine towns were themed after ostensibly European architectural vernaculars (Heynen 1999), attempting to capture a branded logic of new residential development: Bauhaus Germany, Italian futurism or a simulacrum of 'Thamestown', complete with statues of Winston Churchill and a fish and chip shop were built outside the central metropolitan core of the city – a response to central invocation to respond rapidly to the growth pressures of the deindustrialising metropolis.

Supported by high status backing from Shanghai state government each of the sites involves a joint venture between individual district governments and private capital that generates large residential developments of several acres and well over 10,000 homes apiece. They are an architectural curiosity and have not always been seen as major successes. The fish and chip shop in Thamestown never worked, the retail has high vacancy rates and the public spaces are used mostly for wedding photographs. In Anting, 'German Town' was designed in 2001 by the Frankfurt-based architecture firm Albert Speer & Partner. Speer is the son of the eponymous architect who was Hitler's chief architect and minister of armaments and war production during Second World War. Fifty thousand people were expected to live in German Town (with its equivalent statues of Schiller and Goethe), but by late 2011 the site was built out, property sold but it was estimated that only one in five homes were occupied. Others are more successful and the residential property in all of the 'theme towns' has sold. The nine sites are architecturally fascinating but the outcome has been a curious sense of city planning that has almost been overtaken by the spread of much more dynamic developments that have been led at district level and that we explore further in the next chapter. Neither quite free market nor quite old socialism, the 'theme towns' of Shanghai represent one of the experimental hybridisations of state and market that has been tried, not quite worked but still pragmatically become part of Shanghai's urban transformation.

Land and development in southern Shanghai

The sense of the real estate world as extemporised combinations of expert know-ledges and long-term connections can generate some times a sense of creativity. But at other times the knowledge of networks and the combinations of expertise, can lead to rapid wealth creation, complicated legal troubles and exposure of some of the tricks of the trade of real estate dealers. We have drawn illustratively on a range of examples here appearing in the public domain in trade and popular Shanghai press (all translations by Tyler Rooker), most of which relate to the evolving real estate market close to the developing periphery of Shanghai near to the Minhang District where a longer ethnography was conducted.

In April 2001, on the eve of state-owned company Shanghai County Real Estate Corporation changing its system (to joint-stock or private), Zhou Xiaodi's New Century Enterprise Company signed an agreement with Shanghai County Real Estate to obtain 2,536 *mu* (0.07 hectares) in the Pudong Sanlin Yide region, a unit price of 250,000 yuan per *mu* for a total price of 634 million yuan. Without the funds to cover the purchase, Zhou used 'unified development' to obtain some funding. He began to 'catch white wolves with his bare hands' (get rich with primitive means) in land deals. In the Sanlin Yide case, he made three agreements with other companies and not only paid off the 600 million of Shanghai County Real Estate (Zhou paid only 70 million), but his company made 300 million in profit. Zhou was accused and cleared of hiring people to injure others and illegally re-selling land. But another case was brought successfully for the embezzlement of over 160 million yuan. Also accused was chief financial officer of Zhongxiang Company Ding Beili, former party secretary Zhang Yong and earlier partners previously accused of land grabs. Zhongxiang Company was formerly known as Shanghai County Real Estate Corporation. Qin Jinlong was named legal represen-tative and general manager of Shanghai County Real Estate Corporation in 1992. In April 2001, Shanghai County Real Estate Corporation changed its name to Shanghai Zhongxiang (Group) Company Limited, and changed its system (*gaizhi*) from a state-owned enterprise to a privately run enterprise. After changing its system, Qin Jinlong became the legal representative and president of Zhongxiang Company.

A lawyer involved in preparing project documents for these enterprises told *Caijing* that through the 2000s there were in Shanghai very few land transactions that were truly run on the 'bid, list, auction' procedures, and these were all small tracts. Large plots of land went to developers with government background or government *guanxi*. Value was tied to the 'development document' the zoning specification of density and floor area ratios; the property developers could receive billions in profit from a single approval document. There was – he claimed – almost no property available to developers from outside Shanghai in the open market. 'The shares of the original shareholders in the project-purchasing company, while according to central policy are 'disguised land stir-frying'. In truth they show the 'hidden rules' acquiesced to by local government'. If a conflict arises between shareholders, there was no protection to be found from the law (Yang and Chen 2008).

Between 2001 and 2002, changes in the real estate policies and Shanghai local government's resistance to macro-regulation and control efforts lead Shanghai real estate from a low point only a few years before to a triumphant advance. And the value of once-ignored 'Sanlin region' suddenly sky-rocketed as Shanghai won the right to hold the 2010 World Exposition close by – the World Expo region was held in the lower part of the Huangpu River, squeezed next to the two banks of the Sanlin region, so the Sanlin region would naturally enjoy improved transportation, increasing the value of the land. Finally, Shanghai Jinjiang Group and 'Waigao Bridge' joined with the French company Vivendi Group to invest US$870 million in a 'Universal Movie City' park project, which was then under discussion, and they choose a location for the project. As the city expanded in the 2000s major projects in Shanghai at that time, like the Formula 1 Raceway and the Qizhong Tennis Stadium, highlighted the spectacle of government planning a project, preceded state-invested property developments and *minying* enterprises with strong backgrounds grabbing proximate land, waiting for the *grand projet* completion, then either re-leasing the land or developing it themselves.

Sometimes slow: strategies and tricks for 'sitting on land' (Wupan)

The speed of urban change at some times should also not obscure the sense of strategic slowing down of development that can also be found in the real estate industry of cities such as Shanghai. Where the use rights are separated from other property rights the actual 'lease' term may only start when the developer actually acquires the full development rights (which are themselves negotiable). This may lead to situations where it is logical to sit on land (as prices rocket) and stall development to maximise returns – a strategy known as *wupan*. In the real estate ethnographic work we identified four examples of the tricks associated with *wupan*, that legitimise price manipulation tied to the conduct of 'fake sales' that satisfy planning stipulations to start marketing land but in reality mask tricks of sitting on land for speculative purposes in a rising (possibly bubble) market. These tricks included:

- *Trick 1: 'Time delay'*. Receive off-plan sales contracts and not open for business; done to store up customers and pull up the price: scheduled sales contracts do not open up selling of the complex, using the excuses of 'developing a model apartment' and 'decorating the sales department' to delay until the next 'gold September and silver October' period to push onto the market. Cases in the press reported uplifts from 15,000 yuan/m² to 18,000 yuan/m² in less than three months.
- *Trick 2: 'Selling in batches'*. First, push out a small number of units, and gradually push up the price. In one example a complex located in the Tianhe Zhujiang New City area began sales in May 2009. Of the over 300 off-plan sales certificates for units, the first batch only put up 100-plus, and they were distributed in different buildings on different floors to incentivise early purchase but hold supply.
- *Trick 3: Fake Sales*. Developer first buys then sells, creating the false impression of selling like hot cakes. From 2009, the phenomenon of 'fake sales' by developers increased, where 'first buying then selling' is prevalent – that is, the developer unites with an intermediary to first buy the most marketable apartments creating the false appearance of hot sales, then cancels sales and returns apartments; or, once the price has gone up, and it releases the complex onto the market, making healthy profits.
- *Trick 4: Smoke bombs*. Opening the complex immediately 'sells out', and rapidly there is a collector's edition: again examples were found of performed sales that were illusory both to stir demand and to hold on to the developed site in a bull housing market.

Even if *wupan* requires paying more interest to the bank, provided housing prices are moving rapidly, bank interest compared with profits are 'a small witch meeting a big witch' (they pale in significance). A certain well-known real estate expert expressed that, no matter what type of '*wupan*' measure developers adopt, their end goal is to encourage transactions and increase housing prices. Developers set up the phenomenon of consumers 'fighting for scraps', consequently increasing the speed with which consumers make decisions, and achieving the goal of quick sales (Luo *et al.* 2009).

Conclusion

Through historical accident as much as conscious design, real estate markets shape the cities of China in a fashion that reflects the path dependencies of the opening up and reform process. This inflects how we think about post-socialist transition, its particular past and uncertain future.

Path dependency

The new land markets in China reconfigure the bundles of rights at the heart of property prerogatives that generate different propensities of things and define the parameters of the potential for the urban fabric of the city. The 'futures present' in these 'socialist markets' of the city are open to capture, rent seeking, short termism and cronyism – growth models that are premised on local government short term boosterism that leverages local state power and accumulates local government debt. Equally, they generate opportunities for new configurations of the factors of production, alternative relations between land, capital and labour. The market is simultaneously social and economic and the claims on the city and the value of land are mediated by different, frequently competing and often incommensurable forms of expertise: land economy yes, but also the logics and claims to the city of architecture, planning, government and demography. The alternative configurations of property rights generate different understandings of the geometries that define the interaction of public and private in the metropolis.

In the neoclassical economics tradition effective pricing internalises externalities. It is in this sense an effort to eradicate ambiguity, uncertainty and the 'social' dimensions of exchange, though an inevitably incomplete one. It depends on government and law and in this sense law gives form to the economy in the neoliberal project. Reaganism, Thatcherism and their various imitators in the 1990s and 2000s were all in this way state-centric projects (Foucault 2008). Thus Coasian legacies structure the normative models of development economics and emphasise the importance of clear property rights for the optimising of the potential of factors of production (de Soto 2001).

The path dependency of emergent markets in China therefore may encourage a Coasian interest in clarifying property ownership, as the major element in managing city externalities. Coasians develop this beyond the explicit, legal property right, to account also for the tacit dimensions of property forms. In some ways this is not exclusive to China – as we have already highlighted in the work of the legal philosopher Tony Honoré the eleven dimensions of 'ownership' he identifies are rarely all bundled together, but typically distributed across parties (Honoré 1987). Durkheim argued the single defining characteristic of property was that it had the capacity to exclude certain people from use or access – but there are endless ways in which this exclusion can be enacted and constructed (Durkheim 1991), it does not logically rest on the models of private property ownership most often normalised in both mainstream economic theory and urban studies.

For Michel Callon the framing of property keeps the externality at bay, or there is a social overflow. The frames that delineate property rights in China are inevitably less clear cut than that, valued differently by various actors. In Callonian economic sociology, the logics of economics shape the economy and the market emerges performatively but it can be hard in such work to see how Callonian interpretation speaks to (or even wants to speak to) the dilemmas of economic deliberation. By contrast, the commensuration of different justifications of the propensity of the city determines the speed and the nature of urban change. Hence in China, scholars have commented on both the plurality of claims made on property and the ambivalent nature of property rights (Ho 2001). Conventional economic wisdom would see both this plurality and ambivalence as sources of great inefficiency in the system, standard development economics highlights how confused title and property rights can stall development because of the uncertainties it generates. But both some of the empirical evidence in China and the logics of economic sociologists such as Stark or Boltanski and Thévenot might question this, arguing that 'productive frictions' between measures of value and worth can stimulate alternative resolutions of the problems of externality. As we have demonstrated above this is in part about an age-old tension between whether 'markets' or 'hierarchies' best serve the optimal allocation of factors of production in economic systems. But we argue here that it also demonstrates more than this; that the sense of the unknown future demands particular forms of expertise to understand how the city works and anticipate its rapid transformation. Disciplines such as land use planning, architecture and regimes of governance provide not only technocratic models of city engineering, but they also provide justifications of particular urban logics; incommensurable measurements of the territory of the city that are brought to bear on the urban problem in a variety of combinations at different times. Metropolitan experiments in China offer exemplary alternatives to the neoliberal interpretation of property as a private monopoly, and may or may not bring their own competitive advantages with them through the architecture of their markets (Fligstein 2001).

On the nature and limits of national comparison

One way of considering this architecture is by comparison between national models. A sub-genre of economic sociology and socio-economics might compare varieties of capitalism, the relative development 'stage' of capitalism in China and the positive and negative consequences of particular variations seen in China (Hall and Soskice 2001; Fligstein 2001; 2010; Fligstein and Zhang 2010). For Fligstein and Zhang (2010) state capacity for intervention is either 'low' or 'high', network capacity for economic creation similarly dichotomous (see Figure 3.9). In this analysis, China's 'new capitalism' is closer to that of France than the USA. The model in China for Fligstein and Zhang can for them be typologised thus.

While not without value, the problems with such a typology are twofold. First – and perhaps most significantly – the taxonomy of this diagram assumes a sense of convergence of a single China model of development, witnessed in particular sectors and places. Yet one of the defining characteristics of the relational markets that we are describing is their sense of both flux (a notion of infinite contractual relations displacing finite contractual exchange) and *a posteriori* experimentation. What is important about China's experience between 1979 and 2013 is in part about the experimentation and diversity of different ways of modernising the urban. The sense that relational markets allow a localised autonomy and experimentation that we explore further in the next chapter. Cities are increasingly the drivers of economic growth globally. China has a tradition of several thousand years of 'one country, many systems'. Bringing the two together provides a powerful transformative model.

State capacity for economic intervention

	Low		High	
	Positive	Negative	Positive	Negative
Low	**Cell A** Liberal capitalism, economists' dream	**Cell B** Social chaos	**Cell C** Development state (airplanes, cars)	**Cell D** Overly strong state, diffused rent seeking and official corruption
High	**Cell E** Supply chains, industrial districts, small- and medium-sized family business (Wenzhou)	**Cell F** Cartels, local corruption	**Cell G** Flexible state, strong firms (Yiwu)	**Cell H** Crony capitalism (real estate)

(left vertical axis: Network capacity for economic creation)

FIGURE 3.9 Alternative views of China's new capitalism
Source: Adapted from Fligstein and Zhang (2010).

Second, the variable interpenetration of state and market does not lend itself to juxtapositions of 'more' and 'less' in the vector structuring Fligstein and Zhang's typology, it appeals instead to a sense of mutating and experimental institutional form. Such form does not have the conventional boundaries, it has no straight-forward inside or outside, more of an informal structuring that resembles a Moebius strip where there is no boundary between inside and outside. Economic development in urban China and China's economic efficiency has not thus far relied on the creation of formal institutions – and as a result of this the generation of reduced transaction costs – but rather on local experiments and competition between local states. This is no more visible than when it comes to the 1988 amendment of the constitution that grants local states the privilege of selling state-owned land. This was a catalyst for property markets and economic developments but in very diverse ways – a diversity the price of which is institutional contingency.

In this context the territorialisation of the metropolis is structured by temporalities of the city as well as its spatialities. The cultures of change in the city are structured by its ephemerality, a sense that the city in flux privileges a sense of the spatial that is always temporal. This is what Ackbar Abbas has described as 'the city of disappearance' in Hong Kong, in work inspired by the writing of Paul Virilio. It sustains a crisis of representation of the urban through the repeated iteration and slippage between time and space. And what the city might be in the future is qualified by alternative regimes of land use rights. What might be and what is are reflected in the potential of the city, the propensity of things. The facility to realise this potential is the product of particular combinations of urban professional know-ledges, the social production of the forms of expertise of the planners, developers, architects and local government players described here. As the propensity of the city to change accelerates the facility to control its futures depends increasingly on the ability to combine productively these different disciplines in shaping urban change. In this sense the form of the city in China is not simply commodified, it is the outcome of the stable or unstable combinations of these forms of expertise that together – where successful – translate uncertain futures into calculable risks of development. Relating the combination of plural property rights and synthesised (relational) forms of urban expertise become the defining features of the model of urban change that we describe as local state capitalism.

4

LOCAL STATE CAPITALISM?

From urban hierarchy to city markets

不到北京不知道自己官小
bu dao Beijing, bu zhidao ziji guan xiao
If you don't go to Beijing, you don't know how low your official position is

不到上海不知道啥叫乡巴佬
bu dao Shanghai, bu zhidao sha jiao xiangbalao
If you don't go to Shanghai, you don't know what a bumpkin is

不到天津不知道啥叫社会主义好
bu dao Tianjin, bu zhidao sha jiao shehuizhuyi hao
If you don't go to Tianjin, you don't know what the good of socialism is

不到深圳不知道自己钱少
bu dao Shenzhen, bu zhidao ziji qian shao
If you don't go to Shenzhen, you don't know how little money you have

不到重庆不知道自己结婚早
bu dao Chongqing, bu zhidao ziji jiehun zao
If you don't go to Chongqing, you don't know you married too early

Urban hierarchy and socialist markets: the economic logic of China's city growth

Geographical scale is central to the strand of economic thinking that has attempted to model urban change through the development of optimal urban hierarchy. Known in academic neoclassical economics as 'the new economic geography' it has been closely identified with the work of economists such as Paul Krugman and

Anthony Venables (Fujita *et al.* 1999), modelling the agglomeration effects of modern economies. The new economic geography may or may not draw a great deal from the (geographic-based) academic sub discipline of economic geography (Overman 2004). However, the focus on market structure and the nature of price mechanisms in determination of location (Venables 2010) generates a modelling of spatial form that develops for the twenty-first century a sense of optimal location and evolutionary metropolitan growth. The landmark work by Fujita *et al.* (1999) effectively incorporates and updates the mid-twentieth century German geographical tradition of central place theory of Christaller and Losch. But what is shared by this tradition and particularly the new economic geography of the 'The Spatial Economy' (Fujita *et al.* 1999) is the sense that economic development will display trends of spatial agglomeration that will account statistically for predictable forms of urban hierarchy. In both Fujita *et al.* and Christaller's original thinking it should be possible both to read stages of economic development from the arithmetic of urban hierarchy and also to predict the distribution of urban concentration from the scaling of population numbers against geographical pattern.

The China model of urban growth neither corresponds with such arithmetic nor can be predicted by the logics of the new economic geography. At each geographical scale, the DNA of urbanisation in China could barely be more different from this sense of order and urban hierarchy. Pattern in China instead displays situational accommodations of state and market, the outcome of major fiscal decisions that prioritise investment in one area above another. These logics work out at several geographical scales – the region, the metropolis, the city district and the neighbourhood.

There are two possible explanations of the China pattern. One would suggest that the hierarchical organisation of urban form identifies an optimal geometry of resource and urban settlement. In this explanation, urban China's deviation from expected logic must be economically inefficient and developmentally sub-optimal. A second logic might be that what is at stake is more than economic logic alone: that the China model involves a different process of synthesising economic, social and political imperatives. McKinsey's landmark 2009 report *China's Urban Billion*, one of the most extensive reviews of urban pattern in China, draws implicitly on both of these perspectives in its analysis. On the one hand, it stresses that the drivers of China's urban form are 'local' – that the historical autonomy of the China system depends on a coupling of central rule and local incentivisation (McKinsey 2009: 75). On the other, it identifies a typology of three development stages of metropolitan change among the identified 858 cities of China: a taxonomy of 'industrialising', 'transforming' and 'modernising' cities. For McKinsey's analysis the early stage economic development tends to be more state dependent, industrially focused and *ad hoc*, with industrial plants concentrated in central city locations. The move of industrial manufacturing from city centres to peripheral and specially zoned areas outside the city is accompanied by a shift towards more rational land use planning and an increasing dependence on private sector investment. McKinsey suggest that only Shanghai in China is truly 'modernising' although possibly

Guangzhou and Dalian come close (McKinsey 2009: 82). For McKinsey, the four pillars of China's urban growth (land and spatial development, economy and funding, people development and resources) combine in processes that evolve from state socialism to market economy. There is an appealing empirical simplicity to McKinsey's model and it is clearly the case that the move up the value chain and evolution away from heavy industry replicates in China economic development logics globally with correlated consequences for urban form. But this developmental logic displaces the new economic geography's causal connection between urban hierarchy and development with an institutional connection between city development and market completion. Both the new economic geography and the McKinsey model share a particular teleological logic. The former suggests a deterministic outcome of urban hierarchy, the latter a deterministic outcome of market completion. The 'modernising' horizon category of McKinsey's typology should logically find the most complete markets in cities such as Shanghai and a correlation at least between market evolution and growth rates. But the messy realities of today's China do not correspond to this logic, at each geographical scale – the region, the metropolis, the district and the neighbourhood – what appears to have evolved in the recent past and appears emergent in the present is neither arithmetic hierarchy nor market completion in this deeply Western sense of both terms.

At the regional scale, urban growth since 1978 displays strategic macroeconomic fiscal policy choices that reflect the logics of experimental metropolitan growth policies and changing regional influence at the top of the CPC nationally. At the scale of the city, China has tested several pilots of the socialist market in the city. And perhaps most interestingly of all at the level of the district (the *shiqu*), below the level of the metropolis, the most innovative and the most inefficient, the most inventive and the most corrupt emergent forms of capitalism in China display the most dynamic hybrids of state and market. Finally, below the metropolitan districts at the level of the new-build commodity housing organised commonly through *xiaoqu* (literally, small *district*) there emerges both new forms of residential concentration and through the rapidly growing middle class a possible emergence of a novel identity and consumption politics of place.

The post-1978 growth starts with the SEZ, open coastal cities (particularly Shanghai, Tianjin, Guangzhou and Dalian) and open economic regions (Yeh 2000), trialling modes of FDI, privileges and protections for investors and experimental land zoning inside cities. Regionally, there is a clear phasing of investment that reflected both national political influence and stepped change that prioritised in turn the Pearl River Delta (including Hong Kong, Shenzhen, Guangzhou 1978–1990), the Yangzi River Delta (the provinces of Jiangsu and Zhejiang including the cities of Shanghai, Suzhou, Nanjing and Hangzhou 1990–2006), the Bohai Ring (including the cities of Beijing, Tianjin 2000–present), and most recently the development of the interior (Chongqing, Chengdu post-2008 financial crisis–present). Each in turn combined national fiscal license with locally modelled economic development; each in turn structured market liberalisation in a slightly different form. These variations in market formation and path dependency are at the heart of China's economic dynamism. As with other post-socialist models of economic transition there is a sense in which new economic structures are built with the pieces and the ruins of the old system rather than as a pristine new structure on a *tabula rasa* (Stark 1996). In this sense the sort of incremental change that we identified in Chapter Three in terms of relational property rights is just one aspect of emergent structures of economic change that we characterise here as local state capitalism.

From relational property rights to local state capitalism

Deng's 1992 tour of the south signalled a renewed departure from central state planning. Local states and local companies blossomed (Christerson and Lever-Tracy 1997), resulting in economic regions with different characteristics and specialisations (Eng 1999). Partially privatised state-owned enterprises played a central role (Dong and Putterman 2000). Local government officials took shares of the companies, or formed alliances with shareholders. These changes built on the experimental developments of the TVE whose productivity peaked – for Naughton at least – with their 'golden age' long passing around 1996 (Naughton 1996). TVEs were governed by what Oi (1999) describes as 'local state corporatism', characterised by ambiguous property rights, opaque legal enforcement of rule and where *guanxi* relations stabilise uncertainty, oil the nascent market machine and turn incalculable uncertainty into calculable and manageable risk (Walder 1995; Ho 2001). There are similarities between this model of the TVE and the modes of urban governance and development that increasingly structure city growth in China from the 1980s onwards (Walder 1995; Oi 1999; Blecher and Shue 2001; Redding and Witt 2007: 103).

Successive chapters of this volume examine the ways in which this local state capitalism has facilitated the rapid pace of economic growth in China but also defined both its strengths and potential weaknesses. We look at the continued links between emergent companies and the state (involving private, public and hybrid company structures), the detailed relations of risk taking and city making in real estate development companies, how the city through relational markets accommodates massive flows of migration and how the everyday cultures of risk and uncertainty in stock buying and the lives of young professionals are shaped by this form of economic governance. Local state capitalism generates a sense of the socialist market as a form of governance. The main dimensions of such emergent local state capitalism in the cities of China in the first decade of the twenty-first century involved:

1   A 'systemic' set of partnerships between local government and businesses through the development of 'relational markets'. These partnerships are cemented by *guanxi* relations – informal networks of ongoing obligations – trust and intensive inter-personal bonding.

2   A sense of experimental development of combinations of state and market that are trialled at different geographical scales of region, city and district. These variations configure differently the longstanding conceptual tensions between

whether transaction costs between institutions or their organisation through hierarchical configuration are more economically efficient.

3   A step change in flows of capital and labour to the cities. Massive foreign investment, especially from Hong Kong and Taiwan, dovetails with unprecedented migration of labour. Labour stands in a variable relationship to the *hukou*, initially introduced in the 1950s to restrict rural-to-urban migrant flows. Under local state capitalism the *hukou*, effectively a rights-bearing residential registration certificate in a particular city, comes to define a new regime of urban citizenship.

4   The relative autonomy of lower geographical tiers of governance in the development models and particularly the functional autonomies of '*shiqu*' city districts within both the major *mega city* governance structures and the growing city regions.

5   The *danwei* as a predominant source of urban identity is increasingly undermined by the emergence of new patterns of urban residence in the *xiaoqu*. The *xiaoqu* are newly built residential complexes, often initiated by private-sector property developers, whose living units are sold to individuals and families as commodity housing. This trend signals a shift in social identification to the city itself.

6   A new rise of peculiarly urban institutions of social control, as well as actual and potential welfare provision. Social discipline (such as the enforcement of one child policy) may be devolved to *xiaoqu* residents' committees. Health and education are increasingly controlled by district and municipal councils.

Relationality and market transaction

Central to the way that local state capitalism works is the phenomenon of relational markets. As we began to describe in Chapters One and Three we want to understand such relational markets in contradistinction to neoliberal, primarily individualist markets. Such a contrast of 'relationality' to individualism is discussed in some depth by Marilyn Strathern (1992) in the context of Melanesian gift exchange and by François Jullien (1995, 2004) in his influential work on Classical Chinese thought. Yet for us what is at stake is not the pure relationality of gift-giving or traditionalism of Daoism and Confucianism. It is instead a complex combination of relationality and the hyper-modernity of the market. Such relational markets are more long termist than Western markets. In neoliberal markets individuals or individual firms take on risk and are bearers of rights and obligations. In relational markets, there is instead a high degree of risk-, rights- and obligation-sharing between partners to an exchange. Relational markets presume organic, more or less affective, relations of exchange: as much gift exchange as commodity exchange. In relational markets economic agents do not come to the market with clearly defined goals: these are not the classical markets of Max Weber's economic action. There is less a focus on outcome and completed acts and more a focus on process, on activity rather than action. They are not based so much in the transaction (in Oliver Williamson's sense) but in the seemingly never-ending transacting.

We can speak not so much of transaction cost economics, but 'transacting cost sociology'. Trust, ongoing relationships and affective elements require understanding China's market economy through relations/*guanxi* of parties to exchange. In this combination of gift and commodity exchange, we cannot assume utilitarian, benefit maximising action, in which costs and benefits are weighed up in advance. Instead, economic strategy emerges out of particular situations (Jullien 1995). Strategies may be defined less in terms of preconceived costs and benefits than in terms of analysis of the situation itself. The idea is not just to conclude a contract with formally defined rights and obligations on the part of contracting parties. As Hsu (2005) argues situations of high trust and historical *guanxi* facilitate the work of 'capitalists without contracts'. Rights and obligations are left hazy, like boundary objects (*cabianqiu*, literally 'balls that hit the edge [of the table]') that are not once and forever defined. They evolve out of situations over periods of time. A contract is not in principle straightforwardly enforceable by a higher order arbiter, like a court or the state. It is the preservation of the relation, and the trustworthiness demonstrated inducing future and other long-term and processual exchange relations, that are the ultimate enforcers. In a historical sense this is philosophically and jurisprudentially closer to organically evolving common law traditions than the Napoleonic coding of new institutionalism. At a micro scale in everyday life affective bonding takes the form of banquets, singing, drinking and gift-giving. At a macro scale an ongoing relationship between the power of the centre and the autonomy of the local implies an ongoing sense of obligation and responsibility for the state in China even in the context of modernisation, opening up and experiments of market liberalisation. The relation is meant to continue. Its own logic then becomes paramount compared with the goals of the parties of any particular exchange. Yet it is still a market. There are often alternative partners with whom one can contract. There is certain logic of supply and demand. Rights and obligations may be ill defined, but they are rights and obligations. Contracts are constructed with different assumptions and expectations than the West, but they are contracts. These Chinese markets are in some aspects more modern than Western, neoliberal markets. They presume less the equilibrium of neoclassical economics than a process that is perpetually under construction. And we can see the logics and the architecture of these markets in primary research on listed firms and their political ties that we explore in Chapter Five, the real estate markets in Chapter Six and the stocks and share trading in Chapter Seven.

Although less developed there is a growing and parallel sense of the governance implications of such relational markets in the international relations (IR) and politics literature. Conventional game theory influenced thinking and cognitive modelling suggest a Western model in which the efficacy of clear governing rules between institutions can promote cooperation by lowering transactional costs and reduce conflict by increasing predictability and decreasing uncertainty. In contrast Qin suggests that the situation in China model is better pictured by what he describes as 'relational governance' where 'formal rules and institutions are, after all, 'at odds with our generic heritage'. 'Generic heritage' means more in terms of human sociality and human relations, because use of personal ties among human beings is so instinctive. Relational governance provides an alternative approach. Classical Chinese philosophers since Confucius and Mencius have discussed the importance of social relations and maintenance of relations for effective and benign governance' (Qin 2011: 118). As we found in the emergent real estate markets the open-ended nature of the contract and the opacity of legal rule lends an uncertainty to the system that is stabilised by the combination and deployment of city building 'technologies' of architecture, planning, local government and place making.

So the absence of a geographical urban hierarchy in China that is market optimal in the manner the new economic geography suggests is precisely a product of local state capitalism's reconfiguration of the relations between markets and hierarchies. To the extent that hierarchies can displace markets by reducing transaction costs and promoting strategic responses to new challenges the local state capitalism model might be successful. But to the extent that SBC promote sub-optimal allocations of resources hierarchies are conventionally trumped by market efficiencies. To the extent that new economic institutions in China hybridise the separation of market and hierarchy we may be dealing with significant new articulations of this traditional problem of economic organisation. This is true at different geographical scales: regional, metropolitan and city district. From the contrast between different growth models that have emerged in the last two decades, particularly between the city models of the Pearl River Delta and the high-profile alternative piloted in Chongqing, but also between the different districts within a mega city such as Shanghai, scale matters in the structuring of local state capitalism.

Metropolitan scale: Experiments in city growth models in contemporary China

A range of development models were associated with particular eponymous cities and identified with the experimental changes in China from the 1980s and 1990s. The 'Wenzhou Model' in Zhejiang Province was long associated with family company structures targeting specialised markets, generating a pattern of cheap commodities with nation-wide market reach. The 'Sunan Model' refers to the development of township enterprises with strong intervention of local government. The 'Dalian' model (associated with the mayoralty of Bo Xilai from 1992–2000) eased development through managed programmes of demolition and relocation of one million people (in a city of two million) without protests through the development of extensive housing programmes for the poorest. The 'Pudong model' in Shanghai famously used the hope values of anticipated land price uplift from development to finance infrastructure investment (Huang 2011: 572, 593). The 'Dongguan Model' (an early incarnation of the so-called Pearl River Delta model) refers to the rural industrialisation driven by FDI and orientated to foreign demands. Dongguan is located in Guangdong Province, northwest of Shenzhen (Jiang 2011; Naughton 2008). In each case the autonomy of metropolitan government has worked within the framing context of central direction to develop distinctive forms of permeability between state and market, international practice and local vernacular, political culture and market form.

This capacity for individual cities to develop specifically local policy realisations of market development can be illustrated by two examples taken from different moments of the opening-up process: one from the shadow real estate experience of 1980s in Tianjin; the second from 'third hand' development model of 2000s Chongqing (Huang 2011).

The sense of experimentation involved is important. It was seen clearly in the early-stage development of Tianjin. This demonstrates one sense of the permeabilities that link technologies of city building to the emergence of socialist markets in local state capitalism. Transnational disciplines of city building and urban regeneration are brought together in new permutations that articulate local variations on transnational expertise. In the 1980s, as part of the experiment in opening up and modernisation, the China government sanctioned the setting up in London of a property company that would pilot and possibly joint venture in models of city development and capital investment in the UK's own then-experimental urban regeneration of London's Docklands. Links with the Tianjin Economic Development Area (TEDA) were privileged in this exercise.

London Docklands Development Corporation (LDDC) was an urban development corporation set up in 1981 under the authority of then Secretary of State Michael Heseltine. Significant areas of the boroughs of Newham, Southwark, Tower Hamlets and a small part of Lewisham were designated an Urban Development Area under legislation that was based on the development of British New Towns in the immediate post-war era. The introduction of the LDDC reconfigured the relationship between planning, land ownership and property development. Development control powers were vested in the urban development corporation, the corporation was allowed to buy and sell land and the model was used to experiment with fast-tracking urban change, prioritising foreign direct investment (most spectacularly with the Reichman family, the private owners of Olympia and York, and the developers of several large waterfront sites in the 1970s and 80s including Battery Park City in lower Manhattan near Wall Street). Developments of minor and major infrastructure (the Docklands Light Rail and the Limehouse Link tunnel – the most expensive road ever built in Britain) were funded partially on the back of property deals that leveraged private development revenues to generate high-profile projects such as the major new financial district of Canary Wharf and the riverfront retail and residential developments in Southwark's Surrey Docks.

The Tianjin presence in London's docklands was designed to learn lessons directly from London, a notion that experience in the London Docklands of the 1980s and 1990s might inform the working of the TEDA. TEDA focuses on the area of Tanggu District, the free market designated zone, which is now linked by high-speed rail to Beijing (since 2008) and downtown Tianjin but centred in the docks of the city. As the epigraph of this chapter suggests, the reputation of Tianjin (relatively close to Beijing in comparison with Shenzhen or Guangzhou) is for mainstream orthodoxy and so one Tianjin interviewee involved in the experiment suggested that TEDA was chosen because Beijing was more likely to trust Tianjin staffers in experimental joint venture company models in London than they would personnel from other parts of China. But in interviews for this book, key informants from both (formerly the) LDDC and (formerly working for) TEDA described how reality conspired to produce a model of knowledge exchange that was not quite as might have been expected. Although several company structures were developed in London, and even a potential joint venture with Canary Wharf itself explored, the 'Lawson boom' of the 1980s turned into the 'Lawson bust' and the massive downturn in the property market of the late 1980s and early 1990s.[1] Olympia and York went into receivership and much of the nascent developments of Canary Wharf and the old docklands were then held by the banks – particularly Barclays – to prevent receivership proceeding to absolute bankruptcy. The commercial market was particularly strongly hit and the China–London joint venture vehicle was put on hold.

However, as personal contacts and informal links had been developed several of the major players who had been involved in the docklands experiment were invited to translate their expertise in city building back to China. Engaged by TEDA it is possible to see the influence of the Docklands model in Tianjin today. Two examples are particularly significant: the TEDA Administration Centre at the heart of the new economic development area and the masterplanning exercise of the area immediately proximate to this building. Koetter Kim & Associates, a Boston-based architectural practice, had taken on and completed the master-planning of the Canary Wharf site from SOM. After the downturn they were then asked to develop ideas for TEDA. They built the TEDA central administration building, completing in 2000. With flows of people through the ground and top floors overseeing from on high a light-flooded atrium structure, the building displays a familial architectural resemblance to Norman Foster's Reichstag redevelopment in Berlin where tourists walk across the translucent and spectacular dome looking down on the transparent debate below. The Tanggu development that can be seen today combines technological cutting-edge design with an aesthetic and mundane sense of opening up the city hall similarly to forces of transparency. Its permeability is intentional, a design metaphor and an example of the translation of a normatively figured new construction of the city.

Equally interesting is the masterplan and the urban design of the open park adjacent to the administration centre. Through discussion between some of the same actors that had been involved in both Canary Wharf and Tianjin it was agreed to experiment with a model of 'value capture' that was the hallmark of Olympia and York's development practice trialled in Toronto, then New York then London. In this model, a major signature piece of infrastructure was to be constructed before the auctioning of land packages with development potential. In Tianjin's case, a high-quality urban park sits as a centrepiece to the land parcels before they were marketed. Although it would be hard to test counterfactuals on the case, individuals involved in the design and marketing of the site suggested in interviews in 2009 that the returns on the land in the 2000s were between double and treble the value of what they would have been if it had been sold direct to developers before the completion of the park. In this model of value capture the investment in the signature infrastructure more than pays for itself, generating significant returns on capital and a more sustainable – and certainly a more aesthetically pleasing – urban milieu.

Both cases exemplify the ways in which technologies of city building translate international practices in a local context. And powerfully, the Tianjin case exemplifies the manner in which experimentation was at the heart of local state capitalism. Members of TEDA have suggested that the relatively slow transformation of Tianjin's SEZ, in comparison with some of the others, was in some quarters put down to the caution connected with the proximity and suspicion of Beijing; however, the exchange of personnel and practice between London's Docklands and Tianjin captured the sense of experimentation with new models of urban change at the level of the city. In this sense, Tianjin exemplifies the manner in which parallels between London's and Tanggu's docklands are linked by international forms of city building expertise that are permeable to specific social networks, but are embedded in markedly different social contexts.

Similarly, in Chapter Three we have seen how the market opening up of Shenzhen displays specific geographical and historical path dependencies that link Hong Kong FDI and experiments in property rights. That is, the competitive pattern of local governments partly generated by the de-centralisation of authority in 1994 when the tax-distribution system was launched and partly by the national strategic direction that focused experimentation on the Pearl River Delta. Chapter Ten develops this further, considering how the model of 'Shenzhen speed' emerges, incorporating rapid accommodation of migrants to the city and new residential areas.

Step change in flows of capital and labour

In contrast to the rapid development model of Shenzhen, the switch to a focus on the internal regions of China since 2000, and particularly since 2008, has also been connected to a questioning of the scale of inequalities produced by China's urbanisation. In this context, some variations on the local state capitalism formula have attempted to exploit the pluralisation of property rights to develop a more egalitarian model of urban transformation in Chongqing. In late 2011, events in the city of Chongqing attracted international attention following the death of British businessman Neil Heywood, allegedly murdered by Gu Kailai, wife of Bo Xilai, head of the Communist Party in Chongqing. At the time of the death the chief of police and deputy mayor Wang Lijun sought asylum at the American Consulate in the neighbouring city of Chengdu and in the fall out from the 'Wang Lijun' incident Bo was removed from his various positions of responsibility pending further investigation. Bo was one of the princelings associated with the first generation of Party elders close to Mao and had served on the Politburo nationally. He was identified closely with the development of the Chongqing model of city growth and his high-profile sacking as a result of the Heywood incident generated both political turmoil and also considerable debate about the putative value of the economic development model itself. Gu Kailai was convicted of Neil Heywood's murder in August 2012. And if this volume is silent on the historical and political detail of Bo's fall, the Chongqing experiment is important in signalling a quite different form of local state capitalism from that pioneered in Shenzhen and the Pearl River Delta generally in the first decades of opening up and modernisation. Public attention has been often focused on Bo's character and his high-profile cultural campaigns. For some, his encouragement of 'red songs' and other nostalgic practices echoed too closely the cultural revolution. But more interestingly the Chongqing model derived from an analysis of the 'tragedy of the commons' that tried to mitigate the social externalities of economic change through the flexibility of property rights regimes to secure alternative models of urban growth. In this sense, it represents an alternative articulation of local state capitalism. Some see this as a 'leftist' model but in this chapter we want to suggest that the Chongqing model is more interesting because it exemplifies the creative splintering of property rights.

Situated in the interior of China, Chongqing was in a sense a 'wartime special zone'. It was first selected by Chiang Kai-shek as the capital city during the Second World War after Japan occupied Nanjing, and then by Mao as the 'industrial capital city' of the 'Third Frontier' during the Cold War. In 1997, Chongqing was elevated as the fourth municipality city of China, combining provincial and metropolitan status, linked to the completion of the nearby massive hydro-electric infrastructure project on the Three Gorges River Dam project, started in 1994 and completed in 2009: 129 towns were flooded and over one million people migrated because of the project.

In one sense this qualifies Chongqing as one of the biggest cities in the world with a permanent population of 28.85 million (2010), although much of the land mass is both agricultural use and designated by rural rather than urban property rights in the China system. Consequently the 'municipality' contains both 'city dwellers' with *hukou* and a large number of both rural migrants to the city and rural poor living within the Chongqing boundary. Huang estimates that there is a *nongmingong* population of at least four million (with another 4.5 million Chongqing'ites having migrated to the cities of the east coasts).

Partly because of this in 2007 Chongqing was selected (with Chengdu) as a special zone for the development of models of urban–rural integration, as part of national strategy to gradually displace export-focused national emphasis with internal consumption in the China economy. Alongside the flows of rural poor to the city Huang Qifan, Mayor and Head of the local State Assets and Management Commission has leveraged state land to generate major investment deals with 'dragon headed enterprises' (龙头企业) to spearhead developments with Hewlett Packard, FoxConn (Apple's partners), Chang' an (cars manufacturer Ford's partner company) and BASF (the German pharma corporate). Huang Qifan claims that HP investment alone amounts to US$5 billion, while investment for related components will generate further investment ten times that amount, US$50 billion (Huang 2011, 572).

The scale of Chongqing is significant – 82,402 km² – almost 40 times the size of Shenzhen (2,020 km²), 13 times of Shanghai (6,341 km²) and almost twice of the Netherlands (41,864 km²). The rural land use of the metropolitan region leads to a 'city-in-villages' pattern in Chongqing, with 648 km² of constructed urban area – close to that of Shanghai (610 km²), bigger than Shenzhen (396 km²). In 2010 within the permanent population of 28.85 million over 72 per cent are formally registered as rural population (Jiang 2011).

The social theorist Cui Zhiyuan (2009, 2010, 2011) whose writing was central to our theorisation of urban property rights in Chapter Three has both written extensively about the Chongqing model and been engaged directly in its realisation through secondment to the city. Cui sees an analytical equivalence between the 'socialist market economy' and economics Nobel laureate James Meade's 'liberal socialism', in which public assets are used to make profits on markets so that corporation taxes can be kept low yet public services provided. For Cui there are three defining characteristics of the Chongqing model: a land certificates market that incentivises urban densification and rural development, the co-development of public assets by state and market interests in profit share JV and the provision of a new welfare regime, most particularly a massive programme of new-build public housing. From 2011, US$15 billion was identified for 800,000 apartments to be rented out cheaply to the poor. Chongqing is consequently of significance both socially and in terms of Keynesian stimulus.

Thus public ownership of assets has increased in Chongqing from ¥170bn in 2002 to ¥1,386bn in June 2011. These are assets managed by Chongqing's SASAC. Yet at the same time the private sector's contribution to Chongqing GDP rose from 39 to 61 per cent. Apart from such job creation, migration to the city has been incentivised through relaxing urban household registration (*hukou*) requirements. Now the only condition is to have worked for five years in the city. From 2010 to 2011, two million of such migrants changed to urban household registration. This gives them equal access with urban residents for Chongqing city government-provided education, health care, retirement pension and access to public rental housing. Public rental housing been increased from 30 to 40 per cent of Chongqing housing in comparison to say 5 per cent in Beijing (Cui 2011). It is only available to individuals on monthly incomes of ¥2000 or less and families of ¥3000 or less.

Developing the land tax model that incentivises the most intensive use of each unit of land as a factor of production, the Chongqing model is designed to maximise city growth, intensify urban density, enhance ecological sustainability and share the fruits of the development through the separation of (state) ownership property rights from (private) property use rights. Property developers must buy development certificates and effectively transfer resources to peasants through buying equivalent patches of land that are built up but in the formally 'rural' land rights areas. The amount they pay for development rights consequently goes to peasants who will often use the money to facilitate the move from rural to urban Chongqing. This is connected to the other lynchpin of the Chongqing model. This is to maintain the 1.8bn *mu* of cultivated land needed for the country's food supply that Wen Jiabao and the State Council underscored in 2008. This is carried out through the creation of a land exchange market (*tudi jiaoyi suo*). Developers who want to build in urban Chongqing need to buy certificates to do so on this rural land exchange. These developers will typically build on the borders of the city and hence take some rural land out of cultivation. In building on city boundaries, the municipality must use taxpayer money to pay for levelling the land and what they call the 'seven connections' (to road, water, waste, power, gas, communications, rain-drainage) infrastructure. However, business taxes have been kept low in Chongqing at a level of 15 per cent in comparison to more normal levels of 25 per cent in much of the rest of China. By separating use rights from ownership rights, the Chongqing model is said to promote the optimal use of the factor of production. If the 'fruits of the land' are shared there is – at least in theory – incentive simultaneously to maximise the return on land and to socialise the social externalities of development.

The purchase of development certificates ensures that equivalent acreage is put back into cultivation. To sell such certificates peasants must convert rural non-agricultural land – where they may have their houses, storage barns and small factories into cultivated land. Each *mu* that is converted is exchangeable for a certificate. The certificates give developers neither full ownership nor full use rights: they are instead land-development rights. The developer winning such an auction can build in the city and the peasant receiving the money for the sale of the certificate can use the money to fund the move to the city. In principle the model incentivises growth but with redistribution to the rural poor a constitutive feature of the incentivisation of private sector urban growth.

Under Bo Xilai, Chongqing was one of the fastest-growing provincial economies or provincial-level regions in the country (at 16.4 per cent in 2011) and, more controversially, one of China's happiest places (in some state-media surveys) (*The Economist* 2012). The net value of state assets in Chongqing grew sixfold between 2003 and 2009. The private sector share of Chongqing GDP rose from about half in 2005 to more than 60 per cent five years later, roughly the same as the national level. The Chongqing model has not been without its critics and is attacked by some conventional liberal economists as intrinsically flawed (*The Economist* 2012). *The Economist* alleged that while SOE are claimed to have handed over 15 to 20 per cent of profits to the government in the past five years, increasing to 30 per cent by 2015, the mechanisms of SOE contribution is said to be opaque. And whilst the scale of targeting resources at the urban poor is recognised, the city is also typical in hosting China's equivalent of *grands projets*. Chongqing's 'ten big cultural facilities' (begun before the arrival of Bo) echo the appearance in Dalian of 'Bo Grass' in the downtown amenity zones cleared of residences. They include a 'grand theatre' second only in size to Beijing's, said to have cost Chongqing a total of more than $1.5 billion so far. But the economic growth story of the last five years are impressive and for some scholars demonstrates a significant alternative form of market governance in which urban growth can be economically functional and redistribute wealth in theory labour exploits capital.

City district (shiqu) scale: the significance of district-level governance

There is considerable evidence that some of the most important models of city transformation emerge at the scale of the metropolitan district. As Chapter Ten later examines in further detail in the context of migration to the city of Shenzhen, district government frequently is involved in setting up local government investment vehicles (LGIV), which have the facility to deliver combinations of capital and development opportunities. In Shenzhen this has commonly been through joint venture vehicles that secure FDI in major development projects, often linked to manufacturing investment (Cartier 2002).

In the major cities, the size of individual districts can be larger than whole major metropolitan concentrations in Europe and North America. As we explore further in Chapter Ten the flows of migration to the cities make the reliability of official data questionable. However, with *hukou* population counted and those staying less often not enumerated, the official figures are generally thought to underestimate true numbers. Of the 18 districts (*shiqu*) and counties (*xian*) of Shanghai, Pudong, Yangpu and Minhang all have populations over one million. Naughton (2007) suggests that government officials/population ratios are much lower in China than in most other parts of the world – suggesting that there are 32,000 people to one official in China compared with as few as several hundred to one official in many parts of Europe. This sense of a thin layer of governance covering very large population numbers in the city signals the limits of the ability of higher levels of the governance hierarchy to control subsidiary geographical units. Autonomy is in this sense also a product of the sheer scale of China where a population of 1.3 billion and many cities of 5–20 million plus presents extraordinary problems of governance scale.

The governance of the eighteen *shiqu/qu* in Shanghai, reflecting Chinese imperial tradition as much as more recent Communist history, depends on cadres of mayoral office holders and party secretaries at district level that are located in a district for only a few years at a time. As part of the research for this book, we analysed the names and biographies of all the major office holders in the 18 districts and one county of Shanghai over a ten-year period from 1996 to 2006, the period of the city's most rapid growth. The Shanghai Statistical Yearbooks naming district office holders for the years 1996, 1997, 2000, 2003 and 2007 were analysed. The pattern is revealing. Over this period two mayors (Xu Kuangdi 1996, 1997, 2000; Han Zheng 2003, 2007) and three City Party Secretaries (Huang Ju 1996, 1997, 2000; Chen Liangyu 2003; Yu Zhengsheng 2007) served at city level. But at district level, neither District Chiefs heads nor District Party heads appear in three statistical yearbooks successively. Only a minority manage two appearances in succession, though on the one occasion when data were available with an interval of only one year most office holders reappear over both years. In our analysis of all the senior district office holders over the decade the tendency is for senior office holders to last three or four years maximum, sometimes to move up the hierarchy within a single district but they are then more often moved on from one district to another. This has consequences for the governance of the districts. The system incentivises rapid change, with relatively short periods of time for the office holders to demonstrate achievements in office.

TABLE 4.1 Scale and population of Shanghai districts

Name	Area (km²)	Population	Area Code	Street Offices	Residence Committees	Towns (Townships)	Village Committees
Huangpu District	12.41	620,000	200001	9	135	0	0
Luwan District	8.05	330,000	200020	4	64	0	0
Xuhui District	54.76	890,000	200030	12	344	1	14
Changning District	38.3	620,000	200050	9	176	1	6
Jing'an District	7.62	320,000	200040	5	85	0	0
Putuo District	54.93	850,000	200333	6	206	3	8
Jiabei District	29.26	710,000	200070	8	207	1	1
Hongkou District	23.48	790,000	200080	9	255	1	0
Yangpu District	60.61	1,080,000	200082	11	302	1	4
Minhang District	371.68	750,000	201100	3	289	9	166
Baoshan District	415.27	850,000	201900	5	233	9(+2)	165
Jiading District	458.8	510,000	201800	3	89	8	169
Pudong New District	522.75	1,770,000	200135	11	561	13	266
Jinshan District	586.05	530,000	201540	1	60	14	139
Songjiang District	604.7	510,000	201600	4	101	10	120
Qingpu District	675.54	460,000	201700	3	57	8	184
Nanhui District	688	700,000	201300	0	60	14	185
Fengxian District	687.39	510,000	201400	0	65	8	276
Chongming County	1,041.2	640,000	202150	0	52	13	224
Total (approximate)	6340	13,520,000		101	3341	107(+3)	1927

Source: Shanghai (18 districts and one county). Reports to State Council as centrally administered municipality. Most data as of 30 September 2004 (www.xzqh.org).

At times – as with Qingpu (population approximately 0.5 million) in the mid 2000s – a deputy mayor with architectural qualifications was seen to pursue open competitions and a particular focus on the quality of development. Qingpu in the 2000s developed a reputation for high-quality built infrastructure with commissions from outside the normal circuits of preferred planning and architecture companies. More commonly – according to many of the architectural and planning practices in

Shanghai interviewed for this work – the pressure is on officials to deliver high-profile urban-change projects on a short-time scale, while relying on a limited set of urban professionals and demonstrate quick turnaround of real estate led change. The hegemony of economic indicators in the performance management of ambitious officials places a premium on economic growth at the district level in general and *'face'* projects (roughly equivalent to *'grands projets'*) in particular. These are commonly instigated by the development of LGIV, which have the facility to be vested with state resources but also the freedom to raise private finance, enter into joint venture arrangements and address major infrastructure initiatives.

The district is also the level at which many of the variations in quality of the welfare net is determined – in terms of education, childcare provision and health. McKinsey's 'China Urban Billion' suggests that real estate sales are responsible for much of local government's flexibilities around urbanisation (2009: 22). In 2005, 35 per cent of Chengdu's city revenues were accrued from land sales, while redevelopment and reuse pressures also generated both tax revenue and resale revenues. Land sales revenue accounted for, on average, 30 per cent but as much as 60 per cent of China's developing cities' government revenues and for, on average, 15 per cent of the most developed cities' revenues. Moreover, they suggest 46 per cent of local revenues at the district level accrue through local taxes (McKinsey 2009: 468–471), principally through land sales and property taxes. Therefore, the institutional structure promotes both rapid transformation but also fiscal uncertainty that incentivises development that generates local revenues.

The downside of this level of autonomy can be illustrated by the case of the municipality of Jiangqiao in the Shanghai district of Jiading (with a population of approximately 0.5 million) on the north-eastern edge of the city. In 2008, according to the National Audit Office, Jiangqiao and Jiading set up a local government investment vehicle, which in turn borrowed approximately RMB 2 billon (approximately US$295 million) in a loan directly from two separate banks, ostensibly to support the construction of the Shanghai Beijing high-speed rail link. Local governments are (with exceptions) generally not formally allowed to borrow directly from banks but economic development vehicles specially set up for city transformation can do so. In the wake of the fiscal stimulus in China after the global downturn of 2008 this problem has become more pronounced. In the words of Stephen Green of Standard Chartered: 'No one will want to cut off credit to a half-finished project; not only would this guarantee the creation of a non-performing loan, but it would also be politically unpopular. So the bank regulator has to allow banks to continue lending to unfinished projects. But if banks continue to lend to LGIVs for such projects, then the funds could flow to other places too. One cannot exclude the possibility that enterprising local governments might try to intentionally starve a few LGIVs of financing and make sure their problems are exposed, in order to pressure Beijing to keep the credit tap open'. (Alloway 2010).

This sense of competition between districts is replicated in the competition between parts of the city in the metropolitan regions where rural property rights and urban property rights come together. In Chapter Ten we explore in more detail how in Shenzhen the *chengzhongcun*, the villages in the city, act as joint stock companies. With rural property rights distinguished from urban property that is held by the state and where use rights only are commodified, the villages in the city become economic actors in their own right in the urban landscape, specialising in certain forms of production, doing deals with FDI-based corporates and entering into land deals to produce commodity housing

Neighbourhood scale: from Danwei to xiaoqu

For scholars such as Bray (2005) the *xiaoqu* have already begun to displace the *danwei* as the source of collective identity in urban China. *Xiaoqu* (literally 'small districts') tend to be significant developments of 'commodity housing' bought from developers on a 70-year lease. They are frequently marked out by clear boundaries, at times it is suggested they equate to China's developments of 'gated communities' (Wu 2002; Wu and Webber 2004). For Bray they are the nascent units of social organisation of the new middle class, the territories through which logics of neighbourhood and belonging develop and potentially the site of new forms of consumption-based identity politics.

In Shanghai the theme towns referenced in Chapter Three are examples of these major *xiaoqu*. These are large areas of customised development, identified as part of Shanghai's decentralising outward growth in the early 2000s, flagship projects of the emergent global city. They market a lifestyle as well as commodity housing: Bauhaus style in Anting, futurist Italy complete with canals in 'Breeza Citta di Pujiang'. The 'Italian Town' was established close to the site of the 2010 World Expo on a prime riverfront location and sold out rapidly. The design of Breeza Citta maximises the amenity value of an artificially landscaped network of canals that run through the whole complex. At the heart of the *xiaoqu*, close to one of the marketing centres, the history of the development is displayed in a set of models and animated tableaux that link the rationale of the development to the cultural history of Italian dwelling and other OCT developments in China. There are other developers in Pujiang as well that buy into the overall Italian Town masterplan. The marketing motif fuses a Venetian carnival mask to its cousin from China (see Figure 4.1). And outside the marketing centre a raised platform decorated with Italian installation art provides a spectacular view across the canal waterfronts (see Figures 4.2 and 4.3).

New urban institutions of community and social control in the xiao qu

Unlike the theme towns, architecturally, the *xiaoqu* now produced are frequently formulaic; a repetitive patterned combination of majority residential towers, a minority of low-rise town housing all focused on common amenity space. As real estate development moves on to 'commodity housing' sales both the architectural form and the new real estate property market demand some structure through which the *xiaoqu* are maintained and urban life organised. Major real estate

FIGURE 4.1 The marketing motif fuses a Venetian carnival mask to its cousin from China

Source: © Michael Keith.

FIGURE 4.2 Marketing showroom, 'Italian Town', Shanghai

Source: © Michael Keith.

TABLE 4.2 Top 10 Development Companies in China 2005 by assets

Rank	Stock symbol	Company name	Total (billion yuan)	Web	English name
1	中国海外	中国海外发展股份有限公司	27.66	www.cohl.com	China Overseas Holdings Ltd.
2	G万科A	万科企业股份有限公司	21.99	www.vanke.com	China Vanke Co., Ltd.
3	合生创展	合生创展集团有限公司	21.54	www.hopson.com.cn	Hopson Development Holdings Ltd.
4	华润置地	华润置地有限公司	19.55	www.crland.com.hk	China Resources Land Ltd.
5	G陆家嘴	上海陆家嘴金融贸易区开发股份有限公司	11.01	www.ljz.com.cn	Shanghai Lujiazui Finance & Trade Zone Development Co., Ltd.
6	首创置业	首创置业股份有限公司	10.06	www.bjcapitalland.com.cn	Beijing Capital Land Ltd.
7	复地集团	复地集团股份有限公司	9.98	www.forte.com.cn	Forte Group Co., Ltd.
8	雅居乐	雅居乐地产控股股份有限公司	9.62	www.gzagilegarden.com.cn	Agile Property Holdings Ltd.
9	北辰实业	北辰实业股份有限公司	9.13	www.beijingns.com.cn	Beijing North Star Co. Ltd.
10	G招商局	招商局地产控 股股份有限公司	8.94	www.cmpd.cn	China Merchants Property Development Co. Ltd.

Source: China Real Estate 2006.

FIGURE 4.3 'Faux canalside', Italian Town, Shanghai
Source: © Michael Keith.

companies, such as Vanke, develop a plural functional structure with their own
property specialisms in development, real estate facilities management and 'second-
hand' sales. But if the development and resale arms of this structure have obvious
clients, the real estate management function of the *xiaoqu* lends impetus to the
creation of new clients. Residents of the *xiaoqu* become collective consumers of
the urban fabric, whose major capital investments and new mortgages creates direct
interests in sustaining the condition of the estates, the amenity values and the
quality of repairs. It is this common interest that leads some scholars to suggest that
the *xiaoqu* increasingly become the geographical scale at which new forms of
identification pattern will generate a novel sense of urban identity.

The common architectural monotony of the *xiaoqu* form prompts attempts to
distinguish the *xiaoqu* sites through generating place-specific identities. The
branding of residential quarters is not a phenomenon restricted to China but across
Shanghai, Shenzhen and Beijing place branding of *xiaoqu* is now almost universal.
In a study of five *xiaoqu* in the Shenzhen metropolitan district for this research
involving fieldwork in 2008 to 2009 each was marketed through a lifestyle theme
– 'mocha town' (Figure 4.4), 'green town' (Figure 4.6) or, in the case of China
Investment and Trade International Corporation (CITIC) *xiaoqu* in Shenzhen's
Guanlan District, a golfing branding that involved leprechaun motifs in the sales
centre next to a Highland soldier complete with bearskin and kilt (Figure 4.5).

TABLE 4.3 Top 10 Real Estate Companies in China

Rank	Stock symbol	Company name	Total points	Web	English name
1	中国海外	中国海外发展股份有限公司	1.355	www.cohl.com	China Overseas Holdings Ltd.
2	雅居乐	雅居乐地产控股有限公司	1.283	www.gzagilegarden.com.cn	Agile Property Holdings Ltd.
3	合生创展	合生创展集团有限公司	1.14	www.hopson.com.cn	Hopson Development Holdings Ltd.
4	G万科A	万科企业股份有限公司	1.037	www.vanke.com	China Vanke Co., Ltd.
5	复地集团	复地集团股份有限公司	0.684	www.forte.com.cn	Forte Group Co., Ltd.
6	华润置地	华润置地有限公司	0.659	www.crland.com.hk	China Resources Land Ltd.
7	G陆家嘴	上海陆家嘴金融贸易区开发股份有限公司	0.519	www.ljz.com.cn	Shanghai Lujiazui Finance & Trade Zone Development Co., Ltd.
8	富力地产	广州富力地产股份有限公司	0.408	www.rfchina.com	Guangzhou R&F Properties Co. Ltd.
9	首创置业	首创置业股份有限公司	0.326	www.bjcapitalland.com.cn	Beijing Capital Land Ltd.
10	北辰实业	北辰实业股份有限公司	0.273	www.beijingns.com.cn	Beijing North Star Co. Ltd.

Source: China Government official measurements, *China Real Estate* 2006.

FIGURE 4.4 *Xiaoqu* marketing suite, Shanghai
Source: © Michael Keith.

Much of the redevelopment of the major cities such as Shanghai has taken place through the emergence of the new commodity housing sector (see Tables 4.1, 4.2 and 4.3) that drives this *xiaoqu* development. As early as 2005 the turnover of each of the top three real estate companies was over RMB 20 billion (almost £2 billion). Many of these companies such as Vanke exemplify the combination of overseas capital (in this case from Hong Kong) and local government connections. Housing companies commonly have several sites in development across the city so operate both nationally and municipally (see Dahua's Shanghai sites below, Figure 4.7). But as we argue in Chapter Nine, the ethnographic experience focus of the real estate corporate structure in Minhang District of Shanghai and the emergence of the development depends on the manner in which the relational real estate market links the district level of the local state to the developers, the deals that can be done today and the relationships that can be developed for the future. In this sense, the *xiaoqu* become the development form through which local state capitalism is realised.

Conclusion: the limits of local state capitalism?

In Western neoliberal models of economic governance risk in principle is privatised. In theory the unintended consequences of urban growth – the social

FIGURE 4.5 *Xiaoqu* marketing suite, Shenzhen

Source: © Michael Keith.

FIGURE 4.6 'Green town' marketing motif, Shanghai Real Estate Trade Convention, 2008

Source: © Michael Keith.

externalities of city transformation – are priced and allocated. Across the West, the 2008 downturn resulted in the accidental socialisation of risk in the support of financial institutions globally that were 'too big to fail'. Not untypically, in Britain, banking debt exceeded five times GDP and the socialisation of this risk was an unexpected consequence of the 2008 crash, only made visible *ex post facto*. In China, financial risk is socialised *ab initio* through hybrid assemblages of state and market. But the corollary of pluralised local government autonomy is that if the bills of experimental failure exceed the cumulative effects of economic growth then the vulnerability of local state capitalism may – like the consequences of the 2008 crash in the West – also be discovered only after the event. The question that it might be possible to answer only in hindsight is whether or not the innovative experiments in local autonomy at the heart of local state capitalism will be remembered more for moral hazard or for dynamic urbanism.

Local state capitalism has provided a dynamic engine to the rapid growth of China in the period of reform and opening up. The plural form of state market hybridisation, the norms of relationality and relational governance and the sense of continual experimentation at all geographical scales of urbanism provides a flexible model that has fused Western capitalism to China's emergent socialist markets. The power of local state capitalism to drive economic growth is demonstrated in the speed of city transformation in China but this mode of urban governance quite clearly has associated weaknesses as well as strengths.

FIGURE 4.7 'Dahua' real estate investments in Shanghai, Shanghai Real Estate Trade
Convention, 2009

Source: © Michael Keith.

Local government finance – rarely the subject of popular academic scrutiny – lies at
the heart of its possible flaws. China's cities are characterised by debt leveraged local
states dependent on land sales for significant proportions of municipal revenue and
opaque financing that may foreshadow major macro-economic fiscal problems. The
costs of the welfare externalities of a rapidly ageing population are uncertain but it is
sometimes suggested that China will get old before it gets rich. And as the Jiading
example from Shanghai illustrates the flip side of local state autonomy may be cases
of municipal bankruptcy as well as economic success.

The scale of local state debt in China

In mid 2011, Moody's suggested that China may have understated the debt load of
local governments by Rmb 3,500 bn (US$541 bn) and that potentially 75 per cent
of these debts might either make no return at all or would certainly be unable to
repay in full (Rabinowitch 2011). From relatively little debt at the start of 2008,
local governments finished 2010 owing Rmb 10.7 tn (US$1.7 tn) after the national
fiscal stimulus encouraged after the 2008 collapse in the West prompted fears of
downturns in international trade and foreign exchange account surpluses. The
national auditor in China has reported that more than a third of that debt will have

matured by the end of 2012 (Rabinowitch 2012). In early 2012, Fitch had claimed that this unknown scale of local government debt might push the non-performing loan rate of banks in China as high as 30 per cent. As we have seen in Shanghai, much of this debt is held (and sometimes hidden) in LGIV that combine private real estate and local government spin off companies. Financial institutions inside and outside China's central government estimate that such debts probably equate to as much as 25 per cent of China GDP and will in time demand transfers from foreign exchange surplus to cover local government hidden losses (Rabinowitch 2012). Optimistically, in February 2012, central government instructions to banks extended the maturities on local government debt, putting back debt and the aim of fiscal reforms from 2013 to 2016 has been stated openly to translate the hidden sums of local government borrowing from banks into a more clearly regulated arena of local state fundraising linked to marketed bonds with transparent returns.

Land revenues

According to McKinsey (2011: 87) some cities in China may derive over 60 per cent of state revenues from land sales and the average is greater than 30 per cent. Such fiscal models are doubly vulnerable. The finite nature of government land disposals and the potential disruption caused by bubble markets or downturns in property values and real estate markets are considerable. As we have already argued the model of real estate and property rights is at the heart of local state capitalism but the success of the development model longer term depends on the facility to replace diminishing returns from land sales with alternative revenues. The Chong-qing model has demonstrated one attempt to sustain this process through an alternative reconciliation of development obligations and private property rights geared to generate sustainable urbanism, socialised land and a growing, rather than diminishing, public interest in the fruits of economic development. Other combin-ations of fungibility, use rights and exchange rights may inform the local state capitalism models in the future but their success will depend on securing fiscal stability for the engines of local government at its heart.

Ageing

Based on current rates of fertility by the year 2050, a third of Chinese people, 450 million, will be aged over 60. In major cities such as Shanghai this process of demo-graphic ageing is further advanced. The process of demographic transition common to economic development trends globally – where fertility shows lagged decline after falls in death rates – has been accelerated by the one child policy. The process of demographic transition that had taken 50–60 years in France had taken place in 20 years in China. The consequences for welfare safety nets have yet to be fully realised. The BBC in May 2012 claimed that: 'Ten million qualified carers are needed, according to a government committee. So far there are only 100,000 in all of China' (BBC 2012). The absence of a national welfare state limits the fiscal implications of this ageing process but the social and cultural pressures will clearly be considerable.

Where the city begins and ends?

In his landmark essay 'The Politics of Imagining Asia' the social theorist Wang Hui makes a lucid case for being suspicious of using the categories of the European social imagination and the taxonomies of Western political theory for making sense of what is happening in contemporary China. He argues that the continental notion of 'Asia' is in part the antithesis of 'Europe', an invention of enlightenment consciousness, defined in part as being 'not Europe', part of the outside of the European continent. Further, using arguments whose choreography draws from the insights of much post-colonial theory, he suggests that the Enlightenment imaginary naturalises other fundamental units of analysis in a European form, specifically the nation state, capitalism and empire, and in contrast 'the core of the European production of the idea of Asia was made up of the following features: multinational empires as opposed to modern European or monarchical states, political despotism as opposed to modern European political and legal systems and nomadic and agrarian modes of production completely at odds with European urban and commercial life' (Wang Hui 2011: 15). In the Western narrative modernity, the state and the urban regimes of governance are seamlessly linked. The emergence of the state prefigures the agency of the nation and demands an urban realisation (Wang Hui 2011: 16). Wang Hui argues for a new conceptual cartography that sheds this European imaginary and is cautious about alternative continental constructions of 'Asia' in coming to terms with the descriptive complexity of today's China that he prefers to theorise as a civilisation state rather than a nation state.

Wang Hui's thinking is useful in opening up a different frame of reference for the political economy of China's modernisation. It contextualises the paradoxical couplings of the fragility of rule and the power of the Party, economic power and sustained poverty, nationalistic confidence and the uncertainties of ecological sustainability and an ageing population that populate the China area studies literature. It refigures the conceptual and relational geometry of nation, state, city and local state capitalism.

Epistemologically, there is an uncertainty about the scale of development potential generated by future urbanisation (Chan 1999, 2009). Because many of the definitions of what is a city in China follow legal rather than built fabric definitions of the urban some specialists in 2011 and 2012 suggested that more bullish predictions of China's urban growth overestimate the exponential demand for city infrastructure necessary for city growth. However, densities confusingly can be much higher in ostensibly rural non-designated land and the total urban population may become a statistical artefact that overestimates the scale of economic growth still to flow through the more bullish predictions of ongoing urbanisation.

Between moral hazard and innovative urbanism

None of the fiscal weaknesses of local state capitalism are necessarily insuperable or beyond appropriate institutional reform. But they do lend greater uncertainty to the medium term. Paradoxically, this uncertainty implies a sustained iteration in central/local relations, between experiments in the forms of modernisation and growth models adopted at different geographical scales and the institutional forms allowed by central mandate. The tragedy of the commons is configured differently in the cities of China to the privatised cities of the West when property rights secure the formal role of the state in mediating the considerable ecological and social externalities generated by rapid urbanisation. The worry that financial exposure at the local level exemplifies a form of soft budget constraint, a product of the moral hazard generated by the license to experiment and bankroll spectacular urban projects, is only partly countered by the extraordinary pace of economic growth demonstrated by the major metropolises over the last three decades. Such uncertainties demand in turn further forms of (socialist) market stabilisation, optimising transaction costs, the mitigation of risk and the incomplete nature of any single contract; a trend that reinforces the sustained nature of relational property rights and the mediation of developmental risks through the commensuration of alternative regimes of city building expertise, translating incalculable uncertainty into knowable risk.

5

CHINESE FIRMS AND POLITICAL TIES

How much of an executive's working time should be spend cultivating personal relations to a potential business partner? An illustrative case study by Merchant (2008: 60–71) tells the tale of a Chinese executive trying to create good relations with a key manager in a state-owned company, in the process logging several months worth of working hours, spending much money and at least rubbing against several ethical guidelines. Among the activities are researching the manager's background in minuscule detail (looking for a *guanxi* basis as described in Chapter Two), helping the manager's wife with shopping trips and helping his son getting access to a good school to realise his education ambitions. Certainly, developing mutual trust and good social relations with important customers and stakeholders is a major object for most people working in sales or any other form of interface between a firm and its external stakeholders anywhere on the globe. And certainly, these activities often involve drawing on expense accounts and giving gifts. Yet, the case can be made that both the scope and intensity of these practices in the Chinese context, and the fact that often the relation building is with people working in government, put China in a category of its own. In Chapter Two we explored theoretically some of the reasons why *guanxi* ties are of a different kind and degree. In subsequent chapters we explore how enterprises in China are closely tied up with local governments. This chapter takes a break from the on-the-ground quali-tative studies of such enterprises, instead investigating through quantitative analysis whether having political ties brings benefits to Chinese firms. Several such studies exist but none distinguish between ties to central and local government. Precisely because ties to the latter are of particular interest in the context of this book, we here attempt to distinguish between these different types of government.

Creating and using *guanxi*, cultivating and utilising a diverse range of social connections in business operations, is a culturally integral part of life for managers and entrepreneurs working in China. Many studies have documented the importance of managerial ties to various stakeholders for the business operations of Chinese firms (Luo *et al.* 2012). It is therefore not surprising that also personal ties to governmental actors have been found to be related to firm performance (Li *et al.* 2007; Peng and Luo 2000), as such relations are held to mitigate uncertainties and provide access to information. Nevertheless, while studies of business ties (social ties to other business people) generally show that these have a positive effect on earning or other measures of performance, the studies of political ties provide more mixed results. A recent meta-study concluded that while the effect of business ties seems to be more or less constant, the effect of political ties seems to have waned over the last 20 years (Luo *et al.* 2012). The explanation given by Luo *et al.* is as expected, namely that with market institutions being developed, economic transactions become market-based as opposed to coordinated through political networks. When that happens, political ties become less of an asset.

We have in previous chapters emphasised local governments and local state officials as important actors in economic life in China. This emphasis on local government is a poignant reminder that one perhaps should be cautious about lumping all types of political ties together in one category. While most of the studies of political ties have illuminated important elements of business life in China, most of them have also generally depicted a rather crude image of 'government' as a unitary and homogeneous entity. Relations to government are most often measured with little specification of the governmental level and authority in question. In this light, it may not be too surprising that empirical analyses of ties to government and their effect on firm performance have yielded mixed results. Peng and Luo (2000) find that political ties have a positive effect on company performance. Park and Luo (2001) find that political ties are valuable to private companies while ties to the business community are valuable for SOE (as described elsewhere in this book, clear-cut distinctions between private and state-owned enterprises may be questioned). Wong (2010) finds positive performance effects of political connections for firm performance in Hong Kong. Conversely, Fan *et al.* (2007) found that recently partially privatised firms with political connections underperform based on post initial public offering (IPO) stock returns. More generally, it is of course since the utilisation of ties 'hinges on fit with strategy, institutional structures and organisational attributes' (Park and Luo 2001: 456). Liability of foreignness (Xu and Shenkar 2002) seems also to be a factor as foreign companies seem unable to benefit from having successfully established ties, compared with Chinese firms (Hongbin Li *et al.* 2008; Li *et al.* 2007). Li *et al.* (2009) also find that too strong political ties may be counterproductive as this often is at the expense of ties to the business community and/or may hinder strategic agility (this, however, in the study only applies to foreign companies). There are to our knowledge no studies of the possible difference of value between local and central government ties. Lu and Ma (2008), however, study the Joint Ventures (JV) of Japanese and Chinese companies or business groups and the political connections of these JVs to local and central government. They find indicative evidence that ties both to local and central government are beneficial for such groups. In addition, Guthrie (2005) distinguishes between different tiers of (only) local government and finds positive performance effects of companies being controlled by lower-tier local government agencies. Due to the differential role played by central and local government authorities in China, the nature of the benefits obtained by connections may be different. The inability to distinguish between ties from management to government at different levels may be an explanation why studies find mixed evidence of the effects of political connections.

Unlike what happened in the former Eastern Bloc countries, market reforms in China have been gradual (Guthrie 1997: 1295) with the government slowly and very deliberately liberalising the economy in multiple stages and without losing its own control. It has been argued that for this reason social ties have had a more productive role in China than for example in Russia, as ties in China have created trust and hence new possibilities for enterprise rather than having deteriorated into instability and corruption (Hsu 2005). Such a description is of course a gross simplification, but it seems certain that government has in the whole process played an active coordinating role that has compensated for weak market institutions, such as property laws, and which has meant that there has been no sudden transform-ation from a state- to a market-driven regime. And equally certain is the fact that government control over markets remains strong. As noted by Krug and Hendriscke (2008: 100), private corporations constitute approximately 70% of all Chinese businesses, but government (at different levels) nevertheless hold stakes in and maintain a huge degree of control over these businesses. Most of the fast-growing market economy in China is in fact a hybrid between government (at different levels) and market with ambiguous forms of ownership and control (Allen *et al.* 2005: 4). The result is the formation of networks comprising private entre-preneurs and government officials who jointly, and without legally defined distinctions of their respective roles, 'exploit assets' (Krug and Hendriscke 2008: 98). Boundaries are blurred, both in analytic terms where classical theoretical distinctions such as Williamson's between networks and hierarchies become fuzzy (White 2000: 327), but also, more importantly, in the sense that boundaries between private businesses and government mesh. Meyer and Lu (2004) provide an illustrative case of this, even if some of their findings border on the self-evident as their case is a SOE. Among their findings are that a CEO may also at the same time hold a high-ranking position in government, and that companies are part of complex networks which include government agencies. We saw in Chapter Two how both local and central government have created SASAC and other investment vehicles in order to maintain control over nominally private companies. Another tool for doing much the same has been business groups. Not coincidentally, Meyer and Lu's case just mentioned is concerned with a business group. We return in the conclusion of this chapter to some of their findings.

The fact that government still is active is, however, just one factor. Indeed, what government *is* is just as important a question as what government *does*. Govern-ment collaboration with businesses often happens on a local level (Liu 2008; Redding and Witt 2007: 88). Again referring to the 'new' ways for government to control firms, it is noteworthy that state-owned asset management companies similar to SASAC have been much used by local government to maintain controlling stakes in firms (Wang *et al.* 2012: 2). These new institutionalised forms of local government control are a continuation of a long and well-documented trend where local governments are actively involved in the economy. The work of Walder (1995) and Oi (1995) on local corporatism at an early stage documented how TVEs in rural areas formed alliances with local governments in order to further competitiveness and reduce uncertainty (see also Naughton, 2008: 59). Christerson and Lever-Tracy (1997) documented extensive links between local governments and local enterprises in regard to FDI. These findings were repeated a decade later by Du *et al.* (2008) and Krug and Hendriscke (2008) who show how regions and cities compete to attract FDI and how business regimes in various regions create FDI clustering (see also Eng 1999; Sun and Wen 2007; Wang and Meng 2004). Perhaps more crucially, research also shows that the linkages between business and government exist across different types of businesses, that is, among TVEs, SOEs and private businesses (although company size might be a differentiating factor (see Zhou *et al.* 2003).

As seen earlier, there exists a range of different theoretical denominators for this economic structure in which local states have pivotal roles, for example, local corporatism (Oi 1995; Walder 1995), local development state (Liu 2008) and, of course, the term proposed in this book, namely, local state capitalism. As argued by Walder (1995: 295), there is an important distinction between privatisation and (transfer of) property rights. The process in China has not so much been one of privatisation as one of decentralisation with ownership rights and control being devolved and pushed downwards through the tiers of government. The result has been the aforementioned close relations between private entrepreneurs and local, municipal and district governments. China's competitiveness is explained by the fact that low-level government units are granted control with companies. Because of the small scale and resulting limited number of companies over which they have control, these government agencies are unable to allocate capital from the well-performing companies to underperforming (Perry and Wong 1985; Walder 1995; Wong 1991). As a result, the controlled companies face strong budget constraints and hence are moved to increase efficiency and competitiveness. This drive towards local governance of economic enterprises has been accelerated by tax reforms at the turn of the century (Naughton, 2008: 124). The reforms have also resulted in highly heterogeneous provincial governments with different institutional set-ups and mutual competition (Han and Pannell 1999; White 2000). Different regions have chosen various strategies for attracting FDI, different clusters of industry they wish to attract, and the various regions have tried to establish what effectively amounts to trade barriers for companies.

Earlier in this chapter we mentioned that local government officials and private entrepreneurs in close collaboration exploit assets (Krug and Hendriscke 2008). Earlier in the book, we have devoted considerable space to examples of such mutual exploitation, all involving land and property. Indeed, land and property are arguably assets of such importance that they more than anything else have propelled local governments to the fore of economic development (Hsing 2010). The interesting thing about the mutual exploitation of assets thesis is in fact that it transcends a central tenet of social capital theory, namely that political ties are needed to gain either protection for business operations or to obtain information (Adler and Kwon 2002). In both cases this, as we shall describe in detail below, leads to the assumption that the higher ranking or more centrally placed political actors to which Ego has ties, the more the social capital. But in the case of local states, we may be dealing not merely with ties, which provide protections and/or information, *but much more fundamentally with ties that are channels of access or gateways to economic collaboration with government.* Without such access, without mutual coordination or conjunction with political power holders, there may simply not be any economic activity, no access to assets to use or develop. Social capital theory, we argue, only to a very limited degree can capture this aspect of ties as such fundamental channels. By contrast, resource dependence theory (Hillman *et al.* 2009), puts much less emphasis on the exchange of protection and especially information through political ties, yet it maintains that such connections are vital for the survival of a firm. This means that such ties may be needed to obtain protection, but generally they are needed for securing a broad range of resources. In other words, the spectrum of resources is broadened. And more importantly, in contrast to social capital theory, the definition of resource is not a function of hierarchical position in social structure. Instead the resourcefulness of political connections becomes a function of the control over resources. As we have seen abundant evidence of in earlier chapters, local officials hold at least one such crucial resource, namely land.

While there seem to be compelling arguments for assuming that network capitalism in China with the economic reforms has increasingly become capitalism with networks intertwining local government and companies in the fashion described by Walder, Wank, Nee and many others, it remains a fact that China is a hierarchical-centric society with a central government having a marked influence over the economy. This would make ties to central government beneficial. Even a proponent of local corporatism such as Walder (1995) has argued that companies with strong ties to central government, at least in early phases of the market reforms, benefited from central government protection and SBC, a finding which is sustained by Guthrie (1997: 1278). Further, having strong ties to central government can also mean (earlier) access to information on central government policies (Arnoldi and Zhang 2012) as well as protection in cases where contractual disagreement or uncertainty arises. While access to information about general central government policies may be beneficial for a company CEO running the company on a day-to-day basis, it is arguably even more crucial when it comes to making larger strategic decisions. Finally, in spite of the pivotal role of local government in the market developments, it remains a fact that the Chinese system of patronage among the political nomenclature is hierarchical-centric. Allocation of various lucrative posts in the provinces has traditionally been a way for the central power holders to control the vast country by means of creating bonds of loyalty to protégés assigned to these posts. The growth of private business has in a sense reinvigorated this as it has created new possibilities for highly placed political officials to reward protégés, now not with political posts but jobs in business (Naughton 2008). It may indeed be that the weak dissemination of information (Boisot and Child 1996) is not occurring in geographically local networks but in small socially closed networks comprising the elite. Membership of, or access to, such elite groups obviously constitutes social capital, which is a resource at least partially as a function of the hierarchical standing of the dyadic other to whom ego has ties. Social capital may therefore well distinguish between different hierarchical layers, but these are precisely hierarchical either along a top-bottom continuum or a centre-periphery ditto. Hence, ties to central government would by default be more valuable than those to local government. One may, based on this, propose that while connections to local government may well be a prerequisite for operating business in China, the ability to do so successfully on a large scale and over a sustained period will be enhanced by connections to central government. As just stated, this does not rule out the possibility that local government connections are a necessity or prerequisite, but necessities may not represent competitive advantages.

The effect of ties

Theoretical analysis hence finds arguments for why both central and local government ties should be of particular value. We have tested these assumptions through quantitative analyses of listed firms on the stock exchanges in Shanghai and Shenzhen in 2009 using different data sources. We obtained a random sample of 50 per cent of the firms listed at the two exchanges. Researchers take various approaches to how they conceptualise and measure social ties. In the literature on Chinese markets, two approaches to generating data on, and measures of, connections can be found. One is based on survey data and another is based on biographies. Most quantitative studies use a questionnaire methodology where key people in firms are asked to assess the importance of their social ties or the amount of *guanxi* they exercise (Li *et al.* 2008; Luo 2005; Park and Luo 2001; Peng and Luo 2000; Luo 2003; Li and Zhang 2007). The advantage of this approach is that it provides a direct image of how main individuals perceive of their own use of social relations. However, the approach also suffers from shortcomings (Guthrie 2002) as subjective measures of relations may, for instance, be affected by respondents' attitudes towards the practice. Also, studies utilising this approach use general questions on network activity, which typically makes it impossible to distinguish between categories of actors to which ties are formed, for instance, different levels of government. These challenges make it important to consider complementary and more direct measures of social relations in studies of this part of China's business life. In recent studies, ties to government have been measured by party membership (Li *et al.* 2008), committee membership (Wong 2010) and professional background (Fan *et al.* 2007). Besides the advantage of not relying on subjective data, this conceptualisation has the benefit of identifying concrete and specific relations between specific governmental bodies and firms. However, because party membership is often expected of firms' top management members, it is not clear what is actually measured by this variable, as memberships may be instrumental for some while more ceremonial for others.

We have collected data on the professional backgrounds of CEOs, board members and chairperson of Chinese firms to identify their ties to government at different levels (results for board members are not significant and not discussed in the following). Even though relatively little is known about the differential effect on firm performance in transition economies of having key individuals with backgrounds in either central or local government, the importance of director experience has been widely documented in other settings (Boeker 1997; Westphal and Fredrickson 2001). Research has shown how the specific backgrounds of executives have a profound effect and are important in shaping action in subsequent work places (Kraatz and Moore 2002).

We have used two measures of performance in our analyses: return on assets (ROA) and return on equity (ROE). ROA is used as a measure of firm performance in most existing studies of social relations and *guanxi* in Chinese firms. Because firm ROA is sensitive to the fact that we use data on firms from multiple industries, we include industry controls in the statistical analysis. To further explore the robustness of the analysis, we have also conducted analyses using ROE as dependent variable (not reported in this chapter, though mentioned later).

For both dependent variables, we obtained data for 2010 to better reflect causality for our main independent variables measured in 2009. We extracted data from the annual reports of listed Chinese firms in 2009. Based on this information we coded whether CEOs and board chairperson had previously been employed in central or local government. Past work experience in the military, universities and 'other' constituted the remaining three categories. In the few cases where people were stepping down from CEO or board positions and replaced during the year of our observation, the backgrounds of both the persons were coded for. To better reflect causality, the independent variables are lagged by one year.

To isolate the effect of the independent variables, we included a number of controls. Business groups constitute an important element of the Chinese market structure. Therefore, we registered from the annual reports whether a firm was member of a business group or not. Of course, the value of ties may vary considerably between firms, which are controlled by government, and firms that are not. To account for this factor, we created dummy variables for whether the ultimate controller (directly or indirectly) of a firm was either central or provincial government. Firm size is also an important control variable, which is likely to be associated with firm performance as well as the backgrounds of executives and board members. We have included a measure of turnover in the analysis (log transformed due to a skewed distribution). We have also controlled for place or listing by a dummy variable indicating whether a firm is listed on the Shanghai stock exchange, and board size. We have included dummies for six industry types: manufacturing, IT, retail, real estate, financials and conglomerates, which together cover more than 80 per cent of our firms. Finally, regional variations may be important to consider. Due to severe multicollinearity, we are not able to include dummy variables for all regions. We have included the six regions where most firms in our sample are located. Each of these regions is home to more than five per cent of the firms: Beijing, Guangdong, Jiangsu, Shandong, Shanghai and Zhejiang. In separate analyses we tried to include different regions and found that the results reported below are not sensitive to regional variations. Even though we have included a control variable for business group membership, we do not have information on the specific connections between firms. To address this concern, we estimate the models using robust standard errors.

The results of the regression analysis are reported in Table 5.1. The possibility of central government ties having a performance effect is tested in model 2 where the effect of central government background for top management is investigated. Interestingly, only connections formed by the chairperson of the board appear to be related to performance. The coefficient for board chairperson is positive and significant indicating that chairperson ties to central government is beneficial. Contrary to this, central government background for CEOs does not seem to bring benefits.

Model 3 investigates the effect of background in local governments on performance. Contrary to the results for central government connections, a local government connection at chairperson level is not related to performance. However, there is a positive and significant relation at CEO level, which indicates that different types of connections may be important for different parts of top management. Taken together, the results support theoretical arguments both for a particular value of central as well as local government ties. However, while ties to both levels of government appear to be important, they are important for different parts of the firm top management.

We have carried out similar regressions with ROE as the dependent variable. These results generally support the conclusions of the analyses of ROA. Only modest support is found for the relation between central government connections and firm performance. Again, it appears that connections at chair level are beneficial, but the coefficient only reaches levels of marginal significance ($p<0.072$). The results corroborate the findings in Table 5.1 that having a CEO with a local government background is beneficial for performance. On the other hand, this analysis suggests that it is associated with lower ROE to have a *chair* with such a background. All in all, the results of the six models reveal a complex and multi-faceted relationship between political connections and firm performance. However, they do seem to suggest a specific pattern such that central government ties are valuable at chair level while local government ties are valuable at CEO level. This finding holds several implications for research and practice which we will discuss below.

TABLE 5.1 Regression predicting return on assets in listed Chinese firms

	Model 1	Model 2	Model 3
nyroa2009	0.19** (0.08)	0.19** (0.08)	0.19** (0.08)
Business group	-0.16 (0.53)	-0.14 (0.54)	-0.18 (0.53)
Shanghai	-0.82 (0.60)	-0.77 (0.60)	-0.71 (0.64)
lnturn	0.74** (0.29)	0.70** (0.29)	0.75*** (0.29)
Number of board members	-0.13 (0.12)	-0.15 (0.12)	-0.13 (0.12)
Central SOE	-0.68 (0.59)	-0.70 (0.59)	-0.60 (0.60)
Province SOE	0.69 (0.72)	0.84 (0.73)	0.69 (0.68)
Manufacturing	-0.32 (0.52)	-0.30 (0.53)	-0.09 (0.64)
IT	0.41 (1.00)	0.45 (1.02)	0.71 (1.09)
Retail	-1.44** (0.64)	-1.53** (0.63)	-1.36** (0.67)
Real estate	-2.90*** (0.74)	-2.89*** (0.75)	-2.85*** (0.75)
Financials	-3.72*** (1.10)	-4.11*** (1.15)	-3.86*** (1.11)
Conglomerates	-1.52 (1.14)	-1.49 (1.14)	-1.23 (1.14)
Beijing	0.36 (0.64)	0.35 (0.65)	0.36 (0.64)
Guangdong	1.77** (0.85)	1.82** (0.85)	1.79** (0.85)
Jiangsu	0.10 (0.82)	0.20 (0.83)	0.09 (0.82)
Shandong	-0.11 (0.99)	-0.12 (0.99)	-0.05 (0.99)
Shanghai	1.10 (0.81)	1.02 (0.80)	1.03 (0.79)
Zhejiang	1.19* (0.70)	1.22* (0.70)	1.17* (0.69)
Chair central		2.05*** (0.86)	
CEO central		-0.05 (1.30)	
Board member central		-1.33 (2.53)	
Chair local			0.11 (0.65)
CEO local			1.64** (0.79)
Board member local			-0.93 (2.39)
_cons	-9.34* (5.44)	-8.61 (5.44)	-9.92* (5.42)
r2	0.1160	0.1201	0.1203
Number	865	864	864

*** $p<0.01$; ** $p<0.05$; one-sided test for hypotheses, two-sided test for controls. Robust standard errors in parentheses.

Conclusion

The results presented above indicate how connections to government are import-ant for listed Chinese firms and bring a performance gain. They furthermore show that ties to central as well as local authorities are important. It appears that ties to different levels of government are not redundant but related to different aspects of business operations. The results suggest an asymmetric relationship where a background in central government is more important for the chair of the board, while for CEOs it is a background in local government, which is related to higher performance.

Based on common divisions of responsibility between chair of the board and CEO, a viable explanation for this is that connections to central government may be particularly valuable in the boardroom where decisions of more strategic nature with long-term consequences are taken. Such connections may be instrumental because they can mitigate uncertainties associated with general changes in the policy environment or regulatory changes which may affect the strategic decisions of the firm. However, to mitigate uncertainties and dependencies related to the day-to-day operations of firms, they also need relations to local authorities. It appears to be valuable to have a CEO who is knowledgeable about the local environments and who may have the connections and access to local authorities who can secure vital resources. Extrapolating on the results, we argue that the finding that both central and local ties can bring benefits is partial support for both social capital and resource dependency theory. Central tenets of social capital theory would suggest that high-ranking chairs benefit from having ties to the highest-ranking political actors in order to obtain information and at times protection. Resource dependency theory would suggest that close relations and cooperation (which suggests this has to be on a day-to-day operational level) are needed, not necessarily with those at the highest political level but with those that have operational control over vital resources. The proposition that private entrepreneurs in close cooperation with local government officials exploit assets (see Chapter Two) fits well with this line of thinking. This leads to the conclusion that for the operational or executive management of firms (as opposed to strategic), it is contact to local government officials, which are gatekeepers of vital resources, that is beneficial for companies.

There is an interesting difference between social capital and resource dependency theory that concerns institutions. The importance of social capital, especially when applied to the Chinese markets, is by and large seen as negatively correlated with the degree of institutional development, so that social capital increases its currency the weaker the institutions and vice versa. Resource dependence theory only to a much lesser extent assumes such a direct connection between the value of ties and institutional development. As mentioned above, a recent meta-study of political ties finds that the performance benefits of political ties indeed are waning as institutions develop. Corresponding with this, analysis of our data shows that the effect of ties is higher in less-developed regions, suggesting that the importance of ties decreases as market institutions develop (Arnoldi and Villadsen, forthcoming). However, for firms under local government control (a very sizeable group) this effect is absent and the beneficial effect is constant regardless of degree of market or institutional development. The same effect is visible when it comes to the benefits of CEOs with local political background: the higher the development the lesser the value. However, for firms under local government control this effect is absent and the beneficial effect is constant regardless of degree of market or institutional development. Similar results are reported in the earlier mentioned meta-study of *guanxi* ties by Luo *et al.* (2012). This strongly indicates that the influence of local government is constant regardless of economic development. We throughout this book have devoted much consideration to local government's control over land. Earlier in this chapter, we drew on the case study by Meyer and Lu (2004). In that study, one of the ways which the company both used and further cemented its relations with local government was by entering into land-use-for-dividend-swaps, that is, promising fixed return on investment on the condition they were guaranteed use of land. In that case, the local government was a minority shareholder. The findings which we report and reference here suggest that in cases where local governments are the majority or controlling shareholder, close ties to local government become all the more important.

6

PROPERTY DEVELOPMENT

Markets and districts

In the early morning of 27 June 2009, building 7 of the property complex Lotus Riverside in the Minhang district of Shanghai tipped over, crushing a migrant construction worker who was working and living there, killing him. The complex was a product of the Shanghai Meidu Real Estate company, which was founded as a collective enterprise of nearby town of Meilong, the urban administration with ownership rights to the land upon which Lotus Riverside was built (Li Meng 2009). In 2003, Meidu had won a 'bid' for the Lotus Riverside project obtaining land at a price estimated to be only one-third of the price (RMB 604 per square metre versus RMB 1,929 per square metre) of similar land parcels adjoining the area (Liu 2009). In the denouement of this building collapse, it was revealed that the second-largest shareholder in Meidu was also the assistant to the head of the town, a position that was promptly recognised as illegal and rescinded. Members of Meidu and the contracting construction company were arrested, while Vanke took over continued construction of Lotus Riverside and compensation negotiations with toppled apartments' owners were initiated.

On 15 November 2010, at a downtown apartment complex only 10 minutes by foot from the Jing'an Temple in Shanghai, at the intersection of Jiaozhou Road and Yuyao Road, a fire broke out in a 28-storey residential building that was undergoing renovation. The cause was later identified as welders accidentally igniting the foam insulation, and ultimately 58 people died in the flames. The State Council, on 20 June 2011, through its Production Safety Committee Office, issued a circular (Safety Committee Office [2011] No. 22) reporting on the incident. The renovation project originated with the Jing'an district government's Construction and Transportation Commission (JACTC), with Jing'an District Construction General Company as the general contractor, Jing'an Investment Design Company Limited as the designer/architect and the Jing'an Construction Engineering Supervision Company Limited as the supervising unit. Jing'an Construction General, a subsidiary company of JACTC, after being contracted to undertake the renovation job, re-assigned it to its subsidiary (a JACTC sub-subsidiary) Shanghai Jiayi Construction Decoration Engineering Company, who then divided the job into seven parts (heating, windows, scaffolding, window removal, outer wall repair, hall painting and piping organisation) each of which was again contracted out. The indirect cause of the fire, according to the State Council report, was first (among a total of six reasons) that the construction company, bidding enterprise and government agency that invited bidding on the project all colluded with each other, invited a fake bid and fake contracting and illegally re-assigned the bid. In the aftermath, the supervisory bureau of the local Jing'an district government (JACTC) was cut off from its subsidiary (Jing'an Construction General) and sub-subsidiary (Jiayi), both of which were taken over directly by Jing'an District SASAC. It was reported at the time that JACTC had wanted to develop a property adjacent to the Jiaozhou Road address, and had used renovation of the building as a carrot to convince residents.

These two incidents point to a particular path-dependent relationship between government and business in China that continues to this day. Though tragic accidents taking the lives of under-privileged migrant workers and underpaid and 'off work post' (*xiagang*) teachers, they are also brief moments when two failures pulled back the curtain in front of China's particular mode of engaging, transforming and constructing capitalism. They look into the dark side of local state capitalism. In this chapter, we use the two incidents as a painful introduction to a discussion of local state capitalism in the process of real estate development in Shanghai. The discussion below is based on fieldwork from 2007 to 2011 in Shanghai. The following section gives an introduction to the research on real estate development in the districts of Shanghai. It is followed by contextualisation of local state capitalism in terms of development of land, housing and *xiaoqu* in urban China. The subsequent three sections give details of real estate development in Yangpu, Jing'an and Minhang districts. This is followed by a concluding discussion.

Research context

One researcher (Rooker) lived in Shanghai from mid-2007 until late 2011, as a full-time research associate[1] for three years researching the securities (see Chapter Seven) and real estate markets, and subsequently as a full-time employee in a real estate development-related interior decoration supplier. During the three-year period, the researcher conducted participant observation as a general assistant to the CEO lasting between three and six months in three real estate development companies, first in Jing'an district, then in Yangpu district and finally in Minhang district. The characteristics of the districts and companies are given below. In addition, the researcher had multiple discussions with other developers, mortgage and property development bankers, residential property brokers, architects, interior designers and suppliers, as well as attending an eight-week brokerage training class in summer 2008. The researcher also lived in two relatively high-end *xiaoqu*[2] in the

Xujiahui area of Xuhui district and in the Lianyang area of Pudong New Area. The data for this chapter comes from this vast, multi-sited research project.

In general terms, the districts of Jing'an, Yangpu and Minhang are located in three areas of the city – the centre, a secondary centre and outside Shanghai's Outer Ring Road. The structure of economic value-added, equivalent to GDP at the national level, is given in Table 6.1. From the table it is clear that economic structure of three districts is quite varied: Jing'an is highly advanced in service industry, while both Yangpu and Minhang maintain a higher than average amount of industrial manufacturing and low level of services. In addition, while in 2010 the population of Shanghai is some 20 million, Jing'an has a shrinking population of a mere 250,000 residents including those without a *hukou* located there, while Yangpu has some 1.2 million and Minhang 1.8 million.

TABLE 6.1 Average GDP over selected years – Shanghai, Jing'an, Yangpu, Minhang

Average GDP over selected years (2007–2009)

District	Added Value (GDP)							GDP per permanent resident (yuan/person)
	Total (billion yuan)	Primary Billion yuan	Primary % of total	Secondary Billion yuan	Secondary % of total	Tertiary Billion yuan	Tertiary % of total	
Shanghai	1,376.84	10.92	0.79	592.20	43.01	773.72	56.20	72,876
Jing'an	13.37	0.00	0.00	1.55	11.62	11.82	88.43	52,975
Yangpu	67.81	0.55	0.80	37.99	56.03	29.27	43.16	56,819
Minhang	111.03	0.18	0.16	75.35	67.86	35.50	31.98	61,001

Source: Shanghai Statistical Bureau (SSB) (2008, 2009, 2010); Minhang Statistical Bulletins (2007, 2008, 2009); Jing'an Statistical Bulletins (2007, 2008, 2009); Yangpu Statistical Bulletins (2007, 2008, 2009) and authors' calculations.

The forms of local state capitalism in real estate vary across different districts in Shanghai. Table 6.2 shows the different percentages of ownership types for housing in Shanghai over recent years. The statistical survey reveals that, for the first time in 2009, commercial housing – that is, housing bought on the market from real estate developers – accounted for the largest percentage of ownership type. Yet in terms of urban change, the path dependence of the socialist era plays an important role for the context of local state capitalism. And Table 6.2 demonstrates the local variation that is core to our argument about local state capitalism in the real estate sector – districts. For example, in terms of housing, districts across Shanghai vary in terms of their built-up levels before the founding of new China in 1949. Due to its central city location, Jing'an had a massive build-up of private housing prior to 1949. As a result, while some *danwei* chose to locate there, the majority of housing was run by the local government real estate department (*fangguan bumen*) which, in 1992, administered 90 per cent (over 3.8 million square metres) of the district's constructed residential area (*Jing'an Gazette* 1996). By contrast, in Yangpu district, the local government real estate department only administered 60 per cent (7.5 million square metres) of housing in 1990 (*Yangpu Gazette* 1995). Finally, Minhang, reflecting its history as both Minhang town, part of Jiangsu Province, and Shanghai County, is more complex. However, using data from *Shanghai County Gazette* (abolished and merged into a new Minhang District in 1992), Minhang in 1992 had only 22 per cent (920,000 square metres) of residential housing under the administration of the county real estate department, with the majority (74 per cent or 3.1 million square metres) belonging to *danwei* (Shanghai County Yearbook 1993).

TABLE 6.2 Shanghai urban property rights structure (per 100 houses)

Type	2004	2005	2006	2007	2008	2009
Housing Property Rights, per 100 Urban Households	**100**	**100**	**100**	**100**	**100**	**100**
Leasehold public housing	25.9	25.5	23.8	20.4	17.4	16.3
Leasehold private housing	0.7	1.1	1.3	1.6	4.2	3.7
Original private tenement	2.2	2.4	1.3	0.9	0.7	0.7
Reformed private housing	42.9	40.4	40.4	37.3	37.8	37.2
Commercial housing	27.8	30.5	32.4	39.4	39.1	41.3
Others	0.5	0.1	0.8	0.4	0.8	0.8

Source: Shanghai Statistical Yearbook (2007, 2010).

This chapter explores local state capitalism in these three districts through companies operating in them that were accessed by the research. Of the three development companies where participant observation was conducted, one is foreign-owned by a Taiwan insurance company, one is privately owned with a Hong Kong registration and a military background and one is quasi-private in the sense that it is a re-structured spin-off of a district-level government development company. While there has been some research carried out on property development companies in China previously (Li Linyan 2008; Tang and Liu 2005), the attention they draw from academics, policy-makers, media and ordinary individuals inside and outside China exaggerates the 'greed' and 'predatory nature' they are purported to have in the *xiaoqu* literature (Zhang 2010: 159, 199, 215, 209). Instead, conducting research across the crucial district level in Shanghai reveals the variations of local state capitalism, an engine of urban change as well as a site of the sorts of improprieties with which this chapter opened. Combining participation with interviews, discussions and long-term involvement with real estate, the research is unprecedented in terms of access to everyday work and background stories that underlie the eventual *xiaoqu* residences that are produced by property development.

In the following ethnographic research, what is shared across the three examples is an orientation to the local state, particularly at the scale of the district (*qu*) government. The relationship, often viewed as illicit *guanxi* responsible for corruption and inefficiency, is one facet of state involvement in the development of the district. Since their promotion through government ranks is dependent on various factors, including district GDP, pollution, big projects and maintenance of stability, *district* government and its officers are involved in assisting developers to generate sustainable profits. The district government is the specifically urban, intermediary level of government between the municipality – the lowest level policy-making body, often staffed by higher-up levels of party such as the province or central state and the street office (*jiedao*) and residential committee (*juweihui*) that implements policy.[3] A quick look at the district government functions and branches at the district level reveals an astonishing diversity of services and administration concentrated at this level. In the three districts examined here, Jing'an has some 63 bureaus, offices and committees, while Minhang has 38 and Yangpu 27. From the perspective of real estate, the relevant bodies include district level branches of the Development and Reform Committee, the Planning and Land and Resources Bureau, SASAC, the Housing Guarantee and Administration Bureau, the Greenery Bureau, the Environmental Bureau, the Water Bureau, the Education Bureau and the Construction and Transportation Bureau, among others.

Managing the city: land, housing and *Xiaoqu*

The story of Chen Liangyu's fall from power as the Party Secretary of Shanghai is quite sensational, and a small portion of the resulting fall out is covered in the study of a Jing'an real estate company below. It is relevant to bring up here for the link with the comparably, and more contemporary, sensational story of Bo Xilai. For both these powerful municipal party secretaries, their core strategy of economic development involves the idea of so-called 'managing' or 'operating the city' (*jingying chengshi*). In the case of Cheng Liangyu, promoted, importantly, from a position in the Huangpu District government, the rise of local state power during the opening of the real estate market in the 1990s provided the stage for local government to engage in this type of city 'management'. In Naughton's telling (2007c), Chen Liangyu was more guilty of using free or discounted land as an incentive to attract developers and drive growth regardless of the central government's stance on the policy, than any sordid corruption or embezzlement. In a more general explanation of this land-for-local-development phenomena, Bo Xilai discussed his development work in the city of Dalian during the late 1990s. He noted, 'as a mayor, his first responsibility is to grasp the city's essence. A mayor must understand what his most important assets are…a city at its core is also a state-owned asset [like a state-owned enterprise]' (quoted in *Yangcheng* 2001). In this sense, Chen Liangyu's (and Bo Xilai's) fall from power reflects more a local state system of development that here we refer to as local state capitalism in conflict with the central state than with any particular incidents of arrogance, corruption, murder or espionage.

There are two facets to Bo–Chen's style of governance that are relevant here: the opportunities gained for development projects and the ability to enforce government regulations. Urban policy favours local development and *guanxi* ties to local officials facilitate rapid though strict implementation of policy. Often glossed as traditional, cultural heritage or simply as social networks, *guanxi* has become more important and is quite arduous to build and maintain in cities, districts and developments – involving both access to opportunities and adherence to policies (Wank 1999; Croll 2006). Rather than a synonym for the zero-sum game of money-exchanged-for-favours bribery, *guanxi* relations between business and government are developed to facilitate expansion of business and execution of projects. Delays, trouble or excesses do more to destroy *guanxi* (and vice versa) that any amount of gifts, favours or banquets.

'Managing the city'

'In mainland China, property developers were designated as the city builders... successful property development remains a local business' (Tang and Liu 2002: 26).

As used here, 'managing a city' is an experimental principle of urban administration. It refers to a model of development where there is minimal investment by local government, public resources are used to attract capital and construction of the city and development of city's economy is facilitated. Land is one of the local government's most precious local resources. Early in the reform era a popular saying was 'use land to add roads' (*yitu bulu*), meaning government would entrust an enterprise to engage in municipal engineering and traffic construction, and allocate to the enterprise a plot of land along the road as compensation. In 2002, the implementation of 'tender, auction, list' Ministry of Land and Resources (MoLaR) regulations (see below) ended uncompensated transfer of land to developers. In response, municipal governments established land banking organisations (*tudi chubei jigou*). Land banking organisations are used to purchase and sell land locally, and work in coordination with local district-led investment companies – they are established at the district level. Hence the battles that go on in the city today are no longer between former *danwei* socialist land masters (Hsing 2010) and a newly powerful municipal government, but between central government regulation and control measures and local development. This illustrates the importance of local state capitalism. 'Managing the city' is about building bridges, paving roads, opening exhibition halls. At the start, land was conveyed by agreement to some large property developers, so that their influence would have a knock-on effect, and then the district government would use auctions to gain fiscal income since a lot of other developers joined in to participate in local development. But district land banking and local investment allows the local state to retain a stake in development beyond simply income from land – as the tax receipts and employment of local resources take precedence when local developments continue to grow and expand in the future.

The idea of local state involvement in urban development has been discussed before in the literature. It comes from two sources: one, mostly rural, involving local state corporatism (Oi 1999; Smart 2000; Unger and Chan 1999; Blecher and Shue

2001) and the other identifying local growth coalitions (Zhang 2002; Zhu 1999; Lin and Gao 2007; Fu 2002; He and Wu 2005). For the former, the focus is on local conditions that connect with global, national and regional forces through different mechanisms and on different terms – that is, capitalism is local to the extent that the conditions of its existence and operation depend heavily on local embedding (Smart 2000). Yet there is variation in terms of local development-capitalism, since involvement of local government can be strong (Oi 1999) or quite weak when private enterprise and lack of financial capital predominate (Unger and Chan 1999). For the latter, while relying on a neoclassical or neoliberal ideas of markets, they present a China version of Western urban growth coalitions between urban developers and local governments has led to the formation of 'property-led urban development' (Zhu 1999; He and Wu 2005). Zhang (2002: 477) notes that, 'although the government may still be a leading power at the municipal level, at the urban district level, market forces may have a much stronger influence in formulating a development agenda, and many development activities actually take place at the district level'. This is not a transitional or transforming model of economic development in China; instead, as shown in the three ethnographic studies below, it is the emergence of local state capitalism in the form of relations between businesses and the local state, city-making in real estate development and experimental combinations of state and market in emergent urban institutions.

Housing policy and development

There are several elements to the development of the real estate industry in China today, including both the land and housing systems. First, there is the reform of the land system, by which urban land – state-owned since the 1950s – transforms into a transactionable commodity through separation of use and ownership rights. Second, there is reform of the housing system. It is here that scholars have argued for the 'commodification' (*shangpinhua*) perspective, as the vast majority of public housing has been sold to sitting (or at least *hukou*-registered) residents, and new commodity housing is no longer allocated by the *danwei* welfare system. Finally, there is the emergence of *xiaoqu* as a salient location for the provision of housing and for negotiating urban identity. The following sections examine each of the developments in the land, housing and *xiaoqu* industries over the past 30 years. These policy developments are usually discussed with reference to China as a whole, with some studies focusing on particular cities. This chapter, however, while noting the national policies and their implications, refracts land, housing and *xiaoqu* development through the district scale where there is the most variation, the strongest resistance by local stakeholders, and the most visceral changes wrought by the reform.

Land

The crucial feature of China's urban land system is the fact that it is completely state-owned. In the pre-reform era, this meant that land in the city was allocated according to plan on a project-by-project basis to *danwei*, the social-economic control and welfare institutions of the planned economy. Urban land was stipulated in the *Constitution of the People's Republic of China* as being both state-owned and having 'three non-' (*sanwu*) characteristics; land was 'non-compensated' (*wu-chang*, i.e. free), 'non-time-limited' (*wu-xianqi*, i.e. land use was eternal) and 'non-exchangeable' (*wu-liuzhuan*, i.e. cannot be transferred among different users). According to the interpretation of socialism in China prior to Deng Xiaoping's intervention, land was a means of production and hence could not be alienated from its use in projects or as part of projects. At the dawn of the reform era in 1978, land reform in cities was left untouched while in the countryside, the drastic reform espoused in individual household plot contracting system had begun. But in 1979, Deng turned to the city and, for the first time, particularly in the newly established SEZs, allowed the use of land by Sino-foreign joint ventures, with 'site use rights' (*changdi shiyongquan*) deployed as either the China-side investment or as the basis for the collection of fees – this was codified in the 'Sino-Foreign Joint Venture Law' of the same year (Qu and Wang 2004: 53–54; Xinhua Net n.d.). This initial decision, while often unnoticed as simply a part of the Joint Venture law, was important in loosening the ideological constraints on land as an inseparable part of the means of production.

Throughout the 1980s, land experiments in different cities were developed. The crucial and most well-documented moment came in September and December 1987 when Shenzhen sold and auctioned, respectively, the use rights to state-owned land for the first time. The Bureau of State Land Administration, established in 1986, was the primary arbitrator of this system. Yet, despite the State Council's approval of the Shenzhen deals, and clarification that such experiments would take place in Shenzhen, Shanghai, Tianjin, Guangzhou, Xiamen and Fuzhou, it only changed the *constitution* six months later, deleting the statement therein that stated land transfer was illegal and adding the statement that 'land use rights can be transferred according to law'. Modification of the 'Land Administration Law' followed, specifying that a system of compensated land use would be implemented in China. Separating state ownership of land from its use rights provided both the ideological and administrative basis for the compensated, time-limited and exchangeable transference of land use rights in China. At the same time, the Land Administration Law established 'land administration bureaus' at urban district levels throughout the country in 1987–88.

In 1990 and 1994, bookending Deng Xiaoping's Tour of the South, two important land policy measures were promulgated. In June 1990, the State Council issued 'PRC Temporary Regulations for Urban State-Owned Land Use Rights Conveyance and Transfers', affording urban state-owned land exchanges legal protection, and solidifying the commodity nature of land. It was this document that specified time limits for land use as 70 years for residential, 50 years for industrial (or education, science, culture, sanitation or athletics) and 40 years for commercial uses. By 19 May 1991 the formal compensated conveyance and transfer of state-owned land was implemented nationwide (Li Ling 2006: 16). In addition the 'Temporary Administrative Measures for Foreign Investors to Invest and Develop

Land' allowed foreign investment to take over development of infrastructure in return for access to the development of land, an important policy for, *inter alia*, the Pudong New Area's foreign investment-led development (Yeh and Wu 1996; Fu 2002). In 1994, the 'Urban Real Estate Administration Law' was passed by the Standing Committee of National People's Congress. This period coincided with the end of the first real estate 'fever' when large speculation drove up prices of land transfers. The Law also coincided with the State Council's 'Decision on Deepening the Reform of the Urban Housing Reform', a policy discussed in more detail below, which demanded planning and price standards for land transfers.

In 1998, the amended 'Land Administration Law' was issued, though its primary focus was the conversion of rural land and erosion of farmland, requiring local governments to maintain a constant proportion of cultivated land (Lin and Ho 2006). What was more important for urban land development was the emergence of land banking organisations that are used to corner and monopolise the land market (in 1996–97 the first land banks appeared in Shanghai and Hangzhou [see Tian and Hong 2007]). In 1998, the newly minted MoLaR, encompassing the previous Bureau of State-Owned Land Administration, was tasked with implementing the groundbreaking 1998 State Council 'Notification Concerning the Further Deepening of Urban Housing System Reform and Quickening of Housing Construction' that will be discussed in the following section. In its own domain, MoLaR issued an order in May 2002, (MoLaR Order No. 11) that required all state-owned land that was to be used in business projects to be transacted through tender, auction or listing (*zhaobiao, paimai, guapai*, often abbreviated as *zhao, pai, gua*).[4] These regulations were subsequently underscored by the State Council in its 2004 'Decision Concerning the Deepening Reform and Strict Administration of Land' – cited by some researchers as the strictest land policy ever, intended to enforce *zhao, pai, gua* measures (Xu *et al.* 2009: 892). This was echoed by MoLaR itself who claims in its interpretation of the 2007 amendment of the 2002 order that incorporated the new 'Property Law' – that is, 'Regulations for the Tender, Auction and Listing Conveyance of State-Owned Construction Land Use Rights' (2007, No. 39) – that the 2002 order was 'the second land revolution' (MoLaR 2007).[5] The 'State Six Articles' jointly issued by MoLaR and other ministries has brought a renewed attention to land conveyance practices, though the significance of this policy is discussed in the next section.

Housing

On their state-allocated, 'three non-' land, *danwei* built quasi-autonomous compounds (*dayuan*) usually surrounded walls, having guards and exclusive to members of the *danwei*, modeled on the Yan'an self-sufficient army units of the People's Liberation Army in the 1940s and envisioned as a factor of production (Lü 1997; Lu 1998 [1989]). The reform of the housing system opened up this 'patchwork quilt' of *danwei*-cities, creating housing complexes that were owned by multiple *danwei* and purchased rather than self-built. Several policies contributed to this process, building on the reform of the urban land system. In particular, the emergence of development companies and the commodification of housing are of particular significance. As we shall see below the emergence of a new residential form – the *xiaoqu* – becomes an iconic part of this process.

In the 1980s, the only purchaser of housing in China was *danwei* (Bian *et al.* 1997). Experiments in selected cities tried out full-cost sales to individuals or sitting tenants, but even at one-third of the cost price, with *danwei* and municipal government contributing the other two-thirds, the experiments were largely unsuccessful (Chiu 2001; Wang and Murie 1999; Fung *et al.* 2006). In the latter part of the 1980s, development companies emerged in force. For example, in Shanghai there were eight public enterprises in 1985 that were sourced with the task of completing government housing construction; by the early 1990s this had grown to over 90 new real estate enterprises (Shanghai Brokerage Class, June 2008). Yet throughout this period, and particularly up until the late 1990s, the vast majority of customers of these development companies were *danwei* work units, who would then redistribute housing to workers.

From a policy perspective, a defining moment for urban housing came in 1994 when the State Council issued its 'Decision on Deepening of the Urban Housing System Reform' mentioned above. This document explicitly laid out a framework for urban housing reform, including the goal that high-income families would purchase commodity housing, while home ownership overall was promoted. In addition, the policy sought to expand the housing provident fund system (Gu *et al.* 2006) and construct a real estate transaction market for housing. Yet a dual-track of inner- and outer-sales of housing still existed at this time, with only the latter being sold on the market to individuals, while the former continued through *danwei* purchases and redistribution (Wang and Murie 1999). Despite this, the 'Decision on Deepening' forms the major turning point for many researchers examining China's urban housing reform in the late 1990s (Wang and Murie 2000). While highly subsidised rents for public housing continued, the policy initiated a transformation in housing from a publicly (i.e. *danwei*) owned asset to an individually purchased asset (Davis 2003).

The 1998 State Council 'Notification Concerning the Further Deepening of Urban Housing System Reform and Quickening of Housing Construction' (No. 23) covered multiple matters in terms housing reform. In particular, the central government aimed to have the housing system provide housing based on need: low-income households should live in low-rent housing provided by government; middle-income households should live in economical housing; high-income households should live in commodity housing they purchase or rent.[6] The 1998 'Further Deepening' put an end to the *danwei* system of providing housing allocation in-kind, and implemented monetisation of housing subsidies and commodification of housing allocation. After the 'Further Deepening' document was issued ending the allocation of public housing, real estate gradually became a pillar industry of China's economic development.[7] The year often cited when China's real estate industry was born is 1998 (Li Linyan 2008: 83). However, it was only at the end of 2000 that these provisions were fully implemented nationwide (Li Ling 2006: 16). Incidentally, 1998 is also the year claimed for the birth of true 'economical housing' (*jingji shiyongfang*), meant to be a product for middle-income consumption – although Shanghai did not develop any of this type of housing until the late 2000s (Wang Xiaoming, personal communication, 2009).

The 'State Six Articles' (*Guoliutiao*, 2006), the third in a series of 'Articles' starting with the 'State Eight Articles' (2005) and 'New State Eight Articles' (2005), was issued by a coalition of central government departments, starting with the State Council. Initially – the first two Eight Articles – developers did not pay much mind to these regulations, as they were titled 'Notification' and 'Opinions'. While the content of the regulations expressed deep concern with large rises in housing prices, the nature of housing supply and the operation of the real estate market (Chen and Stephens 2011: 6), they did not specify policy measures to deal with the concerns. By contrast, the 'State Six Articles' – issued by seven departments, including the Ministry of Construction, the National Reform and Development Committee, the Ministry of Land and Resources and financial departments – was ominously titled as a residential housing price 'adjustment' (*tiaozheng*). It demanded specific regulatory oversight, engagement by supervisory bodies and a new policy emphasis (such as the provision of low-rent public and economical housing, as well as the 70/90 rule[8]). Despite the general feeling of unease among property developers at any mention of 'State X Articles' (Feng *et al.* 2009: 28), the 'State Six Articles' in particular caused consternation not only about developers' bottom lines but for local states' development model (Naughton 2007b).

Xiaoqu! Xiaoqu![9]

According to Bray (2006; 2005), *xiaoqu* ('little district') emerged in the late 1980s after trials in Wuxi, Ji'nan and Tianjin (see also Cong 1994), and they bear 'an uncanny resemblance to the *danwei* residential compound' (2005: 176). *Xiaoqu* are enclosed residential housing units of the city, often surrounded by walls, protected by security guards, and have internal government representative offices and property management employees. They are sometimes viewed as a form of 'gated community', though this evaluation typically comes from researchers who view China's housing reform as strongly influenced by neoliberalism (Zhang and Ong 2008; Wu 2005).

There is some disagreement about what constitutes *xiaoqu* with, for example, the reference to old *danwei* housing – now reformed as the majority have been sold to tenants and are saleable on secondary markets – as *xiaoqu* (Fleischer 2010). In this chapter, *xiaoqu* are viewed as a more generic form of housing. In everyday language, *xiaoqu* are not simply 'luxury housing units' or reformed *danwei* housing – they can be either. The presence of walls surrounding the complex, guards checking visitors, a *juweihui* or government administrative office and other features depend on construction and ownership of the *xiaoqu*. For example, in Beijing there is a massive economical housing area named Tiantong Yuan. According to *Sina Real Estate* (Liu 2012), Tiantong Yuan has eight million square metres of constructed area (including all types of building) housing over 420,000 people – larger than many urban districts or even some Western cities. An example at the other end of the *xiaoqu* size spectrum is Hugui Yuan in Shanghai's Xujiahui area, where there are 168 house-holds (apartments) on 1,000 square metres of constructed land area, all squeezed into one building (*Anjuke.com*). Certainly, at the expensive, villa and luxury end of the spectrum, walls, well-dressed and managed guards, security-controlled entrances, special clubhouses and even golf courses are features of *xiaoqu*, but it is not these characteristics that define *xiaoqu*.

What is overlooked in defining China's transition from planned to reformed economy as 'privatisation' and neoliberalism (e.g. Zhang and Ong 2008; Wu 2010; Lee and Zhu 2006) is the contested and unique nature of the modernisation process. Chiu (2001) discusses commodification in particular, and distinguishes it from privatisation, the former being the result of markets organising housing allocation (despite the fact that government-backed development companies are building the commodities, and quasi-government *danwei* are buying on the market), and the latter being in fact quite complex. Aside from the complex, plural and differing interpretations of individual/private property rights, even within families (Davis 2010), the process of privatisation entails specific market institutions to be fully realised. As Chiu (2001) points out, privatisation in China's real estate sector only applies to the purchase of housing by sitting tenants from their *danwei*/municipal management company, and even then re-selling said apartment requires a five-year waiting period. Further, even following on some 15 years from the 1994 State Council 'Decision on Deepening' that began the housing transfer process, some *xiaoqu* continue to be populated by mixed housing tenures – i.e. while the majority of tenants bought their apartments in the late-1990s and 2000s, and the five-year waiting period has expired, the presence of a minority who continue to rent (now from a district housing agency) means that one cannot call these *xiaoqu* private in any meaningful sense. This point is underscored by Chen (2006), who notes that a formerly public *danwei* residential *xiaoqu* is plagued by problems (property management fees in arrears, reluctance to invest in the estate, unauthorised works and unsanitary dogs) that result from mixed ownership predominant in the complex.[10]

The system of property development present in the districts of Shanghai is influenced by the policy development of land, housing and *xiaoqu*. These chronicle some of the urban changes and new forms of economic life that this book explores. Local state capitalism involves different district–local business combinations to develop district housing, amenity and environment. The next three sections explore what might be termed this sense of 'managing the district' (*jingying shiqu*) through three companies.

Yangpu – masters of military land: 'the ethnographic detail of nothing happening'

'This PR [public relations, i.e. accompanying government officials], it is even worse than being a dance hall *xiaojie* [girl, also connotes prostitute]. Why? A *xiaojie* can be with you, but if she is unhappy she can also not be with you. [But] if you are in charge of me, I must take care of you'. Real estate developer, cited in Li Linyan (2008: 119).

In what turned out to be a very long-term 'initial' period, ethnographic research was based at a private Yangpu developer named Yangpu Shechi Company. The company is part of a group of allied companies, including two development companies and interior decoration, property management and real estate research consulting companies. While the companies are legally independent from one another, they are all owned and run by, respectively, the general manager and chairwoman of the board – Mr Bin (called 'Executive Bin') and Mrs Shao (called 'Teacher Shao') – a husband and wife team. The employees of the companies are shared, and in the office there is no formal separation between them, although one area where computer-aided designs were created and debated was signed as a 'design academy'.

Executive Bin and Teacher Shao started in the real estate business after Mr Bin – a former ranking officer in the military – decided to 'leap into the sea of commerce' when a company that was formerly directly run by the air force branch of military was spun off in 1997. That was the year when the military control of land began to subside, as one source even claims that 'land ownership was turned over from the Chinese Liberation Army to Shanghai municipal government in 1997' (Xie 2009: 157). Mr Bin ran the company – first named Binshao Decoration, then Binshao Construction and Engineering, combining the two last names of the couple – as an interior decoration finishing company, moving into general construction in 1998, and then real estate development in the early 2000s. Among the projects his company completed prior to reorganising into a Hong Kong-registered group were air force residential buildings, swimming pools and barracks, airport drainage systems and small residential xiaoqu (sold 'internally', or neixiao, to danwei) in the Yangpu district. It is one of those xiaoqu, completed in 1998 and sold soon afterwards, which was the focus one day after returning from lunch with the senior manager. The manager, who had worked with Mr Bin for over 12 years, pointed to the quality of the xiaoqu as we walked back, and how it showed that Shechi was quite experienced in developing property. 'I live in there, too. That is the mark of a good xiaoqu – if the employees of a developer buy an apartment there, you can be sure it is not bad'. The property's location was quite convenient, abutting both vibrant Wujiaochang shopping plazas and the 25-storey commercial building that Shechi has also developed, and where their offices are now located. Yet, there is some controversy surrounding his former and current company, focused in part on that xiaoqu, and several lawsuits have been decided in recent years, while one was still ongoing during the time of the research (2007, 2008).

As a result of lawsuits and some disparagement to the company, Mr Bin and Mrs Shao decided to shut the company. They then set up a new company registration in Hong Kong, combining the old companies into a 'group' of companies. The Shanghai companies were subsequently advertised in promotional materials as the Shanghai branch of a Hong Kong international group, though the Hong Kong company registration had expired by 2012. Reorganising the companies into a group, and locating the group headquarters in Hong Kong, reduces legal liability of any particular company. It would be very difficult, for example, for a partner or supplier to pursue an individual subsidiary from Shanghai to Hong Kong (where there is no office), then back to Shanghai to demand liquidation of another, legally independent subsidiary.

The focus of development during the research and afterwards – continuing today – is the small, high-end Castle Estate *xiaoqu*, composed of several villas and 75 fully furnished apartments in low-rise buildings. Throughout the several months of full-time ethnographic research and even in the year or so afterwards, no clear progress was made on obtaining final approval to begin construction of the development: the site was vacant and ready for development as early as 2007, but construction only broke ground at the end of 2010. The detail of 'nothing happening' belied the veneer of Shanghai's hyper-speed transformation, but was revealing in its exposure of the everyday world of real estate development.

In the State Six Articles, there is concern with the supply of housing, particularly delays in the start of construction, and suspicion that developers were intentionally withholding property from the market to wait for prices to rise (*wupan*, see Chapter Three). The reality is much more complex. In a rising market, as was the situation in 2007 to 2009, there are rational, neoclassical reasons for withholding property from the market. However, in the case of Shechi the delay was not intentional. In an interview in 2010, another developer – from Singapore – noted that the second phase of his Jing'an *xiaoqu* could not get approval from the district Development and Reform Commission for its prices – set at 80–90,000 yuan per square metre – since the government was trying to control inflation, and thus rather than create a sub-standard product the developer was forced to delay finishing the apartments.

In Shechi's case, what caused such a delay? In one sense, delays are quite normal in real estate. Minhang Real (see below) took seven years before it could start construction on a Qibao town site, a very old settlement in Shanghai. In the latter case, however, it was the persistence of *dingzi hu*, 'nail households',[11] which caused the delay by refusing to relocate from their occupied housing on the building site. On the land slated for Shechi's Castle Estate development, however, the only occupiers were grass and weeds. While the roads leading to and from the land to be developed by Shechi were narrow and perilously half-finished, this was due in part to large walls erected to shield the open plain of land for development. In addition, this piece of land, located in the Jiangwan town region of Yangpu district, close to Wujiaochang, was specifically highlighted in Shanghai's Master Plan (*Municipality of Shanghai Urban Master Plan 1999–2020*) as one of four key sub-centres outside the central city for development, hence developing the area was a district and municipal priority. Perhaps, then, the delay was due to the real estate development process itself.

According to numerous developers, in Shanghai, the time to complete this preliminary stage of approvals for a development project takes between six months and well over a year depending on the turnaround and chopped approvals of different district bureaus and offices, and also depending on the size and nature of the project. For larger projects that involve foreign capital, city-level approval is required, while smaller (under 50 million yuan) projects that involve only domestic capital are completely handled at the district level. According to one developer interviewed by the researcher, there were some 90 seals (stamps by bureaus or offices) obtained during this stage; another developer estimated the process typically required over 100 different chops.

Several developers across the city also made reference to the 'five permits and two certificates' necessary for property development, the majority of which are obtained during this preliminary phase. In particular, these are: State-Owned Land Use Permit, Construction Land Use Planning Permit, Building Construction Planning Permit and Building Construction Permit. The final permit and certificates are Commodity Housing Sales (Sale-in-Advance) Permit and Housing Quality Guarantee Certificate and Residential Housing Manual Certificate. Figure 6.1 provides a flowchart of the preliminary stage of real estate project development constructed using Li Ling (2006) and input from Shanghai developers interviewed for this chapter. One of the main variables that determines fast or slow development in this initial stage is the extent to which local government bureaux and offices are motivated to speed the project through various stages or, contrarily, lack motivation such that various designs and forms are likely to get stuck (*kazhe*) at different points in the process. One developer referred to these permits as 'tickets', a particularly poignant metaphor if local state development is regarded as 'high-speed rail'.

Yet, again, the problem for Shechi and its Castle Estate did not lie here – or it did, but only obliquely. Instead of following the normal, codified development process – regardless of any shortcuts from friends in the planning office – this project was caught in what has been called a 'battle' between socialist land masters and district government (see Hsing 2010). And yet the dénouement did eventually follow the well-worn development path noted by other developers. The socialist land master in this case, China's PLA Air Force, had land from the old Jiangwan airport, where during the Second World War Japanese and US forces had separately occupied the area. Shechi had a project, financing and access to the Air Force land. In the middle was Yangpu district, whose approval across multiple bureaux, offices and centres, as well as whose cooperation would smooth the necessary con-struction of infrastructure and traffic networks to attach the development to the city. In addition to the fees paid to the Air Force for land conveyance, the district government wanted a portion of the proceeds– or, in this case, planning input and additional funding – for the transference of land use rights for residential housing. Shechi subsequently solved this problem by inviting a nearby University-related design company to participate in the project execution, smoothing over the uncertainty and the risk 'unknown unknowns' of urban change. It is significant that a compromise was eventually reached, but also that the timing of the approval process was in the hands of the local district government.

In Hsing's (2010) important work, it is the inner city portion, rather than the urban fringe or rural areas, which is relevant to the argument here. More specifically, it is her discussion of the 'battle' between municipal government interests in the form of district governments and the socialist land masters, progenitors of central and

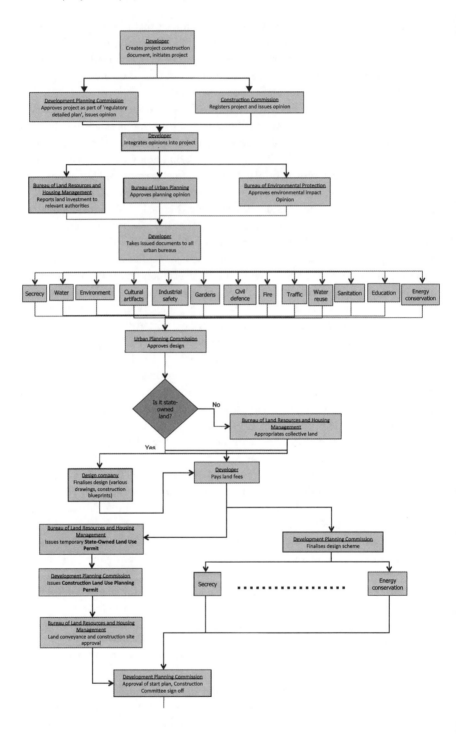

Figure 6.1 Development flowchart

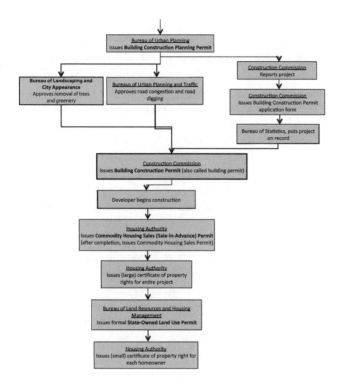

Figure 6.1 continued

provincial *danwei*, as well as public institutions (*shiye danwei*, including military, university, hospital, etc.) that dominated in the pre-reform era (Ibid.: 33–59). In terms of her felicitous but undeveloped temporality of land development in China, the 'land battle in the inner city is between the socialist past and the present market economy' (Ibid.: 23). But, in the case developed here, the evidence seems to argue against one of Hsing's core thesis, that is, that these municipal agents are in a 'battle' with socialist land masters, who occupy a large part of municipal land. The ethnography of the development process revealed a different architecture of urban power. For even in those cases where the latter do transfer land for real estate development, the numerous bureaux of the local district and municipality are core in producing approval, as well the district administrators of urban infrastructure are a core gateway through which developers must all pass (setting up connections to city). Further, transferring land in Yangpu does not mean relocation of the military, as there are generations of military families with a high stake in development of the area, and whom are unwilling to relocate. Hsing's thesis can be fruitfully contrasted with the chronicle of Chen Anjie, former party secretary of Yangpu District, who oversaw the major early conversions of land from military holding to district holding (see retelling by Wang Yi [2010], a military school instructor who lived adjacent to Wujiaochang in Yangpu district for 30 years). Chen Anjie worked tirelessly to coordinate between military units, universities and the district, labouring under the directive of Shanghai City Plan's designation of Yangpu as a municipal secondary centre, Yangpu and Wujiaochang's legacy as an urban–rural bazaar, the concentration of universities nearby and the large swath of land occupied by various branches of the military. Chen celebrated the first auction with the military officials in 2003, though the continuing negotiation of the relationship between military, developers and district government was in evidence through observations of Shechi as the individual parcels of land in Wujiaochang and Yangpu are developed.

It should not be surprising, then, that the two landmark shopping plazas that make up the central Wujiaochang development are Wanda Group and Bailian Group. The former is headed by Wang Jinglin – the 'northern king' of property, with Vanke's Wang Shi as the 'southern king' (Ng 2012) – who has an extensive military background of 17 years, and left the government offices of a district (Xigang) in Dalian in 1988 to run a bankrupt district real estate company, no less. Wanda Group is now one of the premier developers of commercial flagship properties in China. The latter is a large department store developer and supermarket owner, currently under the control of the Shanghai municipal SASAC. As Wujiaochang became a focus for district and municipal development, particularly in the Shanghai 12-year plan, both stakeholders – the military via Wanda and the city government via Bailian – joined in the development process. For Executive Bin, the results could not have been more lucrative. While making a measly profit of only 4 million yuan off sales of the Wujiaochang-adjacent *xiaoqu*, he continues to bring in close to 10 yuan per square metre per month for the commercial tower he completed in 2007 that he maintains ownership of, resulting in an income of some 500,000 yuan per month. The Castle Estate, only 10 minutes away, has enjoyed locational propinquity in its pricing and desirability.

In discussing the importance of maintaining solid relationships with the district government, the assistant to the Executive Bin noted that this was one of Shechi's competitive advantages, particularly in comparison with the Hong Kong real estate company Shui On, which was building Knowledge and Innovation Community (KIC, Chuangzhi Tiandi[12]) just across the road from Shechi's offices. 'They [Shui On] have new people all the time. That is bad for *guanxi* with local officials. They want to know who they are dealing with'. The inability of non-local, and particularly foreign (e.g. Hong Kong), developers to succeed in land development projects is also discussed by Tang and Liu (2002). Just about every government department will have working relationships with real estate enterprises, so in this 'hydra-headed' administrative structure, to have private *guanxi* with every department leader is close to impossible. One day, one of the authors and Executive Bin sat sipping 'Kong Fu tea' (*gongfu cha*, known as such because of the elaborate ritual required to make it) in Executive Bin's office. The matter of the new restrictions that 70 per cent of new apartments should be under 90 square metres (70/90 rule, mentioned above) came up. Executive Bin laughed. 'At first I was quite nervous when I heard about it. But then I talked to some people in the planning bureau, and there are ways around it'. Indeed, two aspects of the policy requirement were pointed out as quite ambiguous:

first, the 90 square metres is dwelling area (*taoxing mianji*; in the brokerage class this was referred to as 'carpet area' – the area where you could lay carpet) rather than constructed area (*jianzhu mianji*). The constructed area is much larger (by 10–15 square metres or more) than the dwelling area, so the requirement of 90 square metres could already be enlarged to over 100 square metres – as pointed out by the head of the Division of Real Estate at the Ministry of Construction only one month after the 'State Six Articles' policy was announced (Shi 2006). This official also pointed out, in a point echoed by Li Linyan (2008: 178), that this 70/90 restriction applied to a region – notable, since a region (*diqu*) is quite ambiguous, being somewhere between a municipal district (*shiqu*) and a *xiaoqu*. The implication is that the policy restriction was sufficiently vague so its implementation is under the purveyance and discretion of local district government.

Pouring hot water over the top of the entire teapot and dispensing the resulting nectar into miniature teacups, Executive Bin continued that there are ways to sell apartments so that they can be folded into one another. 'For example, I can sell two units next to each other that are below 90 square metres, then let the buyer knock down the wall in between. Or do the same thing with a two-storey'. Another option was to leave balconies and common areas uncovered, since according to law, these are only counted as one-half the total area. Once the buyer has the apartment in his possession, he/she immediately covers the balconies and increases the usable/dwelling area.[13] These types of tactics, while quite ingenious ways of 'hitting the ball off the corner of table' (*caibianqiu*, implies the idea of a workaround in the sense of neither hitting nor missing the ping-pong table), are both widespread and require collusion from local authorities. Larger apartments make them more expensive, prestigious and attractive to a different (and assumed more desirable) customer.

Jing'an: selling roots to the city

A second ethnographic study was conducted in the more central Shanghai district of Jing'an. In Jing'an, the development product – the eventual *xiaoqu* – at the centre of attention was the Gaoceng Tower. It dominated the short stay in the sales department (*shoulou chu*) of the field research conducted for this chapter. Following dismissal from the sales team, the research follows Vivian – a precocious Shanghaiese saleswoman (introduced below) – to brokerage class, and from there to a real estate brokerage. These 'intermediary' businesses sit between apartment owners or landlords and their buyers or renters, though with few ties to the city beyond eking out a sometimes quite respectable living and finding life as 'new Shanghaiese'. The appellation is deceiving, as Vivian herself – with family roots over 50 years, and herself born in Shanghai – proves. Nonetheless, as the unwitting researcher discovered at a dinner one night in the Meilong town area with several senior police officers, *bentu ren* ('people of this land', 'real' locals who have hundreds of years of local heritage) speak quite a different dialect from the common Shanghaiese even of those born and raised here. The roots of Shanghai are deep.

In the spring of 2008, one researcher met a young Shanghai woman in her early thirties named Vivian (she prefers to use her English name). She agreed to allow the researcher to tag along on daily work selling the Jing'an Gaoceng Tower, a luxury apartment building (singular) located in the heart of the central Jing'an district, only a 20-minute walk from the famous Jing'an Temple. This location was the lead selling point, and nearby housing mostly consisted of old *lilong* (Shanghai alleyways) broken up by an occasional massive commodity *xiaoqu*. The property was developed by Taiwan MF Insurance, a burgeoning property developer in mainland China that typically focuses on office and commercial buildings. The price of the apartments, at a little over 35,000 yuan per square metre, was average for the area at the time, though a little expensive given the lack of *xiaoqu* walls and greenery. To entice more higher-end buyers, the MF Insurance had decided to fully finish decoration of the apartments for sale. It also planned to install a professional 'hotel-style' property management company, though the property management fee was a whopping 6 yuan (per square metre, per month). The apartments ranged from 90 to 350 square metres, but only eight of the former were offered, three of which were 'reserved' ahead of time by the MF Insurance bosses, whereas 16 massive 350 square metre units were offered. At the opening ceremony to mark the start of apartment sales, only a disappointing dozen or so potential buyers showed up, and only a handful of apartments sold.

The sales team at Gaoceng had to debate with several customers about the rationale for finishing decorating the apartments, including not only floors, kitchens and bathroom fixtures, but walls, lights, windows and even furniture. One potential customer noted that the quality of the apartments – their location, size and management – contrasted too sharply with the level of decoration evidenced in the mock-up apartments on the upper floors. He reasoned that he would have to immediately redecorate upon purchasing of the apartment. In the past, all apartments in China were sold as *maopei* (barebones, i.e. cement floors and no fixtures, lights, etc.). Another developer who is friends with one of the researchers developed a relatively high-end villa complex only a few kilometres from the Minhang Real development (see below). She gave the researchers several tours of the property and villa mock up, as well as inviting researchers to participate in the Halloween, Christmas, New Year's parties and other activities organised at the *xiaoqu* clubhouse. In a discussion about finishing the property rather than allowing the buyer to do it and make their own choices on style and quality, the developer noted that her company had started out in 2007 by selling *maopei*. 'But people kept buying our mock up. I would say "it's just a mock up". But they would insist on buying it exactly how we decorated it. So after that happened a few times, we decided to sell the villas [in the next batch] fully-furnished'. As we drove around the villa complex, several villas had sand, cement and other detritus of interior decoration strewn on front lawns. The developer commented that these villas were sold earlier, and that that was another reason for deciding to decorate new villas for sale: the untidiness and potential risks that individual decoration projects bring to the entire *xiaoqu*.[14]

During the opening ceremony at Gaoceng, the researcher sat down over the course of the six-hour event with several of the MF Insurance managers. In casual conversation, a manager revealed that the company had paid only 200 million yuan for this building. Previously, it was an office building owned by a Shanghai municipal government-controlled transportation construction company, which was listed on the Shanghai stock market. The company paid a premium of over 100 million yuan for the building, but was able to redevelop it into more lucrative residential housing. This was due in part to the fact that the previous office building had been caught up in the Chen Liangyu scandal, involving numerous illicit property dealings with family members and use of the municipal social security fund. Rather than have the scandal bring to light dealings around this building, and influence the credibility of the listed company, officials agreed to the property deal with MF Insurance. 'That is why the use rights period is only for 50 years, instead of the usual 70 years [for residential]', explained the manager. In addition, no planning or construction permits for the work that was ongoing on Gaoceng during the selling process were filed at the Jing'an district or the Shanghai municipal offices. Thus the pace and lack of red tape for MF Insurance in getting to work on construction and sales were facilitated by a 'motivated seller', local government and local enterprise, with ulterior motives for disposing of the property.

When explicitly discussing the subject of relationships with the local government, one manager, speaking Mandarin with a strong Taiwanese accent, noted that they were useful to reducing costs. Pointing up to the ceiling, he indicated the fire lights in the lobby of the building: 'if you have a good relationship, take the fire bureau head out for some banquets, you can install one every two metres instead of every one metre'. Ironically, this instrumental view of *guanxi* betrayed MF Insurance. The developer had no connection with the local area, though it had projects throughout Shanghai and even in the Yangzi River Delta. Sales of the Gaoceng Tower on behalf of MF Insurance were undertaken by a temporary sales team put together for that purpose. All members were Shanghaiese, and had worked together and shared information on housing sales for several years. In addition, MF Insurance had invested quite significantly in advertising, though without a specialised company that engages in consulting and design and planning of the campaign, as will be seen with Minhang. A well-crafted video played in the sales office constantly, and it was displayed on the mini-televisions on the backs of taxi car seats throughout the city. Yet the sales team hired for their *guanxi* could not sell the apartments. The failure of sales to pick up in the months before and month following the open caused MF Insurance to fire the entire team.

Following her dismissal from Jing'an Gaoceng Tower sales team, Vivian invited one researcher to join her in taking preparation classes for the Shanghai real estate broker examination. The classes lasted over a period of eight weeks, being held once a week for six hours. They were taught by local experts both from the industry and academia. While some portion of the time was spent merely reading from the specially prepared internal textbooks, the classes involved rigorous training in real estate general knowledge, discussions with other aspiring brokers and learning about the backgrounds of other real estate businesses in Xujiahui, Shanghai and beyond. The class was run by the Shanghai Real Estate Broker Trade Association and cost over 500 yuan, including books and testing fees. Passing the brokerage examination would entitle the individual to both national and Shanghai certifications to engage in the brokerage business. This examination was restricted to those with a Shanghai *hukou* or those from outside Shanghai (including Hong Kong, Macau and Taiwan) with a Shanghai residence permit who are employed by a Shanghai real estate industry.

There were some 30,000 certified brokerages in Shanghai in 2008, and from half to two-thirds of all real estate transactions are undertaken through a brokerage, making the industry ubiquitous in Shanghai neighbourhoods (Brokerage Class 17/7/08).[15] Brokerages have proliferated in the cities as much as stock trading rooms have (see Chapter Seven) after the mid-2000s with the boom in the values of both markets. They have joined the neighbourhood as regular places of visit – in the case of brokerages, local residents of the neighbourhood, sometimes in their pyjamas, stroll around and stop in front of the stand-up signs, posters, placards and even LED messages that keep them informed of the prices of *xiaoqu* apartments in the area. Brokers' and brokerages' ubiquity is such that, when one researcher moved from Xujiahui to Lianyang, to find a broker all that was required was to go to the entrance of a *xiaoqu*, where several brokerage agents stood everyday passing out information. It was common practice, however, for most local residents to off-handedly ask the price of apartments in a *xiaoqu* and discuss this information in informal conversations. Casual conversations with agents, for example, revealed that smaller apartments – with less area – were more expensive.

Five certified broker licenses are required to start a brokerage, while only one is required to open a franchised branch. Hence for Vivian, this certification was an additional source of income. She was not interested in starting a brokerage, but could 'rent' her license for between 10 and 20 thousand yuan, obtain a monthly income of 1,000 yuan and have her four 'insurance funds' (*sijin*) paid off.[16] 'I wouldn't have to do anything. Just sign any important documents and let them use my certification. They still need me to come out for any important issues so they have to pay'. According to some reports, there are over 100,000 brokers in Shanghai, and the vast majority – over 70 per cent – are unlicensed (Wei and Lin 2004)

Through a contact met at the brokerage class, a subsequent work placement was based for one month at a brokerage (see Tang *et al.* 2006 for introduction to the industry). The work started in a quite nice area to the south of Century Park in the Pudong New Area. The office was a converted apartment in a lovely *xiaoqu*, with nicely landscaped green areas and pathways, and vehicles were forced underground to park upon entering. Given that *xiaoqu* apartments are commonly used as business offices, the guards at the entrance were oblivious to comings and goings, provided the requisite outfit did not fall below the standard of business attire. This idyllic surrounding abruptly changed, however, within two weeks of starting research at the brokerage, and the new locale was even more exotic – the second floor of a 1930s old garden house (*laoyangfang*) on one of the old French Concession's busiest bar streets.

The daily work focused on mastering the markets – the *fangyuan* and the *keyuan*. The *fangyuan*, or 'housing resources', was a supply of housing, either for sale or rent but mostly the latter in this particular brokerage, which was maintained by personal connections to landlords. Individual employees brought in some landlords' apartments, but there was also a concerted effort to *qiang*, or 'steal', landlords from other brokerages. Hence daily work involved viewing the current and emerging apartments available from other brokerages with similar resources and customers. Of secondary importance in daily work at the brokerage was *keyuan*, the supply of customers. Customers mostly contacted the brokerage themselves, while the brokerage spent significant amounts of time in the office updating and expanding online listings of apartments as well as time out of the office showing different properties to customers. In this particular brokerage, the service model was to work as an intermediary between landlord and tenant, such that all housing-related matters would be solved by a broker without the necessity of the two parties contacting each other. In one instance, this broke down because an employee had agreed to give a discount in the brokerage fee to the landlord, such that he brokered the tenancy by himself without using the company contracts and pocketing the intermediary fee directly. The work also required wide, working knowledge of *xiaoqu*'s in the area, as well as those across the city.

The tragedy of the fire on Jiaozhou Road in Jing'an District has multiple significances. The population there, desiring as they did to stay in their neighbourhood and area of the city, were fixed in place. Without district approval, the Construction and Transportation Commission worked with its subsidiary companies – i.e. not companies run by district SASAC or district-administered investment companies – to develop new property while offering residents the opportunity to have a slight renovation to their building. As Zeng and Tsai (2011) have shown, the motivation for local governments to restructure is minuscule unless there are specific incentives – with political advancement and achievements being quite important. The motivation for selling Gaoceng building and allowing its redevelopment is to minimise economic and political fall out in light of the Chen Liangyu scandal. Yet a non-local developer, with no long-term or *guanxi* relationships with local government, found it quite hard to sell off their apartments without a flagship or local development project to which to tie their *xiaoqu*. Brokerages, more organised forms of sales teams like that hired by MF Insurance, reflect a similar attachment to district level development. Contrasting Tang *et al*'.s (2006) view of failure by citywide housing intermediaries, Liu (2007) has shown that *xiagang* ('off their work post') former *danwei* workers were quite adept at organising the filtering of potential tenants and landlords. In observations for this chapter, one *xiaoqu* in Lianyang area of Pudong had started its own brokerage office, as well as managing rental property handovers and payments for gas, water and electricity. Even in housing sectors detached from the local state, the importance of local development and relationality with the local neighbourhood and *xiaoqu* remains key. As the market evolves, the cartography of state and society networks becomes more complex in the socialist market on the ground, transformed nationally but realised in the real estate growth of Shanghai districts.

Minhang: 'A-la Shanghai Ning'[17]

Shanghaiese say, 'In big Shanghai, there are three circles: in the innermost circle, they speak English; in the second circle, they speak outside dialects, though there seem to be quite a few who speak Wenzhou-ese;[18] and 'us Shanghaiese' (*a-la Shanghai ning*) live in the outermost circle' (Real Estate Brokerage class, 12/7/2008).

Gaizhi: restructuring ownership in Minhang district in outer Shanghai

The mid-1990s policy of 'grasping the large, releasing the small' (*zhuada fangxiao*) encapsulated China's national industrial policy, subsequently adopted by provinces, municipalities and lower government levels, that state-ownership of large SOE would be maintained but that medium and small SOE would be sold off and engage in business independently. Of course, at the different scales of state-ownership (central, provincial, municipal, prefecture-level cities, districts and towns), the nature of 'big' and 'small' is quite relative. It was only in early 2000s that this policy of restructuring or reforming the system (*gaizhi*) reached a point where implementation in Minhang district began to pick up steam. At the district level, as with Minhang Real below, the board of directors in the company is exactly the small group of senior managers who ran the state-owned enterprise prior to restructuring. SASAC is not involved here, since in this case a management buyout using a local bank loan was devised as a way for senior management to take control of the enterprise and run it themselves. Interestingly, this mirrors the process of village enterprises re-forming as a shareholding companies with former village enterprise managers becoming board members of the new company, as is frequently seen in *chengzhongcun*. In the latter case, however, shares in the shareholding company are retained by villagers who receive dividends on an annual basis. For district residents, contrarily, this does not occur. While *gaizhi* is often glossed as 'privatisation', this phrasing obscures not only the nature of the process and its results, but the operation of local state capitalism.

Like a *danwei*, the headquarters of Minhang Real (Group) Company, Limited had a cavernous canteen capable of seating over 100 employees where, during the time of the research in 2009, only a dozen or so employees would gather daily for lunch. The courtyard of the headquarters near Xinzhuang – the administrative centre of Minhang District – was vacant on one side, a row of three storey offices completely empty, serving as a reminder of the former joint mission of Minhang Real and the district housing bureau who had relocated after the restructuring. Time spent researching Minhang Real was split between the headquarters of the company and the location of the current *xiaoqu* under development – 'Beautiful Capital' – located some 5 kilometres away in another part of Minhang district.

The story of Minhang Real (Group) Company, Limited is gathered from internal documents and subsequent discussions with Executive Wang, the head of the company. Prior to restructuring, Minhang Real belonged to the district administration, and was incorporated with over 20 companies belonging to the district bureau of housing and land in 2000 under the district asset management bureau. The companies included, most importantly, residential housing development, but also property management, construction, interior decoration, rental, hotel and catering, demolition, consulting and construction materials. In the early 2000s, Minhang Real was a group of companies with over 1,200 employees and 700 million yuan in registered capital at the district level – a large-scale state-owned enterprise group – prior to restructuring. When Minhang Real Company was made to restructure, the district government preferred to sell the company to its managers and employees. However, policy at the time (viz. the State Council's 'Temporary Rules for Transferring Enterprise State-Owned Property Rights to Management Levels', No. 78) required all state-owned businesses to be sold through tender, auction or listing, to prevent corruption and loss of state assets. Hence in 2005 the Minhang branch of SASAC opted for the 'listing' (*guapai*) of Minhang Real's corporate assets at the Shanghai United Assets and Equity Exchange. The initial price was listed as 30 million yuan for 100 per cent of the Real Group Company's assets.

Unexpectedly, two outside bidders arose to compete for the company. One was a real estate developer from Zhejiang, and the other was a real estate company from Hong Kong – although the latter sent two low-profile individuals to bid rather than their company's top brass. After the listing process ended, it was clear that the original managers had been outbid. However, as Executive Wang pointed out, 'We have a lot of historical burdens. All that public housing management, the demolition at Qibao, the bankruptcy of one of our group companies...How can an outside [Shanghai] or Hong Kong company take care of that?' Over the course of several months Minhang district decided that another 40 million yuan would be required to transfer ownership of the company away from the senior managers in order to deal with such historical debts. The two outside companies demurred at any further attempt to gain ownership of the company.

Local development: Zhaoshang Yinzi

The major project under development by Minhang Real at the time of observation (2008–2009) was named 'Beautiful Capital: Holiday Scenic Garden', spanning 244,000 square metres of constructed area and 2,200 households. It has been sold in phases, with the end of 2008 coinciding with the third phase, with each phase entailing the release of another 300 or so units and an increase in price – from under 8,000 yuan per square metre in 2007 to over 12,000 yuan per square metre in 2009. The development included a public pedestrian road in front of the *xiaoqu* that was also to be developed by Minhang Real. The developer controlled the leasing (no sale was permitted, see below) of business fronts on the outward-facing portion of the walls surrounding the *xiaoqu*. For residential sales Minhang Real hired an outside company – Shanghai-based Noble Sales Company, Limited – to assist with PR, advertising and sales.

As related by Minhang Real staff, they were quite pleased with the hiring of Noble Sales to run the phased sale process. On the opening day of each phase, several hundred people showed up, outnumbering the amount of apartments to be put on sale. 'They were lined up outside the door. We told them that we would distribute lots, and that in this way you could pick an apartment regardless of position in line, but they didn't care. There were some fights. We had to hire extra security guards'. As construction continued on the *xiaoqu* complex behind the sales office, the between-phase period of sluggish sales, lack of things to do and sleepy security guards seemed to betray this vivid scene. Of worthy comparison is the scene reported only two years later at a Vanke development in Pudong near the upcoming Shanghai Disneyland. After a reduction in the price of new apartments, buyers who had already bought apartments invaded the sales office and smashed it (Wang 2011). Discussing the original land levelling and start of construction with the business sales manager of Minhang Real, he noted that his company had done quite well with relocating residents. There were two contrasts he raised: 'You know that villa complex up the street? They had a big problem with *dingzi hu*. You were not here then but they actually started building and there was one guy still in his house. They just built around him. His whole house was surrounded by walls and the rest of the construction went on'. The other experience with demolition was a less-smooth process for Minhang Real. 'You like old Shanghai buildings, huh? You should have come to the demolition of Qibao last month. We knocked down a whole bunch. Actually, the [demolition] project has taken over seven years because there are a lot of *dingzi hu* in the area. We cannot do anything, just wait'.

Both this manager and Executive Wang noted the incredible difficulty of managing property in Shanghai these days. Not only are independent (or legally independent but group-owned) property management companies required, but there are multiple headaches involved in dealing with residents. These vary between the old *xiaoqu* that Minhang Real built back when it was a branch company of the district government – where people may refuse to pay management fees and Minhang Real is responsible for fixing potentially dangerous housing and maintenance – and new *xiaoqu* where buying for investment means that the homeowner does not live there, so they do not feel obliged to pay property management fees. Responding to questions about property management and whether owners committees (*yeweihui*) and community (*shequ*) would be involved, the manager said: 'Of course we will manage it. We have no choice. People will move in immediately and there will inevitably be problems to deal with. Who knows when they will form an owners' committee. It is our duty to fill the property management role, and there is no profit in it'. According to another developer who has been working in Shanghai for over 15 years, the old principle of *zijian zifu*, or 'if you build it, you take responsibility for it', still applies, particularly when development is the focus of government interest. In this sense, Minhang Real's property management services were more of an obligation than an opportunity for more income.

For the storefront property that was part of the exterior of the Beautiful Capital project, Minhang Real adopted a different strategy, one more tied directly to the concern with local development (Table 6.3). All business inquiries were directed to the Minhang Real (rather than Noble Sales) manager, who often visited the *xiaoqu* sales office. He revealed that he was only registering companies at the moment, not signing lease deals (they had already signed a Western-style fast-food restaurant and a national bank branch to anchor the storefront) – and certainly not selling the commercial properties. 'If you sell them [commercial properties], you lose control over who can move in. So if the business fails, they might bring in a massage parlor or Chinese-food restaurant with lots of oil and smoke. That would devalue the area'. This strategy is similar to that of Shui On, revealed by the business manager in charge of signing up merchants for the Chongqing version of Xintiandi during a visit by the researchers: it is more about creating a total environment than one particular sale or client. For Minhang Real, a quality environment meant maintaining control over most of the central business area in the new *xiaoqu* and surrounding neighbourhoods. Over lunch back at the large, now noticeably empty company canteen, the general manager of Minhang Real also recalled the intensive negotiations he had in with a massive multi-national European supermarket that eventually moved into a large mall Minhang Real had built nearby Beautiful Capital: 'they wanted a low price, very low. I refused. So, instead, they asked to have the whole building, including storefronts not part of their floor space. Eventually I agreed. [Now] I know, they probably end up paying nothing, since the rent they pay us is offset by rent paid to them by the small storefronts rented by outside businesses, and [the multinational supermarket's] rates are very high because they attract a lot of people everyday'.

Real estate companies that ride on the local government's high-speed rail must learn and interpret local government policy and contribute to local development demonstrated through not only *guanxi* but business and project results. In Minhang this takes the form of 'attracting businesses and bringing in capital' (*zhaoshang yinzi*); this is not a problem of taking officials to dinner and giving them gifts, because local officials want to attract business and bring in capital and tax receipts. This is the *raison d'être* of local government. Government support is given in order to finish construction quickly, so officials want efficiency and no trouble or delays. 'Officials want achievements, enterprises want profits, if the two are in harmony, even bad *guanxi* will become good' (developer quoted in Li Linyan 2008: 138).

Conclusion

This chapter sheds some light on the types of economic life and urban change involved in property development in Shanghai, and the specific role of the district in Shanghai's local state capitalism. This is not documentation of 'traditional' *guanxi* culture and localism that relies on unchanging ideas of family, state and networks. China is forming large, multi-national development companies, and evidence from Yangpu and perhaps Jing'an (in light of the tragedy at Jiaozhou Road) shows local governments are recognising the importance of deploying state assets in the market, in a sense that Bo Xilai, Cheng Liangyu and Huang Qifan[19] would not disapprove of.

TABLE 6.3 Summary of 500 random third-phase transactions of Minhang Real's Beautiful Capital *xiaoqu*

Minhang Real Company			
Analysis of customer transactions, 2008		*Number of transactions*	*(%)*
***Huji* (Hometown)**			
Shanghai		415	83
Outside		85	17
***Huxing* (Layout)**			
Two bedroom		363	73
Three bedroom		98	20
Four bedroom		39	8
Financing			
Mortgage	Provident	103	21
	Commercial	100	20
	Both	142	28
Payments		125	25
All upfront		30	6
Price (yuan)			
700–800,000		33	7
800–900,000		185	37
900,000–1.0 million		152	30
1.0–1.2 million		0	0
1.2–1.5 million		78	16
1.5–1.8 million		52	10

Source: Noble Sales internal documents.

Glossing these processes and practices as either state intervention (Huang 2008) or cultural rules of the game that reflect millenniums of risk aversion (or risk propensity), small family networking and deference to authority (Redding and Witt 2007) belies the variation between districts – even within the singular municipality of Shanghai.

In the phenomenally popular TV soap opera Woju (*Living Narrowness*), an intertwined story of housing development, consumption and (economic) lives lived in contemporary Shanghai is told. A developer commented to a researcher that, 'It is too real (*zhenshi*) [to be entertaining]'. The TV and novel versions have been analysed by Liang (2010), who concludes that Liuliu (the novel author) succeeds precisely because the city's distinctiveness has failed, collapsing into 'anonymous apartment[s] in the concrete jungle' (Liang 2010: 25). This chapter touches little upon *xiaoqu* residents, and so cannot speculate on whether lives lived in Yangpu, Jing'an or Minhang apartments have collapsed into global identities of house slaves, nail households and mistresses, as in Woju. Nor does this chapter discuss the city's migrant construction workers living and working – temporarily – in building sites, apartments being decorated and commercial skyscrapers under construction, whose tales are frequently forgotten or omitted in stories of *xiaoqu* development. But what the chapter can claim is that the processes for creating these 'concrete jungles' have focused on a local scale of urban change and economic life. What the district level of the city develops reflects neither state imperative nor market form straightforwardly. Instead the transition from state socialism reveals path dependencies and differences in company structure, real estate logistics, institutional formation and marketing strategies. They have evolved tentatively not 'from state to market' but from state control to new combinations of state networks and market forms. In this sense China constructs capitalism not simply in the image of neoclassical economics but out of the fabric of an old city. The socialist market is in some ways an accurate description of the interweaving of state powers and market logics. The incidents of death through local state capitalism detailed at the start of this chapter can neither forestall the continuing 'managing' of the city nor glorify its economic and fundamental results. Instead, the stories of Yangpu, Jing'an and Minhang property development amplify the facets of local state capitalism detailed in Chapters Three and Four, revealing its realisation in emergent Shanghai real estate markets. At the same time, this chapter focuses explicitly on the development stories, showing variation in the role of the local state for local property developers, changing relations to the city through *danwei* and *xiaoqu*, and differential benefits to local residents in terms of infrastructure and economic life provision.

What is crucial for local state capitalism is to think through real estate development, through the companies, processes and policies that have been underscored in this chapter, and find the link to an overall system of land, labour and capital that is organising economic and urban life. From the evidence presented here, land is an intensely local commodity in urban China, held dear by both local governments and developers. The right to develop the land of the city invokes a public good as well as asset of private interests. What local governments want is 'governmental achievements' (*zhengji*), perhaps, but those are achieved not simply through GDP growth and spectacular projects but through comprehensive urban development. The complexities of plural property rights and the plurality of public interests consequently combine in multiple ways in emergent real estate markets. Fixed labour (in the form of Shanghai *hukou*), embedded capital (once invested in a project, it is very slow to come back out) and 'fiscal land' (*tudi caizheng*) from land sales and local taxes reinforce local land, housing and governance into a comprehensive system, only parts of which have been brought together and understood before. The chapter certainly builds off previous studies of local capitalism (Smart and Lin 2007) or local government growth coalitions (He and Wu 2005), but it does diverge from them in bringing the comprehensive analytic insight into the local state of capitalism for real estate development companies in Shanghai. Negotiated property rights in urban China are shaped and driven by the *district-level* cadres and developers. In highly urbanised areas of China's cities – that is, urban districts with little or no rural land, where villages and towns have vanished in lieu of Street (sub-district) and Residents Committee (*juweihui*) administration – the district is the lowest level with power and the decisive authority on district affairs, in all facets from urban planning, to construction approval, sales, infrastructure provision and even project development that sustain local state capitalism.

7

TRADING ROOM ETHNOGRAPHIES

Stuck in China

'Two old, dilapidated boats, I'll never buy them'. Old Chen was not looking at anyone in particular when he raised his head from the trading room computer terminal to make this comment, bringing laughter from the circle of other retired factory workers regularly present at a Xujiahui trading room in Shanghai. The Industrial and Commercial Bank of China (ICBC) and the Bank of China (B.C), the largest two banks in China, were the subject of his disdain. 'It is like you hail a taxi, and then have to get out and push!' elicited another round of chuckles.

This chapter examines the non-tradeable share reform (NTSR), known popularly as *gugai* (or simply 'share reform'), and the effect on the stock market from an ethnographic perspective. From both neoliberal and holistic perspectives, it is possible to discuss the development of China's stock markets from 2006 to 2008. Yet these two perspectives share an unwillingness to examine the market as a form of governance and the 'thick' context through which stock trading and investment takes place, examined here in Shanghai. Using the above insights gained from an unquestioned view of the market, this chapter examines the trading room and individual investors not as representatives of the people – in contraposition to the state or big investors – but as active agents mapping stock trades onto regimes of risk and uncertainty through a rationality combining neoliberal market awareness with the 'policy market' (*zhengce shichang*) nature of China's stock exchange.

If there are relational markets, and exchange is really never-ending exchanging, and there is an interrelation between the context of behaviour and its content, rather than particular, singular individual and their investment in a company based on fundamentals – as is argued in the opening chapters of this book – then how do we describe the stock market? There are millions of exchanges of billions of yuan in shares in the market every day during only four hours of trading time. How does this relate to the creation of spatial forms? How to relate the trading rooms to the online trading of stocks, funds, warrants and other securities? And how does this relate to the colourful lexicon of stock trading that the researchers spent time learning in the participant observation in the market?

Individual investors (*Sanhu*): 'A Plate of scattered sand' or 'Three smelly cobblers can best a zhu geliang'

In the overall context of *gugai*, the behaviour of individual investors is important. By observing individual investors in Shanghai's trading rooms, this chapter finds they are not immature but *chao* and *tao* ('stir-fry' and 'get stuck') through major policy changes and reforms. Individual investors do not fit conventional models, so require a rethinking of rationality, uncertainty and market maturity. With *da-xiao fei*, the large and small 'nons' that emerged as a direct result of *gugai*, it is *xiaofei*, the non-controlling shareholders with large chunks of ownership, who pose real danger to the market (the state as the dominant *dafei* holds its shares even if they become tradeable (I return to concept of *da-xiao fei* below). Further, the contradiction between market driven by policy and failure of state to regulate the market, signals the tension between risk and uncertainty and focuses attention on investment behaviour to understand what is really going on. In addition, the significance of small investors and spillover of trading rooms into the city shows the legacy of stock markets in China is not transitional but an alternative way of structuring securities finance.

The incredible rise and fall of China's stock markets from 2006 to 2008 cannot be explained solely by exogenous factors all of which assume a singular yardstick of market functionality, nor can they be explained completely by changes, practices and processes internal to China. This chapter focuses on individual investors, and especially those investing less than US$100,000, as a critical part of the market. One postulate is that it is precisely these 'micro-' investors who, despite the general consensus that China's stock markets are policy markets, keep the state from regulating the market. By examining both urban stock trading rooms in Shanghai, and interviewing individual stock investors, this chapter argues for a different understanding of stock markets in China, as well as engaging the market at a neoliberal level. The spread of stock trading rooms in China's cities points to the production of space through exchange. Something spills over, a form of externality, in the everyday trading in and proliferation of these trading rooms. This chapter adopts an ethnographic approach in order to undertake a discussion about the significance that arises from individual investors. It is also engages the neoliberal perspective even if the goal is to take a standpoint of incommensurability against the normalising neoliberal market perspective in explaining both the rise and fall of the market and the actions of investors in the trading room and beyond.

If China's stock market is a 'policy market', how do we reconcile this with Old Chen's quote above? The disappointment with the 'national team' of ICBC, BoC and other large enterprises, as with football (Lozada 2006), points to a cosmopolitanism of Shanghai investors who consume stocks to engage with economic life on an everyday basis in a changing city, but also as a 'ticket' to ride the fast lane of

China's economic development. But China's 'national team' do not grow or increase in value at the same rate as China's economy. It is possible to draw on general understandings of the stock market that can be called 'shared' understanding. Yet variety exists among individual investors in terms of economic life that is integrated into the city via spillovers from stock trading.

Researching stock trading

The researchers conducted six months of observation in 14 stock trading rooms in Shanghai during 2007 and 2008, with a focus on one particular trading room in Xujiahui, where, cumulatively, over three months of trading days were spent to obtain deeper insight of everyday investment. Aside from actual trading on the market, research data was gained through insight into a dozen other trading rooms throughout Shanghai in different districts. In addition, the authors, in collaboration with Zhang Zhulin and Professor Wang Xiaoming at Shanghai University, conducted interviews with two dozen Shanghai young professionals who invest in the stock market. There were also numerous opportunities to observe interactions with the stock market across multiple portions of research in Shanghai between 2007 and 2010. For example, at an annual meeting for UFIDA (in 2013 renamed 'Yonyou'), one of the largest software companies in China where one of the researchers worked for several years in the mid-2000s, numerous participants were seen checking the market, indices and shares during the conference. During the participant observation at Minhang Real, a real estate company (see Chapter Six), members of the sales team often checked the stock market and made trades during spare, dull moments of morning and afternoon.

Through observational research in a dozen trading rooms across Shanghai, and interviews with young professionals investing in China's stock markets, general understandings of China's individual investors, and the role of the trading room, are ascertained. From the beginning of their investment in the stock markets, if not in stocks than in *rengouzheng*, or '(share) subscription certificates', issued in 1992, people referred to trading stocks as *chaogu*, literally 'stir-frying stocks' (Hertz 1998; Gamble 1997). Colloquially translated as 'playing the market', *chaogu* was believed by early analysts to refer to a buy, short hold and sale, or a cooking of stock prices, in order to earn quick returns (see Hertz 1998). In fact, this interpretation of *chaogu* is correct, but it only applies in a bull, or increasing, market. In 2007, the Shanghai composite index rose 96.66 per cent while the Shenzhen component rose 166.23 per cent, unequivocally bull markets. But *chaogu* obtains different meanings in the context of a bear market, as seen in the first half of 2008. A more precise meaning for *chaogu* is found in the overall attitude towards stock investment held by both the older inhabitants of the trading rooms, and young professionals whose work is unrelated to the stock market. For these individuals, *chaogu* is done to literally 'play' (*wan*) the market, a phrase mentioned by almost all stock investors interviewed. One retired interviewee even referred to stock investing as 'playing to make the heart pound' (*wan de xintiao*). But while this may seem a flippant attitude to hold towards one's paltry savings, especially for old, retired Shanghai factory workers without a social security safety net, the business of *chaogu* is often done in earnest. Some trading rooms' investors wake early to scour morning editions of newspapers for hints about policies, officials' comments, industry news and company reports that may affect the market. Arriving at the trading rooms before the start of trading at 9:30 am, investors gather in small groups to review stocks, discuss rumours and news and test ideas from their 'homework' (*gongke*) of the night before. Among and amid these discussions – which also take place outside the trading rooms in companies among workers and online in chat rooms – there is an important thickening of the meaning of *chaogu*.

While preferring the term *licai* ('wealth management') to *touzi* ('investment'), young workers in Shanghai invest differential amounts in the stock market. To understand the characteristics of investment, a sub-group of *sanhu* were interviewed both semi-structurally and informally. The subjects of the interviews were white collar workers in their late twenties to late thirties, including both Shanghaiese and 'outsiders' (Zhejiang, Anhui, Shanxi), all of whom had purchased an apartment in Shanghai and invested in the stock market. According to Zhao (2012), the interview subjects all lived at or above the threshold for 'comfortable life' – to not be concerned (*bu huangkong*) – in Shanghai, i.e. they had incomes at or above 9,250 yuan/month.

These young Shanghai investors all work regular day jobs, preventing them from paying exclusive attention to the changes in the stock market over regular working days. Yet the proliferation of the Internet in Shanghai, and its connection to most work activity, create the possibility of checking stock share prices and big board indices in real time. The topics of interview questions included not only size of stock investment, sources of information about particular stocks and stock management, but household income, mortgage financing and budget. In terms of the sources of information, young Shanghai investors were asked where they got the information for picking stocks, and how they evaluated it. As their method of trading stocks is Internet software, many of their sources included websites, QQ groups,[1] blogs and stock trading programs. All of our 'comfortable' interviewees used Internet trading, with one exception who used the telephone to make trades. While this group does not frequent the securities companies' trading rooms, they are important for understanding the category of *sanhu* in Shanghai today.

Neoliberal perspectives: stock market orientation, 2006–2008

Howie and Walter (2006) and Walter (2011), the managing director, chief operating officer) (COO) and CEO of JP Morgan Chase in China, chronicles the stock market in the period from 2001 to 2005 as a struggle between China's central bank and the securities regulatory agency for control and (state-owned) business interests. He concludes, as a neoliberal scholar of markets might be expected to, that China lacks relative to the Western capital market model (its adaptation is 'superficial' [2011: 238]), allows state-related entities to 'capture' and 'pervert' markets and, as a result, led to a collapsed market in 2005 (Ibid.: 204). Given his role in this process, it is perhaps understandable that Howie and Walter (2006) initially missed the revolutionary nature of *gugai*, though in Walter's later work (2011) it is quite an obvious omission. Indeed, the early importance he grants to local party and government (Ibid.: 205, 207–8) in influencing the development of the stock market via local enterprises is usurped by his desire to cast non-tradeable shares as the 'Original Sin' (Ibid.: 211), and thus the singular nature of the state – even if its national institutions, the central bank and national securities regulator, differ in terms of control – reflect the singularity of the market.

The singular nature of the state is echoed by Zheng and Kim (2011) in their critique of the state as controlling shareholder of listed companies. Encompassing over 80 per cent of the listed firms on the market are SOE as controlling share-holders tied to government agencies. This leads Zheng and Kim to judge any and all company actions and related-party transactions as malfeasance (with exception of 'cook[ing] the profit figures in order to look good' [Ibid.: 259] or 'show[ing] paper profits' [Ibid.: 261] and 'appear[ing] healthy and profitable' [Ibid.: 263]). But they ignore evidence such as that pointed out by Sutherland *et al.* (2012) that related-party transactions among affiliates are a regular part of business group operations, and can be used for propping up as well as tunnelling away assets and profits for a variety of reasons. The business groups targeted by Zheng and Kim are in fact very common globally, with the dispersed model of shareholding prevalent only in the US and the UK (Khanna and Palepu 1997). This should give us some pause before applying such a yardstick to measure corporate governance. This section shall add to these two perspectives by examining China's stock markets and the period from 2006 to 2008.

Since late 2005, China's two stock markets, in Shanghai (SSE) and Shenzhen (SZSE), have risen over 600 per cent only to fall by close to 60 per cent in 2008 from a peak in late 2007. The race up and down (see Figure 7.1) is reflected in China's macro-economic indicators, but the real story lies with individuals investing in the market. In contrast to past studies of China's stock markets, this chapter argues that individual investors, and especially those investing less than US$100,000, are a critical part of the market. One postulate is that it is precisely these 'micro-' investors who, despite the general consensus that China's stock markets are 'policy markets', keep the state from regulating the market. Put warrants, literally worthless paper in the days before the end of trading, continue to become sites for speculative trading. The 2007 stock market rose 97 per cent, while the 2008 market fell over 50 per cent: the NTSR, allowing large and small holders to trade previously non-tradeable shares, is both boon and bane of the market. Yet the culprits in abnormal trading are not 'individuals', but the companies, often owned by local governments, whom we argue in other parts of this book are the vanguard of China's reform.

China's stock markets have several distinct features that are important to review in discussing the recent movements of the markets. First, both Shanghai and Shenzhen have two types of shares – A-shares and B-shares.[2] A-shares are denomin-ated in yuan, or *renminbi*, while B-shares are denominated in US or Hong Kong

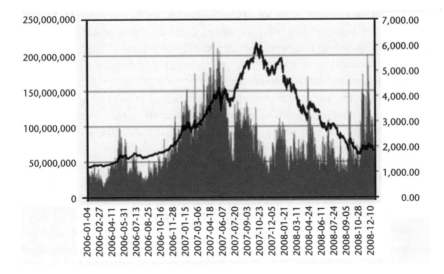

FIGURE 7.1 Shanghai Index, 2006–2008

dollars. B-shares can be bought by both Chinese and foreigners, while A-shares can only be bought by Chinese citizens, companies and institutions.[3] Given that B-shares make up less than 1 per cent of tradeable shares on the market, the focus of this chapter is on A-shares.

In addition to the nominal distinction between A- and B-shares, shares of companies have different ownership categories. This split between ownership categories is of fundamental importance to understanding China's stock markets, as not all shares can 'float', or be traded, on the secondary (or non-IPO) market. As a legacy of the state-owned economy, some SOE that underwent restructuring under the Company Law of 1994 to become joint-stock companies allocated shares in thirds: one-third state-owned, one-third legal person and one third (potentially) available for trading on the markets. The reasoning was that, as former state-owned enterprises, the state is owed a portion of the value of the future company. Further, legal persons, who can be individuals, other companies or the local or central state, also contributed assets, expertise or capital to the formation of the enterprise, and hence are also owed a share of company.

This is a quite amazing clarification of property rights. In the shareholding structure of a listed firm, one can literally see the debts, investments, trading partners, suppliers and customers to the business before restructuring. One need only look at the state and legal-person shareholders listed in company public reports to get a sense of the complexity. Shanghai New World (Shanghai stock code 600628), a company that traces its department store roots back almost to the nineteenth century, and currently is controlled by the Huangpu district SASAC, has had its legal person shares held by customers Shanghai No.1 Department Store and Hualian Commercial Buildings and by suppliers Ganlan cashmere factory and

Caitongdetang Chinese medicine (New World Annual Report 1994) among 145 other smaller legal persons from the outset of its history as a listed company in Shanghai. Thus while Huangpu district SASAC has a share of the listed company as a legacy of local origins and development, other shareholders of non-tradeable shares had debts and interlinked property settled via legal person shares in the listed vehicle. This is an instituted process that is a progenitor of market socialism: clarification of rights but not an end of relationality, as property rights are also obligations – except in cases of pure-profit sellouts, something that does happen after *gugai* in the cases of *xiaofei* discussed below. These common structures of property rights often occurred through exchanging legacy SOE debt owed to external companies for equity in the newly listing company (Qi *et al.* 2000). In practice, this leads to a situation where fully two-thirds of the shares, and market capitalisation, of China's stock markets are non-traded. Legal person shares can be transferred through private deals off-market, a process termed 'two-step privatisation' by some scholars (Green 2005), though a review of the percentage of traded shares and market capitalisation reveals that China's stock markets, especially Shanghai, are still majority non-traded (see Table 7.1).

Gugai: non-tradeable share reform and unlocking market cap

Two key features of China's stock markets prior to *gugai* are that a majority of shares are not traded and that individuals own a large percentage of the tradeable market capitalisation. Here, we draw attention to the significance of reform of the share ownership system, instituted in 2005 and fully completed in late 2007, though with a lag period of three years. The section first explains the reform of share ownership system; it then explores the consequences for both stock markets and China's investors. The magnitudes of these consequences should verify the main importance of policy in the market, and yet, government attempts (through the China Securities Regulatory Commission [CSRC], SSE and SZSE) to control malfeasance remain limited, revealing a major contradiction that continues to influence much of China's economy and especially the securities markets.

The matter of non-tradeable shares has been a target of governmental reform of the stock market since 1999. In 2005, the CSRC finally succeeded by instituting NTSR (also known as the 'Reform of the Split-Share Structure', *guquan fenzhi gaige*), known popularly as *gugai*. It issued the 'Circular on Relevant Issues Regarding Pilot Programs of Non-Tradeable Share Reform of Listed Companies' on 29 April 2005 with approval from the State Council (CSRC, 2008a). At the time, three-quarters of non-tradeable shares were owned by the state. Initial reaction to the idea of two-thirds of market cap suddenly becoming tradeable drove the SSE Composite to its lowest level since 1997, hitting 998 points on 6 June 6 2005. Investor confidence returned soon after, and China's stock markets began a dizzying climb to over 6,100 points near the end of 2007. The following year, however, was a year of decline, with the market falling back below 2,000 points (see Figure 7.1 and Table 7.2).

TABLE 7.1 Shanghai and Shenzhen issued versus floating values

	Listed Companies (#)	Listed Stocks (#)	Total # Issued Shares (bn)	Total # Floating Shares (bn)	Ratio of Floating Shares (%)	Total Market Cap (bn. yuan)	Total Floating Market Cap (bn. yuan)	Ratio of Floating Market Cap (%)
SSE	864	908	1,541.4	491.6	31.9	9,725.2	3,230.6	33.2
SZSE	740	782	344.2	202.4	58.8	2,411.5	1,290.8	53.5

Source: SSE (2009); SZSE (2009). Figures are for end of trading in 2008.

TABLE 7.2 Recent Shanghai and Shenzhen market index values

	SSE Composite Index	SZSE Component Index	Market Cap (trillion yuan)
End of fourth quarter, 2008	1,820.81	6,485.51	12.14
End of fourth quarter, 2007	5,261.56	17,700.62	32.71
End of second quarter, 2007	3,820.70	12,944.23	16.52
End of fourth quarter, 2006	2,675.47	6,647.14	10.75
Non-tradeable share reform (29 April 2005)	1,159.15	3,156.67	–

Source: Shanghai Stock Exchange (SSE) (2009) and Shenzhen Stock Exchange (SZSE) (2009).

The process of making all shares tradeable on the SSE and SZSE involved compensating current tradeable-share shareholders[4] with a package of extra shares, warrants and cash. In addition, all new initial offerings to the public would no longer include non-traded shares. Companies undergoing reform made proposals for compensation, and these had to be approved by two-thirds majority of both tradeable and non-tradeable shareholders (see Haveman *et al.* 2008 for an analysis of compensation packages and their similarity). One could take issue here with some claims (i.e. Howie and Walter 2006) since the requirement of compensation for transforming formerly untradeable shares into tradeable shares signals precisely that the market has *always* valued tradeable and non-tradeable shares of a company in assessing its value, but that this difference in ownership was now calculable and compensation negotiation was the process of equating between two prices.

The first batch of four companies underwent *gugai* on 8 May 2006. The city of Changsha's top machinery company, Sany Heavy Industrial (Shanghai stock code 600031), was the first company to successfully complete its reform (CSRC 2008a). According to the 'Measures for the Administration of the Share-Trading Reform of Listed Companies', issued by the CSRC on 4 September 2005, the waiting or 'lock-up' period for formerly non-traded shares to be traded is 12 months, after which former holders of more than 5 per cent of the total issue can only sell 5 per cent of their total amount in the subsequent twelve months and only 10 per cent of their total in the subsequent 24 months. Practically, this means that the majority of non-tradeable shares only become tradeable three years after the reform is agreed upon by shareholders of a specific company, allowing a significant delay in the actual effects of reform. The schedule for reform varies based on individual companies with Sany Heavy Industrial becoming the first reformed, fully traded company on 18 August 2008, according to public disclosures by the company. Looking in particular at the dates of the *gugai*, the entire market capitalisation became tradeable in the period from 2008 to 2010. According to one source (Li 2008), basing calculations on stock market values from 16 May 2008,[5] 3 trillion yuan in market cap will end trading restrictions in 2008, with 7 trillion yuan in 2009 and 8 trillion yuan in 2010 (with tradeable market cap of the two markets at the time being only 8 trillion yuan).

The share reform has created a new entity in China's stock markets, known in Chinese as *da-xiao fei*, which is translated here as 'large and small non-' (the China Securities Depository and Clearing Corporation [2009, 2010] translated the term as large and small R-share [restricted share] owners). Given the absence of any such entity in Western stock markets, the significance of the concept in China excuses the awkwardness of our translation. A 'large non-' (*dafei*) is a large-scale holder of non-traded shares; a 'small non-' (*xiaofei*) is a small-scale holder of non-traded shares. The term does not have precise definition, but typically large and small are defined as greater or less than 5 per cent of the total stock issue. As should be clear from the above discussion, *da-xiao fei* arise from state and legal person shares pre-IPO, as well as from directed share issues, capital increases and strategic sales. Former state shares are typically *dafei*, since the central or local state takes a minimum of a third of the original issue. Legal person shares, which range from other state-owned companies to institutions and even individuals, are more complex and vary based on the company. However, it is important to note that initial investment made by legal person, is often significantly less than the current value of the stock. The numbers are not publicly disclosed, but some estimates put the investment cost for *da-xiao fei* between 0 and 1 yuan per share, due to long-term dilution. Hence, given the opportunity to sell their shares on the secondary market, *da-xiao fei* have a clear incentive to do so if one-off profit-taking was the primary motive for share reform (Green 2003a, 2004; Howie and Walter 2006).

It is important to further clarify the distinction between *dafei* and *xiaofei*. In many cases, especially with listed companies that are of strategic interest to central and local governments, *dafei* are the state itself, or more precisely SOE controlled by the state. To maintain controlling rights to the company, central or local state agents will not sell their shares. By contrast, *xiaofei* are more numerous for any particular company, and not necessarily interested in exerting control of the company in the future (as their legal person interest or strategic interest may have changed with the course economic development). An analyst at Cinda Securities, Huang Xiangbin, points out that one of the main threats to China's stock markets are *xiaofei*, since they are more numerous, unpredictable and do not publicly disclose information (Ceng and Ma 2008). One should not make the mistake, however, of assuming *dafei* are a unified state shareholder while *xiaofei* are unpredictable civil institutions; in fact, many *xiaofei* are branches of listed or central/local state companies, while *dafei* are state shareholders in a state-owned enterprise that itself is owned by SASAC.[6] Thus, the numerous *xiaofei* of a particular stock do not necessarily share interests with other shareholders – state departments and other local governments – or state securities regulators.

This point can be illustrated by looking at some incidents involving *da-xiao fei* in early 2008. Given concerns about massive amounts of shares suddenly trading on the secondary market, the CSRC issued 'Guiding Opinions For Transfer of Listed Companies' Original Shares Released from Trading Restrictions' on 20 April 2008. In it, the CSRC required that sales of shares totalling over 1 per cent of a company's total issue be executed through the 'block trading system' of either exchange, in order to avoid putting excessive downward pressure on stock prices.

From 20 April to 7 May, three separate incidents of illegitimate sales occurred in violation of these *Opinions*: the Sichuan Hongda incident, the Guanfu Household incident and the Kai Kai Industrial incident. In each case, over 1 per cent of the total issue of the listed company was sold on the secondary market by other companies holding formerly non-traded shares (legal person shares). In fact, in the most astonishing example, 1.55 per cent of Kai Kai Industrial, a Shanghai company that produces clothing and medicine and is controlled by the Jing'an district branch of SASAC, was sold on the secondary market by the Shanghai retail branch of PetroChina, the largest oil company in the world, formerly the Bureau of Oil Industry of the central government and currently controlled by central government SASAC via China National Petroleum Company (CNPC; see Sudan Divestment 2007). One could argue that PetroChina-Shanghai, as a *xiaofei*, actively worked to contravene the policy of the CSRC and make money at the expense of or to destabilise the Jing'an SASAC. *Da-xiao fei* are a crucial concern for *gugai* and the now fully tradeable market cap of China's stock markets (Figure 7.2).

In 2007 and 2008, numerous articles were published in the *China Securities Journal* and other securities newspapers concerning *da-xiao fei* (e.g. Chen 2008; see Figure 7.2). They were also a topic of discussion and concern among many

FIGURE 7.2 *Da-xiao fei* and stock citizens. Tiger reads '*Da-xiao fei* reduce their holdings'; blue-shirted man is *jimin*, 'fund citizens'; red-shirted man is *gumin*, 'stock citizens'; and arrow reads 'the way up'.

Source: Drawing by Tang Zhishun of CNSPhoto; appeared in *China Securities Journal* on 23 August 2008.

individual traders, both in the trading rooms and online. Starting in 2010, the China Securities Depository and Clearing Corporation (2010, 2011) began publishing statistics on the number of *da-xiao fei* and the amount of sales of newly tradeable shares in 2009 and 2010. Indeed, the statistics reveal that while *dafei* only sold 5–6 per cent of their newly tradeable shares, *xiaofei* sold over 40 per cent of theirs. Some 29 billion shares were sold onto the secondary market by *xiaofei* by the end of 2010 (Ibid.). This amount reflects both the path dependency of China's stock markets over this period, and an alternative explanation of the dynamics of the market. In a time of alternating stock jubilation and austerity, the CSRC and major state shareholders of *their own* listed companies have been quite conservative in dumping shares on the market, dampening the effects of *gugai* in terms of reform of corporate governance. Despite *gugai*, many state-owned companies have retained absolute controlling interest (over 50 per cent of all shares) or relative controlling interest (less than 50 per cent, but over 20 per cent). But state-controlled *xiaofei* have ignored this tacit dictum to retain control, revealing that multiple levels of state control operate in quite distinct ways reflecting more an orientation to their own development that to a state-owned system of control or use of stock market to obtain one-off fiscal revenue (compare Wong and Yang 2009).

The consequences of *gugai* are far-reaching, and go beyond other factors, such as excess liquidity, sub-prime mortgage crisis, global economy, companies' re-issues of shares, tightening of monetary policy or Consumer Price Index (CPI) figure announcements, in explaining the meteoric rise and spiralling decline of China's markets. China's stock markets are structurally different from the West: both in their role as financing mechanisms and in terms of the owners of market capitalisation (Rooker 2008). Despite *gugai*, controlling interests in main central and local government enterprises remain in state hands. Yet the interests of state are varied between the centre and local levels, and also between controlling shareholders and legal persons, institutions or minority shareholders. The transformation wrought by *gugai* is still unfolding, as the last batch of non-tradeable shares became fully tradeable only in 2010. However, any notion of 'the state' as a unified actor, particularly in contrast to 'the people' (discussed in next section) is untenable in light of this discussion. What the above account overlooks, however, is the nature of the stock market and stock trading as a form of governance that generates spillovers in the form of urban integration and dispersal of economic knowledge. The widely quoted (Green 2004: 138–9; Hertz 1998: 92; CSRC 2008a: 161) dictum from Deng Xiaoping (1992) is often cited to show a debate over whether stock markets could be socialist, and that China would start to experiment with them.

> Securities, stock markets, are they good or evil? Are they dangerous or safe? Are they unique to capitalism or also applicable to socialism? Let's try and see. Let's try for one or two years; if it goes well, we can relax controls; if it goes badly, we can correct or close it. Even if we have to close it, we may do it quickly, or slowly, or partly. What are we afraid of? If we maintain this attitude, then we will not make big mistakes.

Yet Croll (2006) has pointed out, it was not socialism versus capitalism debate that enthralled people, but defining the 'Chinese characteristics' in the process of transformation.

Trading rooms

Another way to view the stock market is through the trading room. In this section, the research follows early examination of Shanghai's stock market in the first few years of its existence, in the early- and mid-1990s. Despite the brevity of the market's existence both Hertz (1994; 1998) and Gamble (1997) see much more in the stock market than the economical – or neoliberal – singular interpretation. The individual investors, either *gumin* stock citizens or *sanhu* scattered accounts, come to represent a collective nation of 'the people' in a struggle with the state that plays out beyond its reach in the market. Both Hertz and Gamble point to *chaogu*, the buying and selling of shares, and the stock market as referring back to huge social entities – the people, and their boundary expanding work in the stock market that reflects everyday life and the entire reform and change in individual lives, from social status to self-organisation, which has now been freed from direct state intervention. For these scholars, the trading room is a key battleground for the very notions of people as a collective that opposes the state.

The trading room has become a stereotype of individual investors in China. Television news reports, newspaper articles and photographs use images of elderly investors at the trading room to symbolise any news on trading or movement of the stock exchange index (i.e. background of red numbers on display boards for an increase; green numbers in the background for decrease). The trading rooms are the main setting for the two ethnographies on China's stock markets mentioned above (Hertz 1998; Gamble 1997). Depending on the size of the securities branch, trading rooms have between dozens and hundreds of investors who congregate in the general trading room right inside the entrance. All rooms are equipped with a large television or several-metre wide LCD screen, where stock exchange information is displayed (see Figure 7.3). In addition, there are multiple computer terminals running stock trading software, usually the *Qianlong* or *Dazhihui* software programs, allowing anyone with a magnetic stock account card registered with the securities company to make trades on the spot. Most larger rooms also provide seating, though investors who frequent the rooms also bring their own chairs so that they can sit in front of 'their' computer terminal throughout the trading day (see Figure 7.4). The lobbies of securities rooms in Shanghai are both general and local. In general, individuals start to congregate after 9:00 am when the doors to the company open. Volume and activity in the lobby picks up noticeably after 9:30 when the market opens. For some, the entire time in the lobby, from 9:30 to 11:30 and from 1:00 to 3:00, is spent poring over individual computer terminals, checking their shares, viewing big movers and making trades. For others, however, trading on the screens draws only occasional interest, as they engage in reading newspapers, napping, playing cards, sewing or having casual conversations. Yet these trading room lobbies are also intensely local places. The majority of daily visitors are from local neighbourhood. Having resided in the area for dozens of years – or a lifetime – the traders know each other intimately from the time when they were all working at *danwei* under the planned economy. While people of all ages populate the rooms, the regular visitors are majority elderly and are people who live in the immediate vicinity of the securities company.[7] In 2007, the average investor in a Shanghai securities company trading room[8] had between one and several hundred thousand renminbi in his/her stock account.

Securities companies' trading rooms are a ubiquitous feature of urban China today, particularly in Shanghai. There are hundreds spread across Shanghai in every district and major commercial area. According to the CSRC Securities Yearbook (2008), there are 106 licensed securities companies in China with 3,106 business branches and trading rooms. Shanghai Securities Exchange (SSE) (2008) and Shenzhen Securities Exchange (SZSE) (2009) list 3,098 and 3,167 securities business departments representing 109 and 124 securities companies as registered with them, respectively, throughout China in 2008. Yet these branches are found only in China's cities, particularly in cities of coastal regions, and especially in

FIGURE 7.3 View of a trading room in Pudong, Shanghai. The display board indicates this was a particulary auspicious day.

Source: Author's photograph.

FIGURE 7.4 Old Qiu's trading room terminal, claimed by him every day.
Source: Rooker © photograph.

Shanghai, Beijing, Zhejiang (Hangzhou, Ningbo, Jinhua, Wenzhou) and Guangdong (Shenzhen, Guangzhou, Shantou, Zhuhai). Thus while securities trading rooms are a nationwide phenomenon, they are highly differentiated in where they are located. In Shanghai, industry leaders such as Galaxy (Yinhe; with 24 branches in the city), CITIC (Zhongxin; with 12), and Guotai Jun'an (with 22) have concentrated the number of employees and branches there.[9] In addition to providing account opening, fund management and sector research activities, securities companies also provide 'trading rooms' (*yingye ting*), where individuals can monitor the market throughout the day and make trades. Trading rooms are divided into a lobby (*dating*) and middle account and large account rooms. The big room is distinguished from the middle account and large account rooms by its bigger size, lower proportion of computer terminals relative to the number of investors, louder noise and free accessibility by any investor with (or even without) an account.

Besides its generality as a description of playing the stock market, helpful in understanding the context of China's individual investors, *chaogu* also has an important antonym that was accentuated in 2008: *taozhu*, literally 'stuck in place'. To be *tao* (a passive that is usually written or spoken as *beitao* or 'being stuck') is to buy a stock at a specific price, below which the stock subsequently falls, making it impossible or undesirable to sell the stock. For example, one interviewee commented in March 2008: 'I was thinking that everyone would be eating Peking roast duck at the Olympics, so I bought Quanjude [the most famous roast duck restaurant in China]. Now look at it: I am stuck deep (*tao shen le*)' [because the price had fallen below his buy-in price]. Similar usage and examples could easily be multiplied, particularly the large number of people who bought shares of PetroChina when it listed (see below). The point, however, is that in 2008, when the Shanghai composite index fell 48 per cent and Shenzhen component index fell 47 per cent in the first six months of the year, almost all individual investors are *tao*. While they still *chao*, investors are *tao* to the extent that they now refer to themselves as 'long-term investors', though by force and not by choice. At a 2008 stock lecture held at a trading room in Qibao Township of Shanghai, the analyst implored those in attendance not to 'leave their shares of PetroChina to their grandchildren as inheritance' [since that might be how long it takes for them to become unstuck due to PetroChina's massive decline],[10] but instead to free their money by selling (literally called 'cutting off meat' [*gerou*] in Chinese). Visits to different Shanghai trading rooms in 2008 revealed a marked difference from 2007: conversations centred on how *tao* people were, and when they would buy more shares if only to become less *tao* – since buying more shares lowers the average price paid for the total number of shares. A decrease in trading volumes precludes defining *chaogu* solely as a form of quick buying and selling.

The concepts of *chao* and *tao*, stir-frying and being stuck, are central to under-standing China's individual investors in 2007 and 2008. Through observation in trading rooms and interviews, it is clear that these terms are general descriptions that apply differently in bull and bear markets. In the context of stock markets that are profoundly influenced by individual investors, their terms and behaviours are much more significant for the overall market than would be the case if institutional investors and mutual funds dominated the market. The fact that the majority of trading room participants are elderly or retired, and have been 'playing' the market for a decade or longer, lends proof to the contention that these behaviours, represented here by *chao* and *tao*, are not transitional or immature characteristics of a stock market in its infancy. Instead, they point to a different configuration of market players, the state, and the relationship between companies and their stocks. For Hertz and Gamble, the stock market is a form of petty capitalism embedded in the state's tributary mode of production (Gates 1996). This dynamic now represents not just players in the stock exchange but has implications as a symbolic defeat of the state in public life, something that represents new freedom and potential collective society outside state-run *danwei* cities. While not 'uniquely Chinese', since markets and especially stock markets grow out of the global econ-omy, China's stock markets engage and reconfigure the nature of securities markets in an important way, leading the way to a more general socialist market economy.

One view of constructing massive social – national – collectives out of the stock market is Anderson (1991), who draws attention to the simultaneous national experiences of people reading newspapers and using other forms of mass media together. Other scholars have extended Anderson's connection between specifically print media and electronic media to draw further connections between comm-unity and nation (e.g. Feenberg and Bakordjieva 2004). In China, hours are spent in the trading room, with the focus at the terminals on flipping through the screens of one of the software programs, checking candlestick charts, reading public disclosures and calculating price–earnings (P/E) ratios based on current price and reported earnings for the stocks that each investor follows. The red, green and gold numbers and lines on the realtime trading price and trading volume graphs are found on every single computer terminal in the trading room and freely downloaded by every individual stock account holder. This information becomes the most important form of mass media that mediates local communities and a nation of 'stock citizens'. While the securities market has become a national phenomenon, with trading taking place between strangers across the country and beyond – B-shares are purchasable by foreigners across the globe – it is engaged in through quite different social, economic and political factors. The salience of this connection is highlighted by the ubiquitous phrase oft-repeated in both print and television media: 'all citizens play the stock market' (*quanmin chaogu*). But again, the recognition and acceptance (or rejection) by investors themselves casts doubt, as with the neoliberal interpretation above, on its validity as an analytic frame.

The trading room and individual investors

A third view of the stock market, the one adopted here, combines the two previous perspectives, neoliberal and holistic, via the concept of a policy market. A seeming contradiction, the term combines policies made by a government that cannot hope to be followed even by its local bureaus, departments and SOE with the market as a normalising ideal – and China's imperfections and lack of market institutions. The individual investors (*sanhu*) in China's stock market draw on both spillovers from lives spent trading and investing with neoliberal market knowledge to *chao* and be *tao* through policy directives and processing of company information on a daily basis in the context of urban change for economic lives. As Hertz (1998: 93) has noted, 'Those who participate are "in", in sync with the times; those who refuse cannot keep pace with change. Among those who participate, there are those who succeed, those who fail, and those who succeed beyond everyone's wildest dreams'.

According to the China Securities Depository and Clearing Corporation Limited (www.chinaclear.cn), the number of A-share individual accounts increased to 110,060,600 on 28 December 2007 from 69,943,948 to 4 January 2006. Over 59 trading days in April, May and June 2007, an average of 237,591 new A-share accounts were opened each day. While part of the magnitude of these numbers is decreased when one accounts for the fact that a portion of the total number of accounts currently open are inactive or unused, and that a new account usually consists of both a Shanghai and Shenzhen A-share account (and hence each individual is counted twice), the numbers clearly show a unique phenomenon occurred in China.[11] Twenty million new investors entered A-share stock markets from 2006 to 2007 and 75,000 new investors entered per trading day in 2007. Even with a population of 1.3 billion, the ubiquity and pace of individual A-share account created is astonishing.

In contrast to the public lobbies, where anyone off the street can stroll in and check the performance of the two indices or monitor their own stocks' performance, are the middle account and particularly the big account rooms. The researchers observed several of these in multiple Shanghai trading rooms, but perhaps the most poignant example came from a big account trader in a Xujiahui trading room. In 2008, this big trader's room was upgraded, since he had multiple accounts that he administered on the behalf of others totalling several hundred million yuan. He invited one researcher in to view his new digs and talk stocks. The room was approximately ten square metres, at the centre of which was the trader's desk. On the desk were three monitors displaying stock information. In addition, he had a fish tank, mini-television and two extra computer terminals for guests (including the researcher) to check their own shares while sharing time with this trader. There was also a large Chinese character painting above his desk, as well as a selection of tea leaves and tea-making equipment. While this trading room stressed exclusivity and shielding from the 'heat and noise' (re'nao) of the lobby of 'scattered traders', this trader also maintained good relationships with other traders. On several occasions, the big trader took the researcher and several other scattered traders from the lobby out to lunch, and the scattered account traders also came to visit the big trader to discuss market trends, individual stocks or to borrow one of the multiple newspapers that the big trader had delivered every day.

Rooker (2008) has noted that while newly registered investors often choose to register both Shanghai and Shenzhen stock exchange accounts, in Shanghai, for example, there were some 19 million accounts – the same number as the entire population of Shanghai at the time – for *only* the Shanghai exchange, while accounts for the Shenzhen exchange in Shanghai numbered only 5 million. Shanghai added 30 million new individual investors in 2007, while Shenzhen added the same amount (SSE [2008], SZSE [2008c]). Rooker (2008) also shows that the percentage of tradeable (floating) market share in the hands of individuals in China and the UK is quite different – China individuals hold some 51 per cent of tradeable shares in 2007, while UK individuals held only 12.8 per cent. Hence stock trading in Shanghai, while a national or global affair, is strongly orientated to Shanghai, both its stock market and Shanghai companies' shares – a phenomenon Shanghai investors nonchalantly explain as Warren Buffett's (*Bafeite*) 'invest in what you know' strategy. This is an interesting reversal of Lozada's reading of Shanghaiese dislike for local Shanghai football teams. The policy market inverts cosmopolitanism and modernity: since individuals make a difference, they broker neoliberal market knowledge with the strength of individualism ('the People') to find particular routes to investment. This was evident in the hostility one researcher faced from some stock traders in the trading rooms. 'You have come to study our trading and take away the money of us Chinese old one hundred names', one irate middle-aged Shanghaiese trader said after a particularly poor day on the stock market. Yet the shared understandings and comprehension of the market are engaged reflexively in both the trading rooms and individual investment decisions made across the city.

The vocabulary of the trading room and online materials is another resource of the *sanhu*. Like other specialised locations for activity (see Rooker 2006 for a similar argument about Zhongguancun's electronics markets) there is a lexicalisation of practice (see Table 7.3). The most colourful and ethnographically interesting terms are *chao, tao* and *gerou*, and are also the most ubiquitous practices in stock trading, both online and in the trading room lobbies. One investor related a story about having to cut meat after a tip off from a friend did not pan out. She learned that in the short-term, listening to what contacts say must be integrated with an individual's decision-making. Other investors noted that you cannot just read things randomly

TABLE 7.3 Stock terms for *sanhu*

Classification	Chinese	Pinyin	English	Syntax
Types of investor	散户	*sanhu*	scattered account	noun
	中户	*zhonghu*	middle account	noun
	大户	*dahu*	big account	noun
	机构投资者	*jigou touzizhe*	institutional investor	noun
	个人投资者	*geren touzizhe*	individual investor	noun
	庄家	*zhuangjia*	dealer	noun
	老鼠仓	*laoshu cang*	rat hoarder', connected insider	noun
Investor action or situation	割肉	*gerou*	cut meat', take loss	action
	炒股	*chaogu*	stir fry stocks'	action
	买进	*maijin*	buy in	verb
	打新股	*da xingu*	invest in new stocks	action
	套, 套住,	*taolao*	imprisoned in	verb
	跑掉	*paodiao*	sell out	verb
Investor portfolio	满仓	*mancang*	full storehouse/portfolio	adjective
	清仓	*qingcang*	empty storehouse/portfolio	action
	半仓	*bancang*	half a storehouse/portfolio	adjective
Share	龙头	*longtou*	dragon head', top of an industry	adjective
groups/ types	ST股	*ST gu*	special treatment (ST) shares	noun
	认购权证	*rengou quanzheng*	call warrant	noun
	认沽权证	*rengu quanzheng*	put warrant	noun
	大盘	*dapan*	big board	noun
	小盘	*xiaopan*	small board	noun
	板块	*bankuai*	sector, industry, board	noun
Share/ company action	跳水	*tiaoshui*	dive	verb
	杀跌	*shadie*	fall treacherously	verb
	涨停	*zhangting*	rise to ceiling	verb
	跌停	*dieting*	drop to floor	verb
	停牌	*tingpai*	suspension of trading	verb
	粉红	*fenhong*	pay dividends	verb
	重组	*chongzu*	reorganisation	verb

off the internet, because posts are made by moles for *zhuangjia* dealers, trying to inflate (or deflate) a stock price. One Anhui native tried to leverage his hometown connections by using a rumour (*xiaoxi*); he too had to cut meat and noted the need to be cautious. But a QQ discussion involves people known personally to the investor, and so takes on a different tone in the processing of information, market knowledge and policy interpretation, although an individual still makes their own decision.

Across the trading rooms of Shanghai and urban areas throughout China, and for each individual trading online in offices and homes throughout China, they have in common the installation of a particular type of software. These are some of the paths for spillover of market knowledge, where individual investors take up investing to learn and research companies in their spare time. The dominant companies providing this software are Dazhihui and Qianlong. The software provides realtime information on every stock, treasury, bond and warrant in the market. In addition, it provides a wealth of information about each stock, accessed by pressing F10 on the keyboard.[12] It is a common orientation to this software and these categories of information that joins the 'stock citizens' into a common understanding of the market. But this is not sufficient, since this is a policy market. And so trading room investors and individuals access other official sources of information – in the nightly news programmes (particularly Shanghai television's *First Financial* news) that precedes the national news, in stock segments and sections of Internet portals and various newspapers. Individual investors share the knowledge that theirs is not insider information – and that part of what makes them *sanhu* is precisely this lack, an understanding widely shared.

When discussing why they invest, individual investors over and over again pointed to the economic fact that China's economy is growing at a rate of 10 per cent and investors have confidence in China's development and the stock market's ability to reflect it. With the Olympics and the World Expo, China – and its stock markets – will not encounter any strict downturn. At the same time, inflation was at 5–6 per cent or higher, while bank interest rates were at 3 per cent, and it made no sense to put money in the bank. Several interviewees had no savings whatso-ever. 'Invest or pay back the mortgage' were the two options for their money repeated by numerous interviewees. Somewhat contradictory was the oft-repeated phrasing that money in the securities market should be *xianqian* or 'spare money', not life guarantee money. *Xianqian* is contrasted both with money for parents' illness, child school money and emergency money, as well as money paid for mortgage since an apartment is real, long-term and lived in. The confidence in apartment prices was based on a reasoning that Shanghai is, perhaps more so even than China, a dynamic, growing city with high-rate growth of its economy and large numbers of people coming into it who want to buy housing.

One quite thoughtful investor from Shanxi noted the changes occurring in Shanghai and throughout China, specifically referencing the China Merchants Bank put warrant. 'I took classes to learn about specialised things. There was the [China Merchants] warrant incident a while back – many people got into that, and they had no idea what a warrant is…[That is] dangerous. [But] six years ago no one knew what CPI [Consumer Price Index, he uses the English acronym] was, but now everyone knows it. They are learning. Things are changing'. This is the spillover effect of 'all citizens playing the stock market'.

The 'warrant incident' and risk awareness

On 15 August 2007, a researcher visited Old Qiu, a friend at a Pudong securities company in the shadow of the Shanghai Stock Exchange itself. Old Qiu is a more of a loner than the typical *sanhu*, preferring to sit at his computer terminal all day interacting minimally with those around him. Partly, this stems from his relocation to Pudong from Puxi (western Shanghai) after his old *danwei* apartment was demolished, severing links with former co-workers. A stock citizen for over 10 years, Old Qiu has definite views about the direction of the market and particular stocks. His predictions, to the researchers anyway, are often, but not always correct. On this particular day, due to not having seen the researcher in two weeks, and due to a fortuitous event that was to make headlines in securities newspapers, he was particularly animated.

After trading began at 9: 30am, Old Qiu called attention to the warrants board on his terminal. 'Look at this', he said pointing at the China Merchants Bank

FIGURE 7.5 China Merchants Bank CMP1 put warrant trading on 15 August 2007

Source: Author's screen capture of Qianlong software display on 15 August 2007.

CMP1 put warrant (580997), 'it dropped yesterday and now it is going up like crazy' (see Figure 7.5). The Merchant Bank warrant had begun trading on 2 March 2006 and was to be exercised starting 27 August 2007. The exercise price of the 'put' (the price at which stocks underlying the warrant can nominally be sold by the warrant owner, and hence the price which the stock must fall below in order for the warrant to have intrinsic value[13]) was 5.45 yuan. As of 15 August, the trading price of China Merchants Bank stock (600036) was 36.26 yuan. Hence, for the CMP1 warrant to have intrinsic value, its underlying stock would have to drop over 30 yuan in two weeks – unlikely, given the bull market in China's stock markets. The closing price of the CMP1 warrant on 14 August was 0.146 yuan, and it almost certainly would be worth zero at the close of trading on 24 August. That is, as a warrant rather than a stock, there was no underlying company to which investors could cling to in the hopes that price would rise again later. At 3:01pm on 24 August, the warrant would be 'worthless paper'.

'I told her [indicating a female companion behind him] to buy this [warrant] yesterday because I knew it would go up. I bought at 0.10 yuan and I will sell when it reached 0.20 yuan', my friend said. By 9:45, he had sold his warrants. But CMP1 continued upward. 'I can't believe it. I shouldn't have sold', he said by 10am. The warrant had already increased by 80 per cent to over 0.25 yuan. Throughout the rest of the day, we watched the price of the warrant skyrocket. By the close of trading at 3:00, it had increased in value by over 242 per cent while increasing 282 per cent at one point. At three times during the day, the SSE suspended trading for 15 minutes for excessive volatility. At the time, Old Qiu noted, 'It is useless. All that will do is drive up the price even more'. He was right, as the price took steep increases after the 10 minutes of suspension. CMP1 closed on August 15 at a price of 0.50 yuan. On 16 August, CMP1 hit a high of 0.958 yuan. Six trading days later, the CMP1 warrant ended trading at a price of 0.002 yuan, with over 20 million shares waiting to be traded at 0.001 yuan.

From a neoclassical perspective, Old Qiu and the thousands of others speculating on the tail end of an expiring put warrant was unquestionably irrational. The 'worthless pieces of paper' traded back and forth, increased in price by hundreds of per cent. Attempts by the Shanghai Securities Exchange to stop or pause trading only drove the warrant to new heights. It is somewhat ironic that the Old Qiu refers to *bosha* ('greater fool') theory related to John Maynard Keynes (*Kaiensi*) in this context. The idea was that while buying expiring put warrants or highly valued stocks might be investing money in securities that are too expensive, he knew that others were looking at the warrant with great excitement as well, which meant that there were greater fools willing to buy. Intervention by the SSE and risk awareness campaigns by securities companies and banks (see Figure 7.6) only served to underscore the fact that this was an opportunity to be had.

Postings related to risk awareness spread throughout Shanghai, stock media and the Internet in 2007 and 2008. Securities companies, banks selling funds, software programs and investment articles endlessly repeated the phrase 'The stock market has risk; invest with caution' (*gushi you fengxian touzi xu jinshen*). But this phenomenon was interpreted not as a neoclassical lesson on the realities of stock investment, since it was part and parcel of stories of riches made, of dormant accounts of those who suddenly realised they had become rich, by investors in the stock market. There was also a confidence in policy to shield individuals from extreme losses in the market, that the Olympics, the World Expo or a national Communist Party even would prevent the market from falling too far too fast.

Finally, the experience with PetroChina shares some characteristics with Lozada's (2006) presentation of views of the China national football time by individuals in Shanghai. While there is passion for local shares and engagement and rigour that supporting them entails, national champions (both sports teams and companies picked to be winners) are viewed with disappointment – a fact echoed by Old Chen in his remarks on the old, dilapidated boats of ICBC and BoC at the beginning of this chapter. When PetroChina premiered on the secondary market after its initial public offering on November 5, 2007, it started trading at 48.60 yuan, an increase of 191 per cent on its first day. One Xujiahui investor who had 'won' the IPO lottery for PetroChina brought a carton of cigarettes to the trading room to celebrate. PetroChina shares subsequently declined 35 per cent in the first month, and fell to under 20 yuan

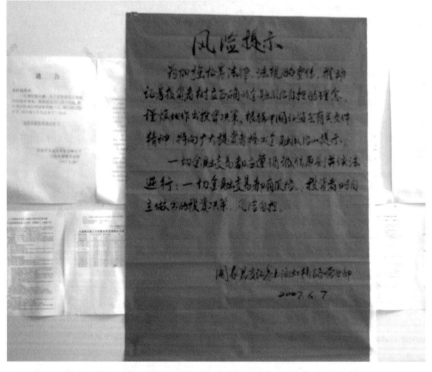

FIGURE 7.6 Risk-awareness campaign at the trading room. A 'red character poster' put up in summer 2007, advising investors to be aware of risk when investing the stock market.

Source: Rooker © photograph.

in March 2008 and to 10 yuan by the end of 2008. This is an example of how *sanhu* read the policy market: Old Chen prefers small capitalisation shares to large capitalisation shares not only because there are more opportunities to make money, but because of an orientation to SOEs and the nation-state. Others prefer to tie their fortunes to knowledge of CPI and its almost double-digit increases in 2007 and 2008 – that money in the bank is losing value – and the national economy, but to their peril. The well-known economic facts about Shanghai, that it is part of high-growth littoral China, is an area of high government investment, and is part of the Yangzi River Delta, provides investors with certainty that underlies the risks on the stock market. One trading room investor commented one way others look at the market is that when the market goes 'down 100,000 – "oh, there goes my Santana"; down 200,000 – "oh, there goes my Passat" '. Hence the stock market provides risks but allows access to the high-speed growth and neoliberal certainties that frame economic fundamentals underpinning the market. It is the policy nature of the stock market that converts these 'truths' into only a part of the overall picture.

The spillover of trading from the trading room is not simply a fever or fad where, temporarily, everyone plays the stock market. Instead, what research on the trading room and individual investors shows is that the images, economic knowledge, government policy intervention, software and candlestick chart modelling and even the 'play' of the stock market have enthralled the city, and thus gained a momentum. The *sanhu* represent the people in a struggle with the state and large, corporate shareholders such as *xiaofei*, but this is the conceptualisation that floats around the city, informing rather than determining investors' *chao* and *tao*. Awareness of themselves as *sanhu*, engagement with neoliberal market models and overarching assumptions that government will intervene in the market through policy, provide confidence that extreme movements in the market will not occur. But the policy market cannot be regulated thus also fleshing out the regimes of risk and uncertainty through individual investors engagement with the stock market.

Stock market significance

This chapter has examined *gugai*, the reform of the split-share system, from three perspectives: neoliberal, holistic and spillover/urban integration. *Gugai* is undoubtedly a transformational moment in the 20-year history of China's stock exchanges, and will continue to influence market direction. While all shares are now 'tradeable', their owners differ significantly, along the lines outlined above: between the state and its variegated local representatives, companies and regulatory bodies, the business interests of companies whose shares are traded and who invest in shares alongside everyone else and the *sanhu* individual investors. These distinctions are important not for their clarification of who is *really* behind the action in the market, nor for measuring the distance between China's stock 'market' and properly functioning capital markets. They are important because they have spilled out of the trading room and overdetermine individual investor behaviour to form part of urban contexts, particularly as investors act with these concepts in mind.

There are structural differences between China's stock markets and those familiar in the West. In addition to A- and B-shares, different types of ownership and investment objectives, China's stock markets play a different role as a financing mechanism for China's companies. The state, in the form of SASAC, local state governments or branches of SOE, continue to hold the majority of shares and market capitalisation, despite *gugai*, especially in companies deemed strategically important to China's economy. If one views central, local and state-owned enterprise interests as unified, China's stock market remains firmly the domain of the state. However, decentralisation of the central state, and pressure for non-strategic SOE to compete, as well as local states competing for their own interests, has blurred the unity of a 'state' in China.

Individual investors are another main pillar of China's stock markets. Despite the rapid rise in the number of new investors in the stock markets, they are not 'immature', blindly speculating on stocks without thought or care. Investors read the larger policy environment through skills honed by years of experience, and *chao* and *tao* through the political changes that affect the direction of the market more than any macro-economic or individual company results possibly could. Slipping out of conventional models, either of investor psychology or of shareholders, individual investors require a rethinking of the concepts of rationality, uncertainty and market maturity.

The trading room and stock market have overflowed their boundaries, in the sense that traders are now found throughout the city and cities of China. Rooker (2008) pointed out that there were some 18 million share accounts in Shanghai in mid-2008, equivalent to the population of the entire city, just for the Shanghai exchange. Not that every man, woman and child has opened an account, but that Shanghai is a centre for trading, even for those outside Shanghai. Trading long ago burst out of trading room – with QQ networks, websites and blogs facilitating this movement, and individuals such as 'Big Brother Role Model 777'.[14] Much like Hertz (1998) in her important study, the stock citizens of the trading room wanted to find an individual or *zhuangjia* lurking behind the manipulation of share prices. There was precedence for this. One individual was discovered to have manipulated share price using over 1,500 share accounts (Zhang 2006). Yet the nature of the policy market makes indefinite any certainty about these dubious individuals hiding behind stock price movements – as is true for the unity of the *sanhu* for Hertz (1998) and Gamble (1997).

Finally, the *da-xiao fei* are crucial to the markets in 2008, and will continue to wield influence as market capitalization is now fully tradeable. While *dafei* in the form of the state branch or organ that holds controlling interest of a company does not pose significant risk of flooding the market with shares, its counterpart, *xiaofei*, certainly does. Whether the 'small non-' are state-owned or not is not the point: examples point to multiple parts of the state working at odds with each other. Hence the further contradiction that while China's stock markets are policy-driven, they remain highly difficult for the state to regulate. This requires a further rethinking of models of risk and uncertainty. The legacy and current configuration of China's stock markets is not a blip on the transition to a Western, or global, model, but a new way of structuring securities finance in the cities of China.

8

KNOWING BUT NOT DOING

The financial sector in China and institutional reform

This chapter is a study of the development of a particular sector of the Chinese financial industries, namely markets for over-the-counter (OTC) derivatives, focusing especially on FX markets. OTC is a term used in juxtaposition to exchange traded. That is to say that OTC derivatives are generally tailor-made products that for the same reason are not traded (as standardised products) on market exchanges but instead transacted in interbank markets, through negotiations between parties, meaning either two banks or a bank and a client. There is hence no open exchange and no market maker involved in such transactions. Derivatives markets generally form arguably one of the most knowledge- and technology-intensive sectors in the financial industry as they rely heavily on pricing models and information and communication technology (ICT).

We have all heard stories from developing countries about, for example, state-of-the-art hospital equipment being donated to an area where there was no stable electricity supply, which made the equipment useless. Without wanting to stretch that analogy too far (China's economy and financial markets have developed much too far to do that), something similar applies to the topic of this chapter. We are here going to study the use of sophisticated financial know-how – namely the pricing models used for creating and valuing derivatives – in a setting which does not fulfil most of the requirements for use of that same know-how. Unlike the example with hospital equipment, the requirements here have little to do with physical infrastructure, but with cultural, political and institutional infrastructure, so the question is not whether derivatives as a technology can function or not in a material sense. Nevertheless, there is still a very substantial conflict between the technology and the environment in which the technology is being implemented as derivatives pricing models, for example, presuppose what in crude terms could be called a liberalised financial market. However, the Chinese markets do not fully fulfil such criteria. This means that derivatives provide a glimpse into the complexities and inherent conflicts of Chinese economic development and global integration. Several of the conflicts, we shall see, hinge on different notions and manifestations of risk.

Derivatives are financial instruments that make it possible to hedge against risks. Similar to insurance policies, derivative contracts enable investors to insure against price reductions of an asset. Unlike insurance policies, it should be added, derivative contracts can be purchased for purely speculative purposes also, that is without owning the underlying asset. FX derivatives are the most common OTC derivatives in China. FX derivatives provide a fixed future price of a foreign currency, which creates an insurance against price increases of that foreign currency. FX derivatives, like all derivatives, are commonly valued using pricing models based on specific probabilistic conceptions of risk: probabilistic knowledge is used to calculate the likely volatility of the underlying asset, which is a crucial metric for quantifying the risk and therefore price. Without pricing models, it would in principle be anybody's guess what a derivative is worth, and that uncertainty would, at least in theory, cripple the market for such contracts. But the models as mentioned rest on a series of assumptions. If the assumptions framing these risks are different from the reality of the markets – for example if the volatility of an asset is limited due to state intervention or if there are limited arbitrage possibilities – then ultimately the derivatives themselves are in conflict with the financial market of which they are part.

The derivatives pricing models have by and large been developed in the West and the assumptions of the models very much reflect that. In relation to China, this creates an interesting friction between market assumptions and market reality because the market conditions in China go against several main assumptions of pricing models. Once more stretching things (this time more than) a bit, creating a derivatives industry in China based on such models is thus equivalent to selling fire insurance policies in a country where it rains all the time, all year round, and where, there, therefore are severe flooding risks but never a fire. Even accepting this stretched analogy, there is a feature of derivative pricing models that may explain why they are being implemented even in settings where they have little applicability at the outset. The reason is that derivative pricing models may be performative (MacKenzie and Millo 2003). This is to say that in contrast to fire insurance in an often flooded country, that cannot change the weather, these technologies may over the course of time come to shape the financial markets so that the reality of the market will approximate the assumptions of the model (and/or prices will approximate the forecast of the models). This would mean that pricing models can be used as drivers of reforms, even drivers that could be used by the Chinese authorities. But as could be seen in the introduction of this book, we are somewhat sceptical of performativity as a sole explanation of the creation of derivative markets in China. It should also be added that unlike fire insurance in an often-flooded country, there is of course a real demand for FX derivatives because of global trade.

This chapter is concerned with a 'sophisticated' financial technology and the attempts to implement this technology in China, which by the standards of the same technology is an 'imperfect', 'inefficient' or 'emerging' market. Our scepticism regarding these somewhat derogatory terms is clear. Moreover, the financial crisis, which unfolded during the research period, has rammed home the fact that these sophisticated financial products are not risk free. Not surprisingly, several of the interviewees would refer to the crisis as proof that the Chinese markets were not that backward after all. Nevertheless, as the viewpoint of the whole chapter is that of Western models being applied to China, we will in this chapter use terms such as imperfect, inefficient, etc., without tiring the reader with inverted commas every times these terms are used. Also the title of the chapter may be interpreted as slightly derogatory as possessing knowledge normally would imply that there is little excuse for not acting accordingly. But the point here is that we are encountering an example of a gradual and rather detached use of economic theories and models for the development of the Chinese economy, meaning that the economic theories are non-performative (see introduction) and that the Chinese economic and political project in China will retain distinctive features. Our main concern here is the clash between, on the one side, theoretical assumptions developed in the West and, on the other, attempts to use models and other tools derived from these theories in China.

China's financial institutions

Institutional economics would hold that the success of an economy depends on a strong and transparent legal and regulatory framework, which can create the best possible conditions for enterprises and markets. The Chinese success with massive growth over a long number of years but with serious institutional voids, however, goes against this thesis (Allen *et al.* 2005b; Faure 2006; Walder 1995). As we saw in Chapter Two, this has led to theoretical discussions on whether China's development should be seen as an emerging economy on a path towards capitalist economic institutions in a Western sense – with many authors arguing that this is not the case (e.g. Khanna 2008; Wank 2001). The Chinese government has not fully privatised the economy, the legal framework is (although developing) still relatively weak and poorly enforced and the financial institutions – which are the topic of this chapter – are still under-developed. The literature that identifies the weak institutional architecture of the Chinese economy and the uncertainties this creates for economic actors often also points to some of the mechanisms, which compensate for these weaknesses or that even turn them into a competitive edge. We saw in Chapter Two that these networks connect industrial entrepreneurs with state officials (Eng 1999; Walder 1995; White 2000), with business partners, suppliers and customers (Chen and Chen 2004; Eng 1999; Huang 2008; Keister 2001; Redding and Witt 2007; White 2000; Zhou *et al.* 2003) and with investors, which forms a shadow financial system (Allen *et al.* 2005a; Tsai 2004). It has also been mentioned earlier that while China's economy largely remains state-run, it is also decentralised, with local government branches competing fiercely. This creates competitiveness and efficiency (Walder 1995).

But while the Chinese markets possess many distinct characteristics, they are also developing and integrating into the global economy and global governance regimes. What will change as markets develop and become integrated in global markets? Are the Chinese markets and their institutions losing their characteristics? It is an indisputable fact that global integration and transnational knowledge transfers are occurring, not least between China and the US (Jongsthapongpanth and Bagchi-Sen 2007), and that foreign companies have exerted great influence on Chinese industries. FDI has, by both the Chinese government that has encouraged it and by scholars who have observed it, been seen as instrumental in transferring knowledge and technology to China and as an alternative way of raising capital – which has been seen as necessary due to the Chinese financial and banking system (Havryl-chyk and Poncet 2007). But as the literature on liability of foreignness and knowledge transfer shows (e.g. Xu and Shenkar 2002; Zaheer 1995), local knowledge and connections are important factors that may hinder performance in unknown markets and make it difficult for multinational firms to transfer knowledge from one country to another as generic knowledge is insufficient. It is therefore no surprise that an often seen strategy for foreign companies has been to invest or form ventures with Chinese companies with strong ties to Chinese government (Lu and Ma 2008). This indicates that global integration is far from a seamless process.

The Chinese financial markets are being developed with some speed but certainly also a great deal of caution on the side of the Chinese authorities. The primary financial markets (equity and bonds) have still not been fully developed, only partially liberalised and only partially globally integrated. As we shall see examples of later, political risks are under these circumstances important factors, simply due to the political control over financial and economic matters. Derivatives are, however, based on financial (i.e. probabilistic) knowledge of market risk, not political ditto, which as mentioned above raises questions about the applicability of derivatives, or to be more precise the expertise (such as pricing models) on which derivatives are based, to the Chinese setting. The Chinese risk environment is radically different from what is assumed by the financial theories on which derivatives models are based.

While proceeding with caution, since initiating economic reforms in the early 1980s China has developed and expanded their financial markets (Bryan *et al.* 2008; Hsio 2009; Neftci and Ménager-Xu 2007). There are at the end of first quarter of 2012 more than 1900 companies listed on the stock exchanges in Shanghai and Shenzhen. There have since the early 1990s been sizeable commodity futures exchanges in Shanghai, Dalian and Zhengzhou. There are treasury bond and FX markets. Interbank or OTC derivatives markets of some size in various structured products have existed since regulatory reforms from 2005 to 2006. China has since 2005 had a relatively liquid FX forwards and since 2006 also a FX swap exchange market. In addition to FX forwards and swaps, the following types are being traded: RMB/FX currency swaps; interest rate swaps; interest rate for-wards; bond forwards; and asset-backed securities. Table 1 shows the growth of FX markets in China and their percentage of world turnover. As is the case in many other emerging markets, FX derivatives markets are the largest OTC markets in China. However, new guidelines from the China Banking Regulatory Commission issued in 2010 have opened up for development of new derivatives products. This new regulation is seen as a significant move allowing the derivatives industry to grow. The expansion of FX derivatives, it must be noted, is very much a function of demand and not just government policy. Reflecting the same demand, FX derivatives trading in Hong Kong has also expanded in the same period. Hong Kong (though hardly in itself an emerging market) is the location of more than 30 per cent of all emerging markets FX derivatives trading (Mihaljek and Packer 2010). Clearly, Hong Kong – and by the way also Singapore – benefit from having both the know-how and the regulatory framework for trading of such products.

TABLE 8.1 Turnover Chinese foreign exchange market

1995	*1995*	*1998*	*1998*	*2001*	*2001*
Amount (billion USD)	Per cent of world trade	Amount (billion USD)	Per cent of world trade	Amount (billion USD)	Per cent of world trade
–	–	0.2	0.0	0	0.0

2004	*2004*	*2007*	*2007*	*2010*	*2010*
Amount (billion USD)	Per cent of world trade	Amount (billion USD)	Per cent of world trade	Amount (billion USD)	Per cent of world trade
0.6	0.0	9.3	0.2	19.8	0.4

Source: Bank for International Settlements Triennial Central Bank Survey 2010.

All of the FX derivatives are traded at the China Foreign Exchange Trade System (CFETS). Foreign banks are allowed to enter the CFETS interbank markets under the Qualified Foreign Institutional Investor (QFII) scheme. The main regulatory body is the China Banking Regulatory Commission (CBRC).

Remarks on data

This chapter is based on 40 semi-structured interviews of which 31 have been transcribed and coded. The research in financial markets was originally guided by an interest in risk cultures, hoping to capture the main characteristics of the risk cultures of Chinese financial markets and participants. As the research developed, this theme became the general background on which more specific questions were formulated. These included: the import of know-how; the impact of generic expertise and conflict between this and local (risk) cultures; the knowledge, assumptions and heuristics that traders use to interpret information and which guide their practices. During the course of the research, the interviews became less structured.

210 Knowing but not doing

The aim of the qualitative interview research conducted was to collect actors' interpretations of knowledge and information, and through this develop an understanding of how actors attribute meaning to knowledge and information (Kvale 1996). All such accounts are necessarily subjective (although objective facts about things such as regulation also were obtained from the interviews), but through analysis that draws on theory, basic premises underpinning the accounts can be gleaned. Hence the analysis does not shy away from using theories to analyse the data (see Silverman [1993: 4] for a support of such an approach). In the present case, the theories largely are of how agents adjust knowledge to different contexts and diverging aims and outcomes and how agents' actions in turn are adjusted by knowledge. This theoretical focus is due to the fact that existing research clearly indicates that organisational practices in finance have been markedly shaped by knowledge (pricing models) and theories about risk. Hence, it seems pertinent to study in detail how agents give account of their use of this knowledge and the organisations and markets in which they operate. The theoretical notion of performativity was therefore the logical starting point for the analysis. Analysis subsequently turns to other theories for further explanatory support.

Access to market participants was a major challenge. Interviewees were found primarily through a snowballing process, although at different junctions interviewees without any connection to previous interviewees were also found. Most were interviewed only once, but eight persons were interviewed twice within an interval of nine to 14 months. Some of the first contacts were to FX traders, and FX derivative markets henceforth became the primary focus of investigation. The interviews were conducted in the period 2006–9 – a period in which the markets went from bullish to bearish and the world economy suffered from the collapse of Lehmann and Bear Stearns. Interviews reflect these changes, but as the focus was on Chinese domestic markets and their particularities, the global turmoil cast less of a shadow than perhaps could be expected.

How Chinese financial derivatives markets are different

The Chinese financial markets are markets where state regulation is heavy-handed yet opaque. The markets also suffer from lack of reliable corporate financial information, insider trading and first-day speculations in just-listed companies as there is an excess of capital and few promising investment opportunities. The regulation, for example, means that trading on stock markets may be suspended if there is high volatility, a measure among other things intended to curb first-day speculation. Short selling has until recently been banned. Chinese markets also have a high proportion of retail investors who display a fundamental lack of knowledge about market fundamentals, including knowledge of derivatives (Rooker 2008 and Chapter Seven). As several interviewed traders made clear, irrational behaviour is, however, not only a trait of retail investors but also lower-rung Chinese banks and other institutional investors.

The most fundamental trait of Chinese financial markets, which we argue resonates with the more general description of the Chinese economy, is that the state is both the most important gatekeeper and the greatest source of uncertainty; most important source of certainty as well as uncertainty. The regulation of the markets, for example, means protection for Chinese banks because Chinese regulators, to quote an official at a large European country's national financial regulation authority that we interviewed, 'are reluctant to let market risks reign'. On the flip side, sudden government changes in economic and monetary policies and arbitrary interventions are great sources of uncertainty. The interviewed traders generally point to the government as the controlling agent. The dominant market participants are, or are seen as being, under government control and hence the prices they offer are, or are seen to be, reflections of government policies and/or inside information. We should note that it does not matter if this in fact really is true. There will in any case be a strong incentive for imitation for the other, smaller market participants who otherwise risk either taking positions, which will be unprofitable because planned government initiatives will work against them or being punished by the dominant market participants who can squeeze third party market makers through their dominant position.

Interviewee: They will think that...it is the practice, no, I just only say the convention, that when Bank of China or the Agricultural Bank...they are all government controlled. We view that when some new policy comes out, they will get instructions first. So that is why all the other market makers will follow. Because they will think that their [the big four] behaviour may instruct something – they [the smaller market makers] just don't want to miss something, new policy or something.

Such forms of imitation, born by hierarchies of the markets participants where some have, or are perceived to have, more control or privileged access to information, are uncertainty reductions. Although scholars have used network analysis to show how social networks of various sorts are constituted in virtually all markets, it is generally the finding that social networks play a more substantial role in Chinese markets than most places elsewhere. And more importantly, there are comparably stronger ties, through which crucial information flows, between market participants and government.

This creates a different perception of risk among Chinese market participants. The following lengthy quotation by a native Chinese, American-trained, investment banker who now has taken up an academic career, sums it up:

Interviewee: Risk in Western institutions, they perceive it as being able to model: statistics, probability. Uncertainty is something you don't really know. There's no model behind it. Here, risk actually is more like uncertainty in the Western mind. There's no model to be made.

> The most developed market [...] in China is the interbank money market. Because there, there is a safe volume and also the participants are institutions and they're considered more rational than individuals. So it's considered to be closer to the market in the Western sense. However, in that market the players are very few compared to the market in the Europe or the US. There [in the West], there are a lot of different features and it's relatively competitive. In China, the money market consists of mainly the banks; they have the majority of the trading volume. So it's more important to know who is trading. So all the traders know each other, they know their characteristics, traditions, and because there are just a few main players. And also the market event, the driving force will change the risk. Mainly the regulations change rather than the market. So that's how people perceive risk in China. The biggest risk is government policies, that for some people is predictable for other people is totally out of the...because if you know the government...people close to the...er...there's a lot of inside trading.

The quotation both assumes that the market price developments are not truly random and hence cannot be modelled – which again means that there is more uncertainty than risk – as well as it implies that networks and social capital are more important in such a market.

It is into this financial system that financial knowledge and technologies are being transferred. Foreign banks who act as market participants, for example, actively disseminate knowledge about pricing models and structured products to clients and market participants (interview data). Traders from foreign banks also state that they take positions on the OTC markets that are not profitable in order to introduce customers to structured products with the hope of in time making these customers interested in or dependent on this expertise. On the side of financial authorities, initiatives such as the creation of the Shanghai Interbank Offered Rate (SHIBOR) index or the decision to allow short selling show a willingness to change the system to increase transparency and liquidity. And for Chinese companies, international trade creates a strong incentive to adapt new risk-management procedures and a need to be able to hedge through the use of FX derivatives (see also above). For this and other reasons, there is a massive influx of financial technologies and knowledge. Yet, at the same time, it is abundantly clear that the Chinese financial system remains so structured that an adaption to a generic 'Western' style of system is not immediately foreseeable. This means that the generic financial expertise is not directly applicable in the Chinese context. For example, the pricing model output does not correlate with the real market prices. As one trader observes, much of this is related to the above-mentioned fact that the few market makers exert a considerable degree of control over the market:

Interviewee: The market expectation accounts for the most…often the pricing mechanism in this market. And I think that […] it's also a market maker driven system in the on-shore market. We [the bank interviewee is working for] are not the market makers but anytime we want to do a forward or swap we are going into the market to see the price quoted by the market makers. But if you calculate it in a formula that you use for other currencies, you can't…it does not work. You can't get the price that you see on the screen from that market. What is the market expectation is the market forecast of the appreciation against the dollar. Another is based on the different liquidity status of each market maker. In RMB swaps there's no correct yield curve because the interest rate market hasn't been liberalised. The PBC still controls the rates for the client and lending. But for interbank there are no restrictions because the interbank price will be decided by the real supply and demand, which means that we have different markets, interbank, funding market, treasury… That is why it's difficult to get a correct and objective…market level.

Note that the 'market expectation' really is a political forecast. It is premised on assumptions about the monetary policy of the Chinese government. This in turn raises questions about the use and function of financial know-how. This question is all the more pertinent given the fact that according to the quotation earlier there is little belief in risk (formal knowledge) and much emphasis on (especially political) uncertainty.

Does formal knowledge affect organisations and institutions?

In the realm of markets and economics, scholars using Actor Network Theory (ANT) have demonstrated the tremendous impact of financial and economic knowledge and technology. ANT not only entails a focus on objects and technologies in the material world, it also reverses the causal connection between object (or technology, or knowledge) and society. Rather than seeing, say, a new technology as being a product of the social, ANT would investigate what kind of social and economic worlds are being created (or at least enabled) by such a technology. This reversal of cause and effect is accentuated in the notion of performativity (Callon 1998, 1999), which has been used successfully in studies of the creation of derivatives markets in the US in the 1970s by Donald MacKenzie and others (MacKenzie 2003, 2004; MacKenzie and Millo 2003). Central to Mackenzie's study of derivatives is the proposition that the Black-Scholes options pricing model, and its extensions, were pivotal in constructing derivatives markets because they create '*agencement*'. *Agencement* is part complexity reduction, part capacity for action, that is, it offers a 'handle' on the markets on which traders can peg their beliefs and actions. Crudely speaking, the function of the models is not that the prices they generate are true, but rather that they reduce uncertainty for market participants.

The models make option prices calculable in an objective and 'certain' manner. Crucially, these prices are not mere social constructions, because when the majority of the market participants subsequently use the models, the market value will come to approximate the theoretical value based on the models. Hence the strength of performative knowledge is that it produces verisimilitude; it produces a correlation between model output and market price. Callon's, and even more markedly, Mackenzie's (2006) definitions of performativity hinge on the ability of knowledge and utterances to impact on the world and produce verisimilitude. The reason for verisimilitude is that more and more traders use the models and hence behave as the models prescribe (although negative performativity may also happen if all slavishly follow the models prescriptions [MacKenzie 2003]). Cause becomes effect and vice versa. The performative power is ultimately a function of belief (Svetlova and Arnoldi 2011): if all market participants believe in the models and act based on this belief, prices will start to approximate the models' output. Mackenzie, however, notes that in the US in recent years the correlation between model and market has decreased as for example the volatility skew on put options means the market no longer follows the Black-Scholes model (MacKenzie and Millo 2003). Yet, MacKenzie argues, in the creation of modern derivative markets, the performative power of Black-Scholes and the model's extensions were absolutely crucial.

Even though there may not ever have been a full correlation between theoretical and market price, there is little doubt that pricing models did boost significantly the derivatives markets in the US and later in Europe because a correlation was quickly established (Braddock 1997: V). Among Chinese market participants there is general agreement that pricing models for derivatives, such as those derived from Black-Scholes' options pricing model, or based on Monte Carlo models, do not really work in China. They simply cannot be applied to a setting with imperfect markets as described above. And of course, because performativity is by and large a function of practitioners' belief in the model, if this is the shared (lack of) belief of the markets, then the performativity thesis itself stipulates that no performativity will occur.

It is in this regard striking that relatively little work has been carried out to develop new models that may provide a better fit or, to make the reverse connection, induce more belief. The big international investments banks as well as the big four Chinese banks do employ (Chinese) quants (a term used to describe people with mathematical and economic expertise whose job it is to develop models) who are assigned the task of adapting the models in the best possible way. But no serious breakthrough has been made and all interviewees questioned on this matter make no secret of the fact that no intensive efforts are being made. One interviewed high-ranking manager of a foreign investment bank stated that employing young Chinese quants was a small expense paid with no real expectation of results.

It is worth noting that Mackenzie at several instances shows how the models are not simply scripts, which are slavishly enacted by markets participants – the notion of *agencement* is more sophisticated than that. The models are held to provide a series of profound insights into the workings of derivatives. One such insight mentioned by Mackenzie is a relatively simple but also fundamental one, namely that derivatives trading is trading of volatility (MacKenzie and Millo 2003: 125). MacKenzie's discussion of the volatility skew also gives an indication (which however, could be developed much further) that while the models may no longer correlate with real market prices, the discrepancy has itself become a metric with which traders gauge the market. However, the crucial factor is that such a metric cannot be performative in the strong Barnesian sense used by Mackenzie (2006). Again, we may explain that with reference to belief. If the model output or rather the discrepancy between real price and the model's output becomes a heuristic tool, a way of interpreting the market, it still plays a role in the trader's decision-making. But it is no longer a basis for uncompromising belief.

Echoing this, one interviewee argued that the function of the models in China is to provide a benchmark of discrepancy. The real measure is hence not the model output but the discrepancy between model output and market prices. In a similar vein, another trader in the FX option market told us that his trading desk used both mark-to-market and mark-to-model techniques 'as an experiment, but not as basis for taking positions', the implication being that the objective was to learn about the market. Such statements indicate that the role of financial know-how is less direct and powerful than concepts such as performativity and *agencement* could lead one to believe. Financial know-how is not used during the development of the Chinese markets to perform or 'act out' trading. It does not produce verisimilitude.

Transfer of non-performative knowledge

If financial models and other forms of expertise do not have any performative, or transformative, power when applied to the institutional setting of China, then why is this knowledge transferred and applied at all? The transfer is a marker of the expansion of the Chinese financial markets and the adoption of new trading and hedging activities among Chinese banks and institutional investors; of an adaptation to a new global regulatory regime epitomised by the Basel II framework; and of a professionalisation of investment banking as a profession – a professionalisation which in the West occurred with the quantitative turn in finance in the 1960s and 1970s (Bernstein 1992; Dunbar 2000; MacKenzie 2006) of which the invention of option pricing models was a crucial part. All three of these aspects fit with general analyses of globalisation processes fuelled by institutionalisation or formalisation of organisational practices (Meyer and Rowan 1991). According to new institutional organisational theory, the adoption of formal procedures, codification of regulatory regimes of practices, professionalisation of staff, and not least implementation of scientific practices (risk management being a case in point) leads to isomorphism, that is, a gradual homogenisation of an organisational field such as a financial market. Homogenisation through adoption of formal organisational practices occurs not only within specific organisational fields but also across nation states. As such, institutionalisation is a driver of global integration (Meyer 2009). Scientific knowledge plays a pivotal role in this (Drori *et al.* 2003; Strang and Meyer 1993). Institutionalisation most often happens through the application of scientifically grounded meanings and frames to organisational practices (Meyer and Rowan 1991: 42–3; Powell and Dimaggio 1991b: 15).

The diffusion of financial models and their application in China can to a wide extent be explained as such an institutionalisation of formal organisational practices. According to the theory, the driving force behind it is the great authority, which is bestowed on science in modern society (Drori *et al.* 2003) – in this case financial and economic theory. The diffusion is part of a more general, and global, integration of financial systems (see account of global integration above), which includes implementation of regulatory regimes, accounting standards, certifications, etc. As described most extensively by John W. Meyer and colleagues (Drori *et al.* 2006; Drori *et al.* 2003; Meyer 2009; Meyer and Rowan 1991; Strang and Meyer 1993), these institutionalised rules and practices are diffused around the globe, which means that even the least-developed countries have adopted such regimes. But in many such cases these institutionalised practices have limited utility. Organisational reality is often sharply decoupled from the institutionalised scientific 'myths'. The formal practices lend scientific and/or normative authority, but 'the more inspiring and universal the values and claims at the institutional level are, the more bounding and decoupling at the practical level are likely to result'. (Drori *et al.* 2003: 15).

New institutional theory would hence explain the proliferation of formalised institutional practices by the symbolic power of science and other rationalised 'myths' of modern institutions. These myths are often very loosely coupled to the level of organisational practice. Earlier outlined statements regarding the perception of risks already provided ample evidence of a decoupling, in these cases decoupling between on the one hand the real market perceptions of risks and pricing assessments and on the other an institutional level where formal, codified knowledge and conventions are applied. But other and perhaps more fundamental forms of decoupling can also be found. It is for example implied by one interviewee that the very creation of derivatives markets can be interpreted in this light:

Interviewee: They want to free the interest market but the government always do things like step by step. And before they free the interest market they announced they will establish a forward market. The order is wrong (laughs).

The result of such decoupling is, needless to say, a strange dual reality (Arnoldi and Zhang 2012) to which market participants have to relate, navigating both a state-controlled market and modern financial instruments brought into the markets prematurely. Two of the factors mentioned earlier in this chapter, namely lack of belief in pricing models and knowledge of volatility skew, also add to the decoupling. As one interviewee remarked, the models 'don't even work in America' (former FX trader now academic in a Chinese business school). Another lost patience with me for keeping the conversation on the pricing models and interrupted:

Interviewee: Look, I don't think…you should not spend so much time on models. Models rely on us […] humans are very complex creatures…

Dealing with uncertainty

The limit of such a theoretical explanation is on the other hand that the decoupling may not be permanent. For example, even if derivatives markets were created much before markets were liberalised and mature enough for that to make sense, with time the initial wrong order of creation will matter very little. Even though the institutionalisation of formal pricing models may at the beginning be decoupled from the day-to-day operation in the markets, and even though the model does not have any performative power, the decoupling may be lessened over time. Another objection is that pricing models may have a purpose and meaning for those that use them even if they are decoupled from the underlying financial markets. That objection may in fact be less of a criticism of institutional theory than an extension of the same. Uncertainty is often mentioned as a reason or impetus for institutionalisation of scientific knowledge. In the following we suggest an augmented version of that hypothesis.

Even if the complex models do not work properly, the structured instruments themselves can still be used for hedging or speculation, and models can provide insights into the workings of the instruments. We have already seen indications that if there is uncertainty about the prices and the market prices diverge from the theoretical values, this discrepancy is something which itself calls for interpretation and explanation. Hence, traders use the divergence between market and theoretical value as a metric with which to gauge the market. Similarly, it is clear that both the use of the instruments and the gauging of discrepancy require an understanding of the theoretical fundamentals on the basis of which the instruments are created. Seen from this perspective, the models do not function as concrete pricing tools, which render these tools performative, nor are they simultaneously institutionalised and decoupled from everyday trading techniques. Rather, they function as general concepts for valuating and negotiating prices of structured securities and subsequent use of the same for strategic investment. Traders working in China are faced with uncertainty and complexity precisely because of the market imperfections and lack of applicability of the pricing models. In such situations they adopt various strategies including imitating the market leaders who (are held to) enjoy privileged information. But they also abstract from the diverging specificities in order to gain a general understanding. And abstraction requires theory and theoretical concepts. The following is an excerpt from a former trader and now academic who was asked why there was little development of models given the fact that the existing did not fit. The answer was that it is because traders do not so much depend on the models for precise pricing but rather for providing 'conceptual insights'. When the interviewee was asked to explicate, the importance of abstraction became clear:

Interviewee: Black and Scholes taught us that the value of an option has got nothing to do with your directional view but the volatility you try and hedge…this…is a real conceptual breakthrough.

Interviewer: But this means that Black-Scholes is important not only because it is a practical tool for pricing but because it is a concept that you can unfold in different concrete situations and apply in different contexts, to generate new and creative ideas…

Interviewee: For example capital structure which is an interesting idea right now.

Interviewer: You know, there are some social theorists that see Black–Scholes as the cornerstone of modern derivatives markets because it kind of gives traders a script that they can follow. But what you are saying about the conceptual breakthrough…

Interviewee: It means that it is even more important.

Interviewer: Yes.

Interviewee: Anyone can value a forward and in an option anyone can value the intrinsic value, so the real mystery lies in the time value, which is a function not of expectations but a function of liquidity and the pricing gap, so these two things explain everything. And this is a real conceptual insight.

In this quotation, the performative function of models, pricing, is pushed aside as almost trivial. The real importance, instead, lies in the conceptual insights, which the models provide. That conceptual insight would be important also in context where the performative function did not exist

The basic assumption of the so-called convention school is that human beings are able to relate all specific – often conflicting – events or experiences to abstract values, which create equivalence. Any particular event can hence be compared with others, and particular events or problems can be evaluated with reference to some form of standard or principle of equivalence. Such discussions about common standards, conventions or principles of justice, might invoke notions of stable norms, which uphold social order, but this is not the hypothesis of convention theory. Rather, convention theory invokes a 'notion of coordination which is much more open to uncertainty, critical tensions and creative arrangements than the ideas of stabilised and reproductive orders' (Thévenot 2001a: 406). Consequently, convention theory is more aligned with phenomenology, symbolic interactionism and above all pragmatism.

This very general theory has been applied in more detail to economies and markets by the economist Laurent Thévenot and colleagues. Thévenot's focus is hence the market regime, one particular regime of worth. With this comes also a focus on uncertainty and the valuations (in the context of the market regime, the regime of economic value, we no longer need to talk of evaluations) through which agents seek to reduce uncertainty. Apart from the enhanced focus on uncertainty, Thévenot and colleagues make at least three important additions to the general convention school. First, markets function not so much because market participants subscribe to one great abstract principle of equivalence that becomes the yardstick for all evaluations but more through a plurality of standards and other principles of equivalence which include texts, legal corpuses, accounting units and evaluation tools (Eymard-Duvernay et al. 2005: 6). Pricing models belong to this latter category. Second, this focus on what we will refer to as small-scale conventions leads to a focus on the technologies in which small-scale conventions are embedded and sustained. Thévenot refers to these as investments in forms. These are objects and materials that create generalities and standards over time and space, which again facilitate coordination (Thévenot 2001a: 187). In this area there are significant similarities with ANT, but according to Thévenot, the construction of what Callon would call calculative devices (Callon 1998, 1999; Callon and Muniesa 2005) is dependent upon the prior construction of a general principle of equivalence (Thévenot 2001a: 408). Third, this prior construction of small-scale conventions often happens through a gradual bottom-up process. Thévenot describes such practices, the result of actors intentionally striving to reduce uncertainty, as a three-stage process. It starts with an agent experiencing a given thing in the world, human or objective. This is best described by the phenomeno-logical notion of intentionality. Thévenot stresses the open-endedness of such an experience but adds that 'new configurations of links do not emerge without the identification and development of some sort of new equipment of humanity' (2001a: 409–10), be this equipment cognitive or instrumental. The next phase will then consist of a strengthening of this equipment, in the first instance through further generalisation through e.g. language or money, or algebraic formula for that matter. It may also evolve through investment in forms, that is, through the construction of technologies (spanning from the invention of paper to the personal computer) that can sustain the conventions. The result is conventions about worth, and, in the case of markets, value principles that are intellectual or human resources. Even though there of course are conflicting valuations in a market, there must be some form of mutual agreement on the fundamental principles of value (Eymard-Duvernay et al. 2005). This is certainly all the more important in the case of complex derivatives where 'conceptual insights' as described in the quotation above, are necessary for comprehending the structure of the securities.

Convention theory in many ways gives a more modest account than new institutional theory and ANT. Unlike ANT, the conventions or investments in form do not necessarily structure or construct the organisational field. This also means that the conventions are relatively more independent of context: while a pricing model only can generate a credible output if the market context coheres with the assumptions underlying the model, the general concepts on which the model is based are of interest also in cases without such coherence. Even in an imperfect market like the Chinese, there have to be principles of equivalence with which securities can be created, correlations can be assessed and prices negotiated. In order for the latter to occur, the principles have to be mutually known so that they can 'facilitate negotiation amongst sophisticated participants', as Mackenzie writes in a sentence which echoes convention theory (2009: 15). Here, we see an element of convention theory, echoed in MacKenzie's later work, which places much emphasis on social embeddedness, on mutuality in social ties. Moreover, unlike new institutional theory, the conventions are not seen as necessarily being institutionalised (although that possibility is not ruled out either) and they are to an even lesser extent seen as leading to codification or an institutionalisation of technologies/investment in forms. Finally, comparing all three theoretical perspectives used in this analysis, we find a confluence when it comes to uncertainty and a need for a common conceptual framework that can coordinate valuation and negotiation. New institutional theory sees institutionalisation as being accelerated in transactional environments with high uncertainty (Powell and Dimaggio 1991a: 77), and both ANT and convention theory place great emphasis on market devices (which for the convention school primarily are conceptual) that reduce uncertainty. Hence, even under conditions, which require or are characterised by decoupling, uncertainty may accelerate diffusion of formal, scientifically grounded, techniques and expertise.

Mutuality or equivalence is also important in another respect. Conventions are standards of equality and fairness between market participants, and such conventions of fairness sustain markets. A market maker may for example not quote different prices to two different brokers simultaneously. Such principles also apply to imperfect markets like Chinese derivatives markets. The prices may be far from the models' prescriptions, but as one trader in the FX forwards put it, 'nowadays all the banks they quote prices based on this market [rate]. So whatever the price I get, the prices we get are the same as the prices quoted by the other banks'.

Conclusion

One of the seven theses on the economic development in China presented in the introduction of this book was that (Western) economic theories do not make any performative interventions. We believe that we have provided one case of this here in this chapter. Practitioners simply do not believe in the pricings models' ability to provide the 'correct' price in the Chinese context, just as they are aware of deviations of the theoretical price also in Western markets. Because of this lack of belief, the models do not shape the market in their mould. Yet, in spite of this lack of performativity, a knowledge transfer is ongoing. The development of the Chinese OTC derivatives (and by implication the financial sector as a whole) is in many ways to be seen as an institutionalisation of an organisational field. This is a process that includes implementation of regulatory regimes and practices, adoption of knowledge and technologies and professionalisation of actors working in the field. However, absence of performativity means a clear discrepancy between this general institutionalisation and individual markets participants' view of the markets and the price dynamics. This discrepancy may be theoretically explained as decoupling, yet we suggest that there may be more to the story. There are clear institutional and regulatory differences compared with Western markets, an important one being the dominant position of the big four Chinese banks and the control that government can exert through these. But if decoupling can be explained as the necessary result of the overarching political structures in China, then the real concern is what drives the formal institutionalisation, in this particular case of course the diffusion of pricing models, which nevertheless occurs?

One suggestion would be that uncertainty and the need for uncertainty reductions should be the starting point for any deeper explanation of the process and the role of derivative pricing models in that process. Conventions and concepts, which can be used to valuate securities, are needed. Even if market rates do not correlate with these resulting theoretical values, the structure of the instruments needs to be understood and the market needs to be assessed. The pricing models, the concepts and theoretical assumptions on which they are built, and the very spread between the real market prices and the theoretical values of the models become heuristic 'handles' or metrics with which the market can be gauged (see description of the volatility skew above). Uncertainty generally provides fertile ground for the diffusion and institutionalisation of scientific knowledge (Powell and Dimaggio 1991a; Strang and Meyer 1993: 492), and the more abstract the knowledge, the speedier the diffusion (Strang and Meyer 1993: 495). Both conditions are certainly present in the current study. Yet, that uncertainty reduction functions without any performative shaping of the markets in the image of the model. As mentioned above, performativity boils down to one essential factor; namely belief. Many interviewees gave various reasons for why models only had limited applicability to China. When pressed further, they (as mentioned above) would refer to the volatility skew in US option markets or even simply make a general reference to the financial crisis in the West, mentioning that the derivatives industry in the West was not exactly efficient either. In other words, the pricing models are studied and the underlying concepts supporting the models are used and understood, but there is no performativity of the models because the traders are analysing and observing the models rather than basing their actions on them. There is a certain detachment, a certain scepticism towards the models. This is not to say that there is no scepticism, at times frustration or sarcasm, voiced over the state-influenced and networked power structure that permeates the financial markets in today's China. But there is just as much cautiousness towards any idea that these problems can be easily fixed by creating a market similar to the American or European. In other words, the sceptical attitude to Western models is certainly not only an attitude held by the government. It runs also among the practitioners in the industry in China.

This detached and cautious attitude to the financial market construction – what we may term construction without belief – in many ways reflects the development of the Chinese economy at large. It is a cautious process – we have mentioned Deng's crossing the river one step at a time several times before – and the government maintains a great deal of control. Integration and modernisation does occur, and is certainly demanded by actors dissatisfied with the inefficiency of the current market institutions. However, those who voice this scepticism are just as wary of many elements of Western capitalism (in this case pricing models). Hence, it seems likely that the further development of Chinese finance will be a cautious approach towards Western and global conventions – so cautious, in fact, that the here-described Chinese characteristics are likely to remain in place for a good while to come.

9
RISK CULTURES
Production of Shanghai space

Risk regimes: winners and losers

Hai Heng (English name Robert) is Shanghainese. He is 29 years old and works for a privately owned fabric trading company – owned by a Shanghainese woman, who is married to a famous local television presenter. This helps give her a 'good political background'. The fabric company, which has ten employees, does not manufacture at all. They export fabrics: they are a 'middleman' company. They buy and sell. If a client's order is below a certain amount, Robert's company buys from the factory, pays the factory and then sells onto the client. Some orders, however, are over US$1m. In these cases the buyer pays the factory directly and pays Robert's company a commission. He says 'US$1m', in a 'LC' (letter of credit) because in 2008 buyers were paying only in US dollars. Buyers want to do business in euros too, but at the moment are only set up to do US dollars. All the suppliers are from neighbouring Zhejiang and Jiangsu provinces – from not Wenzhou, but Hangzhou, Ningbo, Jiaxing in Zhejiang, from Wujiang and Suzhou in Jiangsu province: from Huzhou which sits on the border of Jiangsu and Zhejiang provinces. Perhaps the secret of Shanghai's (comparatively) fabulous wealth is its positioning between these two economically super-vibrant provinces. They – especially Zhejiang – provide a labour force for Shanghai of middle-class, very ambitious lower and middle management. In Shanghai's periphery, factories make the stuff that Shanghai sells. These are more often than not light industry factories. Silk from Hangzhou and Jiaxing, which are important trading cities on their own. Robert's company does two lines: silk and beddings, for example, duvets. Robert is head of beddings.

Shanghai, along with the southeast part of Jiangsu and northeast Zhejiang make up the global economic powerhouse of the the Yangzi River Delta. These YRD factories are not just anywhere in the massive Jiangsu and Zhejiang provinces. They do not for example include Nanjing or Wenzhou. They constitute a factory periphery around increasingly post-industrial Shanghai, comprising in total some 75 million people. The YRD has two of the world's five busiest ports by cargo tonnage.[1] If there is a motor of the world economy, it may be here. About 20 years ago Saskia Sassen wrote some about the global city – about New York, Tokyo, London. In 2013, none of these make the world's top twenty ports. At stake now is not the global city but the *mega*city: Shanghai, Mumbai, Sao Paulo, Mexico City. At stake primarily may be no longer a New York–Tokyo–London axis, but the Shanghai–Hong Kong–Singapore axis. This is a question not only of cargo tonnage, but also increasingly for finance and a range of products moving up the value-chain.

This chapter is about 'risk biographies' – based on detailed interviews with 60–70 Shanghai residents. This is supplemented by another 70 interviews more closely structured around just housing and stock markets. These 'risk biographies' overlap experience in markets: labour, housing and, in many cases, stock. In their cross-hatched and networked accumulation, these risk narratives are constructing Shanghai. They are producing the city on an urban, para-urban and ex-urban level.

Robert's company's buyers are mostly from India and, secondly, Australia. Robert's boss negotiates with the buyer, while Robert deals with the suppliers. With trading companies, the suppliers depend on the buyers: you always start from the buyers. You meet with buyers in a well-appointed Shanghai office. With suppliers you take trains and buses or drive on poorly maintained B-roads out to factories in the provinces. Robert has excellent English, as does his boss and her TV-presenter husband. They hope soon to develop US clients. The boss has connections with very large Indian trading companies that 'sell stuff all over India', that 'dominate many local Indian markets'. These massive Indian trading companies deal with a number of smaller Shanghai trading companies. This saves the Indian traders the hard work of chasing out to the Chinese factories with non-English speaking managers. Sometimes the Indian trading companies 'put their own label on the product': they 'brand it and re-export to Europe or the US'. These companies never pay in advance. Robert's company, when there is a big order, must pay the factory a 30 per cent deposit. The Indian companies will not pay until they see the product: they lay the risk off onto Robert's firm. Robert mediates for them on quality: he knows what the buyers' standards are. If he does not like the quality, he asks the factory to improve it. Full payment is made only when the quality is right. Once it is, the Indian traders pay for everything and Robert's firm makes its percentage.

Some of Robert's bedding suppliers are medium–large factories with over 200 workers, some private, some (local) state owned. His most important relations are with the smaller, always privately owned, factories. Robert's base salary is ¥5,500/month plus an annual ¥7000 bonus. He supplements this income by doing quality inspection work for the supplier factories. For this he receives a not-contracted '*hongbao*', a red bag, or money wrapped in red, similar to the gift most interviewees give to their mother and father when they return to their villages or small towns for Spring Festival. It is part of a taxless 'gift economy'. SOEs and large private firms do not give Robert *hongbao*. Middleman companies like Robert's are very important to these smaller factory owners: they 'want to make a long-term relation'. These are not 'home factories' but plants of 100–150 workers. But if the quality of the fabric is not good – and this happens in 10–15 per cent of cases – Robert will give the *hongbao* back. *Hongbao*, normally some ¥2,000, happens about once per month. With bonus and *hongbao*, Robert's monthly income is about ¥8200. With a low-earning wife, you are struggling a bit on ¥5,500 in Shanghai: even in the outer districts where Robert lives. The extra ¥2,000 makes a difference.

Robert studied at Fudan University, a sort of applied business studies course with English-language training. He subsequently enrolled in a business studies course in Amsterdam, returning to China in 2005. While sourcing buttons in Shanghai's South Bund Fabric Market, he began to chat to the girl in the sales stall. They fell in love and scandal ensued. His parents would not accept her: the girl 'had no education'. She was from a village in Fujian, 'so far from Fuzhou' – Robert visits for Spring Festival – that 'there was no supermarket, no shops, no China Unicom signal'. She was *de facto* a girl *nongminggong*.[2] Robert's mum and dad are Shang-hainese. His father has a diploma from a two-year technical training course. His father and mother were accustomed to the risk-regime of the old *danwei*. Robert's dad worked at Baosteel and they had always lived in north Shanghai near the Baoshan District. The *danwei* provided Robert's father with a security regime. Subsequently social security had come from the municipality, guaranteed by their Shanghai *hukou*. Robert's fiancé, without *danwei* or urban *hukou*, was without 'social citizenship': no school subsidies, no health subsidies, no pension. His grandmother and uncle and aunt – who only finished middle school – were also against the girl. Thinking them 'selfish', Robert broke with his family and married the girl. He moved out and they rented a flat. A short time after, Robert began to bring his new wife home for dinner – just every one to two weeks. She 'showed kindness' to his parents: she 'washed dishes, cooked, did housekeeping'. Things began to improve.

In Robert's company, the 'boss pays in ¥1,500 per month' for his (Robert's) social security on top of his salary. 'Police officers or telecom employees get pensions of ¥3,000 per month'. His wife gets nothing. His in-laws in rural Fujian, 60 years old, get nothing. He brings them a Spring Festival *hongbao* with ¥1000 each for father- and mother-in-law. Ulrich Beck's 'risk society' is thus also about security-systems: security-systems for illness, old age, education and perhaps, above all, housing. Robert with his Mum and Dad had a *danwei* flat from Baosteel. They 'made application at the end of the 1980s to the Baosteel *danwei*' for a larger flat. Dad was a technician so had the 'right' to a three-room flat. This still was only an 87 square metres flat, near Fudan University, just south of Baoshan district. In 1999, Baosteel sold the flat to them for ¥40,000 (US$7,000). 'But there was nothing there then'. Subsequently the whole area is completely built up, with private residential high-rises, shopping districts, offices, cafes, restaurants. The same flat by 2008 was worth ¥500,000. The flat is now in Robert's name and his wife has moved in: they have one room, mum and dad one room and the third bedroom is kept empty for a future baby. Robert's mum has had a work-related blood disease for 20 years, and is on ¥1,100 of disability per month; his Dad's salary at Baosteel was ¥2,500–3,000 per month, his pension now (paid not from Baosteel but Shanghai municipal authority) is ¥1800 per month. With mum's bad health, it makes sense for wife to do housework rather than work. For her 'low education there are no good jobs': 'sales girl and waitressing pay about ¥800 with no social security'.

Robert bought shares in Baosteel. His father was required to buy a minimum of 1,000 shares at ¥2 per share. This was 1999, just prior to Baosteel's IPO. Robert and his dad chipped in and bought ¥4000 worth. Robert sold at ¥6.5 in 2001 and used the money to pay for further study in Amsterdam. By 2007 Baosteel stood at ¥20. Robert again invested on his return to China in 2005, this time in China Unicom. He only buys in 'big state-owned companies': he reckons, these companies are 'stealing from me, so I'll get some back'. How stealing from him? First, on taxes he pays to subsidise them and, second, in the low salaries. Robert is only interested in long-term investment. He starts from the understanding that 'China will never let the key sector – oil, steel, telecoms – be privatised'. He thinks China Unicom is 'ripping off' its subscribers with high monthly fees for low levels of service. He wants his back. He bought 1,000 shares at ¥5. China Unicom peaked at ¥18 in 2007, and is now in 2013 at ¥9.51. Robert is aware of the dip (in June 2008) of the Exchange to 3,555. But he reckons the CPC will not allow it to sink much further. The Shanghai Exchange index peaked in September 2007 at 6,000. Robert reckons one day it will reach 10,000 to match the New York and Hong Kong exchanges.

Zhang Lei, 23 years old from Nanyang in Henan province lying just south of the Yellow River – west of Shandong – is studying for an accounting certificate. He grew up among peasants, whom he sees as, if not risk averse, living in a very 'limited' regime of risk. In 'the villages there are no markets, they just produce for themselves'. 'They sell a little bit: very few transactions': there is 'no risk, no gain' in the village. Zhang's elder brother age 29 now, 'did not know how to send text messages till last year'. He says this is a bit like 'corporate bonds versus investing in government bonds: higher risk, higher return'. Zhang is a *waidiren* (person from outside of a given locality) in Shanghai. *Waidiren*, 'in the big city' 'take more risks. Zhang wants to define his own risk regime in opposition to his father's. His dad's risk regime was defined by the People's Liberation Army (PLA). Born 1947, his father – unusual for rural Chinese of his generation – was an upper school (*gaozhong*) graduate, who also spent several years as a mid-level manager in a beer factory. Joining the PLA meant that he was away from family and 'paid them little attention'. Quite different from Western armies, the PLA includes intellectuals and what would seem to be people with quite non-military profiles. The PLA is itself a regime of, not risk, but of security. PLA membership meant dad could finance Zhang Lei's education, not in Henan, but in the adjoining Hubei in Wuhan. Lei studied Marketing at Wuhan Engineering Institute: fees were ¥4,000 per annum: but with living expenses cost was ¥80,000 over four years. Zhang has chosen a painful and individualised risk regime. He refuses to depend on his father and alongside his studies works part time in Shanghai. He has forsaken his Wuhan friendship network for the loneliness of a part-time student. His last job was in sales for a Japanese manufacturer. He would liaise with sales teams to obtain orders and then get back to his company's factories to meet the orders to designated specifications and quality. He has just moved to a job in an English company. He can 'always get another job'. Shanghai's labour market is thriving. Many of our interviewees were between jobs and unworried about it. But Zhang is earning only ¥3000 per month and, while studying, working 50 hours plus per week. He observes, 'risk-averse' Shanghai girls, unlike Wuhan girls, are 'looking for money'. 'Cute Shanghai girls grew up in a city with so many attractions'. One Shanghai girl said directly to him, 'no serious relation is possible if you don't have money'. This girl wants 'to go to France to study: her parents will pay. They work for the government. Make lots of money'. Similarly father's PLA security-regime has ensured an excellent pension and a three-storey villa.

Zhou Wei was born in Xinjiang Autonomous Region, between (Outer) Mongolia and Kazakhstan in China's far northwest. Xinjiang is an autonomous region due to minority ethnic-group dominance: the Turkic-speaking Uyghurs. Zhou is Han Chinese, China's majority ethnic group: age 16, he and his father moved to Shanghai in 1982. Zhou's family had been in the far northwest for generations. His great-grandfather had a business in neighbouring Ningxia Autonomous region, 'specialising in products for the region's Muslim community'. Zhou's dad was a teacher, who transferred to a Shanghai work-unit. 'There was more mobility in the 1980s than there is now'. Zhou Wei went to middle school in Xinjiang, but senior high school in Shanghai. This made it possible for him to take his university entrance exam in Shanghai. He studied design at Shanghai University Art College, after which he joined an architectural design house as a project manager. Zhou is an intellectual: he reads books, knows Western architecture and the Chinese contemporary art scene. He has researched and written on the evolution of Shanghai architecture. In the late 1980s, Zhou joined another, this time Hong Kong-run, architecture and design firm as project manager. In each case these private design houses, need ' to offer some share to Shanghai government'. Zhou's present company collaborates with a state-owned publisher. Private sector firms cannot publish unless they have a licence from a (local) state-owned publisher, whose licence costs are quite varied. Prohibitive Shanghai and Beijing rates means the city's private sector firms often buy their licenses in less expensive – in Zhou's case Jiangsu – provinces. After two to three years Zhou moved onto a Swiss ad firm: specialty industrial magazines. Their public-sector partner's licence will give them access to advertising rights for their other magazines.

Zhou's currently working in environmentally friendly design: for a firm, run by a Hong Kong manager, using Australian-model environment certification system and US environmental design. They renovate old estates: model estates in office format. They retain as much as they can of the old building, an exercise in preservation. 'Looks very chic'. Half of its work is as a certification agency. It almost seems like an art organisation. They design events and temporary theatre. They had a

Shanghai Expo 2010 project: some interior work on the Chilean Pavilion, including logistical support.³ They do it 'cheap' to 'enhance their profile'. The pay is not great.

Most of his new firm's employees are from other provinces. 'More hard-working', says Zhou. 'You need less pay'. Shanghainese seldom go elsewhere: as a major university professor on ¥12,000, you can afford relatively expensive private schools. Zhou Wei has a Shanghai *hukou*. He actually 'bought it' around 1990, 'when you could'. Now in 2010 it is more a question of formal requirements.

In Ulrich Beck's risk society there are 'risk winners' and 'risk losers'. Zhou is a risk loser. He has failed at business. Also, tragically, his wife died (he is now 44 years old) and he has no children. China's is a family-based risk culture. Communism with it Legalist lineage, its *danwei*, set itself against filiality and the family. The Cultural Revolution – kill the father, kill the teacher, kill the bourgeois – took it to extremes. But this was a regime of the utmost insecurity, and was experienced as such. Hence, Wen Jiabao in March 2012 accused Bo Xilai of endorsing a new cultural revolution. Subsequently, however, especially buoyed by the institution of now near universal urban home ownership,⁴ the family is back with a vengeance. If Western risk culture is based on life choices and reflexive individualism, then in China first and foremost it is about reproduction and the family. Zhou has lived for past six months with his mother and father, who bought a 93 square metres flat in a perhaps less salubrious corner of the very upmarket Jing'an district. They (recently) paid ¥875,000 (US$140,000) on a ¥1.5m flat. This is in a modern residential *xiaoqu*.

Many of these respondents have had a 'risk event': a life-defining risk event. For Zhou Wei, this was starting his own business. He started this business with a female cousin, who had worked for a US laboratory. She (they) spotted a lacuna in the market for sourcing Chinese medical research laboratories with lab animals. Cousin and Zhou purchased monkeys, rabbits and rats, domestic and overseas, with overseas purchase on commission. Moving animals by commission yielded low profits, so they decided also to raise their own monkeys and rabbits. They raised capital, borrowing as much as they could from family and friends, 'at very high interest rates'. Cousin and Zhou borrowed long term and paid over 10 per cent interest. They used a broker for some of this at even higher rates. Brokers in principle are not Shanghainese: they often are 'underground'. They are *waidiren* often from Zhejiang. 'You have to know these brokers from your own network'. The business broke down because they had no *guanxi* with local government. Government regulators came to require a licence for farms doing foreign and domestic trade in lab animals. Zhou sourced partly from 'plantations' in remote mountainous regions, paying farmers in advance for the animals. Now these farmers could not obtain the licences. The farmers then shut down shop without paying Zhou back. He had contracts with his own clients. These had penalty clauses for non-delivery and Zhou quickly had a mountain of debt. He could not pay back relatives, friends and moneylenders. He thought of running away. But did not because he (at that point) had a wife. Over many years he paid his penalty fees. The licensed farms provided animals at unaffordable prices. What was behind this? The government began to regulate because they wanted to develop their own lab animal companies. To start with there were just vaccines, etc. for the lab animals, but even these were not obligatory. Then, all at once, a whole range of standards had become obligatory in order to obtain a licence. Zhou's supplier farms could not afford to change their procedures plus the effective tax that government was demanding as certification fees.

Zhou was ruined: a risk loser. With political relations with local government, he thought, he could have had some subsidy for his sourcing. Business was moving in the right direction. But the unpredictability of regulation destroyed Zhou.

The state itself was a source of uncertainty. But where does security come from in the Chinese economy? This market, this budding and emerging market for lab animals was not secure. For Harrison White's economic sociology, markets do not tend to equilibrium. They are instead metastable systems. Yet there is a strong dimension of stability in them: there is a reasonable measure of predictability, without which no one would invest. Frank Knight – who distinguished risk, which is insurable, from uncertainty, which is not – is perhaps White's foremost influence. In Beck's risk society most choices are not insurable: they are more like uncertainties than risks. Risk here is a question of *investment:* a question of leaving yourself exposed to great loss so that you may gain future returns. The question is under what circumstances are investment and risk-taking possible. For Weber thus capitalism requires a certain level of stability and predictability. Where is this stability coming from in China? In Zhou's case, the market – because of unpredictable state action – did not provide this. This stability needed instead to come from local-government *guanxi* relations. In the absence of these Zhou met with disaster.

Risk and housing

Wang Rui (Margaret) lives in a *longtang*, in inner-ring (*neihuan*) Shanghai, in a now very fashionable neighbourhood where the former Luwan district meets with Xuhui and Jing'an. She calls this the old 'French Concession' (*fazujie* – 法租界). Margaret, however, is quintessentially Shanghainese: from generations of residents of Luwan. Though there are 'lots more *waidiren* now', she went to middle school near her *longtang*. A lot of people who were locals here 'had to move – especially to Pudong'. She grew up in the *longtang*, where there was 'lots of communication'. 'Neighbours can help each other'. It's 'all about communications and knowing your neighbour'. A '*longtang* is not like a *danwei*: more like a *xiaoqu* but with low buildings'. 'You open your window, you saw your neighbour'. 'Maybe two or three of the neighbours 'work for the same company, but most do not'. 'Now foreigners want to live in *longtang*'. In the nineties, she says, '90 per cent of people seemed to live in *longtang*'. 'Then after the reforms, you get very high buildings'. The *longtang* is three stories high: 'often five to six people lived in one room, just 20 something square metres'. Wan Rui and her father and mother have two rooms in their flat. Neighbours told them their *longtang* was lived in by Russians originally.[5] 'Most of Shanghai before 1949 was foreigners'. Many Russians, seemingly paradoxically, lived in the French Concession. Margaret and family moved here in in 1992, when she was nine years old. Previously they and her father's younger sister lived in her grandfather's *longtang* flat. This consisted of three rooms, one family per room: 28 square metres per family. 'We didn't feel crowded. We thought this was ok for a family. We were happy, I had "loads of friends". Now they have 45 square metres and two rooms. Her family owns the flat: they bought it, 'cheap', in 1992.

Their Shanghai *hukou* and flat are sources of security. So is Margaret's father's CCP. He and his sister have a business: a company that tests buildings – factories and offices – for environmental standards. This private company is *de facto* outsourced from the state (Barry 2000), hence the necessity of Party membership. Their local government contact is also Shanghainese, a friend of Margaret's father and sister. Her Dad earns ¥8,000 per month. Born in 1954, he was sent to a farm in the northeast near Harbin in the Cultural Revolution and could not go to university. He lived there seven years: 'nothing to eat, he almost froze'. Margaret's mother could stay in Shanghai, and when father returned, they married and he found his way into the Party. Their company, with some 50 employees, checks and ensures light and air standards in factories. The factories pay them testing fees: they are 'subcontractors' for 'government standards'. If standards are not met, the (Shanghai) government will close the factory. Her father's company uses labs and the government certifies the company's and its labs' standards. Every few months, the government checks these lab standards. The factories (often in electronics) and office buildings, for whom they check and ensure standards, are mostly in the Shanghai region and mainly employ Shanghainese.

Wang Rui wants her own flat. The one she is in is too noisy and she cannot study in the *longtang*. People are always 'decorating, renovating'. She is in her fourth year at East China Science and Technology University ('*Ligong Daxue*'), with campuses nearby in Xuhui.[6] Her university is best known for research in chemistry. Had her marks been better she could have majored in computing. As it turned out her marks were only good enough for an English major. *Ligong Daxue* is 60 per cent *waidiren* – Jiangsu, Beijing, Dongbei. People come to Shanghai to study, 'for the opportunities after graduating'. At age 19, just after senior high school, Wang Rui went to study in Malaysia: at a private, business, Chinese-language college near Kuala Lumpur. For this, her parents paid an exorbitant ¥60,000 per year over two years. This was her (and her family's – and most Chinese risk biographies are very much *family* risk biographies) biography-defining risk. It failed. The college's only 'aim was to make money'. It was 'like a factory'. 'No education'. Margaret now works part time as an assistant, teaching Mandarin to foreign residents. She charges ¥40–50 per hour for these lessons. She advertises them on Craig's List. Margaret wants to set up her own business. She thinks Shanghainese are risk-averse, and want to make a decent income straight out of college. She would rather be poorer and more ambitious. Take a worse paid job where you can learn as much as possible. She would like to set up a science and technology business: say, a standards business like her Dad.

Shanghai is so much a city of young professionals. We are opening up a window on this in this chapter through recounting a number of urban-risk biographies. These are integrally tied up with housing regimes. The big shift since the mid 90s to privately owned housing markets and the mass building of commodity housing in suburban *xiaoqu* has brought with it a certain individualisation of such risk regimes. It has on the other hand, reinforced the traditional role of risk-sharing through inter-generational families based on private property in housing.

Let us have a closer, and more historic, look at how housing works. Let us consider the case of Liu Yan a guard, a *bao'an* in an affluent *xiaoqu* in Xuhui District, a ten-minute walk from the massive upmarket Xujiahui shopping mall. The *longtang*s (literally alley-space or lane-hall) in some ways look similar to Beijing's famous *hutong*s. The *longtang* is more literally an alleyway than a *hutong*. Both *longtang* and *hutong* are formed of alleyways and courtyards, but the courtyards feature more in the *hutong* than *longtang*. The *hutong* courtyards are the traditional *siheyuan*, literally a courtyard surrounded by four buildings. The *longtang* is on the *hutong* model, whose origins are in pre-Song Dynasty city planning. Emperors planned Beijing according to a model taken from the social classes of the Zhou Dynasty in the first millennium BCE. The term *hutong* only appeared in the thirteenth century under the Yuan Dynasty. The *hutong* was the lowest-level urban administrative division. In the Ming Dynasty Beijing was divided into 36 *fang*, each fang divided into a number of *pai* and each *pai* into a number of *hutong*s. *Hutong*s were connected one to the other by alleyways. This changed in modern China as divisions according to population and household displaced geographical divisions. Each *fang* however had a guard and gates: they were *de facto* gated 'boroughs'. Shanghai is a more modern city and heir to China's newer outward-facing 'second modernity', subsequent to a first modernity that arguably began to surface under Song. Shanghai is also a colonial city. While wealthy French and English 'colonialists' lived in villas, many among the popular classes inhabited *longtang*s, which were partly displaced by Maoist *danwei* and Dengist *xiaoqu*. Even today's *danwei* are often guarded. For example, today, Nanxiucun – literally 'South Excellent (or elegant) Village' is still a University *danwei* in Nanjing. It is in a *danwei* comprising nine building complexes surrounded on the north side by an alley, also paradoxically called Nanxiucun, which leads to the West gate of the University, on the south side by Hankou Road and on the east side by Pingfang Alley: these alleys presumably from previously existing *longtang*. The buildings are most all residences, many for retired university teachers and still-working employees and their families. There are two entrances to this *danwei*: all are guarded. Gates close between 23:00 and midnight, and you need to arouse a guard from his sleep to gain entrance. Most of the university staff no longer live in this *danwei*. Many have joined private sector housing markets.

Liu Yan is one of 24 guards[7] in this Xujiahui *xiaoqu*. This is all private housing, unconnected to any workplace: very high-rise, 15–20 floors. There are no restrictions on when you can come in at night, and the guards are not intrusive – or are at least a lot more discreet about residents' business and private lives. There is thus a measure of individualisation. Liu Yan keeps a record every day. Liu's boss is Shanghainese manages the *xiaoqu* on behalf of its Shanghainese private owners. Liu Yan, for his part, does not consider himself to be Shanghainese. His mother and father were born in Jiangsu, and came to Shanghai in 1950. His father – and many others – came to Shanghai as an ordinary PLA soldier. At this point in time, there were were low levels of urban density: not just *longtang*, but until 1985, in most of Xuhui there were *pingfang* (平房). The '*pingfang* were bungalows, like adobe houses' for rent. In China they are literally one-storey houses, as distinct from multi-storey apartment buildings or *loufang* (楼房). With the *pingfang* 'there were no courtyards, just buildings'. The '*pingfang* were built in the 1950s'. 'They built them themselves'. 'No one cared'. There were 'no regulations'. 'There was just empty space, and you just built your own house' and lived in it. Liu's father thus built their *pingfang*. He was no longer in the PLA but was a staffer in a hospital, actually on the now very elegant Huaihai Xilu. He built the pingfang near what is now Xujiahui. You could build effectively anarchically in the 1950s. But this was communism and 'you could not *maimai*'; you couldn't buy and sell. 'Beijing government forbade *maimai* in the 1950s' and later. They started to raze the *pingfang* and by 1989 they were replaced by *loufang*, by six to seven storey buildings. These were *danwei* flats. Liu's father worked for the hospital *danwei*: enclosed, but nothing like a dedicated big factory *danwei*. People from different work units lived in these buildings. Yet it was, not commodity (*shangpin* – 商品) but public or '*gongfang* (公房) housing': seven to eight years later Liu's family bought their flat from the *danwei*. 'People only paid ¥20,000–¥30,000 for these flats'. They 'have unlimited use rights, not just the 70-year lease'. 'Now people sell these for ¥850,000'.

In the early to mid 90s, when the *danwei* flats first went on sale, no one bought. Renting cost ¥200 per month. If you bought you only needed to pay the building's property management fee of ¥6 per month. There were 'no mortgages then'. There 'were no banks'. Liu was then about 40 years old. He had been working in a large Shanghai municipality-owned belt factory, with several hundred workers, only some of whom had flats in the *danwei*. Liu's family bought their flat: no mortgage, they had to pay the whole ¥20,000. They paid however with 'Provident Funds', into which *danwei*, state and the individual workers paid into. The factory went bankrupt just after Shanghai government sold it to a Hong Kong entrepreneur

So Liu got a job in this affluent Xujiahui *xiaoqu*, not very far from the only 28 square metres flat, where he and his wife (a printing factory employee) live. Their salaries are far below the Shanghai average, where, say, a taxi driver earns ¥3,000 per month. Liu earns only ¥1500 and his wife ¥1000. They, Liu's aged parents and their 20-year-old son – an IT student – live in the flat. This may be private housing and they may have a private shower, but everyone knows it is not commodity, but *danwei* housing. The *xiaoqu*, where Liu is guard is commodity housing: most flats are 98 square metres of 'constructed area'. Ninety-nine per cent of the flats, including 200 square metres two-storey units, are for purchase. There are 18 buildings in the *xiaoqu* – eleven-storey buildings, two flats per floor: 584 flats in all. Who owns them? Many *waidiren*: Jiangsu, Zhejiang, Shandong. 'Wenzhou people come and buy several of the flats and then resell at a profit'. At least a dozen *waiguoren* also live in the *xiaoqu*: Taiwanese, Hong Kongers, a Spaniard, Korean, American, Japanese, Italian. The *xiaoqu* is not far from the prestigious Shanghai Jiao Tong University, more than few of whose professors have bought the flats.

The juxtaposition of *danwei* and *xiaoqu* in contemporary urban risk regimes for Wang Xiaohong, who is in his early thirties and lives in Zhabei distric in the middle ring of Shanghai districts, just north of Jing'an. I visit him and he receives me in his father-in-law's flat, with father-in-law and his nine-month-old child.[8] His father-in-law was born in Jiangsu in 1940. He came to join his grandfather who had moved to Shanghai to work as an engraver in 1946. In 1953 his mother and father followed. His grandfather worked for a private engraving company, but then in '1956 all the companies became state-owned'. The company gave him this *danwei* flat, though both call it a '*xiaoqu*'. Before 1985, the older man had a flat, also in a *danwei*, in the adjacent Hongkou district. The older man speaks Shanghainese. His father-in-law had worked for his entire work life for a state-owned construction materials firm, which gave him a flat first in Hongkou and then in 1988, this Zhabei *danwei* flat. There was no *maimai*: it was given to him '*mianfeide*' (免费的), for free. In 1999 he bought the 40 square metres flat at minimal cost. The construction materials firm subsequently closed and the Shanghai government took over the father-in law's pension. The minimum pension 'Shanghai government pays is ¥1000'. The grandfather and his wife look after Wang's baby daughter.

Wang and his wife live in their own ex-*danwei* building about 15 minutes walk away. When he married, he sold his bachelor flat and bought the Zhabei flat, again in an old *danwei* early 80s building. Theirs is 31 square metres, which Lei thinks is inadequate. 'A normal flat is now two bedrooms plus a living room, 90 square metres. The price for this now is about ¥1,500,00. The building society says you need to pay 'a 30 per cent or 25 per cent deposit'. 'They want to minimise their risk'. Wang has just changed jobs and now earns a solid ¥8,000 per month. He could sell his present flat for about ¥400,000: enough to meet the deposit. But the monthly mortgage payments – 10 year mortgages seem the most common – would be crippling. Wang bought his present flat 'second hand'. A second hand, '*er shou*' (二手), flat is in a very different market. This house had only 30 years left on a 50-year lease. Once the lease runs out, the house reverts back to local government. Then 'the government might not move you out', 'but you would need to buy a new 50-year leasehold from government, if not for the flat, a least for the space'.

In some cases, housing-related risk regimes are overwhelmingly insecure. For example, Chen Yaya (English name is Casey) is 22 years old and an international trade and finance student. Her parents came to Shanghai from Taizhou, Zhejiang. Our young urban professional respondents largely comprised *Zhejiang* and *Jiangsuren,* but a lot more Zhejiang than Jiangsu. Jiangsu has a lot higher proportion of state-owned enterprise than Zhejiang. *Zhejiangren* are seen typically as very ambitious. Several of our respondents were from Taizhou. Shanghai is the pivot of the YRD, which includes Hangzhou and northern Zhejiang. Taizhou is towards south Zhejiang, closer to Wenzhou, whose connections are perhaps with Fujian as much as Shanghai and the YRD. Yaya's parents came to Shanghai when she was two years old; however, they still have no Shanghai *hukou* so have no access to an array of welfare services and payments. Her parents are vendors, with a stall in the same South Bund accessories market where Robert met his wife. It is unimaginable how they have been able to help pay Yaya's university fees. The parents further fear this incredible investment risk, their biggest and perhaps only, will not bring any returns: because Casey has not yet got a good job. Unlike some market booths, her parents' booth is not doing very well. They are not 'natural communicators', 'get impatient with customers', she says. She teaches English to make ends meet, though she is studying trade and finance.

Her parents have a Taizhou *hukou*, where they lived in the rural counties. Taizhou, overwhelmingly rural when they left, now has 5 million residents and 1.5 million urban residents. Taizhou municipal government is buying out ('forcing out') collectively-owned urban peasant villages and converting them to state-owned freehold, in order to sell the leaseholds. As this happens, previous counties (*xian* – 县) become urban districts (*qu* 区). As city government takes over welfare functions from the *danwei*, they do this for all *hukou* holders, both rural and urban. City government only reaps revenues from lease sales from the areas that are *qu*, hence the conversion strategy. City, unlike *danwei*, welfare is only partial. You now have to pay a portion of your own hospital and education costs. Yaya's parents, with only a Taizhou *hukou*, had to pay the full costs for her Shanghai primary and secondary education. Her university fees are an exorbitant ¥15,000, three times those of many Shanghai institutions. Casey's course is in a non-state university, a 'joint venture' of Chinese business-studies educators and an Australian university. Casey's economically successful aunt came to Shanghai from Taizhou and paid ¥1m for a 120 m square flat in 2000. Casey's parents and grandparents are peasants become market traders, and still cannot afford to buy a flat.

If you do not own a flat, you have no security. Prospective partner's families will surely take into account Casey's family's poverty, who will not be able to contribute to any possible marriage. For our interviewees, flats often cost as much as ¥1,000,000, of which typically 40–50 per cent was paid up front. Say ¥400,000. The groom's parents, even if subsequently they move in, must find this kind of money. Often it is the bride's parents who stump up another huge sum of money for the flat's furnishings. Grooms' parents may sell their old, say 40 square metres *danwei* flat, for which they originally bought at a quarter market-price, and put the payment on the 75 square metres *xiaoqu* flat. But Casey's, originally peasant, parents had no *danwei* flat to sell.[9] Their only choice was to put all their resources into education. Rural *hukou* holders can have more than one child and Casey has a 20-year-old brother studying at Zhejiang Normal University. Casey and her brother went to middle and high school in Huangpu district, in central-most Shanghai, where she and her parents still live. They live in a *longtang*, near the market, the four of them crammed into 30 square metres. The *longtang* she estimates is about 80 per cent Shanghainese; 20 per cent *waidiren*. Casey's family pay rent to Shanghai owners who have moved to larger premises elsewhere. Most Huangpu and inner-ring Shanghainese had their *longtang* houses pulled down, were compensated and bought flats in the suburbs. This is not the case, however, for Casey's *waidiren* family.

Casey is in the fourth year of her studies. The first year after graduating she can make ¥3000. But 'even ¥10,000 is not enough', given her family's disadvantaged status and Shanghai prices. She prefers sales work. She applied at a Mitsubishi trading company, but her Japanese-language skills were inadequate. There seem to be an overwhelming number of Shanghai jobs in trading companies of one kind or another. A number of these are small and medium sized, and are sourced from factories up the Yangzi River. Some are divisions of vast industrial firms like Mitsubishi, or Baosteel itself, which, like many SOE, has its own dedicated trading companies. Where will Casey's security come from? She has not been asked to join the Party. The *Gongchandang* 'doesn't want me'. 'Lots of people compete to be in the Party. 'You need to be very academic'. Many of her friends from her class in upper school and university have applied to join the CCP. Only a few succeed. Casey's best bet is to eventually get a job in international sales.

Risk regime and urban space: a city of traders

For students coming out of the city's many universities, opportunities are to be found in some aspect of international trade. If Beijing's universities such as Tsinghua produce engineers, many of Shanghai's produce international traders. Finishing university in Shanghai, you can get work in a foreign company, hence the incentive to learn English. Shanghai comprises a massive, middle class, university-trained workforce, many of them risk takers from outside Shanghai, balanced by the different risk-regime of native Shanghainese, both sustained by an underclass of *nongminggong*.

Bachelor Steven, age 33, has set up some of his own small shops in the garment sector. Steven lives in the very northeast corner of Putuo district, again the middle ring of Shanghai districts. Steven and his father paid ¥500,000 (¥4,500 per square metre) for the 118 square metres flat in 2005, just as the property market was reaching its height. Mother and father consequently moved into the flat with Steven. When he marries and has a child, all five will live there. The flat is now the cornerstone of the generations. What was property in land for many generations has become property in the *xiaoqu* flat. Steven started a small garment company two years ago,[10] working with a small factory in Songjiang, a former county now a district in far west Shanghai. Steven's father, a professor at Shanghai University of Engineering Sciences, retired in 2008. He once started teaching but does not want a 'boring professor job' like his father. His father earned ¥6,000 a month; his mother, a *gaozhong* teacher, ¥3,500 monthly. But Steven's father had a large and comfortable university *danwei* flat, which he bought cheap and sold dear. With earned money and father's contribution, Steven, age 28, went to Macquarie University in Australia for a two-year Masters in Business Studies. Expenses and fees were ¥150,000 per year, some seven times China's out-of-province studies fees. Steven had saved, finding a job 'on the internet', working for an US IT goods and electronics marketing company in Pudong Lujiazui. The salary (¥20,000 per month) was so high it did not matter that Steven had no Shanghai *hukou*. The job was 'too much pressure' so he quit and went to Australia, doing kitchen help to pay his university fees. Steven's English is appalling, so we speak mainly Mandarin. He could not get a proper job in Australia, so he came back to Shanghai in 2007 to work for an international garment trading company, earning ¥6,000 per month. After betting his family's life savings on this Australian education, Steven came back with poor English and at a lower salary. The following year he began his own company: trading clothes and fabric, exporting globally to the US and Germany. Sometimes he imports fabrics from Japan. He uses Guangzhou tailors: 'Shanghai tailors are good, but Guangzhou are better'. 'Chanel styles are made there'. He is in the loop with the boutique shops in Maoming Road. Steven's friend, who owns a shop in the fashionable Huaihai Road, is also owner of a factory in suburban Songjiang. Steven buys items of fabric mainly from this factory; he gets them made up and sells them. With savings from his previous IT-marketing job, he had ¥70,000 with which to start his business. Much of this goes for renting his three shops: one in Beijing Road – north of Nanjing Road and just south of Suzhou Creek; the second near Zhongshan Park, further west and a bit north in Changning; and one in Chengdu Road – near the east section of Huaihai Road, just north of Xintiandi. Each of these shops is just off the beaten track so rent is not exorbitant. His original capital also serves to buy fabric items from Songjiang and other factories. His English is poor, so he uses contacts (Shanghai-based Indians) – from his previous garment trading company job – to intermediate sales. Steven has a girlfriend: not a Shanghai girl to please his family, but a much younger Henan girl. 'Shanghai girls want too much'. In Australia he had a Romanian girlfriend: 'European girls don't want babies'. Steven 'wants a stable business' before he marries: 'in marriage the *families* marry one another'.

Yang Dian is a venture capitalist (VC). He is 29 years old and just joined a Taiwanese-led Shanghai VC firm. Wang had previously worked as an engineer for oil companies: initially in California and after for another international oil company in China. His English is perfect. He studied engineering at Shanghai Jiao Tong University. This elite university gave him immediate entry into a top international company job. 'They used to recruit just from Tsinghua and Beida (Peking University)': 'now they recruit from Shanghai Jiaotong, Fudan and Zhejiang Universities'. He was able to land an international salary, earning an astonishing ¥40,000 per month. However, 'engineering was boring' and 'I wanted to try my hand at finance'. His VC firm focuses on 'IMT, IT, media and technology'. 'Eighty per cent' of the firm's 'energy' is in Shanghai, thought they have a 'joint-venture' firm in the Wuxi (Jiangsu) area. They are YRD orientated: 'looking for early stage companies'. This 'is where we are different from private equity [PE]'. Yang estimates 'there are more than 300 VC or PE companies in Shanghai'. 'The economy is bad now [February 2009]'. 'Local, international, small and big VCs and PE used to make a lot of profit. Not now'. This VC firm comprises just 15 staff globally: 10 in Shanghai. Just VC: not PE. Most 'of the companies they invest in are

Mainland: some in Taiwan'. They have a lot of 'good relations from the Harvard Business School (HBS)'. 'The leading guys in the firm all did MBAs from the HBS'. Yang 'found the job online: after university he undertook 'hard labour-market work'. Some of his colleagues who worked in (oil) Africa 'got even more'. There is always a chance (of an international salary) if you, for example, 'work for Dutch Shell'. You get 'this by moving around international jobs. They hire from all nations, all get the same salary'. 'After graduation you do the first, the second round, the third round of interviews: if they like you and you are lucky, you get a Western salary'.[11]

Yang has taken a big risk moving to a VC firm. Who do they invest in? 'They pay attention to recent graduates and new start-ups coming from universities, but do not "invest in them a lot" '. They 'focus on guys, who have had experience in one or two start-ups: there is more chance of success. You "judge people as well as an idea" '. 'You hope for IPOs but also look to make money through M&A[12] and selling our shares'. We 'prefer IPOs on the Shenzhen Exchange, because "it's easier (than Shanghai)" '. 'Government relations are important. A VC firm can negotiate for a company wanting to IPO on the Shenzhen or Shanghai Exchange'. You 'negotiate with the exchange'. 'The market seems not very open, but in fact it is open'. His company has no IPOs yet on the Shenzhen exchange 'because in fact they are a very young company, just set up four years ago'. His Taiwanese boss has been on the Mainland three to four years. He 'moved here, thinking it would be a great market'. The 'average investment in a start-up is three to five years. We don't borrow money: we have a fund'. The fund 'is other people's investment'. Part of the job is 'to build the fund', especially through 'limited partners' (LP). These 'are different from managing partners'. When there are 'profits, the limited partner will take a major share, and we as managing partner will take a minor part'.

'For start-ups and investors they look at Hangzhou, but are Shanghai focused'. 'If two start-ups are about equal we will invest in Shanghai first because the managing partners are here. You can get to the company easier if it's on Shanghai. Proximity is important'. In terms of jobs and life chances, 'Shanghai is open to all the provinces'. 'If you come from outside and can live here, it's proof of your ability'. 'Zhejiang developed earlier: the atmosphere was better'. But Shanghai people 'work for others: for international companies. There is a different lifestyle [here]'. There are 'lots of risks on start-ups'. 'Are you brave enough?' People 'from other provinces are the biggest risk takers'. They have already conquered the difficulties of moving to Shanghai. So why not take another risk? Yang is from Shandong: his mum and dad both from Shandong. His father 'used to be a farmer'. But now 'moved to the city'. He 'was born in the countryside', moved to the city when he was eight years old. His dad is 'now retired'. Although a '*waidiren*', Yang's oil company got him a Shanghai *hukou*. He has stayed near Jiaotong University in Xuhui, paying only ¥2000 per month rent. He 'needs to buy'; 'needs to get married'. He will pay as much as he can but 'needs a mortgage'. He is looking to go to a part private bank for this: CMBC: Zhaoshang Yinhang. He wants to live in *neihuan*.[13] A flat will cost him about ¥1,000,000. But to get married, 'you need to own'. His earnings have taken a hit from top dollar in the oil company to the commission pay of a VC in a troubled market.

Gendered risk

Shen Yangxie (沈阳协) was born in Shanghai. We meet near the Shanghai Indoor Stadium in Xuhui district's unfashionable southwest corner. Yangxie is 25 years old and has for some time worked in wholesale for a Hong Kong-owned upmarket stationery company. Their products 'are made of good PVC material'. The office where she works is nearby; the factory that makes the stationery and office goods is in the far northwest corner of suburban/rural Shanghai Jiading district. Yangxie's clients are nearly all foreign – Japanese, European, Taiwanese. Every month she organises factory visits for clients to come see the quality of goods and equipment. The factory employs almost all *waidiren*. This is a high-margin business, with upmarket clients, such as Textwriter, Tapei's leading retail stationery shop. The biggest Hong Kong retail stationers and office equipment firms buy from them. Yangxie sells stationery to retailers in Japan, in Dubai, in the United Arab Emirates. The Japanese and, for example, Italian clients come to the factory, but not the Gulf clients. With them it is selling only by email. Thirty per cent of business is with Japanese clients: Yangxie studied upper school Japanese and is reasonably fluent. The hardest thing is to increase her sales. Her immediate boss is Shanghainese and 'annoying'. The 'big boss', from Hong Kong, is 'kinder', but 'his daughter is not so good'. The Hong Kong owner gave his 35-year-old daughter a managerial post. (She) 'does nothing: just shouts at other people'. The owner 'is an engineer, so he knows the technical side. They have a house in Hong Kong, one in Shanghai and houses in other cities'. 'Every year he goes to Hong Kong and Japan and Germany and Finland for stationery expos'. Also to Chicago and Los Angeles. You 'get customer information from the expositions'. Yangxie goes to the Hong Kong and Japan fairs. They sell sometimes also to mass retailers like WH Smith and Walmart. Yangxie meets people at these expos, who can see her company's products. Buyers are interested in both quality of the raw materials and price. Sometimes the client will ask them to change the raw material, often sourced in Thailand; sometimes the price. The factory's purchasing agent handles sourcing. When Yangxie is handling orders – telephone work with clients is in English and Japanese – negotiations are mostly on price. She works through email, mostly in English, even with Japanese clients. Their biggest competitor is Stabilo, the American stationery and office equipment manufacturer. There are 'lots of Chinese competitors: usually very small factories near Ningbo that sell at very low prices'. There 'is no IP in China' so these companies can do cheap knock offs. We have to compete with them on price and with Stabilo on quality.

Yangxie started with this firm while a History student at Shanghai Normal University from which, surprisingly, 70 per cent of graduates do not become teachers. She is now paid well – ¥7000 per month. Living at home, she saves all of it. Born in the elegant Jing'an district, which was a lot less elegant then, her family was middle class. Her father could not go to college following the Cultural

Revolution, in which the eldest son from each urban middle-class family was sent to work in the countryside. This was Yangxie's father's older brother who was sent to freezing Dongbei. When she was a child, they moved from their Jing'an *danwei* flat to Putuo district, towards the northwest of Shanghai's middle ring road, where they moved into a flat owned by Yangxie's grandfather. The five of them live together now in this purchased *danwei* flat. Yangxie earns extra on Saturdays as a translator for Japanese clients – from English and Chinese to Japanese. Her 'mission is to give the most happiness possible to her parents'. Meaning 'to get married'. 'Not too many years to go on this' so she 'needs to hurry'. In 'China women need to get married before twenty-five: in Shanghai before thirty'.

These Shanghai interviews have oversampled for 1) people between jobs, who had time for the interviews, 2) single women or women without children, 3) those working in the export sector and 4) those who had some English.[14] Thus we oversampled for individualised, cosmopolitan respondents, and the most modern of Chinese risk regimes. These types of risk regimes will probably become more pervasive in the future. There may be more pressure for women to get married in China than the West. But urban life makes it possible for women *not* to get married. It makes it possible for them to have regimes of security that are not entirely dependent on a male breadwinner.

Mary, who we interviewed in Pudong, was born in about 1980 in Chuzhou, Anhui, some 25 kilometres northwest of Nanjing. She has not got a Shanghai *hukou*, but her earnings are so high that she does not need one. Her (biological) uncle lives in Shanghai and when Mary moved there in 2002, she stayed with him and his wife. The uncle also from Anhui, met his Shanghainese wife in Chuzhou when she was a girl, sent there during the Cultural Revolution. So many of Shanghainese, and Chinese big-city regimes of risk and (in)security have to do with the Cultural Revolution and its memory. Marriages and mobility were contracted then. Mary's aunt brought her husband back to Shanghai afterwards, where he obtained a Shanghai *hukou*. Mary never properly went to university: she 'wasn't so good at her studies'. She moved to Nanjing at age 18 to work for Ping An, China's largest life insurance company. Ping An was already starting to take on market colours and Mary worked entirely on commission. We spoke of risk. She said that life insurance, that *baoxian* was seen as 'an investment'. 'You get the money back after 20 or 30 years. 'We never speak to clients about their death', but 'about a long-term investment'.

   Mary 'learnt English by herself'. In a 'self-study system', she 'passed courses'. She enrolled in full-time study at a Nanjing English language school, obtaining a diploma (not a BA) in 2002. This helped her get a job in Shanghai at JD Power, the global marketing company, recently acquired by McGraw-Hill.[15] JD Power does research on consumer behaviour and publishes education books. They pay her ¥10,000 per month. She writes, for example, press releases for media and keeps up close relations with Chinese media. She started in an 'administration' position and got promoted to a marketing position – hence her salary. JD Power employs 800 people worldwide, 40 of which are in Shanghai: two Taiwanese – the research director and senior project manager; all the rest Mainlanders. The Shanghai branch mainly carries out research on China's consumers, their focus automotive and retail banking. Eighty to ninety per cent of China's automotive companies are their clients, for whom they write press releases and 'syndicated reports'. The press releases detail which cars give the most consumer satisfaction. Consumers wants to know which is best and the (automotive) manufacturers need to know if they are the best. They are not rewarded for flattering clients. We 'need to be honest'. What counts is not how clients feel, but 'their sales results'. 'Our risk is if a big automotive company is not happy with their sales results': it is losing a major client. She will soon mainly focus on retail banking. They will be doing research for the big state-owned banks and also a number of foreign banks. Mary thinks 'a number of the state-owned banks will not survive'. The biggest risk for McGraw-Hill is the' 'digital transition'. She is aware that the main arena of competition for publishers is increasingly education. McGraw-Hill need 'a new way of marketing for education'.

Mary is single. Her uncle still lives in Puxi.[16] She bought a flat in a Pudong *xiaoqu* in 2003. There 'are many foreigners here'. The café, where we talk, is probably 70 per cent European – you hear German spoken. Her mother and father have moved from Anhui into her flat. They paid the down payment, or more than half of it. Mary meets the monthly payments. What is risk? You can win or lose. 'If your friend is ill, that is not risk, it is more of a danger'. We speak about whether investment in education pays off. Her answer, part in jest, is the famous horse story: the mythic story of the old man who lost his mare. The Saiwengshima (塞翁失马) story. This is also known as the 'Story of the Daoist Farmer'. It goes a bit like this, though it has many versions:

> A man named Sai Weng owned a beautiful mare which was praised far and wide. One day this beautiful horse disappeared. The people of his village offered sympathy to Sai Weng for his great misfortune. Sai Weng said simply, 'That's the way it is'. A few days later the lost mare returned, followed by a beautiful wild stallion. The village congratulated Sai Weng for his good fortune. He said, 'That's the way it is'. Some time later, Sai Weng's only son, while riding the stallion, fell off and broke his leg. The village people once again expressed their sympathy at Sei Weng's misfortune. Sai Weng again said, 'That's the way it is'. Soon thereafter, war broke out and all the young men of the village except Sai Weng's lame son were drafted and were killed in battle. The village people were amazed as Sai Weng's good luck. His son was the only young man left alive in the village. But Sai Weng kept his same attitude: despite all the turmoil, gains and losses, he gave the same reply, 'That's the way it is'.

The notion of risk in this story is instructive. It is something quite different from the Western 'risk society' that Ulrich Beck (1992) has so aptly described. The risk society is very much a creature of Western and modern cosmology. The assumptions of Western risk theory are less ancient and Greek than modern, almost

Protestant. In antiquity man lived in nature, nature had reason, had pattern. In modernity, as especially Blumenberg (1985) shows, but is also implicit in Hegel, we have on the one hand God and on the other chaos, or contingency. Reason, if there is reason, is – through a glass darkly – in God as Absolute Spirit. This reason of Absolute Spirit is of course shifted onto Descartes' cogito, whose lineage is in the Weberian social actor and finally the decision-making individual in Beck's risk society. Here we have, not God, but modern agency attempting to control the contingency in his or her risk-taking decision-making. We have also the unintended consequences of the former creating new contingency or uncertainty. But to think like Mary's Daoist farmer is different. At stake is not risk-management and unintended consequences. It is some notion of 'fortune': a sort of 'what will be will be', yet all the time thinking that it may be worthwhile to take certain initiatives. This is all prior to the opposition of freedom, on the one hand, and necessity, on the other, that has been so historically widespread in Western modernity. There is something Daoist to this notion of risk: to the *Dao*'s *wu wei* of the *yin* and the *you wei* of the *yang*. Yet every clear and distinct risk-taking decision of the *yang* is already in the process of disintegration, of decomposition onto the flow and flux, the *wu wei* of the *yin*. This is *not* an 'unintended consequence'. The *yang*, the *you wei* is not something that happens that is followed by the consequence of the *wu wei*. This is underscored in Jullien's (2009) *The Great Image Has No Form*. Here we see that in Song and Ming Dynasty landscape painting, Renaissance-like form is at the same time disintegrating flux. This is not the stuff of the Protestant God, on the one hand, and contingency, on the other. In the *dao*, risk-taking decision-making is already contingency, is already its unintended consequences. Risk-taking has inscribed within it these unintended consequences. They, the Chinese, know this when they risk-take. They know that every 'action', every decisive action is at the same time built-in contingency. They further also know that the most flux-imbued situation has the acute distinction of the *yang* built in: that the flow and flux also has a 'propensity', what Jullien called the 'propensity of things'. The sort of activity, the *wu wei* that is not action but activity and is at the same time always a mix of *wu wei* and *you wei* works like this. This is at the same time to build islands of security in which this non-dialectic of risk works. Confucian filiality can build such islands.[17]

We are not arguing that the whole of Chinese risk culture is a question of such Daoist/Confucian forms of life. Of course there is considerable individualisation, lots of Westernisation. The Chinese have a term for every Western concept. For example, our idea of the subject is in Chinese the *zhuti* (主体). *Zhuti* is literally ownership of the body. The subject as a body-owner is not a million miles away from our Lockean property rights as based on the self-owning subject. Yet China without a transcendental God that needs to put order on the chaos, does not need a self to control the chaos of the body. Indeed the body is not first about contingency or chaos or even mechanism. In the West the modern is set up as the destroyer of the ancient. The ancient was Greek reason, and for Hegel, for Weber, for Foucault, the modern is fundamentally Christian. In China, unlike the West, the modern is overlain onto the ancient. In the West the Augustinian Church closed down the schools of philosophy. The old ontology of reason and harmony and different levels of teleology in nature disappeared, displaced by nature as contingency (mechanism) and God/man as reason. The West may be Greco-Christian. But the Christian – as Blumenberg describes and Foucault knew – killed off the Greek. In the East, Daoism and Confucianism co-exist and are grafted onto one another: as is the modern onto the ancient. This is Wang Hui's thesis. Is China an ancient empire or modern nation? The Kyoto School say 'modern nation' and this is very much the case for Japan. In China it is the one that is grafted into the other. The Ancient persists in the modern.

Zhang Jinping is from Shandong province, about an hour's drive from Qingdao. Her father was a PLA officer and was stationed in Beijing for about five years, where she was born in 1977. They returned to Shandong because Jinping's mother 'was an only child and needed to be near her parents'. Jinping's maternal grandmother had given birth to a younger brother for her mother, but the boy died in childbirth because they had no car and her grandmother could not get to the hospital in time. Jinping's mother for her part, despite the one-child policy, was determined to have a second child. So Jinping got a younger brother in 1980. And her mother nearly lost her job because of it. Her mother is a doctor, while her father retired in 2007: both are 'Communists, materialists'. Jinping is a Christian, 'for more than ten years now'. Was 'baptised' in Xiamen in 2006. For her Shanghai is 'too materialist'. Primary school in small-town Shandong was not ideal for learning, so her family moved to the city when her brother came of school age. With an education handicap, Jinping could only get limited tertiary education at Qingdao Normal College, which, without university status, could only award a two-year diploma. Afterwards Jinping taught *zhongxue* for seven years, at which point she began to study Japanese. Salary at the middle school back then was just ¥280 per month.

Aged 24 in 2001 she took annual leave. She 'needed something new: needed further education'. Lacking a BA she could not gain admission to Shanghai MA programmes. The best she could do was a college near Qingdao. There, an electronics major, she turned out to have remarkable linguistic abilities and was top of the class in English. This raised her profile and Xiamen Normal University accepted her.[18] Aged 26 she moved to Fujian and stayed on to undertake an MA in Chinese in Fuzhou's Fujian Normal University. This was not Chinese literature but comparative language study: her focus was ancient Chinese calligraphy, going back to the bone inscriptions. Fujian government subsidised her MA. She wanted subsequently to do a doctorate in Ancient Chinese at the prestigious Zhongshan University (Sun Yat Sen University) in Guangzhou, but her Xiamen tutor did not think she was qualified for this.

Completing her MA in 2006, Jinping wanted to move to Shanghai, but was unable to afford it. She needed to work and found a job, in a furniture factory doing international business.[19] The pay was bad, ¥1,600 per month, and she had to hide her education. She worked there only three months, laid off when she fell ill.

She then moved to another, locally and privately owned export firm, specialising in hand-made furniture, working in international and sales. There were problems. First, she was the only English speaker, causing major distrust for fear that she will steal clients (75 per cent of business is in exports) if she left the firm. Her supervisor was two years younger and was especially mistrusting. Worse, the owner made his own son general manager. The firm moved their English-speaking employees from department to department, every two to three months or so, so they did not have time to develop relations with overseas clients. The firm once had stores in every major Chinese city, but mismanagement and employee distrust has created crisis, shrinkage and debt.

The interview is near Jinping's flat in Pudong. She has no Shanghai *hukou*, which hurts low earners like her. Although born in Shandong, her *hukou* is from Fuzhou, Fujian. She finally made the move to Shanghai in 2008. She had taught some English classes in Fujian to make ends meet. Now, self-employed in Shanghai she makes approximately ¥3,000 per month. Although some months she makes only hundreds of yuan. She was interpreter for the Egyptian ambassador, yet was paid only ¥100 per day. She has taught English in adult education. Here she needs to teach six hours to earn ¥400. From Monday to Friday she can do some translation or interpretation. For translation she is paid only ¥65 per 1,000 words. To boost earning power, she is preparing her exam for a government-awarded interpretation certificate. She shares a 60 square metres flat with her brother: one bedroom each in Pudong; each paying ¥100 per month. Her brother, with an MA in gene technology from Beijing's China Agricultural University, is 30 years old and, like her, unmarried. He makes ¥4,000 per month. Until a month previous to our interview, they shared an attic apartment with no air conditioning so they could not sleep. Yet as a Christian she enjoys 'freedom and peace and rejoices in her freedom from material goods'. Her brother 'lends to her sometimes'. Jinping observes, 'Shanghai is an aging city. It is hard for the city to pay its pensions. Medical care costs so much; people need to save up for old age health care'. She is especially at risk because as a freelance, she pays into and gets no pension. Her brother and she 'share each other as a burden'.

Conclusion

Harrison White is a Knightian. He works from the opposition of, on the one hand, 'risk' and on the other, 'uncertainty'. Risk presumes not just the insurance principle. It presumes that a particular is subsumed under a universal. This is of course also the insurance principle in which a great many particular cases are subsumed under a universal. The universal is in a sense the insurance company and the particulars are the individual policies. When an individual makes decisions he/she is at the same time subsuming the particular of the contingency of the experienced world under the 'universalism' of the agent. In uncertainty there is no such subsumption. You are a particular or even a singularity in a sea of singularities. If risk is science, uncertainty is art. You are not even judging by subsuming particulars under universals, but instead making inferences from the previous case. In risk as science, there is the calculation of the Kantian understanding: in uncertainty it is instead the imagination. Chinese risk biographies it would seem are much more a question of Knightian uncertainty than Beckian risk. They do not subsume empiricals under universals. Instead of transcending the empirical for risk's universal, you instead live with the uncertainty of the empirical. You have no choice but to put yourself into the grain of the empirical and see what emerges. Risk has an *a priori* logic. The logic of uncertainty is in contrast very *a posteriori*, very empiricist.

Italian Marxism in the work of Antonio Negri has focused on the concepts of 'formal' and 'real subsumption'. Thus in Volume I of *Capital* and the *Grundrisse*, Marx speaks of handicrafts and manufacture in terms of the formal subsumption of the worker to the means of production as capital in large-scale industry for its part there is both formal and real subsumption. This is from the point of view of capital. But if we understand handicrafts and manufacture, with Smith, in terms of markets and labour-intensive market production – and not in terms already of capital – then this formal subsumption becomes no subsumption at all. It is the non-subsumption of the worker by the means of production. If the means of production are not yet capital then they are not yet a universal, subsuming the worker as particular. They are an empirical coming up against another empirical: a Humean or Smithian juxtaposition of empiricals. Risk follows a logic of subsumption while uncertainty does not. Risk, as an insurance principle, presumes the subsumption of particulars under universals.

Chinese risk regimes are regimes of uncertainty that do not privilege Knight's individual entrepreneur. In place of Knight's individualism is instead Smith's inter-subjectivity of moral sentiments, of economic and moral sentiments. Smith gives us an inter-subjectivity, not a transcendental inter-subjectivity that Husserl's phenomenology struggled to achieve, but an empirical inter-subjectivity. Yet, in contrast to Smith, at stake in China is a much more embedded inter-subjectivity of not just myself and another but a web (and not a network) of others. This is not to say that there is not a strong current of subsumptive thought in Chinese culture. Legalism from the fourth century BCE has bequeathed to us Weber's theory of bureaucracy, in which universals, especially that abstract universal which is the office, attached to general rules, subsume particulars. Mohist thought is sharply analytic this time logically with universals subsuming particulars. And these two paradigms pop up time and again in Maoism, not to mention the 'Westernisation' of contemporary Chinese capitalism. But the two overwhelming and persistent tendencies of Daoism and Confucianism, and Weber knew this, lead to rather different risk regimes. Weber captured this in his ideal-types of traditional and affective action.[20]

We are now in a position to outline a sort of ideal-type of risk regimes in urban China in comparison to their Western counterpart:

- These risk regimes are far less individualised than in the West. They are especially governed by *filiality*. This is mostly of Confucius's five filial relations of father–son, but the husband–wife and sibling-to-sibling filiality is also very important. Filiality is perhaps the central unit of security (and of course risk-sharing). But the filial unit rather than the individual is more often also the unit of risk. The unit of risk-taking is you, your spouse, your child and your and your spouse's parents. Often seven people rather than one. This becomes all the stronger since the advent and immediate spread of mortgages and flat ownership from the mid 1990s. This strengthens filiality as parents put up the 30 per cent deposit and sometimes more. And the children often then move the parents in with them.

- *Guanxi*: local state capitalism. This has become much more important from the 1990s. The connection here is typically between private sector firm and municipal or district government. In the West, we see in Harrison White's work, markets themselves are sources of security, in the context of which individual take risks. Markets and contracts are so uncertain in China, partly due to (local) government, that private firms need to work closely – in also a gift-giving, affective and long term, not to mention sometimes corrupt relations – with individuals in local government and local Party.

- The *hukou*. Anyone in any city has a *hukou*. But to have a *hukou* in a rich city like Shanghai, Beijing or Guangzhou is to have your local state as a major source of security – that is a local welfare state. With the eclipse of the *danwei* as provider of education, health and pensions, local government takes over. But without an urban *hukou* you pay a lot more for education and medical care, and you do not get a pension. The approximately 5 per cent of urban dwellers who are in the CPC have an extra source of security, not to mention *guanxi*. The PLA also is a space of security.

- Housing is at the centre of contemporary urban Chinese risk regimes. Private ownership has skyrocketed from 0 per cent to perhaps 90 per cent in a space of about a decade (1994–2004). In Shanghai, there has been a movement from *longtang* to *danwei* to *xiaoqu*, each coming with its own attached risk regime. The *danwei* flats went on highly subsidised sale in the mid 1990s, giving people another sort of state-provided housing security.[21] *Danwei* housing was built in the 60s, 70s and even 80s. But from early to mid 90s came the boom in private housing. The *xiaoqu* increased individualisation, but it also vastly strengthened family and filiality.

- Gendered risk changes. With home ownership and reinforced filiality, there is a reinforcement of women as gendered, as wife, in a husband–wife relation. Yet individualised, more pervasive inclusion of women in middle-class labour markets makes divorce possible. The rise of consumer culture leads to gendered spending patterns. The one-child policy leads to heavy family investment in daughter's education, increasingly in education abroad. Finally Shanghai's status, and everybody wanted to be Shanghainese, leads to inward marriage patterns. A Shanghai girl needs good reasons to marry a non-Shanghainese.

- Urban housing and urban space (local state capitalism) not only is a factor constituting risk regimes of individuals and others. But these risk regimes themselves in their scaling, in their up-scaling and out-scaling are themselves a motor of production of urban space.

Chinese risk culture starts not from the disembedded decision-taking individual, but instead from the situation, in which subjects find themselves. To start from the disembedded actor of neoclassical economics makes sense in the West but not in China.[22] This is a disembedded individual, a 'world-less' subject-verb-object individual who acts, ideal-typically rationally through the subsumption of particular cases under universal cognitive concepts. In China you need to start from the initial embeddedness of such a quasi-Confucian filiality as further embedded in a situation. This is not the disembedded actor of positivism but again the patterns, the ways of doing and of making sense, the background of an 'empiricist' recasting Wittgenstein's forms of life of phenomenology's life-world.

10

SHENZHEN DWELLING

Arrival and migrant urbanisms

Informal cadastre[1]

One day in late 2008 in the *chengzhongcun* (village in the city) of Guanlan, in the northern district of Shenzhen, we took a lunch break and drove out to the edge of the *cun* (village). In the surrounding area some of the local government speculative property initiatives have included the Guanlan Lake Golf Club Holiday Inn, a spectacular luxury leisure complex. The hotel is next to another local state-backed initiative, Mission Hills Golf Course, which boasts 11 championship golf courses and was until recently host of the annual Omega Mission Hills World Cup. A major water-based tourist development of holiday homes, also based on a *shiqu* (city district) local-government investment vehicle, is just up the road focused around a beautiful lake of diminishing depth and an aspirational green tourism.

The logic of urban form in this part of *Bao'an* district is not straightforwardly discernible. Landscape moves seamlessly from dense residential blocks to a field of barely visible crops and back to brick, all in the space of a few hundred metres. But after ten minutes drive the land is barren and barely cultivated at all. We talk for a while about where the *cun* ends. Sherlock Holmes laughs. Sherlock (he used his own 'English' nickname for himself) works for the *cun*'s management committee. His father had been elected to the committee that month, turning over an old regime in the nascent democratic arrangement of village affairs. He then tells a story about the boundaries of the *cun* that it is hard to provenance but revealing for its substance and its subtext. At the time of Deng's 'reform and opening up', the villages in the city in Shenzhen and other parts of the south were encouraged to expand autonomously economically. The logic linked to the growth of township and village enterprises in the same decade.

Government inspectors had been sent round to turn reform principle into economic practice, confirming the cartography of local landholdings. The inspection-based cadastre was to regularise those privileged in the first wave of SEZ exemplified by Shenzhen. Guanlan itself lay outside the 'collar' or old boundary (*guan nei*) that separates inside the special zone (*tequ*) from outside (*guan wai*) and is still marked by old, barely used forms of passport and identity control. It sits half way to Dongguan, a city famous for the fierce autonomy of local government that prompted several interventions from Beijing to rein in local government affairs in the 1990s and 2000s. However, its proximity to the growth area meant the village had the potential and the interests in attracting investment in manufacturing and the facility to accommodate the workshops and factories along with the large migrant populations and sweated labour.

The border of the *village* defined the territory for Guanlan's potential development, the geographical limits to the property rights of the village 'clan'. Before the days of geographic information system (GIS) and satellite technologies, in the wake of the moves to experiment with the growth of Shenzhen, the cadastration process was mapped out by visiting inspectors who stayed as the guests of the village's committee. Because the precise boundaries of villages in the area owed more to tenure than secure landholdings, legacies of the histories of the late-twentieth century, each *cun* was to be defined by the limits of its cultivable area. So according to Sherlock, the elders would take the inspector out during the day to formulate the map of the cultivation of a particular lychee tree. After a long lunch and hospitable dinner the inspectors went to sleep at which point a number of local families went out in vans and trucks and dug up the lychee trees in one set of plots and created afresh a new landscape of lychee trees in a different sector of settlement. They moved in turn from north to west to south and east of the village, ensuring on each occasion the *cun* made a land grab based on the fictitious cultivation of the lychee. And that is why – as Sherlock boasted – the boundaries of the *cun* are so extensive in comparison with most other villages in the region.

The story may be apocryphal but it captures a sense of the balance between local solidarities and suspicion of central authority, valorises the wit of the local to fool the bureaucrat. The story almost mimics a plot line in Gogol's nineteenth-century play 'The Government Inspector' that sketches the ambivalence and venality of both central power and local autonomy. It captures the sense in which Guanlan sees itself as a site of potential, the possibility of attracting affluence resting on the authority to develop, transact and leverage the potential of the land. As Helen Siu (2007) puts it in a study of the 'uncivil urban spaces' of post-reform China, the focus of the villages has changed in the last 30 years: 'Their main livelihood, as a villager puts it, has shifted from cultivating crops (*gengtian*) to cultivating real estate (*gengwu*)' (Siu 2007, 331).

The story also illustrates how the *chengzhongcun* has become an iconic urban form of contemporary China (Zheng *et al.* 2009). It brings together particular combinations of property rights, urban fabric and migrant demography. The particular assemblage of housing supply and cultural flows allows the city to accommodate simultaneously both extraordinary migration numbers and the dynamics of urban change; to allocate the externalities of demographic change through a particular configuration of the metropolis. The villages accommodated the massive flows of people into the city but migrant status is conditional and qualified. The costs of sustaining the migrant-driven change (the welfare externalities) are largely displaced back to sending rural districts where frequently children and sometimes wives or (less often) husbands sustain family ties and reproduction at a distance in hometowns (*laojia*).

In this chapter, we explore the manner in which the migrants to the city and built form come together to create new urbanisms in today's China. The empirical material draws on an intensive three-month period of research tracing the life histories of migrants to the city of Shenzhen that focused on four of the *chengzhongcun*. The four locations exemplified very different urban forms. In Guanlan, on the outer periphery of contemporary Shenzhen, the village economy was based significantly on the assembly of electrical manufactured goods. A single corporate venture was based in a large factory, complete with dormitory accommodation for many of its migrant workers. The village had been split in two by a major new road construction and the emergent local politics was similarly divided between the two factions who had just recently fought out control of village management, with those associated with Sherlock's father on top at the time. In Dafen, the village had famously specialised successfully in oil painting and was now the site of a host of factories that produced production lines of 'original' copies of old masters and popular modern art that is exported to the west on a grand scale. In Xiasha, the local economy was moving up the value chain with new employers locating now demanding workers with degree qualifications for their IT-based manufacturing plant. A village that was once seen as particularly lawless and notorious for sex workers and illicit trading was moving upmarket, now more respectable and the site of a form of gentrification, Shenzhen style. And in the final location in Shuiwei the proximity of the border and mass transit links to Hong Kong had driven a process of increasing residential affluence. Built into the bricks and mortar new build of luxury residential apartments blocks and *xiaoqu*, tenants and residents commuted in labour markets that increasingly linked Hong Kong and Shenzhen as a single travel to work area.

In each village (*cun*), working in collaboration with Shenzhen Academy of Social Science, over 150 migrants were interviewed about their home place of origin (*laojia*), their employment, tenure, family structure, work security and expectations of how long they planned to stay in Shenzhen. In each village a full day interview was spent with the committees that controlled the village, the families (or 'clans') that ran the villages. Through formalised joint stock companies they exercised several of the conventional property rights of 'ownership'. Village families were assigned specific plots, developments that were largely rented and sometimes sold to incoming migrants. Each village described the methods through which these joint stock companies and similar institutional forms had been developed – owned by the villagers themselves – to run the affairs of the village.

We also returned to Shenzhen two to three times a year over four years (2008–2012), repeat interviewing 16 senior planners working in the city who described the city's evolving attitudes, fears and aspirations for the villages. We worked over the same time with a range of the city's architectural and private planning practices and companies that had been asked to address the 'problems' of the *chengzhongcun*, which had been stigmatised in much journalistic discussion, paradoxically valorised in some architectural characterisation, but beyond controversy host a significant majority of Shenzhen's population, a pattern typical of the two major metropolises of Guandong province. In the Pearl River Delta's two major cities there were 139 urban villages in Guangzhou in 2006 (Hsing 2010) and 'urban villages in Guangzhou and Shenzhen make up more than, respectively, 20 and 60% of their planned areas providing homes to 80% of migrants in these cities' (Zhang *et al.* 2009, 426).

The argument of the chapter is that the process of migration generally – and the material cultures of the urbanisms of the new villages more specifically – provide a powerful lens through which it is possible to understand the relationship between the emergent city, informality, the evolving economy and the new demographies of urban China. There is an organic and paradoxical power to the village*s*. They have proved to be powerful 'integration machines' (Saunders 2010, 2) facilitating the incorporation of migrant numbers into the workings of the new China. Yet this incorporation is conditional, qualified, partial and differential. It reflects and reproduces the legacy of the *hukou* system in stratifying citizenship rights, even in its residual and reformed working. The flexibility of the urban form is predicated on insecurities of tenure, the fungibility of land use and development rights, the ownership of the land by few, the limited and partial citizenship rights of many, the development interests powerful and the capacity of the city form to evolve extraordinary (Cheng and Selden 1994).

Migration to cities in China is the major driver of demographic change but migration involves complex differences – not just between the skilled (state sanctioned) and unskilled (floating population) but also between wide-ranging matters of geographical scale (proximity) and variegated *hukou* status. There is a small but increasingly significant international flow of migration to the cities of China (Aiyar 2007; Bertoncelo and Bredeloup 2007; Bodomo 2009; Jing 2003; Le Bail 2009; Lyons *et al.* 2008), but this is dwarfed by the scale of rural–urban movement. Technically this latter migration is internal (national) rather than international but migrant journeys may range in distance from movements from local counties to a nearby metropolis to migrations that are effectively continental in scale as with the great 'exporting' of large numbers of people from Sichuan (Zhang 2001, 2008; Ma and Xiang; 1998; Xiang 2005). Analytically, the theoretical factors central to migration studies internationally are reproduced at the continental scale of China's 'civilisation state'.

Consequently, although the term is used generically in much journalistic – and some academic – description, there is no singular 'floating population' in China as such, but instead a series of increasingly discrepant status forms of migrant life (Zhang 2001). The nuanced categorisations of formal and informal status, tenure, employment and residence become important here. They reflect the importance of patterns of informality in structuring the cities of the global South (Roy 2004). The 'migrant urbanisms' of China also combine objects and cultures, bricks and mortar. Urban form is not just a *tabula rasa* shaped by migration flows or a determinant of migration cultures but instead is a synthesis of legal status, individual behaviour, cultural formation and land economy. Material anthropologies of home and belonging are consequently central to the emergent metropolis. And welfare externalities of the new markets are mediated by these migrant urbanisms in ways that distinguish the cities of China from the migration structured metropolis of Europe or the US.

In this context, we might contrast the ambivalent sense of the geographies of the villages in the city in this chapter with the pejorative sensibility found in disapproving characterisation of the *chengzhongcun* typified in vernacular journalistic description. In one formally sanctioned piece that diagnosed the problems for Shenzhen:

> A typical urban village in today's China has absolutely no planning. The residents used to be farmers but now are mostly landlords and the majority of residents are migrant workers. The streets, if they can be called that, are narrow, dirty and lined with all kinds of small shops selling fake or shoddy merchandise. It's the birthplace of much of a city's sweatshops and crime cases. Like bankrupt State-owned enterprises (SOEs), these villages are remnants of the old times, when urban planning was non-existent and suburban farmers scraped a living from growing vegetables and peddling to city slickers. But unlike the SOEs, few solutions have worked.
>
> If you demolish them without proper compensation, there will be unrest among the residents. If you pay market price, the cost will be prohibitive since urbanisation has driven them into prime real estate. And since municipal governments can hardly afford the job, they'll hand it over to developers, who can be unscrupulous and ruthless in kicking out the original residents. In cities like Shenzhen or Guangzhou, the housing complexes villagers built have such narrow passageways that only one bike can go through them. Stairways are dark all day long and corridors are cramped and piled with all sorts of junk. Fire hazards are everywhere and there's little chance a fire truck could get close. Suddenly awash with easy money, some of these landowners and sellers have turned to business ventures, but stories of gambling and drug binges also abound. A distant relative of mine died of overdose while squandering his 'land money' on drugs. Some of his old neighbours are still spending their entire days on mahjong games. Desperate for a way out, some cities have turned to consultants from Western countries. Surprisingly, these experts say, 'Don't change a thing'. This is how people live and interact. It reflects a lifestyle that should be respected…
>
> So, are 'urban villages' a cultural heritage or an eyesore? They are not on anyone's tourist routes, and the renting public inside them don't live there because they like to, but because they cannot afford a better place. Would a Western consultant say, 'Don't clean up a slum because gentrification will change the way people interact?' Probably not. Allow me to be blunt: these 'urban villages' are virtual slums.
>
> (Zhou 2006).

Guanlan is far from unusual in this sense. In the opening-up process, Shenzhen has grown from a site of tentative urbanisation of a few hundred thousand in 1978 to an estimated current population of somewhere between 10-15 million today (depending on the cartographic definition of the metropolitan area and the numbers of migrants counted as resident). It became a city with its own prefectural administrative status in 1988. By the year 2000, Liu claims Shenzhen was ranked nationally in China:

- fourth in GDP among Chinese large and medium size cities;
- fourth in total industrial output;
- second in total value of industrial profits;
- second in tax revenues reported to the central government;
- third in local fiscal income;
- first in total export and import value;
- first in per capita GDP; and
- first in per capita productivity.

(Liu Kaiming 2007)

Liu Kaiming (2007) has characterised the growth of the city in terms of four phases. In phase 1 (from 1979–1985) the focus was on the construction of large-scale urban infrastructure. Initially, most migrant workers came from other parts of Guangdong province and concentrated on work at construction sites, stone and sand quarrying and transportation. From 1983, the city saw the development of export-processing factories, the system known as *sanlai yibu* (three imports and one compensation). Imports from Hong Kong of raw material, unassembled components and prototype models with the one compensation the provision of technical equipment in exchange for land and labour, and eventually factories to be turned over to locals. The model was state-led enterprises (Cartier 2002), linked to (frequently Hong Kong-focused) FDI, which grew in number, adopting an even more flexible employment policy and tended increasingly to hire young female workers (Pun 2005; Rofel 1999). Migrants began to come from further afield, increasingly from beyond Guandong Province, but the gendered division of labour was sustained. In what Kaiming describes as phase 2 from 1986–1992 more factories and enterprises appear, developing a wider geographical focus but remaining largely within the special economic zone area. In phase 3 (1992–2000) and phase 4 (2000–present) the city is characterised by rapid restructuring; the factories and production systems move up value chain and systemic factory relocations begin. In the most recent phase (2000–present) the focus has been on human capital. The city has an increasingly upskilled labour force. In the early 2000s it was sometimes alleged – if with questionable provenance – that there were more PhDs in Shenzhen that in rest of China combined (So 2002; Liu 2007).

In 2003, the majority of migrant workers stayed in Shenzhen for an average of three years. The average annual turnover rate of workers was 30 per cent in Shenzhen's factories and enterprises (in some enterprises the turnover rate reached

TABLE 10.1 Changes in Shenzhen's resident and temporary resident populations, 1979–2000 (10,000 persons)

	Shenzhen city (including SEZ population		Shenzhen SEZ	
	Shenzhen hukou residents	Temporary residents	Shenzhen hukou residents	Temporary residents
1979	31.26	0.15		
1980	32.09	1.2	8.41	1.00
1981	33.29	3.30	9.83	3.30
1982	35.45	9.50	12.86	7.80
1983	40.39	19.00	16.50	12.00
1984	43.53	30.61	19.14	14.61
1985	47.86	40.29	23.19	23.79
1986	51.45	42.11	25.74	23.13
1987	55.60	59.84	28.68	31.29
1988	60.14	93.00	32.19	46.21
1989	64.82	126.78	36.20	66.49
1990	68.65	133.29	39.53	61.45
1991	73.22	165.31	43.21	76.59
1992	80.22	180.68	47.28	74.73
1993	87.29	207.30	52.14	66.80
1994	93.97	241.54	56.52	91.01
1995	99.11	245.96	59.96	91.22
1996	103.38	255.10	63.28	97.02
1997	109.46	270.18	68.12	106.98
1998	114.60	280.36	71.48	113.14
1999	119.85	285.29	74.81	115.38
2000	121.48	579.36	76.59	166.76

Sources: *Shenzhen Statistical Data Yearbook* (Beijing: China Statistical Publisher, 2001); Shenzhen Fifth Census.

50 per cent). In 2007, 70 per cent of migrant labourers were in Shenzhen for less than three years, and 70 per cent were 22 years old or younger, while 5 per cent were 35 years old or older. Twenty-eight per cent make RMB 700–900 per month, while 39 per cent make 900–1,200 and 19 per cent make 1,200–1,600 (Shenzhen Labor Service 2008). The city consequently captures a sense of China's economic change less in microcosm than amplified and magnified. An extraordinarily young population is subject to both the extraordinary growth rates of the local economy at above 20 per cent per annum for most of the last three decades, and the city doubling in size every four years. But it is also subject to rapid re-structuring, acute insecurity and the flows of people characterised by secondary status in the city itself and sustained links to a homeplace sometimes at great distance.

Migration to the city in China

As Cindy Fan has pointed out, the extensive research literature on migration in China has highlighted how the *hukou* has structured the 'two circuits of migration': one of 'privileged migrants sponsored by the government and the other consisting of peasant migrants relying on their own resources' (Fan 2008, 1). But this simplicity belies quite how graded the multiplication of migrant status has become in today's China. The categories of belonging, the associated rights and the links between new sites of settlement and conditions of bare life make such binary subject positions more complex. There is also no word in Chinese that directly translates 'migrant'. The closest, perhaps, is *qianyi renkou*, which refers to the moving population – although this refers specifically to the officially moving population as allocated in planned quotas and under specific rules (for details, see Chan and Zhang [1999]). Below is a sample of some terms used by a variety of sources to refer to migrants, mostly from rural areas, entering the city to work.

TABLE 10.2 Terms used to refer to migrants entering the city to work

迁移人口	*qianyi renkou*	moving population
流动人口	*liudong renkou*	floating population
农民工	*Nongmingong*	peasant workers
外来人口	*wailai renkou*	population arriving from outside
外出务工者/员	*waichu wugongzhe/yuan*	people leaving to work for others
进城务工者/员	*jincheng wugongzhe/yuan*	people entering the city to work for others
打工妹/仔	*dagongmei/zai*	working girls/boys
暂住人口	*zanzhu renkou*	temporary population
边缘人	*bianyuan ren*	marginal figure

According to the China Statistical Yearbook in 2007, China's 2007 population was 1.32 billion, with 594 million in urban areas and 728 million in rural areas. However, population statistics based on status in the *huji* systems (the general system that determines one's individual *hukou*) are neither complete nor reliable. In Shanghai, for example, there are now four categories defined to represent the urban population: *changzhu renkou, huji renkou,* and *wailai renkou* (long-term living population, *huji* or '*hukou* in area' population, and 'coming from outside' population). The final category is broken up in another section into over six months long-term living population (*changzhu renkou*) and less than six months floating population (*liudong renkou*); though, by definition, floaters of less than six months cannot be accurately documented by a yearly publication. By contrast, data from Beijing (Beijing Statistical Yearbook 2008) does not give specific figures for distinguishing between *wailai renkou*; instead, there is a category of *changzhu renkou*, of which *wailai renkou* is a sub-category, while the category of *zanzhu renkou* or temporarily living population is a sub-category of a population numbered by *huji* (Beijing also uses the category of *huji* population in other sections). That the temporary population in 2008 was 5.549 million, while the *wailai renkou* is only 4.197 million, leads one to believe that these are representing similar categories to Shanghai, though this is not made explicit.

TABLE 10.3 Population by *hukou* (2007)

Region	Population	Residing in the townships, towns and street communities with permanent household registration there	Residing in the townships, towns and street communities for more than 6 months, with permanent household registration elsewhere	Residing in townships, towns and street communities for less than 6 months, with permanent household registration elsewhere, having been away from that place for more than 6 months	Residing in the townships, towns and street communities, with place of permanent household registration unsettled
	Total surveyed	*Percentage of total*	*Percentage of total*	*Percentage of total*	*Percentage of total*
National total	1,188,739	90.38	8.44	0.69	0.48
Beijing	14,554	58.81	38.31	2.38	0.49
Shanghai	16,708	69.73	28.66	1.36	0.26
Tianjin	9,896	86.32	13.41	0.22	0.04
Chongqing	25,850	92.79	6.62	0.18	0.41
Jiangsu	69,503	89.17	10.09	0.27	0.46
Zhejiang	45,844	82.54	15.73	1.21	0.53
Guangdong	85,649	69.10	25.64	4.29	0.97

Data in this table are obtained from the *2007 National Sample Survey on Population Changes for 2005*. The sampling fraction is 0.900‰.

Subject categories are recorded differently in different cities at different times: the category *wailai renkou* appears in the Shanghai Statistical Yearbook 2006 but not in the 2005 version or earlier, though floating population categories were recorded in the Fifth Census conducted in 2000. So undercounting – or *inability to count* – the floating population, as well as their emergence in recent statistical yearbooks, are two statistical artefacts. The formal record and the informal reality rarely correspond. Shenzhen in its Shenzhen Statistical Yearbook 2007 uses the cryptic category of *fei-huji renkou* (non-*huji* population) to represent its substantial, but very fluid and changing, population (8.5 million long-term living population in 2008, of which 6.5 million have a *hukou* elsewhere as of 2006).

This means that while the term *'liudong renkou'* is commonly used as a shorthand for the country's 'floating population' the subject position of the floating population is both more complex and more differentiated by geographical scale than it commonly appears. Comparing the figures that Naughton (2007: 129–130) gets from Liang and Ma (2004, *China's Floating Population: New Evidence from the 2000 Census*), suggest a 144 million floating population; 65 million are 'local', away from their place of residence but in same county; 36 million 'out of county but inside province' migrants; and 42 million who move outside the province of their residence.

In the National Bureau of Statistics (NBS, 2002) – Department of Population Social Science 2002 report on the 2000 census, we find that, of the 42.42 million inter-provincial floating population, 16.4 per cent come from Sichuan, 10.2 per cent come from Anhui and 10.2 per cent come from Hunan; along with Jiangxi, Henan and Hubei, the six provinces provide 59.3 per cent of all migrants who cross provincial boundaries. A significant 35.5 per cent float into Guangdong (the growth region of the Pearl River Delta including Shenzhen and Guangzhou), while 8.7 per cent float into Zhejiang, 7.4 per cent float into Shanghai, 6.0 per cent float into Jiangsu (the later three are Yangzi River Delta, making up 22.1 per cent of destinations), 5.8 per cent into Beijing and 5.1 per cent into Fujian (a total of 68.5 million interprovincial floating migrants float into these six destinations). Of the total 121.07 million 'floaters', 32.67 million are urban. Hence the term 'peasant worker', or *nongmingong* does not apply to these statistics.

TABLE 10.4 Migrants' origins, by place and percentage

Sending area	Sample number	Percentage of inter-province national	Percentage of all national
Sichuan	77,350	11.69	3.98
Anhui	76,044	11.49	3.91
Hunan	61,637	9.31	3.17
Henan	59,690	9.02	3.07
Jiangxi	49,054	7.41	2.52
Hubei	47,014	7.10	2.42
Guangxi	37,468	5.66	1.93
Chongqing	30,786	4.65	1.58
Guizhou	30,603	4.62	1.57

Source: 2005 1 per cent survey compiled by Tyler Rooker.

In some ways, the major metropolises of Beijing and Shanghai are poor examples with which to understand the floating population, if such a stable categorisation or

subject is to have ontological meaning. As municipalities under the direct administration of the State Council, they lack rural hinterlands (in the statistical accounting
sense) and so the majority of 'floaters', if defined as those who leave their hometowns
to work elsewhere, are not found there. Instead, intra-county and intra-provincial
movement is more common. If *inter-provincial movement* is the definition of floating
then the total population of floaters in China reduces significantly and in 2005 is
between 40–50 million, or only 4 per cent of the population of China. This makes
the significance of the floating population – symbolically powerful – analytically both
more questionable and more mutable for an understanding of China. However, if one
takes 600 million (or 60 million for urban floaters, assuming all inter-provincial
migrants float to cities, and adding 10 million for short-term, non-registered floaters)
as the urban population of China in 2005, floaters make up 10 per cent of city population, making them an emergent minority in any understanding of urban China,
though perhaps their importance is overemphasised due to scholarly attention to
Beijing, Shanghai, Guangzhou and Shenzhen where they are a much higher
percentage. This speaks to the heart of the imperative to recognise the 'different
Chinas', or the role of local states, in understanding and making 'formal' the 'subject'
of the floating population. In an analysis of migration, legal status is one of the major
determinants of differing life chances and the complex and localised patterns of
migrant status make visible the power of regional and city-by-city differentiation of
migration status.

As might be expected, *hukou* registration has a negative effect on permanent
migration though not on temporary migration. Yang (1993) explains the relationship between *hukou* and types of and reasons for migration. Even with strict control
of *hukou* transfer, post-reform people can move freely throughout the country. It is
the lack of social services, employment and schooling in which the *hukou* is
embedded that makes permanent living in the city by migrants more difficult (and
allows local government to maintain control over population). Using a study of
Zhejiang province in 1986, Yang defines migrants as those who have moved minimally across township (*xiang*) boundaries, with permanent migrants staying longer
than one year and temporary migrants staying less. The reasons for migration of
permanent migrants with non-agricultural *hukou* are employment and return from
countryside (following Mao's re-education movement); while agricultural *hukou*
migrants move for help, marriage, military or looking for a job. Temporary migrants
are more motivated by seeking of employment. In general, non-agricultural *hukou*
migrants are less likely to move for simple economic reasons since they historically
paid their *danwei* a fee for long absences (though this has been reformed). The
results clearly show that non-agricultural household registration significantly
increases the probability of permanent migration. However, once its function as a
control of migration disappears, such as in the case of temporary migration, the
type of household registration loses its significance (Yang 1993, 814). In this sense
the *hukou* has lost its role as an absolute regulator of migration. To some extent
migrants are largely free of government regulation since destination governments
have few rights to regulate and local governments have trouble locating migrants.

Ma and Xiang (1998, 560) suggest that the links between migrants and their home place remains strong, the sense of *laoxiang* (*tongxiang*) and native place. More often than not, migrants from one place tend to move to a city in small groups rather than as individuals. *Laoxiang* have shared experiences, place of origin and dialect. In their study, 75 per cent found first job networking through relatives/ *laoxiang*; 77 per cent moved to city in organised groups of two to five people. Construction teams are recruited from fellow *laoxiang* into teams of contracted workers who do construction jobs from massive, official, state-owned company construction, to interior decoration (see also Yuan and Wong 1999). Native place can be viewed as a 'container' in which kinship relationships (*xueyuan guanxi*) geographic relationships (*diyuan guanxi*) are fostered (Ma and Xiang 1998, 562; 2000). Migrant enclaves consist of migrants from the same county or even village (not province), and are the result of migration across province boundaries (Zhang 2001) In this sense migration to the modern city builds on China's traditional relationships of *diyuan* and *xueyuan* (based in place and kin). The vernacular use of the 'floating population' as a singular analytical subject masks many forms of status and distance of travel. Across China – although as we have seen the data need to be treated carefully and the regional variations are pronounced – the majority of migrants are within county or within province (long-distance migrants tend to be one-third of all migrants). And there is no stable state. As cities grow rapidly, the numbers change but also national, regional and local reforms and amendments restructure the formal and informal status of new arrivals in the metropolis.

As the 1980s witnessed the end of the rationing of grain and the emergence of new markets China also saw the emergence of migrant enclaves in cities. These linked to the patterns of location-specific migrant employment described. Most significantly they create a sense of the rural in the city – linked to dual systems of entitlement and nuanced forms of 'cityzenship'. As cities expand, the transition from collectively owned rural land to state-owned urban land restructures tenure patterns but only when property rights are redefined (Naughton 2007, 118–120). In many parts of China villages at the edge and in the middle of the cities create a juxtaposition of rural property rights sustained inside the metropolis in the *chengzhongcun* – the villages in the city. The contrasting property rights at the heart of the villages in the city and in new urban residential districts (or *xiaoqu*) create different ways of dwelling in the city. And the process of urban migration in particular can only be understood through this link between personal status, property rights and these villages, as this chapter goes on to examine.

Material anthropologies of home and work

Four scholars in particular have focused on the interplay between these flows of people and the gendered spatialities that they reproduce and challenge: Pun Ngai, Ching Kwan Lee, Dorothy Solinger and Zhang Li. Their scholarships works mostly through the conventions of cultural anthropology but also speaks to the intellectual work that has tried to make sense of what it means to make a place, shape a home or an identity through the fabric of the changing city. Solinger's most noted work highlights the differential status the city endows on new arrivals (Solinger 1999) and while Zhang's study is of migrant entrepreneurs (not migrant workers), she considers workers explicitly in the chapter on gender (Zhang 2001). Lee and especially Pun focus particularly on women workers, with Lee's study a comparison between two factories (one in Hong Kong; one in Shenzhen) of the same electronics company, and Pun's an ethnographic study of a Shenzhen factory located in a *chengzhongcun* with Pun living in the workers' dormitory and working alongside them in the factory.

Lee (1998) finds that matron workers in Hong Kong and maiden workers in Shenzhen utilise different networks (familial versus localistic) to engage the types of discipline imposed upon them (hegemonic versus despotic). Work and product are similar in both places but in Hong Kong, the middle-aged workers view the factory as a place to work casually with expectation that family has priority over work and factory discipline is loosely enforced. They cover for one another when family problems arise in contrast to the maiden workers of Shenzhen that are single, immature, unmarried young migrants. They work in the factory with low aspirations and seek to escape the village, acquire skills and explore freedom (with some entrepreneurial aspirations). The factory regime is the source of a 'discipline' of physical control, timing of labour and the docking of wages for rules/discipline violation. Workers are involved in localistic networks based on native place, province/county of birth and whether northerner or southerner. Localistic networks in such scholarship have efficacy, they facilitate the first trip to Shenzhen, obtain permits, recommendations for changing jobs, financial assistance and running errands. Different institutions (family/localistic) translate into shop floor practices producing two factory regimes.

Pun (2005) presents a substantial challenge to existing research and theories of migration. She foregrounds the emergence of *dagongmei* ('working girls') as a social identity in China at the heart of Chinese modernity, post-socialist transformation and global capitalism. *Dagongmei* are young, normally single, women migrant workers concentrated in residential dormitories and working long hours in export-focused factories. In socialism, the ungendered *gongren* was one of the vanguards of the revolution. The *dagongmei* is a gendered, exploited, a looked down upon emerging subject. Socialism for Pun is in retreat to capitalist global economy that relies on regulations, class, rural–urban differences and sexual relations; the city of Shenzhen relies on the particular exploitation of female labour. Despite the formal separation of factory and dormitory, Pun claims that their propinquity increases worker dependence, trapping them in the company. Most *dagongmei* quit for marriage and return to village, though this fate is resisted. Cantonese, Chaozhou and Hakka are distinguished like Sichuan, Hunan or Hubei workers. These are identities based on *tongxiang*. The value of 'working' (*dagong*) is determined by market forces and surplus value is extracted as component of capitalist profit. In Pun's work, Shenzhen factories are known as 'peach orchards' – factories filled with young, docile girls. Eighty per cent of factories in Shenzhen are owned by Hong Kong capital (Pun's good friend, Mr Zhou, was the major shareholder and company director of the factory where her research was conducted). Her research took place over eight months in 1995 to 1996 but some of the cultural formations were replicated, in some of the *chengzhongcun* migrant life stories picked up in our research decade later, particularly among the young women working in the factory of SAGAM in Guanlan – one of the sites of the research that informs this book.

Urban form and migrant urbanisms

The *chengzhongcun* of Shenzhen provide a fascinating lens through which to examine the migrant urbanisms of the new metropolis. Although Shenzhen's chief planner (interview April 2012) suggested that all land in Shenzhen has now been made formally 'urban', the city is structured by several hundred villages in the city, each effectively an economic actor driven by family associations – commonly organised as joint stock companies – that have secured the property rights of the *chengzhongcun*. Companies are bound by legal and formal sanction, report annually and are structured around share ownership distributed between members of the villages. But the villages vary greatly in their urban form. Some – such as Shuiwei – are constituted by tracts of land indistinguishable from the fabric of the city of Shenzhen, where redevelopment has erased almost all marks of the old infrastructure and whose boundaries can only be traced on a map. Close to the Hong Kong border, Shuiwei is effectively part of Shenzhen but also residentially a commuter suburb of Hong Kong. In contrast Guanlan appears more of a throwback, formally urban but distinguished by low density and peripheral location beyond the Shenzhen 'collar' that marks the old enterprise zone border. Xiasha is gated off from the rest of Shenzhen, dense residential build surrounding a major public square, but is located on a main road connecting residents to the city Metro system in walking distance. Dafen is an hour journey by car from downtown Shenzhen across unoccupied rural landscapes but is now densely built up with the oil painting factories, showrooms and hotel spaces for the purchasers of the village's export and a mass transit connection to downtown imminent in 2009.

Reading urban form and migrant urbanisms

Le Zheng (2008) has suggested that the *chengzhongcun* in Shenzhen function like a sponge, accommodating migrant flows and then squeezing them away from the city at times when growth slows and factory relocations occur. Potentially, this systemic integration of migrant labour minimises the welfare externalities of flows of people at minimal costs. It is sustainable when labour supply is plentiful and cheap. It speaks to the insecurities of the Shenzhen labour market that have been publicised in the post-2008 fiscal crisis period with a focus on labour unrest, deaths in some plants, 'suicide' nets outside other blocks and a scrutiny of the labour process of IT giants such as Apple in their Shenzhen production sites. But the urban form of Shenzhen is more subtle than the caricature. In this section of the chapter we argue that the propensity of the city to accommodate migration flows generates migrant urbanisms that are neither state controlled nor market generated and that reflect the increasing differentiation of Shenzhen society.

If the status of people who move is pluralised and there is no straightforward vocabulary of 'who is a migrant' – as research on migration in China suggests – then the urban form that accommodates these flows of people to Shenzhen is equally complex. In the four *chengzhongcun* where research was carried out for this study it is common to see dominant rental stock housing migrant workers alongside the proliferation of the sorts of new residential *xiaoqu* described in Chapters Four and Nine. It is a restless landscape. A powerful element of the *chengzhongcun* phenomenon is the ability of the urban fabric to evolve in relationship to the functional demands of the local economy. The central argument that we suggest here is that the built form, migrant status and the dynamic economy need to be understood synthetically. The *chengzhongcun* in Shenzhen concentrate power and affluence in the hands of small numbers of Guangzhou clans and the living conditions of many of the 'floating population', the 'marginal characters' of Liu Kaiming's (2007) scholarship, are commonly precarious and grim. But as demonstrated above the commonly invoked binary flows of migration are complicated by both the rapidly changing economy and the nuanced characteristics of the migrants themselves. The extraordinary pace of social and economic change in Shenzhen has been both realised and facilitated by the residential pattern. The *chengzhongcun* in this way have both the facility to drive economic change in their own right and the potential both to drive the reshaping of the urban fabric and to accommodate changing demand. Precarious tenure and cyclical migration to the country and back lends itself easily to selective upskilling of labour markets, laying off the less skilled and bringing in new labour, incremental changes to existing housing stock and wholescale plot transformations through demolition, displacement and redevelopment. In this sense, the *chengzhongcun* demonstrates a particular relationship of the urban system and the 'socialist market'. Small parts of the system combine localised power with architectural and planning logics that emerge from the interest of the village rather than those of the city. This constellation of 200–300 discrete village interests across the city relate to City Hall, the planning department and the state. This geometry generates a different organic sense of the metropolis, neither idealised nor demonised, but an urban form that is flexible and constantly mutating and provides as much an institutional element of 'Shenzhen speed' referenced in Chapters 3 and 4 as the rhetorics of rapid real estate development.

In institutional form each urbanised *cun* has a *juweihui*, a committee run by the families of the clan that have original responsibility for the village (previously a *cunweihui*). The parallel CP structure runs through the same form – in most of the *cun* the head of the *juweihui* was also the head of the CP locally. In one case – Guanlan – the *juweihui* had been fiercely contested in democratic elections as factions disagreed on how to persuade Japanese FDI not to move away from the village. Each village tends to run property development through a joint stock company, with a fixed number of shares (share holding company) allocated across the families of the village. In the villages studied, individual families had share allocations linked to specific plots of land. In some of the villages 'marrying out' resulted in loss of rights to pass on share holdings, in others more flexible inheritance of property was possible. In some villages women held shares; in others they did not. But in each village there is a sense of family continuity, curated history and a strong sense of property lineage and genealogies of interest.

In most of the *chengzhongcun*, the village committee constructs a narrative and an exhibition that tells the story of the village itself and the triumphs of the particular clans that have been in charge. In Guanlan this was present in a small hall, whereas in Dafen and Xiasha and Shuiwei, grand municipal buildings display panoramas of architectural models that describe the local history, complete with pictures of famous visitors (for example, Bill Clinton visited Xiasha). In Shuiwei, a cultural history wall marks the boundary of the main public square. As with several spots in Shenzhen – and not without controversy – the figure of Deng Xiaoping is given equal prominence in representational space of the wall with the figure of Mao. 'History' becomes a visual genealogy of – in Shuiwei – the Guang family. The wall displays in miniature an unrelieved triumph of the victories of the local Guang family, one of whose members described to us in detail each section of the wall. And then a slightly embarrassed silence as we came to one panel, paused a second after a brief description in heavy *Guandong-hua* (Cantonese) – not translated – and then moved on. This was the section describing the putative invasion of Shenzhen by the British in 1908, an excursion from Hong Kong that was ostensibly defeated by the villagers of Shuiwei.

On repeat visits we spend a few hours at a time with the village elders. Some passed the time 'cultivating' their real estate by collecting rents in the new developments, playing cards and sending their children overseas for education. This is the image of the indolent rural clans, empowered by the serendipity of Shenzhen's geography that spreads the city like toothpaste to the north of the colonial legacy of Hong Kong. But more often the *juweihui* were interviewed and described detailed architectural masterplans, negotiations with city hall and new initiatives for the village. In this sense they mediate between the forces of change in Shenzhen as a whole and the changing social landscape of the city. They exemplify the evolving location of the *chengzhongcun* within an implicit urban hierarchy that is neither market rational nor state controlled but something of a hybrid between the two. The urban form of the *chengzhongcun* serves not only as Le Zheng suggests as a sponge for the absorption of migrant labour. The morphology itself becomes an actor in the evolution of Shenzhen through the pluralities of emergent economic specialisation and differential integration of migrants into the city.

FIGURE 10.1 Shenzhen Districts (Shenzhen City Government)

Shenzhen districts

Guanlan, Bao'an

Guanlan was the *chengzhongcun* studied that was furthest from Shenzhen's downtown areas of Futian and Luohu. Much of the employment was dominated by the major factory of SAGAM, said by our hosts to be backed by Japanese money. While we were interviewing migrants and the *juweihui*, negotiations with the company were ongoing about their site lease. The company were considering relocation and in the face of the 2008 downturn were negotiating hard with the village about the terms on which they were prepared to stay. Migrant workers interviewed from the factory described how they were assembling electronics and telecommunications/mobile phone parts. A web search reveals SAGEM to be a subsidiary of a major transnational telecommunications company with production facilities in Shenzhen but not at this *chengzhongcun*. Whether SAGAM was a derivative copy of the SAGEM brand was less clear.

A lot of the workers corresponded closely to the *dagongmei* described in Pun's work (2005). Early in the morning and at meal times the streets were flooded with factory workers with identical green uniforms. So many, so young. And in interviews again the sense of the fragility of the jobs and the uncertainty around the future was palpable. Most of the workers interviewed stayed in the dormitories linked to the factory though several lived with boyfriends in privately rented rooms outside. Visually, sartorial uniformity generated a sense of numbers and a sense of solidarity. The sea of workers at lunch time and home time lent an appearance of security that was clearly not felt by the workers themselves or those with an insight into the stories of the factory in recent months. Many testified that they faced a choice between schooling costs in Guanlan and schooling costs at home. And in tight times the financial costs of education outweighed the social costs of separation and mothers and fathers described how they sent their children to school in *laojia*, their extended parents or extended family providing the childcare.

The micro-geographies of the village were also powerful. Two interviews were conducted with landlords who were both visibly affluent and also sanguine about the future of the village. Conducted within the view of a very large rat standing just behind the hangout of the two villagers, we sat together while they spared the time for the interview after they had spent the first part of the morning under a canvas shooting the breeze, passing the time of day. Both were relatively comfortable, both not too bothered about the migrant population, both owned their own blocks. Sherlock – our link with the joint stock company – took me to the blocks owned by one of the men, smiling when I asked him why the 'strict' building codes with heights zone-limited to six floors were flagrantly contradicted by manifest examples of eight and nine floors of what are known as handshake apartments (*woshou fang*), where the gaps between buildings are so narrow that you can reach across to the tenant across the way. Several of the migrant workers agreed to conduct interviews inside their rented accommodation – normally no more than a small room shared by several people, or the back room of a ground-level retail space in the village. Small spaces were domesticated in circumstances that were striking. Two women boiled hot water that could be sold both straight from the fire or purified for a small mark up. While the interview was conducted they carried on feeding the fire with small pieces of wood gathered from local waste, the stove still covered in green leaves, a young boy selling water by the small bottle and large bottle. In another back room one evening a couple living in the back of a shop had taken home hundreds (maybe thousands) of parts of wire connectors to put together by hand while sitting over the kitchen table. They described how they were paid piece rate for this work but had no idea of the purpose of the parts they were assembling. One of their neighbours suggested that it is common for this sort of 'leakage' from the factory to feed the informal economy of electronic parts and circuits produced locally also. In another small space, a phenomenon replicated in other villages was the presence of a 'paying' mahjong table located in the interstices of one of the handshake apartment blocks; the host coordinating the game and taking a small percentage for the function. There was also some evidence of migrants both finding rental spaces through networks of chain migration that reproduced the kinship relationships (*xueyuan guanxi*) and geographic relationships (*diyuan guanxi*) described above (Ma and Xiang 1998, 562; 2000) although it was less clear the extent to which these generated specifically migrant enclaves from particular regions as opposed to micro-geographies of the networked *chengzhongcun*.

Dafen Cun

In Dafen *Cun* there are over 5,000 painters producing over five million paintings per year, generating an export surplus of more than RMB 100 million per year. By 2007, over RMB 380 million in oil painting and painting-related goods were exported from Dafen, 60 per cent to the international market (Financial Times 11 December 2008). In 1989, a Hong Kong entrepreneur started up the first 'art college' locally, training gifted painters to reproduce existing masters, directed mostly to the global circuits of the hotel and corporate world. Huang Jiang, originally from Guangzhou, had migrated to Hong Kong and ran a commercial studio there but experimented with a new site in what was then the rural outskirts of Shenzhen. The chances are that if you have stayed in a mainstream hotel chain – not just in Hong Kong or Singapore – but in Cleveland or London or Frankfurt – you will have seen at least one product of Dafen on your wall.

In terms of urban form, the village is small, it only occupies 0.4 kilometre squared and is surrounded by countryside even though literally designated as a village in the city. According to interviews with one of the authors with people working, selling and starting up their own business in the village, most artists come from all over China, not just from the south, frequently migrating to Dafen after moving first to Guangzhou. As several people said, the 'top ten *laoban*' (bosses) in the art world locally are from Hong Kong.

The pattern of mass production and the labour process of the factory assembly line have been extended to the work of oil painting. Assembly lines sit in over 30 factories in Dafen. A line may generate thirty copies of a Van Gogh *The Starry Night*, a piece of classic calligraphy or a Picasso. All are hand-painted, collectively copied, each painter specialising in a nose or a border, a colour, a pattern or an eye. The products are sold by the crate and by the container, it is possible to buy 50 Miros, a hundred copies of Constable's *The Hay Wain*, each individually copied, 'the work of art in the age of personal reproduction'. Over the years the early factories in Dafen have been challenged by new sites, many of the painters have gone on to set up their own production lines. And some of the streets display individual artists that increasingly produce 'original' oil painting work, although the genres of such work commonly describes itself in genre terms – 'post-modernist oil painting' or 'Russian Art' (see Figure 10.1).

The village now boasts a major exhibition space designed by the architects Urbanus. With no major permanent collection and only a series of socialist realist celebratory images of the triumph of Shenzhen in general and Dafen in particular exhibited inside, the gallery space has struggled slightly, although the knowing

FIGURE 10.2 Images of Dafen *cun*
Source: © Michael Keith.

embossed images of Greek Classics and Van Gogh's *Sunflowers* speak to the local vernacular. The spatial form of the village is now wholly structured by the art business. Migrant 'handshake apartments', the *woshou fang* 握手房, have in some parts been demolished and replaced by more up-market developments such as hotels for the visiting buyers and dealers. As the economic drivers of art production keep prices cheap as the factories compete on the basis of price and speed, the skilled workforce demand increasingly higher wages. Street signs are now in English and Mandarin focusing on the central quasi-public space of 'Art Square'. Next door in a large plot of land sold off by the village a gated *xiaoqu* is marketed in what has become a more centrally suburban location as the city of Shenzhen has expanded all around the old village.

The form of the *cun* has moved upmarket, shaped by its new population. According to the promotional video that Dafen produces to narrate its extraordinary rise, when Huang Jiang first came from Hong Kong the average annual wage of the 300 'indigenous' population was no more than RMB 200 per month (approximately US$35). While the money that has come into the art industry has been mostly from Hong Kong, the local farmers cultivated their real estate, rented out their property to the growing artistic labour of the new factories. But they made so much money they went even further. At the end of one day of interviews with migrants to Dafen, one of the landlords invited me home. 'Home' was Dafen *Xin cun* ('new village'). About ten miles down the road, close to the new rail connection to central downtown Shenzhen, Dafen Xin Cun is where most of the 'indigenous' families live now. It is a residential development of luxury apartments, mostly 150–200m. sq. each. The development is complete with gym, basketball courts, tennis courts, five-a-side football pitch and swimming pools. The density ratios are unusually low, the facilities extremely high quality but the location itself was not that great, sandwiched between another *cun* with characteristic handshake apartments and a new development site, fronting on to a motorway between the new village and the special enterprise zone (military-guarded) boundary (*guannei*). It had been designed and built with a logic all of its own, a small piece of luxurious urban fabric with a singular locational rationale that emerged largely from its proximity both to the original Dafen Cun and the new road and rail infrastructure being built in 2008 to access downtown. This particular village in the city was so successful at replicating that they had copied the entire village and moved it down the road, leaving behind an authentically fake simulacrum of art retailing; a space of consumption and a site of a particular kind of migrant urbanism spectacle.

Xiasha

Planner Wang Shi (anonymised) was explicit about the history of Xiasha. It had been a place of ill repute, historically a site of contest between local power networks and the Shenzhen city authority and definitely somewhere to be cautious at night-time. In contrast to the showcase model of Dafen there was a strong sense of wariness about relations with the local *juweihui* although it was suggested that this had changed significantly in the 2000s. As with much of Shenzhen, the reputation of Xiasha had been significantly influenced by the early boom years of the 1980s. Local politics had focused around the few families that controlled the village. Notorious for drinking, drugs and sex workers there had been several confrontations in the 1980s and 1990s between city authorities and the families in Xiasha.

More recently, in the early 2000s, local interests had responded to pressures from city authorities about the reputation of the village. The *juweihui* had introduced and funded a local patrolling and policing practice in the village in response to these reputational concerns. Officers would walk around the village to monitor the behaviour of people locally, particularly regulating conduct in public. The street pattern of Xiasha revolves around a pentagonal open space that at its apex has a space of commemoration for the ancestral families of the village. On an autumn evening people will sit around, play cards and music and gather together in the formal dancing exercises characteristic of many open spaces in China. Architecturally it is one of the more attractive of the Shenzhen *cun*. The urban fabric retains some sense of proportionality. The village clan leader has a luxurious residence just off the main square, complete with satellite TV and a big garden. But in general the scale of the development in much of the village is mediated by some open space. The village is marked by clear entrances from the main road system that

FIGURE 10.3 Xiasha *cun* panorama (civillagety)
Source: © Michael Keith.

are gated and so the unity of the spatial configuration is generated by an intro-spective aspect to the built form. Most of the fabric combines pedestrian and car traffic better than in many cities in an unruly compromise. Some work carried out for the Shenzhen planning by Columbia Architecture School in the mid 2000s suggested that the density in some of the *chengzhongcun* was greater than anywhere else globally and in the South of the village there is a plot plan of 40–50 six to eight storey migrant *woshou fang* cheek by jowl that makes such a claim at least plausible. As the photographic images below suggest, density – as measured by site ratios – is demonstrably extraordinarily high in these parts of the village. Urban density is conventionally measured by floor–area ratio (FAR), the ratio of total floor area of buildings on a certain location to the size of the land of that location, or the limit imposed on such a ratio plot ratios in planning law. It is less the height (seven to eight stories) than the line up of these buildings one next to another, separated by narrow alleyways of no more than a couple of metres that renders density so high, where it is almost possible to lean out of one building and reach the neighbours across the way.

But immediately to the south of this densest development area, the village has sold a major site to the prestige developer Vanke. Annual revenue returns on hand-shake apartment rentals were displaced by a single sale capital return on a site that has generated a luxury development on the edge of Xiasha, complete with its own internal *yeweihui* or residents' committee – democratically elected – that can hire and fire the management company of their own *xiaoqu*. Vanke have a corporate structure common to many developers (as seen in Chapter 4); profit centres around the development site, the real estate marketing and the real estate management are separated into 'companies'. Some of the functions – such as the sale of 'second-hand apartments' and even the facilities management can be carried out by different companies, although in Xiasha the Vanke management team described how it was difficult to persuade owners of the apartments to participate in the running of the *xiaoqu* because, for many, the apartments represented second or third homes, investments frequently held by people working elsewhere, whether in downtown Shenzhen or in Hong Kong. The Vanke *xiaoqu* was almost entirely self-contained and in some respects conformed with some of the caricatures of Shenzhen life – affluent Hong Kong investors, weekend golfers and women sometimes derogatively characterised as *ernai* (literally 'second breasts', or mistresses), moving to Shenzhen and being kept in upmarket apartments by their Hong Kong backers.

But the Vanke development was only one element of an increasingly graded residential pattern. Planners suggested that one reason the red light industry was now not as punitively treated as it had been was possibly linked to co-operation with government on other matters, particularly around land development and the policing of public spaces. More recently, Tian An Digital Electronics had invested in the area significantly in a plant that was walking (or certainly cycling) distance from Xiasha. In contrast to the experience in Guanlan, the factory was outside the village boundary and was expanding rapidly and recruiting skilled workers. A significant number of the new arrivals recorded in migrant history interviews in 2008 in Xiasha were graduates that had first degrees and low salaries, renting in some of the old handshake apartments while they saved to place a deposit on their own apartment. There was in this sense a very local process of gentrification at work. Sometimes these graduates lived in small handshake accommodation but rented two or more rooms, doubling the conventional migrant space, sometimes adapting the space architecturally in discussion with their landlords. One block owner in Xiasha described how he was refurbishing his own block and joining up some of the smaller rooms into new configurations of apartments inside the building – hardly luxurious but some distance from the characteristic backrooms of the floating population or the single-room multi-occupancy sites behind some of the retail shopfronts.

Shuiwei

The configuration of Shenzhen is an almost horizontal development focused on a number of clusters that follow the Hong Kong border. Shuiwei sits close to the Hong Kong border, almost on a line joining two of the earlier nodes of the city's development. Though clearly distinguishable as a village in the 1970s and with land development pattern that can be traced retrospectively, it is effectively indistinguishable from the bustling streetscape of Shenzhen. One of the richest of the villages in some respects, the old village is now in many ways functionally a suburb of Hong Kong. Development deals have been worked in joint ventures with several real estate companies, generating a landscape of high-rise dense apartment blocks that sell at the upper quartile of the rental range and now cover almost half of the village's administrative area. Yet the *woshou lou* migrant housing was some of the smallest that we saw, an exceptional corner of open space colonised by another pay and play mahjong game. This juxtaposition of migrant squalor alongside migrant gentrification in the space of tens of metres throughout the *cun* was powerful. The handshake apartments here were a residual form and may not survive the next wave of redevelopment of the village. The family network in charge of the village has both a strong sense of many centuries of history and a keen commercial eye. The stock company has a family museum of stones and gems and one space of the *cun* has a cultural history wall that is 15–20 metres long, tracing the family name Guang through centuries. Spending a day with the management committee of the stock company that runs the *cun*, we discussed the potential reconfigurations that would further diminish the area covered by the migrant apartments and their imminent demolition was clearly on the agenda.

Unlike in Xiasha – where a section of the village had been sold to Vanke housing development and so the geographical area had been diminished – the joint stock company were proud of taking the lead on developing its own commodity housing joint ventures. Although the geographical boundaries of the *chengzhongcun* are invisible because the development is now part of seamless urban fabric, its geographical intensity is sustained. More significantly, the joint stock company retained a revenue interest in the commodity housing through their own investment vehicle that combined external capital with local ownership rights and a separate business spin-off retail development. The particular combination in Shuiwei of share company, governance structure and the forms of mediated development are one more form of experimentation in local state capitalism. It is now possible to use the Metro network to commute to downtown Hong Kong in slightly less than 80 minutes. The Chinese University of Hong Kong is even closer on the direct line that crosses the ever more permeable boundary. One of the interviewed 'migrants' in Shuiwei lectured there and described his commute as convenient, the prices of Shenzhen preferable to Hong Kong. In some ways the village becomes incorporated into a wider and emergent megalopolis of Hong Kong/Shenzhen where the historically functional interdependency is strengthened. Over time the travel to work and commuting might flow increasingly both ways across the border.

Conclusion

How does Shenzhen evolve? At one level the city has realised the strategic ambitions of rapid growth, exemplifying state directed 'opening up'. 'Shenzhen speed' has become a catchphrase for the economic success story of the 1990s and 2000s. At another level, a form of systemic urban flexibility concentrates the accommodation of migrant millions on the villages in the city, which mediate both economic growth and labour demand. As we have seen in Chapter Four, pattern is not driven through the emergence of a *natural* urban hierarchy. The cartography cannot be read off from Ricardian rent theory or the locational logic of settlement that was modelled first by Christaller and Losch and, most recently, refined in the spatial economics of Tony Venables and Nobel laureate Paul Krugman (Fujita *et al.* 1999). Neoclassical rent theory would suggest that land prices decline with distance from the prime site at the city centre and a rational structuring of city form and urban hierarchy that falls out from such geographies of price. Shenzhen is, by contrast, a product of state strategic focus on the Hong Kong border and an *a posteriori* marriage of experimental urban governance and extraordinarily rapid economic growth. The FDI-driven economic transition has already moved rapidly towards an economic model that develops human capital and promotes domestic consumption.

The *chengzhongcun* is a remarkably flexible urban form and has been functionally significant to this urbanism of flux. It has a degree of autonomy that can be traced directly to the ownership of the village land by the small collective. This has allowed both an extraordinary opportunity for economic specialisation (as with Dafen) and experiments in local democracy within the strict framing of the stock company structure itself. Within the family network that controlled Guanlan the democratic elections to the board that ran the *cun* were fiercely contested. The small collectives that control the *chengzhongcun* act in their own self-interest. They have the facility to negotiate with major developers (as with Vanke in Xiasha and similar *xiaoqu* in the other villages).

In conventional Western urban-planning logics the part of the city is functionally subservient to the interests of the whole metropolis. In some ways the Shenzhen logic inverts this. The metonymic relationship of this urbanism makes the whole subservient to the parts. What we have seen is neither exclusively market- nor state-driven urban growth but does possess a particular logic of interdependency between the metropolis and the villages, the formal and the informal, economic life and social change. It is not possible to suggest that the *chengzhongcun* is either planned in the European style or 'unplanned' in the Anglo Saxon or US sense. Instead, the metonymic relationship between the part of the city and the whole works through different geometries and distinctive dynamics working in parallel. The relative autonomy of the villages permits a certain sense of the informalities of rapid change. These come with the gross exploitation of some strands of migration flows but also with an extraordinary flexibility of the built form. The villages are, paradoxically, sites of informality and creativity as well as the means of selective incorporation and subordination. Functionally, they serve the interests of the city. Economically they mediate welfare externalities of migration. Significant costs of the reproduction of labour are borne by the hidden systems of support in the rural sending regions where children are sent home to be educated, the partial and incomplete models of 'cityzenship' that proffer provisional and partial membership and limited access to the rights to the city to new arrivals.

Institutional readings of the built form

In an important article Li Tian (2008, 282) argues that 'maintaining collective land ownership in *chengzhongcun* has been socially and economically costly, but a redevelopment strategy without a complementary affordable housing scheme may be problematic'. Li Tian's argument is based on a paradoxical recognition that the city needs migrant labour to drive growth but the imperative of labour reproduction is based fundamentally on the systemic selective and partial incorporation of migrants into the culture and economy of the city. This is effectively a rephrasing of an argument made by Manuel Castells in a classic text of urban studies *The Urban Question* many years ago (Castells 1977). The reproduction of the city depends in part on processes and patterns of collective consumption, including the right to dwell in the metropolis. But whereas Castells argued at the time for the revolutionary refiguring of the spatial order of the urban – and then later for the empowering of social movements and the grassroots – the migrant urbanisms of today's China highlight analytically a slightly different problematic. For at the heart of both the desirable and undesirable aspects of the *chengzhongcun* are the regimes of property rights that privilege what we might pejoratively characterise as the *rentier* class of real estate cultivators but we might also understand as the drivers of city change. When Li Tian goes on to argue that 'in order to solve the problems of *chengzhongcun*, an institutional reform of collective land is required' there is at the heart of the argument a return to the problem of property rights but within a neoclassical framing that sees the *chengzhongcun* as discrepant, irrational and wasteful figurations of urban land because of the suboptimal use of the land factor of production where property rights are ambivalent or ambiguous and '…when legal rights remain poorly defined, the collective and villagers are motivated to maximise their economic rights in the informal markets, leading to the mushrooming negative externalities in *chengzhongcun*' (Tian 2008, 301). Yet Tian's argument on closer analysis is only correct if welfare externalities are given moral force as well as economic measure. It is quite possible for the villages to be economically functional but morally costly.

Li Tian provides a framing that asserts as much as assumes the priority of clear property rights and enforceable legal systems as the necessary if not sufficient condition for the release of the engine of economic growth. In academic theorisation of property markets this argument accords with the perspective of new institutionalists, adapting rather than rejecting the neoclassical economic theory of Coase and his successors (Nee 2005; Nee and Cao 1999). It valorises the formal city over the informal. In this framing the informalities of the arrangements of Shenzhen (and other *chengzongcun*) promote rent seeking from those favourably placed in the urban hierarchy and negative externalities of selfish interest that maximise the 'tragedy of the commons'. In such an argument the rational city and the optimal spatial ordering of the urban should logically emerge from the proper market pricing of development and its consequences.

But if we look at Shenzhen it is hard to suggest *a priori* that the negative externalities of these pieces of urban form have hindered the urban growth rate thus far. The relationship between the *chengzhongcun* and the city is interesting in its institutional realisation. The companies that supervise the interests of the villagers are a structured form with obligations to their shareholders. They organise the relationship between the city government and the spatial configuration of urban change. The city is an assemblage of cultures and objects, buildings and people, migrant flows and mutating urbanism. It is not just an urban territory shaped by the agency of migrants or the power of markets. The *chengzhongcun* is an intermediary institution between the city and the people – so just 'reforming' premised on legal accountability and clear property rights – is not quite so straightforward. How does this make us think about state theory or the triangular relationship of states, markets and social structure in the *chengzhongcun?*

The city of Shenzhen structures a particular market form. Whether or not it might be correctly characterised as the socialist market might be moot but the organisation of *chengzhongcun* alongside the powerful city state figures the relationship between market and hierarchy differently. The urban system allocates costs through the intermediary institutions of the villages in the city. They are flexible institutional forms, at times opening up new economic opportunities on a global scale (as with Dafen), responding quickly to the residential demands of economic change (as with Xiasha) and the changing locational implications of mass transit (as with Shuiwei). They are based at times on the systemic exploitation of people whose access to the rights to the city are circumscribed by the residual *hukou* system and the *de facto* discriminations against rural migrants. But equally this highlights the ambivalence of a purely economic conceptualisation of welfare externalities that is invoked to understand migrant flows and urban form. In its economic analytical form externalities may be costed and priced. The pricing of these costs is measured only in the utilitarian logic of market measures of value. In purely economic terms the relationship between market and hierarchy mediated by the *chengzhongcun* provides a very flexible machine for the cheap allocation of the welfare externalities of migrant labour and the very rapid reconfiguration of spatial form in purely economic terms. As interviews with senior planners in Shenzhen made clear, the power relationship between city and the villages remains on the table, subject to potential reforms of land zoning and property rights. This generates negatively a sense of uncertainty; positively an incentive to co-operate. The relational market that results serves to generate a sense of relationship between the village and the city in an endless infinite iteration. The losers – normally the migrants themselves – only 'count' in economic terms if the measurement of economic value in welfare externalities is supplemented by the incommensurable measures of dignity that measure the handshake apartments and the situations of precarious life in a calculus of moral not financial worth.

In mainstream urban theory, the arguments for the 'pure' market logic that uses the market to cost risk and putatively price externalities produces the neoclassical (conventionally US) city of real estate markets that reflect the geographical symmetry and simplicity of Ricardian geographies of rent and the hope values contingent on technological change, transport infrastructure and redevelopment.

The 'rational city' of European land use planning attempts to accommodate public interest in this ideal type, socialise externalities and spatialise the metropolitan ordering of workplace and homeplace. But the *chengzhongcu*n migrant urbanisms of Shenzhen and some other cities in China confuses both these forms of spatial ordering and the particular measurement of the welfare externalities of migration. Both the critics of the *chengzhongcun* and the architectural advocates of its form are confused by the intellectual assumptions at their heart because of the way they tend to separate migration from city form, not recognising the simultaneous realisation of built form and cultural formation (the material cultures of migrant life) both qualifies the criticism of the *chengzhongcun* and complicates the process of possible reform. The classical institutional theories of real estate are challenged intellectually by critiques of institutionalism in property theory (Haila 2008). But such critiques of classical real estate reform cannot be blind to their social and economic context.

There are analyses that highlight the limits to the formalisation of property rights in understanding metropolitan change in the cities of the South (Mitchell 2002; Sundaram 2005). They tend to share a sense in which the clear boundaries between internal and external market formations in Egypt (for Mitchell) or India (for Sundaram) tend to overflow their separation with dysfunctional consequences. But in some ways the ambivalent combinations of discrepant property rights of development, densification, exchange (fungibility) and use incentivise co-operation between metropolitan state and village stock companies. The villages work as intermediary institutions, mediating between city and economy; city and demography. They bridge the formal and the informal city. The share companies at the heart of the model have formalised but less than certain legal status. According to city planners significant proportions of the buildings in the *chengzhongcun* are almost certainly in breach of development control restrictions. In 2012, a senior planner of Shenzhen municipality suggested that all the rural area of Shenzhen was now formally to be considered urban and that in these terms the greater proportion of the built fabric of Shenzhen and the network of *chengzhongcun* were in breach of development control legislation. The planning scenario developed by the city hall from 2012 onwards to consider the expansion of Shenzhen over the next two decades has identified both the geographical limits to the expansion of the metropolis and the complex mosaic of formal property rights and *de facto* tenure as major barriers to the planning process. But in reality this points to an inevitable negotiation between local state units – the combination of people, property and migrants in the *chengzhongcun* – and the state in determining the future of the city. Property rights, migrant rights and cultural form combine through the bricks and mortar of the villages in the city. Paradoxically they represent a model that contradicts most Western models of economic efficiency. Yet thus far they have not only facilitated but also driven 'Shenzhen speed'. Whether the urban form that has worked so well for the economic growth of the last three decades is adaptable to the imperatives of the next three is of course of both analytical interest and ethical significance.

CONCLUSIONS

China and the neoclassical subject

What are the lessons from this book in terms of thinking about China? Perhaps just as important is what are China's lessons for how we might more generally think about both economic life and urban change? We have argued in this book that some of the contours of mainstream debates about China are unhelpful, anachronistic or redundant. At the heart of the book is an argument that the current processes of modernisation in China fundamentally change the workings of capitalism and consequently how we will come to think of the relationship between economy and society in the twenty-first century. In making sense of China Constructing Capitalism we are focusing on the diverse social and economic changes of today's China but in doing so argue that we need to rethink the basic categories of analysis and thought across the social sciences. The significance of patterns of relationality, situated propensity and 'empiricist' sociality and incremental reform we see in today's China will speak to the socio-economics of the West's future as well as the developmental trajectories of the globe.

There are three reasons why the empirical investigation and theoretical arguments of this volume point in a different direction to much discussion of contemporary China.

First, any notion that China can be understood in the language of neoclassical economic orthodoxy is implausible. We have shown that the concept of the *neoliberal* is not always that helpful in understanding contemporary patterns, drivers or outcomes of the new China. In literatures of journalism and economic sociology the neoliberal can perform the role of a boundary object, marshalling its defenders and critics in relation to its nostrums, defining the geometry of rhetorical discourse and the choreography of arguments in relation to itself. China is seen either to replicate the ascendancy of neoliberal governance or alternatively be in need of further reforms that follow neoliberalism's logic. But in reality the complexities of neoliberalism's ideologies, genealogies and practices need to be unpicked, the power, the logic and the limits of neoclassical economic conventions understood and the particular trajectories of China freed from the conceptual vocabulary of the term. We have argued instead that the combination of the long historical trajectory of statecraft and culture in China, the geopolitics of capitalism's globalisation and the scalar politics of the continental and the local in China render such thinking ephemeral to the processes of modernisation that shape economic change.

Second, the literatures that consider the developing forms of economy and society in China in terms of the transition away from socialism are also problematic. The transition from socialism found in Eastern Europe and the former Soviet Union offer some important lessons about path dependence and the sense in which economy and society are built from the ruins of an old order. But the reform process in China is also fundamentally very different. The teleology implicit in the notion of an *emergent market* that implies an eventual replication of Western behavioural norms and institutional forms is contradicted by the gradualism that characterises China's reflexive process of modernisation and reform and refusal to surrender a central role for state power in shaping the economic order. Not only has the CPC sustained its political base, reinforcing the political order of the last six decades, more significantly the political configuration in China has for many centuries been characterised by a delicate and, at times unstable, balance between centre and periphery. China's first political imperative is always to sustain the unity of the civilisation-state, building on traditions of the last millennia. Governance and statecraft for China's twenty-first century consequently rescales the relationship between the global, the continental and the very local in a manner that disrupts the nation-state logics of discrete economies and societies through which much Western thought has been theorised.

Third, building on this long history of social and political tradition, the variation across the landmass of China is phenomenal, the canvas on which contemporary China emerges is epic and the scale of processes structuring today's China continental. All belie national comparison or a nationally 'comparative' perspective. The contrast between cosmopolitan affluence of some districts of Shanghai and the rural poverty of parts of the provinces of central China provide data for some of the most extreme Gini scores of income inequality to be found anywhere today. But also this geographical variation has a historical resonance, the corollary of the focus on the preservation of the civilisation-state has been the development of 'one country, many systems' long before the British withdrawal from Hong Kong was covered with the modesty blanket rhetoric of 'one country, two systems' – capitalism and communism alike in parallel. More profoundly, the *longue durée* of history has shown the facility for the country to experiment with multiple models of development within the framing logic of state stability. In this sense we are arguing that China is an ongoing economic experiment. Through scale variations between regions and between districts within cities these experiments in modernisation are plural, developing diverse institutional forms, none which are converging towards a Washington Consensus model, but instead evolve towards several types of political market regimes. The book has sought to tease out some basic socio-cultural-economic drivers behind this by looking at and theorising relationality-propensity and relating this to empirical studies of primarily local government embedded in economic life and urban development. In so doing we are not arguing for a statist China model but instead suggesting that we see a range of dynamic experiments that have powered the last three decades.

As Heilman and Perry (2011) have argued China has been characterised by ceaseless change, tension management, continual experimentation and *ad hoc* adjustment. China is more tolerant of informal institutions than many of its erstwhile counterparts else in the world with far greater bottom-up input than would be predicted from its formal structures. The invisible hand of Mao leaves its legacies, tamed, tweaked and transformed, to be sure, but his guerrilla policy style still plays an important role in China's governing practices. In effect, localities are generally left to fend for themselves, receiving only erratic and episodic central support. Heilman and Perry go on to suggest precisely that there is no ready-made 'Chinese development model' defined by replicable institutional variables but instead a fluid, context-, situation- and agency-based *modus operandi*, a method of policy generation and implementation based on an acceptance of pervasive uncertainty, a readiness to experiment and learn (even from enemies and foreigners), an agility in grasping unforeseen opportunities, a single-mindedness in pursuing strategic goals, a willingness to ignore ugly side effects and a ruthlessness in eradicating unfriendly opposition (Heilman and Perry 21–22). Whether these experiments succeed or indeed whether they unsettle the stabilising framing of economy and society that makes local diversity possible is less clear. Long-term outcomes are less certain. Experimental models have promoted extraordinary processes of urban agglomeration and economic growth but the consequent problems of economic, ecological and political sustainability are profound and particular to the path dependences generated.

We have argued that the dynamism of China's modernisation is to be found in the cities but these cities demand an attention to the cultural forces that shape China constructing capitalism for the twenty-first century, the socio-economics that reflects both cultural legacies of centuries and new institutional forms that emerge from the recent history of Communism. In the contemporary city, the cultural, political and economic governance of property is central to this dynamism. The complexity of property reflects the bundle of rights long analysed in jurisprudential theories of property, but the new combinatory powers of China's markets reframe state prerogative and markets freedoms, reinventing what it means to consider the propensity of the city to host a novel pace of economic development and a new calculus of risk and uncertainty. The relational markets of China owe a particular debt to the path dependence of both the socialist market transition and the enduring power of China's cultural traditions. This is reflected in both the scholarship that has addressed an economic sociology of China (discussed in Chapter Two) and our own characterisation of the emergent real estate drivers of metropolitan change examined in detail in Chapter Three. The particular combinations of relationality, state enterprise, local government entrepreneurialism and urbanism we defined in Chapter Four as *local state capitalism*; an institutional form of many different guises. Indeed, the plurality of local institutional forms exemplify the experimental nature of state/market hybridisations seen in the salience of local state ties of firms described in Chapter Five. The detailed ethnographic consideration of three real estate companies in Chapter Six amplified further this sense of experimentation of models of economic development and the pillar driver of the real estate market in structuring new urbanisms. The continued sense of an affective capitalism shaped culturally and instrumentally building on many centuries of China's traditions is reinforced in the focus of Chapter Seven on the emergence of a new shareholding class and everyday culture of stock gambling and in the demonstration of Chapter Eight of how knowledges of financial markets, derivatives and mathematical models are instrumentally implausible but might shape the future market in part through their performative power. Chapter Nine similarly traces how new risk cultures that are determined by this configuration of new institutional forms and old cultural traditions in the everyday lives of young professionals who reveal in a series of depth interviews their own sense of 'futures present', an understanding of the reflexive sense of shaping a personal life and a financial horizon. The capacity of the city to accommodate the flows of several hundred million people through incorporation of migrant populations and rapid urban development was seen in Chapter Ten both to reproduce at the level of the metropolis the trade off between migrant rights and flexible labour markets and to demonstrate the inventive powers of China's migrant urbanisms in Shenzhen.

What all of these exercises in empirically rich economic sociology demonstrate is that there is no sense in attempting to explain or understand China's contemporary reconstruction of global capitalism through either an anthropological lens of China area studies alone or through a conceptual vocabulary rooted in Western economics, anthropology and sociology. The combinatory power of Western knowledges and cultural traditions of China synthetically combine to form plural and experimental models that are reshaping what it means to live in a capitalist order of the future, what it means to be urban in the twenty-first century. It is why in the rest of this conclusion that we demonstrate the limited reasoning that informs an analysis of contemporary China also demands a rethinking of the basic categories of economic reason and sociological models of the sovereign self.

Decisive in this context is that the neoliberal paradigm is grounded in the assumptions of *neoclassical* economics. And it this – as much or even more than the critique of neoliberalism – that has been at stake in this book. So much sociological analysis and urbanism – as well as a paradigm in regard to which maybe most of us live our lives – is grounded in the same neoclassical assumptions. The fundamental assumptions of neoclassical economics that emerged with its founders – William Stanley Jevons, Carl Menger and Leon Walras – are the assumptions of marginalism. Menger, perhaps the most powerful of the three, is the founding thinker of the most influential neoclassical paradigm, the Austrian School of Economics, which came to include von Mises, von Wieser, Böhm-Bawerk, Schumpeter and Hayek. From this would emerge, three generations down the line, neoliberal thought, with Hayek the pivotal figure, bridging Vienna and Chicago (Van Horn and Mirowski 2009). Menger was father of not just the neoclassical economic actor but also the social actor, bequeathing to Max Weber the notion of the 'ideal type' that would structure the method and understanding of rational social action. (Gane 2012a).[1] We think that China can help us think the critique of neoliberalism and this neoclassical notion of subjectivity that pervades Western culture. Note, this is not the subject of classical political economy that Marx dealt with in *Das Kapital*, grounded in factors of production and exploitation at the point of production. It is instead the neoclassical utility-maximising paradigm that pervades not just in the economy but, more generally, life in contemporary Western capitalism. So if in the middle of the nineteenth century, Marx needed to work via the critique of classical political economy, we at the beginning of the twenty-first century must work via the critique of neoclassicism.

Learning from China helps open up some space in such a critique. In this context we can speak of perhaps six dimensions of this neoclassical subject. Let us address this via 1) subjective utility versus embedded subjectivity, 2) juridical subject versus bundles of rights, 3) rationalism versus empiricism/pragmatism, 4) equilibrium versus non-equilibrium, 5) performativity versus forms of life and 6) politics and (social) justice.

Subjective utility versus embedded intersubjectivity

What we saw consistently in our investigations ran very much counter to the idea of the disembedded, individualist, rationally choosing economic actor of neoclassicism. Instead of the individual we see inter-subjectivity. This is evidenced in the *guanxi* relations of real estate developers and officials from local and district government. This is not a disembedded but an embedded inter-subjectivity. We see this in the risk-sharing between generations in families (Chapter Nine) that has so strikingly resurfaced since the pervasion of mortgage housing since the mid 1990s. At stake here again is not economic action *per se* as evidenced in the decision of the one-off or the short-termism of the contract, but instead economic forms of life that are culturally embedded as we saw in our ethnography of the local stock trading rooms in Chapter Seven. These are longer-term webs: less economic action than economic *life*, of forms of economic life. Here value is neither objectively determined as in classical political economy nor subjective as in neoclassical, indeed value is something that is not fully determinate, nor even understandable in terms of determination. Value is instead inscribed, embedded in forms of social life themselves.

Of the neoclassical founders it was Menger whose focus was the most specifically on the subjective determination of value. This stands in contrast to classical political economy – Smith, Ricardo and Marx – for whom value was a question not of subjective utility maximisation, but instead was *naturally* produced through land, labour and capital (Bittermann 1940). In China we have seen not an individualistic but a relational economy: one that works less through networks but through webs of social relations between entrepreneurs and the local state. For neoclassicals it is the subjective perception of the marginal utility of an additional unit of a given good that determines its value. Jevons, Walras and Menger did not use the word marginal utility. None of these forefathers spoke of marginal utility *per se*. Jevons spoke of units of value as 'utils'.[2] Walras gave us the general theory of equilibrium and Menger the subjective theory of value. In the Austrian School value and the debate with Marx's theory of value in especially Böhm-Bawerk was at centre stage. Not till Menger's student Von Wieser was there literally, marginal utility, or *Grenznutzen*. When supply and demand is summed in a perfectly competitive market, these summed subjective marginal utilities at a certain price bring the forces of supply and demand into equilibrium. The model here of course is Newtonian physics. The market thus resembles the physical forces acting on an object, which when in equilibrium will result in the object continuing on its path, according to the law of inertia, the first law of mechanics

The shift of neoclassicals from the naturalism in political economy to the subjective is important, as they were explicitly neo-Kantians (especially Menger); however, they differentiated themselves not only from the holism of the Historical School of Economics, but also from natural-science views of Hermann von Helmholtz. For Menger (1950: 114–20) in what was for him an 'epistemology' (*Erkenntnistheorie*), every science must have an object, and the object of economics was the structure of individual wants, or individual needs. Unlike the later more exclusively *a priori* investigations of von Mises, Menger insisted on empirical work. Hence his focus on Kant's idea of experience: on empirical experience. This centrality of experience also differentiated economics from mathematics and metaphysics. To start, such subjective experience can be much more than a psychology. Kant's starting point of the condition of possibility of experience ruled out a psychology. The neo-Kantians took psychology more seriously. Like the other neo-Kantians, the neoclassicals start from subjective value and wind up with an objective science. Thus Hermann Cohen's foundational Marburg neo-Kantian *Kants Theorie der Erfahrung*. The point was to develop a basis for an objective science, as a reaction to Historical School and Hegelian metaphysics. This subjectivism is less a psychology than an axiomatic that in tandem with empirical data will yield an objective science. This resurfaces in the fact-value debate surrounding Max Weber in the separation of objective social science from morality. It was very much the case in the separation of legal norms from ethics in Hans Kelsen's (1997) neo-Kantian pure theory of law. Here an axiomatic of subjective value could be a foundation for an objective science of economics. And an axiomatic of subjective instrumentally rational and ultimate value-rational action could be a basis for an objective sociology.

Menger's subjective value is based on a structure of human needs and action through the maximisation of utility. J. S. Mill's utilitarianism is a philosophy rooted in a notion of subjective judgement. This is the judgement of value more then the classical factor-input value naturalism. Mill's idea of utility already largely breaks with metaphysical notions of classical economics' underpinnings of Aristotelian substance (Schumpeter 1994: 408). Again you start from subjective value and move towards objectivism, in Mill's case positivism. The neoclassical lineage to Hayek and the decisive founding of neoliberalism in the Mont Pèlerin Society is not Smith or Hume or Locke, and their empiricist liberalism, but Mill and his positivist liberalism (Plehwe 2009). Mill insisted on a rationalist, a deductive approach to counter what he saw as the weaknesses of inductivism. Still he, like Menger, was a rationalist with an empirical referent: Mill was the founder of the notion of falsification. For Mill, who knew St. Simon and corresponded with Comte, metaphysics would be a stage before the objective science of positivism. Smith gave us labour as value-substance – and Marx uses the term *Wertsubstanz* repeatedly in his *Grundrisse*: their attendant naturalism is of a piece with natural law notions of individual freedom that originate Locke's political philosophy. Mill has broken with natural law for a very rule-bound paradigm of legal positivism, whose focus is not on natural rights but the positive law of the state. Mill attended the lectures of John Austin, the first great legal positivist jurist. For his part, Austin's biggest influence again was the father of both legal positivism and utilitarianism, Jeremy Bentham. Bentham of course was the designer of the famous Panopticon that Michel Foucault so intensively wrote about in *Discipline and Punish*. The neoliberal society is not just the society of bio-political governance, but also the panoptic society. With Bentham again we get a theory of subjective value and judgement in utilitarianism and the hard objectivity of positive law. Thus Foucault's notion of the juridical subject rings ever truer as the notion of the neoclassical subject itself.

It is not just neoliberals, but economists on the left such as Paul Krugman who begin from these neoclassical assumptions. Thus Krugman's urban economics proposes a regime of externalities (see Fujita *et al.* 1999) of the unintended consequences of economic exchange. The problem is that Krugman, like neoliberal Ronald Harry Coase, is starting from the wrong place. Krugman also starts from the economic exchange, the rational economic actor, from implicitly the clear and distinct rights of the property owner. He is starting from the internal. In China you need to start instead from the external. From the background propensities and the situation. This situation is Cui Zhiyuan's bundle of rights. It is a web of urban and economic activities that become such bundles of rights. These background bundle of rights are very much of a piece with the secularised ritual activities that we discussed in Chapter One in Wang Hui's alternative Chinese modernity. If in the West it is the internalities as it were that count and the externalities are their consequence, in China the web of external economic life is predominant and it is from here that the derivative internal sphere of preference schedules and the rationally choosing economic actor *per se* emerges.

Rationalism versus empiricism

Sebastian Heilmann and Elizabeth J. Perry (2011) in *Mao's Invisible Hand: The Political Foundations of Adaptive Governance in China,* explore influences from US pragmatist philosophy and especially from John Dewey on Mao and the CCP. They point to the experimental one step and one place at a time approach to reforms, which goes on in tandem with a powerful and all pervasive party-state capable of centralised executive orders with imperative coordination. The relations between pragmatism and empiricism are close: indeed one of pragmatisms' classic texts is William James's *Radical Empiricism*. Heilmann and Perry's book betrays Smithian empiricism in its title. This empiricism is very opposite to the neoclassical and neoliberal rationalism of the Chicago school and their all at once *a priori* rule bound interventions elsewhere in the developing world – in Russia, Argentina, Mexico and especially Chile. This empiricism is what Foucault (2008: 279) called the 'blindness' of the invisible hand that contrasts with the all-seeing character of the rational bureaucratic firm. Hence Alfred Chandler (1977), who with Coase ranks as benchmark theorists of the hierarchical (and neoliberal) firm, called his major book on the rise of the modern corporation *The Visible Hand*.

Smith's famous statement using the invisible hand in *The Wealth of Nations* was in the context literally of the wealth of the *nation* and the preference of domestic versus foreign industry. China started about with this sort of Smithian domestic model historically while Europe used foreign trade and precious metals. Here Smith was already talking about the *Nationalökonomie*. In such a context the neoclassical rationalism stands out in contrast to the *Historische Schule der Nationalökonomie* in Germany's famous *Methodenstreit*. The first *Methodenstreit* was between Menger and Gustav Schmoller. Weber (1976) in 1904, at about the time he was writing the *Protestant Ethic*, was also refining his methodological position in a minor work on Wilhelm Roscher and Karl Knies who were first-generation Historical School scholars. Their contemporary, Karl Marx, writing the *Critique of Political Economy*, still purveyed a naturalist factor-input labour theory of value. Roscher and Knies tried to look at economic development in terms of a number of institutions, legal, political and cultural. The second generation and Schmoller became the economists of the newly unified Germany, in the *Reichsgrundung* in 1871. They saw society as a whole or totality *Ganze*, but were more concerned with policy than method: their work supported both Bismarckian social welfare and a strong Prussian state (see Tribe 1995). Hence their *Verein für Sozialpolitik*, is literally the Association for Social Policy. They remained politically dominant in Germany but when they effectively lost the *Methodenstreit* with the Austrians. The Historical School also partly prefigure the neoliberal *Ordoliberalen* (Plehwe 2009). The Ordoliberals could mix Austrian neoclassicism with the social market assumptions of the new *Bundesrepublik*. The Historical School not only opposed Menger's idea that economics could be like a natural science, but also saw no need for an economics as a separate science apart from history. For the Historical School values as part of a sort of social totality were inseparable from facts. It was Menger who was separated fact from value and focused on method, and the *Streit* came with Schmoller's hostile review of Menger's (1963) *Über die Methode der Sozialwissenschaften und der politischen Ökonomie insbesondere* in 1883.

The second or *jüngere Methodenstreit*, this time about value-freedom, again featured Schmoller, but this time pitched against Max Weber. Here Weber, with Menger, was on the side of value freedom. This debate began inside the value-laden *Verein* in 1909, but already formulated in the Weber's methodological essay on objectivity in 1904. It was pivotal in deciding to set up the much more value-free *Deutsche Gesellschaft für Soziologie*. Thus neoclassical economics is at the basis of the social actor as rational as rational, as *zweck-* and *wert*-rational: The subject of Weber's action types is very much the neoclassical subject. If anything stands in radical contrast to this, it is China. Here the individualist disembedded neoclassical subject is displaced by an embedded relational inter-subjectivity. This is an empiricist inter-subjectivity, with an eye more on the last case than to an *a priori* set of rules. In terms of Weber's ideal types, in China there is a much larger component of traditional and affective action. With the rise of mortgages, as we saw in Chapter Nine this is not going away. As China modernises and hyper-modenises, the more traditional and affect-laden economic relations do not necessarily subside. Fact and value in China are much less separated than for Weber: interest and ethics are not binary opposites. China is much closer to a Hume or Smith state of affairs in which interest and value are made of the same cloth, in which value emerges from interested social and economic activity, and interest emerges from the heavily value-laden activity such as the aforementioned secularised rites and ceremonies.

Singular juridical subject, plural property rights

In *Birth of Bio-politics* and its companion volume, *Security, Territory, Population*, Michel Foucault identities two paradigms: with 'political economy' and 'population': not just discourses of political economy and population, but that at this point there actually emerges a political economy, a wealth of nations, and that for the first time population itself becomes important. These two Foucauldian principles of modernity, as it escapes the claws of the Christian confessional and absolutist *raison d'état* and sovereignty, are *natural*. This modern regime of political economy and population displaces a previous absolutist constellation of what Foucault calls 'sovereignty' and 'territory' associated with post-Westphalisan *raison d'etat*. The old regime is still tied up in a Christian *problematique* of divine right and the confessional. For Foucault the old sovereignty and the confessional is displaced by the naturalism of the hidden hand, which he insists is fully unlike the hand of God. The hidden hand, Foucault insists is 'blind', whereas, like the later Panopticon, God is all seeing and omniscient.

In this context liberalism and empiricist political economy gives us a 'subject of interest' that Foucault contrasts with the 'juridical subject'. The subject of interest emerges with the birth of bio-politics and 'population' and a more general the paradigm of the popular. Neoliberalism (and not liberalism), developing from neoclassical economics, is a mode of bio-political *governance*. Here neoclassical economics is much more than performative: it is in large part *constitutive* of today's neoliberal and juridical subjectivity. Marx showed how saw classical political economy was ideological, in hiding the extraction of surplus value from workers.

But the constitutive effect of neoclassicalism is much more thoroughgoing: colonising political discourse, urbanism, law, politics and education. Indeed the notion of instrumental reason comes from neoclassicism. Bio-politics, born with naturalism, only becomes bio-political governance as this natural is juridified. Through the social contract population becomes *le peuple*. The subject of interest becomes the 'subject of right' (*droit*), contracting out its interest in the social contract to the Rousseauan or Hobbesian state. This contracting out is also a 'transfer', unlike Locke, Hume and Smith's empiricist subjectivity, which is for Foucault 'non-transferable'. There are indeed two empiricist Lockean subjects of right: the one from contract theory, but the other that presumes (untransferable) rights in the self. For Marx in *Theories of Surplus Value* this is a basis for the labour theory of value.

Foucault's (2008) 'subject of interest', which is also the subject of desire, sense, and sentiment and sensation 'overflows' juridical subjectivity. At the end of any line of juridical reasoning comes the non-juridical painful/not-painful. At about the same time as these lectures on bio-politics, Foucault is writing the second and third volumes of the *History of Sexuality*. The first volume is about the Christian confessional, whose lineage is to the psychoanalytic situation as a mode of governance of the soul. But the second and third volumes, *L'usage des plaisirs* and the *Le souci de soi* are situated in late Antiquity and talk about an effectively non-juridical subjectivity. The juridical subject for its part corresponds to the neoclassical system of formal law. What this system of formal law does – as Carl Schmitt (2005: 27) noticed in Max Weber's work – is to give a space of predictability, a 'calculability' for firms to invest. This is what Weber also meant by 'formal rationality' of the law. Firms are protected from violent incursions of gangs on the one hand and the arbitrary interventions of the government on the other. In Shanghai and elsewhere firms and individual stock market investors were perpetually aware of what sometimes seemed to be arbitrary intervention by government. The idea for them was to try somehow to predict what seemed so often like a random arbitrariness.

Property relations are at the heart of what we have called local state capitalism. This is very different from the clear-and-distinct regime of property found in Western 'new institutionalist' urban studies. Such a paradigm is based on a pronounced dichotomy of the internal and the external, which privileges the internal (Haila 2007). Thus the 'internality' of property rights determines the externality of those excluded from property rights. By contrast, property in China is complex: the proliferation of interests distributes the bundles of rights at its heart. When the stakeholders are pluralised and interests distributed, the boundaries of the external and the internal may be less clearly marked. The line dividing internal and external changes. The dimensionless line becomes a much thicker boundary. Mutual exclusivity and exhaustiveness yield to a semi-permeability. These bundled rights must be understood in contrast to Coasean new institutionalist rights that are at the basis of neoliberal law, economics and urban studies. Coase is the father of new institutional economics, whose (1937) idea of the firm was influential in arguments against anti-monopoly law under the Reagan administration. This internal sphere of Coasean law is also the space of economic decision-making and exchange. Such 'internal' economic action has side effects or externalities. These are 'social costs' that for Coase (1960) can be solved through well-defined, i.e. unbundled, property rights. The point is that in China this sort of regime of property is simply not operative. Yet with seemingly arbitrary state and absence of well-defined rights, Chinese economies and cities (in some senses) work. China's *de facto* property regime and their meaning is perhaps quite analogous to Wittgenstein's natural language. In language games, Wittgenstein insists, there is no need of clearly defined concepts for words and sentences to be meaningful. Property is not clear and defined but like language is intelligible only against a social backdrop. Like Wittgenstein's (1958: 45) language it can be 'vague' and intuitive yet still work. Thus local councils, privately owned firms, local state-owned firms and various hybrids, as well as district government can all effectively have rights in the same unit of property.

Equilibrium

Equilibrium comes from the first law of motion in Newton's *Philosophiae Naturalis Principia Mathematica*. Galileo, *contra* Aristotle, proved that a body would move as a constant speed in the absence of an active force: that an equilibrium of forces acting on a body results in inertia. Yet classical political economy persisted with a metaphysical notion of value as substance (Mirowski 1989: 238–9; Lash 2010: 103). 'Natural price' then followed from the value substance of a commodity. What classical political economy could not explain was the divergence of natural price from market price. It was the neoclassicals and the 'marginalist revolution', which took on the Newtonian model. What the neoclassicals did was to collapse natural price into market prices. Now an equilibrium price was decided by the forces of supply and demand. This was, like in Galileo and Newton, a static equilibrium. Here forces in equilibrium so to speak on a body – a good or service – yielded a value to this good or service, which was its equilibrium price. Thus when supply and demand is summed, these summed subjective marginal utilities at a certain price bring the forces of supply and demand into equilibrium. Here we have both the demand-side and the supply-side maximisation of utility, the forces of demand and the forces of supply. Sociologists, and not just sociologists, like to think about systems in equilibrium: hence Talcott Parsons' theory of the social system. Systems language seems to come into ideas of equilibrium not so much in Newtonian mechanics but in thermodynamics, and the idea of dynamic equilibrium. Here when reactions occur at a rate that compensate each other, while there is dynamism, the system stays at a steady state. neoclassical economists, especially growth theory, have taken on related ideas of dynamic equilibrium (Schumpeter 1994: 970). In regard to equilibrium, you need a system – and a forms-of-life-based economy like the Chinese economy is fundamentally unsystematic. There is, also, unlike in Smith, Ricardo and Marx, no notion of value substance. No Greek, no Aristotelian background, no notion of substance. The closest words in Mandarin for substance are *wuzhi* (物质), *shiti* (实体) and *shizhi* (实质) all of which are derived terms. Wittgenstein forms of life had little to do with systems, the latter presupposing clear and distinct parts. Yet in Chinese economic life, whose lineage is as much Legalist and Mohist as it is Confucian and Daoist, there is a constant movement from the vague and intuitive to the clear and distinct and then back again.

But what about far-from-equilibrium self-organizing systems? Here the result can be entropic disintegration or negentropic moves to higher levels of energy of speed. And in urbanism it is such a mode of thought that we initially encountered in China, in Rem Koolhaas's *Great Leap Forward*. China is at the same time embedded in sort of pre-modern, neo-Confucian forms of life and engaged in an historically unparalleled constellation of hyper-modern speed and acceleration in both city and economy. For us this conditioned our own methodological choice of the far-from-equilibrium economic sociology of Harrison White. In White's work a post-neoclassical dynamic disequilibrium is at stake: a disequilibrium sometimes magnified in China by a seemingly arbitrary state. Harrison White speaks of 'producer markets' – in which price and quality are in large part a consequence of the signalling of producers to one another. The metastable outcome of such producer signalling is not just a measure of disequilibrium and uncertainty, it also is a large measure of security: sufficient security for investors to take the risk of actually investing. In China, the relative absence of rule of law and relative preponderance of seemingly arbitrary state intervention makes markets so unstable as to discourage investment. In this sense China has some way to go in order to achieve 'market completion'. Yet in China there are alternative sources of security in play, what White once spoke of as 'networks' (which are not actor-networks), but are instead long-term exchanges and culturally bound webs of economic activity.

A number of the chapters in this book are about Shanghai. We have understood urban change in Shanghai for example as a sort of up-scaling and out-scaling of the risk-regimes of households and individuals. It is this sort of scaling that constitutes Shanghai as an urban economy. This urban economy is at the same time what Castells (1977) understood as a regime of meaning; it is an aggregated urban risk regime. But most important Shanghai itself as a city is a 'propensity'. An urban regime is in this sense a propensity. We are in agreement with the urbanism in, for example, Sanford Kwinter's (2002) *Architectures of Time* and Patrick Schumacher's (2011) *The Autopoeisis of Architecture*. Is Shanghai itself such a self-organising, autopoetic city? Perhaps in some ways. But it does as a whole constitute an emerging urban propensity, not just a situation but also a propensity. In this neo-Daoist paradigm, propensities are also as it were de-propensities, urban regimes like Shanghai also have entropic moments of disintegration and disorganisation.

Politics and social justice: against abstraction

Where are the politics in all of this? And politics there are. 2012 experienced this decade's handing over of power to a new generation of leaders. This has rarely taken place without strife: in example the changeover at the end of the 1950s, signalling the end of the Great Leap Forward; at the end of 1960s and 1970s that punctuated the beginning and end of the Cultural Revolution and the end of the 80s and

Tiananmen Square. The present handover in part has juxtaposed the social paradigm some have seen in the 'Chongqing Model' – whose predecessor was Shanghai Pudong – versus the free market 'Guangdong Model'. The political demise of Bo Xilai may not have heralded the end of the Chongqing Model.[3] In 2011 Guangdong's CCP leader, Wang Yang, and Bo Xilai had entered into more or less open debate. This was publicly portrayed in terms of a pie: Wang Yang proposing increasing the size of the pie, and Bo Xilai the more equal cutting of the pie. Increasing the size of the pie works if there is rapid growth. Yet no one in the old or new leadership thinks that China can continue to grow at 10–12 per cent. All realise that the inevitable 5–6 per cent growth will mean more equally cutting the pie. Thus Hu Jintao spoke of Sun Yat-sen's concept of *minshengzhuyi*, the 'principle of people's livelihood'. Among Sun Yat-sens Three Principles of the People, it is the *social* principle. So the question of politics in China is very much also the question of social justice.

Some among today's generation of Chinese youth are aligned with neither left nor right. Coming from popular culture, with backgrounds in music, art, video and new media, this generation wants neither Chongqing nor Guangdong Model (Hui 2012). The political inspiration here comes from the Arab Spring, the Indignados and Occupy. Its inspiration is less communist than anarchist. Occupy proposed a politics without demands, a politics without ends. So what kind of politics follow from our analyses of China and their implications for the critique of neoliberalism and the neoclassical, juridical subject? It is signal that Carl Schmitt's notion of the political is a direct confrontation with Hans Kelsen's pure-law legal positivism. Schmitt's state of exception is in this sense also a space for the emergence of a political subject that evades juridical (neoclassical) subjectivity. Walter Benjamin's 'Critique of Violence' (1921) and Schmitt's *Political Theology* (2005) run in parallel. In 1916 in 'On Language as Such and the Language of Man' Benjamin counterposed instrumental language, where language was a means to an end to a notion of language of pure means that was at once ontological and divine. Schmitt opposed to formal and liberal law a political ontology, which is also a political theology. Both Schmitt and Benjamin were influenced by the writings of Georges Sorel. Thus Benjamin's idea of pure violence drew in large part on the anarchist assumptions of Sorel's *Reflections on Violence* (1999). For his part, Schmitt wrote that formal legalism, the juridical political subject in our sense, was no longer tenable in the age of 'mass democratic movements', of both left, and the right. In this vein Schmitt was anti-liberal but also suggests a different notion of democracy.[4] So we are looking at not just a critique of neoliberalism and its utilitarian-juridical subject but also a possible new kind of democratic politics: at a new political subjectivity. If the subject of neoclassicism, formal rights and the Rechtsstaat can be understood in terms of an extensive democracy, perhaps this critical subjectivity is connected with what might be called intensive democracy.

Foucault breaks with not only legal positivism but also natural rights discourse in his *Birth of Bio-politics*. This is because his 'subject of interest', which is also the subject of sensation and desire, as well as the 'popular subject', transfers parts of its sovereignty over the self to the state in the social contract. Walter Benjamin puts a similar argument in the 'Critique of Violence'. He rejects not just legal positivism, in which law is a 'system of means', but also natural law, as a system of ends. Both are means-ends type thinking, which Benjamin rejects as both are modes of governance and iterations of the juridical subject. What Benjamin proposes instead is a notion of justice as a system of means.[5] This is Benjamin's notion of 'pure violence'. It is a politics of means without ands. Thus there is Occupy, which will occupy but not state their ends or demands. Thus Sorelian or French/Spanish revolutionary syndicalism can come to power without an end state of dictatorship of the proletariat, indeed without any state at all. Thus the *syndicat* (union) in revolutionary syndicalism are means for organising production and distribution. Forms of life are means: they are ways of doing for Harold Garfinkel they are ways of accomplishing, methods for accomplishment. A politics of means, a notion of justice as suggested by Benjamin and Occupy and revolutionary syndicalism is a politics of forms of life. Thus the Chicago warehouse space from which Occupy hosted the anti-NATO protests in April 2012 was a space of alternative health practices, of alternative food, of ways of assembly holding to the two-minute rule and anti-rhetoric rules. Occupying itself was *living* in a space and setting up forms of life in and producing such space.

Thinking about Adam Smith in Beijing[6] may also have political implications. If Smith can be instructive for understanding economic life, perhaps he can be equally instructive for understanding political life. If we are looking for a politics in China we should not be looking for one that is set up as opposite to economic life but one that instead is inscribed in economic life. Likewise for an ethics or idea of justice. This should not be seen as outside of, or a 'subtraction', from the empirical or experience, as in the ethics of on the one hand Rawls and Habermas and on the other Alain Badiou. Smith's ethics, Smith's 'moral sentiments', grow out of the subject of interest: they are not set up in opposition to this subject. China as Max Weber said gives us, in contradistinction to Abrahamic beliefs, a this-worldly religion. In economics or politics in China we should not be looking for the otherworldly. The same is true of law and the rule of law. China has had unprecedented growth with neither well-defined property rights nor an abundance of the rule of law. Although we strongly support of course the rule of law in China, it is perhaps not primarily there that a possible democratic politics might emerge. Such a politics is more likely to emerge from more localist, on-the-ground practices, of protest, of online criticism.

Democracy in the conventional sense, to the extent that it emerges in China may not at all come from a Western-type institutional complex of civil society, the rule of law, formal parliamentary institutions. Western commentators may well be off the mark in their discussions of the moral basis of economic relations. Western thinkers often see this moral basis as inscribed in formal institutions of contract, property and the rule of law. In China as we have discussed at some length, the morality, the ethics are embedded in the very process of economic exchange itself. These forms of life, about both habits and ethics, are a question very much of the background propensities that we have understood as the residues of Confucian rites, filiality, of the Daoist *wu wei*. Secularised rites may be the operative concept, and perhaps the development of rights in China, including democratic rights, will have perhaps less to do with disembedded civil society than with such background practices. When you look at political organisation around the 2008 Sichuan Earthquake or in Shandong against the excesses of one-child policy this may be evident.

'Thus we should look to rights' are as inscribed not in the proceduralism of governmentality or governance, but rights inscribed in the symbolism, of secularised rites, of forms of life. Rights in Mandarin (*quanyi* – 权益, *renquan* – 人权) are closely associated with sovereignty (*zhuquan* – 主权). Perhaps rights and democracy are also about the workings of sovereignty. In the West, modernity was counterposed against antiquity, against tradition. In China modernity is superimposed on tradition. The ancient is preserved in the modern. Thus for Wang Hui, China is a combination of two types of sovereignty: ancient imperial and civilisational sovereignty and the modern sovereignty of the nation state. Ancient sovereignty was inscribed in tribute between nations. The sense of modern sovereignty and the Westphalian system was based on treaty and contract. Wang here is looking back to this more meaning-laden rather than procedural idea of sovereignty. This applies not just to nations but to individuals. We are, one the one hand, the possessive and utilitarian individuals of procedural law, and, on the other, what Georges Bataille understood as 'sovereign' individuals, situated in excess of the utilitarian and restricted economy. It is as sovereign individuals, outside of the logic of governmentality that we are possessed with not property but dignity. The point here is that sovereignty which is not a question of governmentality alone but more around meaning and symbolic exchange and right which are very much bound together. The very situated propensity of economic life and urban change – and implicitly economic and urban justice – that this book has addressed is inscribed in forms of life that can also be a basis for political change and any future democracy in China.

NOTES

Introduction: China versus neoliberalism

1 We are grateful to Michael Dutton on this point.
2 Though also see, e.g. P. Mirowski and D. Plehwe (2009).
3 Cui Zhiyuan, who has worked in close collaboration with the implementation of the social Chongqing Model, is inspired pointedly by the work not of John Maynard Keynes but James Meade. Cui underlines that Meade understood himself as a 'liberal socialist'.
4 Brazil, Russia, India and China comprise the BRIC, coined famously by Goldman Sachs' Jim O'Neill in 2001.
5 *Xiandai zhongguo sixiang de xingqi*.
6 Gary Hamilton (2006) for many years has challenged Weber's theses.
7 The lineage of the faculty of understanding that is so central to Kant goes back to Locke's *Essays on the Human Understanding*. Kant of course wanted to cut through Locke's empiricism and Leibniz's rationalism for his own transcendental yet not ontological notion of the understanding.
8 In this book, too, we reflect on the Confucian influence on contemporary China, but in a decidedly different way. The attempt in Chapter Two is to construct social theory from very distinct strand of Chinese thinking. In fact, Chapter Two is neither descriptive nor empirical – it is a theoretical intervention in the development of social theory in the West, as much as about Europe as it is China.

1 – Chinese thought, cultural theory

1 Lyotard in Jullien (1996: 22).
2 Ricoeur in Jullien (2001: 217–19).
3 *Sittlichkeit* is literally 'customariness'.
4 This is a point that is continually made in the work of Michael Dutton.
5 We do not want here to underestimate the importance also of Mohism and Legalism in the desacralization and infusion of a certain analytic logic and utilitarianism into the syncretic Confucianism that dominated from the time of the Han Dynasty (206 BCE to 220 CE).

4 – Local state capitalism?

1   Nigel Lawson was Chancellor of the Exchequer in the UK from 1983–1989.

6 – Property development

1   The authors were supported by the 'Risk Cultures in China' project, funded by the World Economy and Finance programme of the Economic and Social Research Council (ESRC).

2   Both *xiaoqu* were commodity housing, and rent was approximately 5000 yuan per month.

3   Towns, such as Meidu, are urban areas in an otherwise rural county. Currently, Chongming Island is the only remaining 'county' in Shanghai, with the rest being urban districts.

4   'Listing' refers to the process of tendering a price for a tract of land and then publicising it, for example on the China Land Listing website, www.landlist.cn, and subsequently updating the various bid prices over a certain period, minimally 10 days (see MoLaR 2005).

5   Presumably, the 'first' land revolution was Mao's nationalisation of all urban land and collectivisation of all rural land, though this is not stated by MoLaR.

6   Fung *et al.* (2009: 44) refer to two 'sandwiched layers' (*jiaxin ceng*), meaning the groups of people who sandwiched between these neat divisions into low-, middle- and high-income housing.

7   From the brokerage class, pillar industries are those that are the backbone and supporting industries for national economic development. The regular definition of pillar industries must include the following four conditions: 1. The industry has a wide inter-relation with other industries, so it strongly promotes effects on them; 2. It makes up 5 per cent or more of the gross national product; 3. It fits with the evolution of the industry structure, and benefits optimisation of structure; and 4. In terms of national economic development, it has significant importance from its position. Directed and indirectly related to the real estate industry are over 60 other industries, a multiplier of 1.95, such that 100 yuan of construction investment creates 170–220 yuan of demand (Brokerage Class, 4/7/2008).

8   The 70/90 rules refers to the demand that 70 per cent of commodity housing be under 90 square metres in area.

9   A residential *xiaoqu* has a technical definition, used for reference; namely, a population of between 5,000 and 15,000 people, taking up between 12 and 35 hectares. There is also a residential group (*juzhu zutuan*) type of residential area. This is typically the size of a residential committee (*jumin weiyuanhui*), namely 3,000–5,000 people. Finally, there is a hybrid between residential *xiaoqu* and group, which are *xiaoqu* made up of two to three residential groups.

10   Sub-section title borrowed from Cong (1994) article title.

11   The phenomenon of *dingzi hu* is widely known in China. It describes households targeted for demolition and relocation who refuse to leave their homes, even under threat of demolition of neighbouring buildings, cutting off supplies of water, electricity and sometimes even violence. The refusal to leave leads to metaphor of their 'being nailed down' to the area. A much-publicised case in Chongqing during 2007 spread rapidly through the internet, giving a drastic image – a single household perched on top of a steep hill, around which all ground had been excavated – to exemplify the *dingzi hu* (see Hess 2010).

12   A '*tiandi*' literally 'heaven and earth' is a branded development of the Shui On real estate group. Its most famous incarnation is Xintiandi, in the Luwan district of Shanghai. Xintiandi selected particular aspects of Shanghai's history as cultural artifacts and surrounds them in a museum with high-end shopping, commercial, hospitality and residential buildings in a coordinated development effort in league with the local district government (see He and Wu 2005 for a fuller discussion).

13 This practice was common in Shanghai, and was observed upon multiple visits to friends, neighbours and customers. One real estate agent commented, 'you can tell if the apartment is bought for investment, since only in that case would the balcony *not* be covered'.

14 On a visit to a Suzhou villa complex, one researcher observed that a notice of violation (*weigui*) had been attached to the front door of a wealthy factory owner's villa. He brushed it off as irrelevant, and was not embarrassed in the least. The violation was for actually extending the size of upper stories of the villa, a rather major 'interior' decoration. This was also observed in one of the most expensive villa complexes in Shanghai, located adjacent to Century Park, where several owners expanded or reworked the existing structure of their villas prior to decorating – notable, in this case, including the head developer who was said to have demolished the new villa he bought and rebuilt it.

15 By 'neighbourhood' we refer loosely to the concentrations of *xiaoqu* and retail stores, restaurants, convenience stores and wet markets that pepper the geography of Shanghai.

16 The four insurance funds are pension, medical, unemployment and housing provident. They are the individual contributions to the system of 'five insurance funds and one fund', viz. pension, medical, unemployment, accident and maternity insurance funds and housing provident fund.

17 The phrase translates as 'Us Shanghaiese' but using well-known Shanghai dialect terms.

18 A tongue-in-cheek reference to the influence of Wenzhou *chaofang tuan*, or house-frying groups. *Chaofang tuan*, particularly from Wenzhou, emerged in public consciousness around 2003. Their mode of operation is to act collectively in investing in real estate in particular areas, often in particular *xiaoqu*. They use the scale of investment to bargain lower unit prices, then wait for prices to rise due to induced scarcity and they then sell out to make large speculative profits. Whether or not they are at work, rising prices in China are often blamed on these speculators. See Feng *et al.* (2009) and Liu (2008).

19 Huang Qifan is the architect behind both 'Pudong Logic' and Chongqing Model. See Huang (2011).

7 – Trading ethnographies

1 QQ is the dominant software for Internet and mobile phone instant messaging and chatting, including both individual and group chats. It is developed by Tecent (*tongxun*), a Shenzhen-based company listed on the Hong Kong Stock Exchange.

2 In addition to A- and B-shares, China companies can have N- (New York-listed), H- (Hong Kong-listed), S- (Singapore-listed) and L- (London-listed) shares (CSRC [2008a]).

3 An important exception to the restriction on purchases of A-shares by foreigners is the qualified foreign institutional investor (QFII) programme, which began in December 2002. Under it, approved foreign institutions can purchase up to US$10 billion of A-shares on the secondary (Shanghai and Shenzhen) markets.

4 That is, all individual investors and any other type of investor who had bought shares at the initial public or secondary trading on the market.

5 The number of shares that end restrictions on sales is constant, but their value (i.e. market cap) depends on the value of the stock on a particular day. These figures have declined significantly prior to the publication of the chapter, Li (2008) cited the number of shares ending restrictions is 118.1, 663.7 and 121.3 billion for 2008, 2009 and 2010, respectively.

6 The State Assets Administration and Supervision Commission (SASAC), is a state asset ownership body that was established in 2003. Importantly, it has branches at the central level, but also at the provincial, municipal, prefecture and district levels. While it is 100 per cent owner of state-owned enterprises that are controlling shareholders of listed companies, its ability to impose its will on SOE boards is limited (see Naughton 2007 for an example).

7   According to the SSE, there are 455 Shanghai securities branches that trade on the SSE, while the SZSE reports 404 registered Shanghai branches (SSE [2008]; SZSE [2008b]). Of course, in places such as Tibet, where only one branch is reported by SSE and two branches are reported by SZSE, there is no guarantee that the people in the trading are local. However, the focus here is on *regular* visitors to the trading rooms, therefore it is assumed that they all live nearby.

8   Although *yingye ting* includes the big room and the middle accounts and large accounts rooms, for the remainder of this chapter we refer exclusively to the big room as the trading room. When middle accounts or large accounts rooms are referenced, they will be done so explicitly.

9   Sources for the numbers of branches in Shanghai for these companies are their respective company websites under the business addresses section.

10 PetroChina is the largest oil company in the world by market capitalisation. Since its debut on the Shanghai market, however, it has fallen precipitously. From an initial price of 48.62 yuan on 5 November 2007, PetroChina fell to 14.94 yuan at the end of June 2008.

11 The magnitude is further diminished by the fact that institutional investors and private stock funds often disguise their strategies by opening hundreds of small accounts.

12 The categories of information are: Required Reading for Stock Trading, Financial Perspective, Business Analysis, Industry and Products, Restructuring Situation, Analyses from All Directions, Company Situation, Management, Latest Quarterly Report, Entry-Exit of Shareholders, Shareholder Structure and Dividends, Capital Operations, Related Guarantees, Information Brief and Past Development.

13 For a call warrant, the opposite is true. That is, the underlying stock of a call warrant is set a particular price that, upon exercising the warrant, allows the warrant holder to buy the stock at the price specified in the warrant issue. Hence a call warrant has intrinsic value when the underlying stock is trading at a price greater than the price specified in the warrant. Usually, warrants with intrinsic value are settled as the cash difference between the price specified by the warrant and the trading price of the stock.

14 *Daitou dage 777* is an individual named Wang Xiujie who created hundreds of QQ groups, which investors would have to pay a fee in order to join. He then provided stock information and tips. He was charged with providing securities consulting without a license and sentenced to three years in prison in 2008 (Zhou 2008).

9 – Risk cultures

1   The two ports are Shanghai and Ningbo. In 2009 Shanghai was world number one with 506,000 metric tons and Ningbo number five with 372,000 metric tons. Guangzhou and Hong Kong are the next two. Seven of the top ten metric ton ports are Chinese. The eighth is Singapore. Only one, Rotterdam, is non-East Asian.

2   农民工, migrant worker, literally 'peasant-worker', sometimes a term of abuse.

3   Interview January 2010, four months before Expo.

4   Apart, of course, from migrant workers.

5   By 1934 there were 8,200 Russians in the French Concession. Most were emigres from the Revolution, but also others fleeing the Japanese occupation of Manchuria. Huaihai Lu was called Avenue Joffre in the French Concession.

6   We need to say here and at a thousand points in this book how much we owe to Jiang Jun. Former editor of *Urban China*, we have reconnected with Jun at every step of this research. This book is dotted with his insights.

7   Including cleaners.

8   Co-author Scott Lash.

9   In this sense, Casey's parents were effectively *nongminggong*. Early *nongminggong* who went into market trading rather than semi-casual work.

10 Hayami, 'The Great Transformation. Social and Economic Change in Sixteenth and Seventeenth Century Japan', *Bonner Zeitschrift für Japanologie 8* (1986), p.6.

11 Interview in 2010.

12 It is common for firms (Mainland and foreign firms) to pay their Western Taiwanese and Hong Kong staff salaries three to four times more than their Mainland Chinese staff.

13 Mergers and acquisitions.

14 Shanghai's inner ring.

15 McGraw-Hill had just sold *Business Week* to Bloomberg.

16 Fifteen of Shanghai's 16 districts lie west of the Huangpu river, hence Puxi (浦西). Where the *pu* refers to the *Huangpu He* (黄浦河) and *xi* (西) means west. The exception is the fast-growing Pudong district, meaning literally east (dong 东) of the Huangpu.

17 This of course works for the individual who is embedded in such filiality. But largely the individual is not the 'unit of risk' at all: the family becomes the risk unit, becomes the risk and security unit. It is prior. And it has been so strongly reinforced by the ubiquitous property owning, the necessary flat from the mid-1990s.

18 Shifan Daxues are ubiquitous in China. *Shifan* (师范) means teacher training. These are translated into English as 'normal universities', in say East China Normal University. Some of these teacher training institutions are just colleges and award not BAs but diplomas. Others have become proper research-driven universities, in which teacher training is now only a peripheral activity. For example, East China Normal and Central China Normal University in Wuhan figure in China's QS top 40. Nanjing Shifan Daxue is particularly distinguished.

19 Given the economic success of the Bohai Ring, Pearl River Delta (PRD) and Yangzi River Delta (YRD), it is easy to forget thriving economies in Shandong, locked in between the extended YRD (Jiangsu, Shanghai, Zhejiang, and Bohai Ring and Fujian, south of the extended YRD and just north of the PRD).

20 At stake is something much more hermeneutic like Wittgenstein's forms of life than the positivist nature of the classical social action. Wittgenstein's shift from logical positivism to natural language philosophy and forms of life is paved by his observation. In logical positivism, universal rules are applied to concrete particular things in order to have knowledge. Wittgenstein asks, but where is the rule that tells us how to apply the rule? The answer is not only an infinite regress, but that there is no such rule. Agamben (2009) notes this in Continental European Law and the Roman Law tradition, in which unlike in Common Law, there are universal rules or laws that are meant to decide in particular cases. Applying these rules however is a different story. In fact Roman and Continental lawyers then also refer to past cases to make and justify decisions as to how to apply the rule.

21 Indeed it could be argued that massive investment in urban infrastructure is a form of security. Compare, say, Mumbai and Delhi with Shanghai and Beijing, and absence of urban transit, of plumbing, etc. is striking.

22 Weber's term for this was *zweckrational*.

10 – Shenzhen dwelling

1 *Cadastration* is conventionally the process of mapping and formalising the formal property ownership, particularly for purposes of governance, taxation and regulation.

Conclusions

1 Heinrich Rickert directly of course influenced Weber on the ideal type. But Weber's idea is very much like Menger's notion of the 'pure type'.

2 Jevons had already understood utility as not cardinal but ordinal (Schumpeter 1994: 628).

3   We are indebted on these points to discussions with Wang Xiaoming.
4   See Agamben (2005).
5   Hence the attraction of Schmitt to left intellectuals, such as Agamben and Chantal Mouffe (1999).
6   See Agamben (2011).

BIBLIOGRAPHY

Acemoglu, D. (2006) 'A simple model of inefficient institutions'. *Scandinavian Journal of Economics*. 1084: 515–46.

Adler, P. S. and Seok-Woo Kwon (2002) 'Social capital: prospects for a new concept'. *Academy of Management Review*. 271: 17–40.

Agamben, G. (2006) *The Time that Remains*. Stanford, CA: Stanford University Press.

Agamben, G. (2005) *States of Exception*. Chicago: University of Chicago Press.

Agamben, G. (2011) *The Kingdom and the Glory*. Stanford, CA: Stanford University Press.

Aiyar, P. (2007) 'Shaoxing – little India in China'. *The Hindu*. 17 April 2007.

Alchian, A. A. (1961) *Some Economics of Property*. Santa Monica, CA: Rand Corporation.

Alchian, A. and Harold, D. (1973) 'The property rights paradigm'. *Journal of Economic History*. 331: 16–27.

Allen, F., Qianm, J. and Qian, M. (2005a) 'China's financial system: past, present, and future'. In: *The Transition that Worked: Origins, Mechanism, and Consequences of China's Long Boom*, Loren Brandt and Thomas Rawski (eds). Available at: http://fic.wharton.upenn.edu/fic/papers/05/0517.pdf (accessed 29 August 2011).

Allen, F., Qianm J. and Qian, M. (2005b) 'Law, finance, and economic growth in China'. *Journal of Financial Economics*. 77: 57–116.

Alloway, T. (2010) 'China's great central economy, and big local problems'. *Financial Times*. 24 March. Available at: http://ftalphaville.ft.com/blog/2010/03/24/184741/chinas-great-central-economy-and-big-local-problems/ (accessed 10 June 2012).

Anderson, B. (1991) *Imagined Communities: Reflections on the Origin and Spread of Nationalism*. London: Verso.

Anjuke.com 安居客 (n.d.) 'Hugui Yuan' 沪贵苑. Available at: http://shanghai.anjuke.com/community/view/1706 (accessed 26 March 2012).

Arnoldi, J. and Zhang, J. (2012) 'The dual reality of the Chinese knowledge economy'. *International Journal of Chinese Management and Culture*. 3(2): 160–73.

Arrighi, G. (2009) *Adam Smith in Beijing: Lineages of the 21st Century*. London and New York: Verso.

Aspromourgos, T. (1986) 'On the origins of the term "neoclassical"'. *Cambridge Journal of Economics*, 10(3): 265–70.

Bacon, F. (2000) *The New Organon*. Cambridge: Cambridge University Press.

Badiou, A. (2003) *Saint Paul: The Foundations of Universalism*. Stanford, CA: Stanford University Press.

Balazs, E. (1964) *Chinese Civilization and Bureaucracy*, trans. Arthur Wright. New Haven, CT: Yale University Press.

Barry, A. (2001) *Political Machines*. London: Continuum.

Barthes, R. (2012) *Travels in China*. Cambridge: Polity.

BBC (2012) Available at: www.bbc.co.uk/news/world-asia-china-18091107 (accessed July 2013).

Beatley, T. (2000) *Green Urbanism: Learning from European Cities*. Washington, DC: Island Press.

Beck, U. (1992) *Risk Society – Towards a New Modernity*. London: Sage.

Benfield, F. K., Terris, J. and Vorsanger, N. (2001) *Solving Sprawl: Models of Smart Growth in Communities Across America*. Washington, DC: Island Press.

Benjamin, W. (1999) *Critique of Violence*, trans. Edmund Jephcott, In: *Selected Writings, Volume 1*, M. Bullock and M. Jennings (eds). Cambridge, MA: Harvard University Press.

Berger, P. L. and Luckman, T. (1991) *The Social Construction of Reality*. London: Penguin Books.

Bernstein, P. L. (1992) *Capital Ideas*. New York: Free Press.

Bertoncelo, B. and Bredeloup, S. (2007) 'The Emergence of New African "Trading Posts" in Hong Kong and Guangzhou'. *China Perspectives*. 1: 94–105. Available at: http://chinaperspectives.revues.org/document1363.html (accessed 7 September 2009).

Bian, Y. (1997) 'Bringing strong ties back in: indirect ties, network bridges, and job searches in China'. *American Sociological Review*. 623: 366–85.

Bian, Y. (1994) *Work and Inequality in Urban China*. Albany: State University of New York.

Bian, Y., Logan, J., Hanlong Lu, Yunkang Pan and Guan Ying (1997) '"Work units" and the commodification of housing: observations on the transition to a market economy with Chinese characteristics'. *Social Sciences in China*. 184: 28–35.

Bittermann, H. (1940) 'Adam Smith's empiricism and the law of nature'. *Journal of Political Economy*. 48: 703–34.

Blecher, M. and Shue, V. (2001) 'Into leather: state-led development and the private sector in Xinji'. *The China Quarterly*. 166: 368–93.

Blumenberg, H. (1985) *The Legitimacy of the Modern Age*. Cambridge, MA: MIT Press.

Bodomo, A. (2009) 'The African presence in contemporary China'. *The China Monitor*. 36: 4–9.

Boeker, W. (1997) 'Executive migration and strategic change: The effect of top manager movement on product-market entry'. *Administrative Science Quarterly*. 42(2): 213–36.

Boisot, M. and Child, J. (1996) 'From Fiefs to Clans and Network Capitalism: Explaining China's Emerging Economic Order'. *Administrative Science Quarterly*. 414: 600–28.

Boltanski, L. and Thévenot, L. (2006) *On Justification: Economies of Worth*. Princeton, NJ: Princeton University Press.

Braddock, J. C. (1997) *Derivatives Demystified*. New York: John Wiley.

Braudel, F. (1993) *La Méditerranée et le Monde Méditerranéen à l'Epoque de Philippe II, tome 1: La Part du Milieu*. Paris: Le Livre de Poche.

Bray, D. (2005) *Social Space and Governance in Urban China: The Danwei System from Origins to Reform*. Stanford, CA: Stanford University Press.

Bray, D. (2006) 'Garden estates and social harmony: a study into the relationship between residential planning and urban governance in contemporary China'. Urban Development and Planning in China: China Planning Network CPN 3rd Annual Conference, Beijing, China, 14–16 June 2006.

Brumagim, A. L. and Wu Xianhua (2005) 'An examination of cross-cultural differences in attitudes towards risk: testing prospect theory in the People's Republic of China'. *Multinational Business Review*. 133: 67–86.

Bryan, P. D., TieCheng Yang and Wang, L. (2008) 'An update on China's derivatives markets'. *The Journal of Structured Finance*. 134: 49–59.

Buckley, P., Wang, C. and Clegg, J. (2007) 'The impact of foreign ownership, local ownership and industry characteristics on spillover benefits from foreign direct investment in China'. *International Business Review*. 16: 142–58.

Buiter, W. H. (2009) 'Negative nominal interest rates: three ways to overcome the zero lower bound', Working Paper 15118, National Bureau of Economic Research: Cambridge, MA.

Burt, R. S. (2004) 'Structural holes: the social structure of competition'. In: *The New Economic Sociology*, Frank Dobbin (ed.). Princeton, NJ: Princeton University Press, 325–48.

Cai, Yongshun (2011) 'Distinguishing between losers'. In: *Going Private in China*, J. Oi (ed.). Stanford, CA: Walter H. Shorenstein Asia-Pacific Research Centre Books, 71–93.

Callon, M. (1998) *The Laws of the Market*. Oxford: Blackwell.

Callon, M. (1999) 'Actor-network theory – the Market Test'. In: *Actor Network Theory and After*, J. Law and J. Hassard (eds). Oxford: Blackwell, 181–95.

Callon, M. and Muniesa, F. (2005) 'Economic markets as calculative collective devices'. *Organization Studies*. 268: 1229–50.

Callon, M. (1999) 'Actor-network theory – the market test'. In: *Actor Network Theory and After*, J. Law and J. Hassard (eds), Oxford: Blackwell, 181–95.

Calthorpe, P. (1993) *The Next American Metropolis: Ecology, Community, and the American Dream*. Princeton, NJ: Princeton Architectural Press.

Calthorpe, P. and Fulton, W. (2001) *The Regional City: Planning for the End of Sprawl*. Washington, DC: Island Press.

Carruthers, B. and Ariovich, L. (2004) 'The Sociology of Property Rights'. *Annual Review of Sociology*. 30: 23–46

Cartier, C. (2001) ' "Zone fever", the arable land debate, and real estate speculation: China's evolving land use regime and its geographical contradictions'. *Journal of Contemporary China*. 1028: 445–69.

Cartier, C. (2002) 'Transnational urbanism in the reform era Chinese city: landscapes from Shenzhen urban studies'. 39(9), 1513–32, 2002 Development. *Canadian Journal of Development Studies*. 9: 313–24.

Castells, M. (1997) *The Urban Question*. London: Edward Arnold.

Ceng, Zijian and Ma Yufei (2008) 'Reducing Holdings as Fiercely as a Tiger: Lethality Rankings of Large and Small Non- [*Jianchi meng yu hu: da-xiao fei shashangli pai hangbang*]'. *National Business Daily* [Meiri jingji xinwen]. 12 May 2008. Available at: www.nbd.com.cn/_NewShow.aspx?D_ ID=106341 (accessed 14 July 2008).

Cha, A. (2007) 'Chasing the Chinese Dream'. *Washington Post*. October 21 2007, A16.

Chan, K. W. (2009) 'The problems with China's population data'. *Financial Times*. Available at: http://blogs.ft.com/dragonbeat/2009/07/14/the-problem-with-chinas-population-data/#axzz1vOS68JQg (accessed April 2012).

Chan, K. W. (2010) 'Fundamentals of China's urbanization and policy'. *The China Review*. 10(1): 63–94.

Chan, K. W. and Zhang, L. (1999) 'The *Hukou* system and rural-urban migration: processes and changes'. *China Quarterly*. 160: 818–55.

Chan, N. (1999) 'Land use rights in mainland china: problems and recommendations for improvement'. *Journal of Real Estate Literature*. 7: 53–63.

Chandler, A. (1977) *The Visible Hand: The Managerial Revolution in American Business*. Cambridge, MA: Harvard University Press.

Chatterjee, P. (1986) *Nationalist Thought and the Colonial World: A Derivative Discourse*. London: Zed Books.

Chen, A. (1998) 'China's urban housing market development: Problems and prospects'. *Journal of Contemporary China*. 717: 43–60.

Chen, J. and Stephens, M. (2011) 'The Shanghai housing and mortgage markets: a preliminary assessment'. 23rd ENHR Conference, 5–8 July, Toulouse. Available at: www.enhr2011.com/sites/default/files/Paper-Chen-Stephens-WS01.pdf (accessed 20 May 2012).

Chen, L. (2006) 'Management of sold public housing in urban China: a case study of railway new estate, Shanghai'. Paper presented at ENHR International Conference, Ljubljana, 2–5 July 2006.

Chen, Qi (陈奇) (2008) 'Stock citizens fear *Da-xiao Fei* the most' (股民最怕大小非). *China Securities Journal*. 13 November.

Chen, Xiao-Ping and Chao Chen (2004) 'On the intricacies of the Chinese Guanxi'. *Asia Pacific Journal of Management*. 21: 305–324.

Cheng, T. and Selden, M. (1994) 'The Origins and social consequences of China's *Hukou* system'. *China Quarterly*. 139: 644–68.

China Financial Market Development Report Committee, PBC Shanghai Head Office (2008) *2007 China Financial Market Development Report*. Beijing: China Finance Press.

China Real Estate Top 10 Research Group (2006) 'China Real Estate Top 10 Listed Companies Research Report'. Available at: http://industry.soufun.com/ (accessed 17 October 2008).

China Securities Depository and Clearing Corporation Limited (2006) *Monthly Work Statistical Report, December 2006*. Available at: www.chinaclear.cn/main/03/0304/1177571818885.pdf (accessed 27 July 2008).

China Securities Depository and Clearing Corporation Limited (2008) *Monthly Work Statistical Report, June, 2008*. Available at: www.chinaclear.cn/main/03/0304/1216609584495.pdf (accessed 27 July 2008).

China Securities Depository and Clearing Corporation Limited (2009, 2010) 'China Securities Registration and Settlement Statistical Yearbook' 中国证券登记结算统计年鉴. Available at: www.chinaclear.cn/ (accessed 15 May 2012).

China Securities Journal (2008) 'It will be difficult for the southern air put warrant to change from "worthless paper" to "gold"' [*Nanhang rengu quanzheng "feizhi" nanbian "jin"*]'. 11 June 2008. Available at: www.cs.com.cn/xwzx/03/200806/t20080611_1488285.htm (accessed 1 July 2008).

China Securities Regulatory Commission (2008b) 'List of QFIIs'. Available at: www.csrc.gov.cn/n575458/n4001948/n4002195/n4003695/n4003770/n4003860/10671763.html (accessed 27 July 2008).

Chiu, R. (2001) 'Commodification of Housing with Chinese Characteristics'. *Policy Studies Review*. 181: 76–95.

Christerson, B. and Lever-Tracy, C. (1997) 'The Third China? Emerging Industrial Districts in Rural China'. *International Journal of Urban and Regional Research*. 214: 569–88.

Coase, R. H. (1937) 'The nature of the firm'. *Economica*. 416: 386–405.

Coase, R. H. (1960) 'The problem of social cost'. *Journal of Law and Economics*. 3: 1–44.

Coleman, J. (1988) 'Social capital in the creation of human capital'. *American Journal of Sociology*. 94: 95–120.

Collins, R. (1998) *The Sociology of Philosophies*. Cambridge, MA: Harvard Belknap.

Cong, Y. 从亚平 (1994) 'Xiaoqu! Xiaoqu! A Beautiful Housing Dream' 小区！小区！美丽的住房梦. *China Quality Ten Thousand Steps* 中国质量万里行. 11: 33–5.

Corbett, J. and Corbett, M. (2000) *Designing Sustainable Communities: Learning from Village Homes*. Washington, DC: Island Press.

Croll, E. (2006) *China's New Consumers*. London: Routledge University Press.

Cui, Z. (1993) 'China's Rural Industrialization'. Available at: www.cui-zy.cn/Recommended/Personalpapers/CuiRURALIndu.doc (accessed 22 November 2009).

Cui, Z. (1998) 'Whither China? The Discourse on Property Rights in the Chinese Reform Context'. *Social Text*. 55: 67–81.

Cui, Z. (2009) 'Liberal socialism and the future of China: a petty bourgeoisie manifesto'. Available at: www.networkideas.org/featart/jan2006/liberal_socialism.pdf (accessed September 2012).

Cui, Z. (2010) 'From scholar to official: Cui Zhiyuan and Chongqing City's local experimental policy' (interview with Emilie Frenkiel), 6 December 2010. Available at: www.booksandideas.net/IMG/pdf/20101206_Cui_Zhiyuan_EN.pdf (accessed September 2012).

Cui, Z. (2011) 'Partial intimations of the coming whole: the Chongqing experiment in light of the theories of Henry George, James Meade, and Antonio Gramsci'. *Modern China*. 1–16.

Dahles, H. (2007) 'Creating social capital as a competitive disadvantage'. In: *Business Networks and Strategic Alliances in China*, S. Clegg, K. Wang and M. Berrell (eds). Cheltenham: Edward Elgar.

Davies, W. (2010) 'The politics of externalities: neo-liberalism, rising powers and property rights'. COMPAS Rising Working Papers, University of Oxford. Available at: www.compas.ox.ac.uk/fileadmin/files/Publications/Research_projects/Flows_dynamics/Rising_powers/Will_Davies_Rising_Powers_working_paper_Final.pdf.

Davis, D. (2000) 'Introduction: a revolution in consumption'. In: *The Consumer Revolution in Urban China*, D. Davis (ed.). Berkeley, CA: University of California Press, 1–22.

Davis, D. (2003) 'From welfare benefit to capitalized asset: the re-commodification of residential space in China'. In: R. Forrest and J. Lee (eds). *China Urban Housing Reform*. London: Routledge, 183–96.

Davis, D. (2004) 'Talking about property in the new Chinese domestic property regime'. In: *The New Economic Sociology*, S. Garon and P. Maclachlan (eds). New York: Russell Sage Foundation, 288–307.

Davis, D. (2005) 'Urban consumer culture'. *China Quarterly*. 183: 677–94.

Davis, D. (2010) 'Who gets the house? Renegotiating property rights in post-socialist urban China'. *Modern China*. 36(5): 463–92.

Davis, M. (2006) *Planet of Slums*. London: Verso.

Deleuze, G. (2009) *Difference and Repetition*. London: Continuum.

Demsetz, H. (1967) 'Toward a theory of property rights'. *American Economic Review*. 572: 347–59.

Deng, X. (1992) 'Excerpts from talks given in Wuchang, Shenzhen, Zhuhai, and Shanghai'. *Selected Works of Deng Xiaoping, Volume III 1984–1992*. Available at: http://english.peopledaily.com.cn/dengxp/vol3/text/d1200.html (accessed 1 July 2008).

East Money (2008) 'Xing u pin *dao* [New Stock Channel]'. Available at: http://stock.eastmoney.com/xgss/newstock.html (accessed 1 August 2008).

De Soto, H. (2000) *The Mystery of Capital: Why Capitalism Triumphs in the West and Fails Everywhere Else*. London: Bantam.

Derrida, J. (1967) 'Violence and Metaphysics'. In: *Idem, Writing and Difference*. London: Routledge, 79–153.

Ding Jinhong, Yang Hongyan, Zhou Shaoyun, Zhou Jixiang, Lin Kewu and Zhang Yuzhi (2004) 'On the special characteristics and direction of foreign marriage in China in the new period: the case of Shanghai'. *Lun xin shiqi Zhongguo shewai hunyin de tezheng yu zouxiang: yi Shanghai wei li Zhongguo renkou kexue.* 3: 66–70.

Dirlik, A. (1985) *Culture, Society and Revolution: A Critical Discussion of American Studies of Modern Chinese Thought.* Durham, NC: Asian/Pacific Studies Institute.

Dittmer, L. and Xiaobo Lü (1996) 'Personal politics in the Chinese danwei under reform'. *Asian Survey.* 36(3): 246–67.

Douglas, M. (1966) *Purity and Danger.* London: Routledge & Kegan Paul.

Dunbar, N. (2000) *Inventing Money.* Chichester: John Wiley.

Drori, Gili S., Meyer, J. W. and Hokyu Hwang (eds) (2006) *Globalization and Organization: World Society and Organizational Change.* Oxford: Oxford University Press.

Drori, Gili S., Meyer, J. W., Francisco O. Ramirez and Schofer, E. (2003) *Science in the Modern World Polity.* Stanford, CA: Stanford University Press.

Du, J., Lu, Y. and Tao, Z. (2008) 'FDI location Choice: Agglomoration vs. Institutions'. *International Journal of Finance and Economics.* 131: 92–107.

Durkheim, E. (1968) *Les Forms Élémentaires de la vie Religieuse.* Paris: PUF.

Durkheim, E. (1991) *Professional Ethics and Civic Morals (2nd edn.).* London: Routledge.

Durkheim E. and Mauss, M. (1903) 'De quelques formes primitives de classification', *Année sociologique.* 6: 1–72.

Dutton, M. (1999) *Streetlife China.* Cambridge: Cambridge University Press.

Economist, The (2012) 'Chongqing rolls on a city's deposed leader had tried to be different. But was he?' 28 April 2012. Available at: www.economist.com/node/21553495?zid= 306&ah=1b164dbd43b0cb27ba0d4c3b12a5e227 (accessed September 2012).

Egger, S. (2003) 'Globalisation and the sustainability of cities: a methodology for determining their relationship'. Presented to MODSIM 2003, Townsville, Australia, 1–2.

Elkington, J. (2008) 'Interview with Peter Head of Arup on Dongtan'. Available at: www.sustainability.com/insight/article.asp?id=438 (accessed 15 November 2009).

Eng, I. (1999) 'Agglomeration and the local state: the tobacco economy of Yunnan, China'. *Transactions of the Institute of British Geographers, New Series.* 243: 315–29.

Espeland, W. N. and Stevens, M. L. (1998) 'Commensuration as a social process'. *Annual Review of Sociology.* 24(1): 313–43.

Eymard-Duvernay, F., Favereau, O., Orléan, A., Salais, R. and Thévenot, L. (2005) 'Pluralist integration in the economic and social sciences: the economy of conventions'. *Post-Autistic Economics Review.* 12.

Fan, C. Cindy (2002) 'The elite, the natives, and the outsiders: migration and labor market segmentation in urban China'. *Annals of the Association of American Geographers.* 92(1): 103–24.

Fan, C. Cindy (2007) *China on the Move: Migration, the State and the Household.* London: Routledge.

Fan, Joseph P. H., Wong, T. J. and Tianyu Zhang (2007) 'Politically connected CEOs, corporate governance, and post-IPO performance of China's newly partially privatized firms'. *Journal of Financial Economics.* 84: 330–57.

Fan, J. (2008) 'Guotai Jun'an raises the buy-in fees for southern air put warrant'. *Guotai junan tigao Nanhang guzheng mairu shouxufei. Caijing Magazine.* 6 June 2008. Available at: http://magazine.caijing.com.cn/20080606/67926.shtml (accessed 1 July 2008).

Fan, Y. (2002) 'Questioning guanxi: definition, classification and implications'. *International Business Review.* 115: 543–61.

Farrer, J. (2002) *Opening Up: Youth, Sex, and Market Reform in Shanghai.* Chicago, IL: University of Chicago Press.

Faure, D. (2006) *China and Capitalism.* Hong Kong: Hong Kong University Press.

Fenby, J. (2012) *Tiger Head, Snake Tails.* New York: Simon and Schuster.

Fei, X. (1992) [1948] *From the Soil: The Foundations of Chinese Society Xiangtu Zhongguo.* Berkeley, CA: University of California Press.

Feenberg, A. and Bakardjieva, M. (2004) 'Virtual community: no "killer implication"'. *New Media & Society.* 6(1): 37–43.

Feng, G. and NOffice (冯果川) (嗯工作室). (2009) 'Keywords of China housing' 中国当代住房关键词. *Urban China* 城市中国. 34: 28, 33, 39, 40, 44, 45, 51, 61, 68, 73.

Feng, Wang, Xuejin Zuo and Danching Ruan (2002) 'Rural migrants in Shanghai: living under the shadow of socialism'. *International Migration Review.* 362: 520–45.

Fleischer, F. (2007) '"To choose a house means to choose a lifestyle." The consumption of housing and class-structuration in urban China'. *City and Society.* 192: 287–311.

Fleischer, F. (2010) *Suburban Beijing.* Minneapolis, MN: University of Minnesota Press.

Fligstein, N. (2001) *The Architecture of Markets.* Princeton, NJ: Princeton University Press.

Fligstein, N and Jianjun Zhang (2010) 'A new agenda for research on the trajectory of Chinese capitalism'. *Management and Organization Review.* 71: 39–62.

Fong, V. (2004) *Only Hope: Coming of Age Under China's One-Child Policy.* Stanford, CA: Stanford University Press.

Forrest, R. and Lee, J. (2004) 'Cohort effects, differential accumulation and Hong Kong's volatile housing market'. *Urban Studies.* 41(11): 2181–96, October.

Foucault, M. (1975) *Surveillir et Punir.* Paris: Gallimard.

Foucault, M. (1969) *L'archéologie du Savoir.* Paris: Gallimard.

Foucault, M. (2009) *Security, Territory, Population.* London: Palgrave Macmillan.

Foucault, M. (1998) *The History of Sexuality, The Will to Knowledge, Volume 1.* London: Penguin.

Foucault, M. (2008) *The Birth of Biopolitics.* London: Palgrave Macmillan.

Francis, C.-B. (1996) 'Reproduction of *Danwei* institutional features in the context of China's market economy: the case of *Haidian* district's high-tech sector'. *The China Quarterly.* 147: 839–59.

Fraser, D. (2000) 'Inventing oasis: luxury housing advertisements and reconfiguring domestic space in Shanghai'. In: *The Consumer Revolution in Urban China.* Deborah Davis (ed.) Berkeley, CA: University of California Press, 25–53.

Frenkiel, E. (2010) *From Scholar to Official: Cui Zhiyuan and Chongqing City's Local Experimental Policy.* Available at: www.booksandideas.net/IMG/pdf/20101206_Cui_Zhiyuan_EN.pdf (accessed September 2012).

Frege, G. (1892) 'Über Sinn und Bedeutung'. *Zeitschrift für Philosophie und philosophische Kritik*, NF 100: 25–50.

Frisby, D. (2001) *Cityscapes of Modernity.* London: Blackwell.

Fu, Z. (2002) 'The state, capital, and urban restructuring in post-reform Shanghai'. In: *The New Chinese City: Globalization and Market Reform*, John Logan (ed.). Oxford: Blackwell, 106–20.

Fujita, M., Krugman, P. and Venables, A. (1999) *The Spatial Economy.* Cambridge, MA: MIT Press.

Fung, G. and NOffice 冯果川 嗯工作室. (2009) 'Keywords of China housing policy'. *Urban China.* 34.

Fung, Hung-Gay, Huang, A., Qingfeng Liu and Shen, M. (2006) 'The development of the real estate industry in China'. *The Chinese Economy.* 391: 84–102.

Fung, K. K. and Forrest, R. (2002) 'Institutional mediation, the Asian financial crisis and the Hong Kong housing market'. *Housing Studies.* 172: 189–208.

Gadamer, H. (2004) *Truth and Method.* London: Continuum.

Gamble, J. E. (1997) 'Stir-fried stocks: share dealers, trading places, and new options in contemporary Shanghai'. *Modern China.* 232: 181–215.

Gamble, Jos. (2007) 'Guanxi and ethical business issues in China'. In: *Business Networks and Strategic Alliances in China*, S. Clegg, K. Wang and M. Berrell (eds). Cheltenham: Edward Elgar, 272–89.

Gane, N. (2012a) *Max Weber and Contemporary Capitalism*. London: Palgrave Macmillan.

Gane, N. (2012b) 'Property and neoliberalism: from Hayek to Coase and beyond'. Theory, Culture and Society workshop, Property Rights, Naples, September 2012.

Gates, H. (1996) *China's Motor: A Thousand Years of Petty Capitalism*. Ithaca, NY: Cornell University Press.

Gillham, O. (2002) *The Limitless City: A Primer on the Urban Sprawl Debate*. Washington, DC: Island Press.

Glaser, E. (2010) *How Our Greatest Invention Makes Us Richer, Smarter, Healthier, and Happier*. London and New York: Penguin.

Gold, T. (1985) 'After comradeship: personal relations in China since the cultural revolution'. *China Quarterly*. 104: 657–75

Gold, T., Guthrie, D. and Wank, D. (eds) (2002) *Social Connections in China*. Cambridge: Cambridge University Press.

Goodwin, P. B. (1997) 'Solving congestion when we must not build roads, increase spending, lose votes, damage the economy or harm the environment, and will never find equilibrium'. Inaugural Lecture for the Professorship of Transport Policy, University College, London, 23 October 1997.

Graeber, D. (2002) *Towards an Anthropologial Theory of Value*. New York: Palgrave Macmillan.

Graeber, D. (2011) *Debt: The First Five Thousand Years*. New York: Melville.

Graham, A. C. (1989) *Disputers of the Tao*. Peru, IL: Open Court.

Granet, M. (1958) *Chinese Civilization*. New York: Meridian.

Granet, M. (1975) *The Religion of the Chinese People*. New York: Harper & Row.

Granet, M. (1989) *La Pensée Chinoise*. Paris: Albin Michel.

Granovetter, M. (1985a) 'Economic action, social structure, and embeddedness'. *American Journal of Sociology*. 913: 481–510.

Granovetter, M. (1985b) *Getting a Job*. Chicago, IL: University of Chicago Press.

Green, S. (2003a) *China's Stock Market*. London: Profile Books.

Green, S. (2004) *The Development of China's Stock Market, 1984–2002*. London: Routledge.

Green, S. (2005) 'The privatisation two-step at China's listed firms'. In: *Exit the Dragon? Privatisation and State Control in China*, S. Green and Guy Liu (eds). London: Chatham House/Blackwell, 100–130.

Greenhalgh, S. (2008) *Just One Child: Science and Policy in Deng's China*. Berkeley, CA: University of California Press.

Gu, Junqing, Sun Lan and Shi Meicheng 谷俊青 孙兰 施美程. (2006) 'The current situation and development of China's housing provident fund system' 中国住房公积金制度现状与发展. *China Real Estate Development Report* 中国房地产发展报告, No. 3.

Guardian, The (2011) Available at: www.guardian.co.uk/business/blog/2011/jan/17/mitsk-economies (accessed 19 March 2010).

Gunder, F. A. (1998) *Re-ORIENT*. Berkeley, CA: University of California Press.

Guthrie, D. (1997) 'Between markets and politics: organizational responses to reform in China'. *American Journal of Sociology*. 1025: 1258–1304.

Guthrie, D. (1999) *Dragon in a Three-Piece Suit*. Princeton, NJ: Princeton Unversity Press.

Guthrie, D. (2002) 'Information Asymmetries'. In: *Social Connections in China*, T. Gold, D. Guthrie and D. Wank (eds). Cambridge: Cambridge University Press, 37–55.

Guthrie, D. (2005) 'Organizational learning and productivity: state structure and foreign investment in the rise of the Chinese corporation'. *Management and Organization Review*. 12: 165–95.

Guthrie, D. (2006) *China and Globalization*. London: Routledge.

Haakonssen, K. (2002) *Introduction to Adam Smith, The Theory of Moral Sentiments*. Cambridge: Cambridge University Press.

Haila, A. (1999a) 'City building in the East and West: United States, Europe, Hong Kong and Singapore compared'. *Cities*. 16: 259–67.

Haila, A. (1999b) 'Why is Shanghai building a giant speculative property bubble?' *International Journal of Urban and Regional Research*. 233: 583–8.

Haila, A. (2008) 'The market as the new emperor'. *International Journal of Urban and Regional Research*. 311: 3–20.

Haila, A. (2009) 'Chinese alternatives'. *International Journal of Urban and Regional Research*. 332: 572–5.

Haila, A. (2007) 'The market as the new emperor'. *International Journal of Urban and Regional Research*. 31: 3–20.

Haila, A. (2000) 'Real estate in global cities: Singapore and Hong Kong as property states'. *Urban Studies*. 37: 2241–56.

Haila, A., Bo-sin Tang and Wong, S.W. (2006) 'Housing intermediary services in China: the rise and fall of Fang Wu Yin Hang'. *Journal of Housing and the Built Environment*. 214: 337–54.

Haila, A. and LeGalés, P. (2005) 'The coming of age of metropolitan governance in Helsinki'. In: *Metropolitan Governance. Capacity, Democracy and the Dynamics of Place*, Hubert Heinelt and Daniel Kübler (eds). London: Routledge.

Hall, P.A. and Soskice, D. (eds) (2001) *Varieties of Capitalism*. Oxford: Oxford University Press.

Hamilton, G. (2006) *Commerce and Capitalism in Chinese Societies: The Organization of Chinese Economics*. London: Routledge.

Han, Sun and Pannell, C. (1999) 'The Geography of Privatization in China, 1978–1996'. *Economic Geography*. 753: 272–96.

Hansen, C. (1992) *A Daoist Theory of Chinese Thought*. Oxford: Oxford University Press.

Hanser, A. (2008) *Service Encounters: Class, Gender, and the Market for Social Distinction in Urban China*. Stanford, CA: Stanford University Press.

Hardt, M. and Negri, A. (2000) *Empire*. Cambridge, MA: Harvard University Press.

Harvey, D. (2005) *A Brief History of Neo-Liberalism*. Oxford: Oxford University Press.

Hass-Klau, C. (1993) 'Impact of pedestrianization and traffic calming on retailing: a review of the evidence from Germany and the UK'. *Transport Policy*. 11: 21–31.

Haussermann, H. and Haila, A. (2004) 'The European city. A conceptual framework and normative project'. In: Yuri Kazepov (ed.). *Cities of Europe*. London: Blackwell, 43–63.

Haveman, H., Calomiris, C. and Yongxiang Wang. (2008) 'Going more public: ownership reform among Chinese firms'. Available at: scripts.mit.edu/~cwheat/ess/papers/Haveman_10.pdf (accessed 24 March 2012).

Havrylchyk, O. and Poncet, S. (2007) 'Foreign direct investment in China: reward or remedy?' *The World Economy*. 1662–81.

Havrylchyk, O. (2006) 'Foreign direct investment in China: reward or remedy'. Working Paper. Paris: Centre D'études Prospectives et D'information Internationalee, 20.

Hayami, S. (1986) 'The great transformation: social and economic change in sixteenth and seventeenth century Japan'. *Bonner Zeitschrift für Japanologie*, 8: 6.

Hayhoe, R. (2009) *China's Universities 1895–1995: A Century of Cultural Conflict*. London: Routledge

Haynes, K. E. and Enders, W. (1975) 'Distance, direction, and entropy in the evolution of a settlement pattern'. *Economic Geography*. 514: 357–65.

He, Shenjing and Fulong Wu (2005) 'Property-led redevelopment in post-reform China: A case study of Xintiandi redevelopment project in Shanghai'. *Journal of Urban Affairs*. 271: 1–23.

Hegel, G. W. F. (1952) *Philosophy of Right.* Oxford: Oxford University Press.

Hegel, G. W. F. (2008) *Lectures on the Philosophy of Religion.* Oxford: Oxford University Press.

Heilmann, S. and Perry, E. (2011) *Mao's Invisible Hand: The Political Foundations of Adaptive Governance in China.* Cambridge, MA: Harvard University Press.

Heilmann, S. and Perry, E. (2011) 'Embracing uncertainty: guerilla policy style and adaptive governance in China'. In: *Mao's Invisible Hand,* Sebastian Heilmann and Elizabeth Perry (eds). Harvard, MA: Harvard University Press, 1–29.

Henderson, G. and Cohen, M. (1984) *The Chinese Hospital: A Socialist Work Unit.* New Haven, CT: Yale University Press.

Hennis, W. (1987) *Max Weber: Essays in Reconstruction.* London: Routledge.

Hess, S. (2010) 'Nail-houses, land rights, and frames of injustice on China's protest landscape'. *Asian Survey,* 50(5): 908–26.

Heyhoe, R. (1991) *China's Universities, 1895–1995: A Century of Cultural Conflict.* London: Routledge.

Hofstede, G. (1984) *Culture's Consequences.* Sage: London.

Horkheimer, M. and Adorno, T. (1997) *Dialectic of Enlightenment.* London: Verso.

Hsing, You-tien (2010) *The Great Urban Transformation.* Oxford: Oxford University Press.

Huang, P. (2011) 'Chongqing: Equitable development driven by a "third hand"' *Modern China.* 37(6): 569–622.

Huang, Y. (2005) *Selling China.* Cambridge: Cambridge University Press.

Huang, Y. (2008) *Capitalism With Chinese Characteristics.* Cambridge: Cambridge University Press.

Hume, D. (2007) *An Enquiry Concerning Human Understanding.* Oxford: Oxford University Press.

He Yue (2009) 'Yunnan jingnei de waiguo liudong renkou taishi yu bianjiang shehui wenti tanxi'. *Yunnan Shifan Daxue Xuebao.* 1: 18–25.

Hertz, E. (1994) The trading crowd: an ethnography of the Shanghai stock market. University of California PhD, unpublished dissertation.

Hertz, E. (1998) *The Trading Crowd: An Ethnography of the Shanghai Stock Market.* Cambridge: Cambridge University Press.

Heynen, H. (1999) *Architecture and Modernity: A Critique.* Cambridge, Mass: MIT Press.

Hillman, A., Michael, J., Withers, C. and Collins, B. J. (2009) 'Resource dependence theory: a review'. *Journal of Management.* 356: 1404–27.

Ho, P. (2001) 'Who owns China's land: policies property rights and deliberate institutional ambiguity'. *China Quarterly.* 394–421

Hoffman, L. (2006) 'Autonomous choices and patriotic professionalism: on governmentality in late-socialist China'. *Economy and Society.* 354: 550–70.

Honoré, T. (1987) *Making Law Bind: Essays Legal and Philosophical.* Oxford: Clarendon.

Horkheimer, M. and Adorno, T. (1997) *Dialectic of Enlightenment,* London: Verso.

Howie, F. and Walter, C. (2006) *Privatizing China: Inside China's Stock Markets.* Singapore: John Wiley & Sons.

Hsio, M. (2009) *Financial Regulation of Banking Derivatives, Securitizations and Trusts in China.* Toronto: Carswell.

Hsu, C. L. (2005) 'Capitalism without contracts versus capitalists without capitalism: Comparing the influence of Chinese guanxi and Russian blat on marketization'. *Communist and Post-Communist Studies.* 383: 909–21.

Hsu, C. (2007) *Creating Market Socialism: How Ordinary People are Shaping Class and Status in China.* Durham, NC: Duke University Press.

Huang, Y. (2005) *Selling China.* Cambridge: Cambridge University Press.

Huang, Y. (2010) 'Rethinking the Beijing consensus'. *Asia Policy.* 11: 1–26.

Huang, P. (1993) '"Public sphere"/"civil society" in China?: The third realm between state and society'. *Modern China*. 192: 216–40.

Hughes, N. (1998) 'Smashing the iron rice bowl'. *Foreign Affairs*. 77(4): 67–77.

Hugo, G. (2008) 'Trends in Asia that will influence its future as a source of skilled migrants'. *Canadian Diversity*. 3: 41–6.

Hui, Yuk (2012) 'Collective individuation: a new theoretical foundation for the social web'. Available at: www2012.wwwconference.org/proceedings/webscience/wwwweb sci2012_hui.pdf (accessed September 2012).

Hume, D. (2007) *An Enquiry Concerning Human Understanding*. Oxford: Oxford University Press.

Husserl, E. (1973) *Experience and Judgment*. Evanston: Northwestern University Press.

Husserl, E. (1983) *Ideas Pertaining to a Pure Phenomenology and to a Phenomenological Philosophy First Book*. Dordrecht: Kluwer Academic Publishers.

Hutton, W. (2008) *The Writing on the Wall*, London: Abacus

Ip, D. and Lever-Tracy, C. (2005) 'Diversification and extensible networks: the strategies of Chinese businesses in Australia'. *International Migration*. 433: 73–96.

Ivakhnyuk, I. (2009) 'Crises-related redirections of migration flows: the case of the Eurasian migration system'. Paper at 'New Times? economic crisis, geo-political transformation and the emergent migration order', Centre on Migration Policy and Society COMPAS annual conference, Oxford, 21–22 September 2009.

Jacques, M. (2012) *When China Rules the World, 2nd edn*. Harmondsworth: Penguin.

James, I. (2011) *Paul Virilio (Routledge Critical Thinkers)*. London and New York: Routledge.

Jaspers, K. (1994) *Vom Ursprung und Ziel der Geschichte*. Munich: Piper Verlag.

Ji, You (1998) *China's Enterprise Reform*. London: Routledge.

Jiang, Jun (2011) 'From Chongqing to Shenzhen and back: the evolving "China model" ESRC centre on migration policy and society'. University of Oxford: COMPAS Rising Powers Working Papers.

Jing, C. (2003) 'Penetrating the situation and social problems of China's foreign population in the time of globalization'. *Zhengfa xuekan*. 3: 56–62.

Jing, J. (2000) *Feeding China's Little Emperors*. Stanford, CA: Stanford University Press.

Jing'an District Gazette Editorial Committee (静安区地方志编纂委员会编) (1996) *Jing'an District Gazette* (静安区志). Shanghai: Shanghai Academy of Social Sciences Press (上海社会科学院出版社).

Jing'an District Statisical Bureau (2008–2010, 2007–2009) Statistical Bulletin of Economic and Social Development Jing'an District, City of Shanghai. Available at: www.jingan.gov.cn (accessed 12 May 2012).

Jongsthapongpanth, A. and Bagchi-Sen, S. (2007) 'US-Asia interdependencies: a study of business and knowledge links'. *Journal of the Asia Pacific Economy*, 122: 215–49.

Jullien, F. (1993) *Eloge de la fadeur*. Paris: Le Livre de Poche.

Jullien, F. (1995) *The Propensity of Things: Toward a History of Efficacy in China*. New York: Zone Books

Jullien, F. (1996) *Fonder la Morale*. Paris: Grasset.

Jullien, F. (1999) *The Propensity of Things*. Cambridge, MA: Zone Books.

Jullien, F. (2001) *Du 'temps'*. Paris: Grasset.

Jullien, F. (2002) *Traité de l'efficacité*. Paris: Le Livre de Poche.

Jullien, F. (2004) *Detour and Access*. Cambridge, MA: MIT Press.

Jullien, F. (2009) *The Great Image Has No Form, or on the Nonobject through Painting*. Chicago, IL: University of Chicago Press.

Kant, I. (1956) *Critique of Practical Reason*. Indianapolis, IN: Bobbs Merrill.

Kant, I. (1999) *Critique of Pure Reason*. Cambridge: Cambridge University Press.

Keister, L. A. (2009) 'Interfirm Relations in China'. *American Behavioral Scientist*. 5212: 1709–30.

Keister, L. A. (2001) 'Exchange structures in transition: lending and trade relations in Chinese business groups'. *American Sociological Review*. 663: 336–60.

Keister, L. (2002) '*Guanxi* in business groups: social ties and the formation of economic relations'. In: *Social Connections in China*, T. Gold, D. Guthrie and D. Wank (eds), 77–97.

Keister, L. A. (2007) 'Inter-firm relations in business groups: group structure and firm performance in China'. In: *Business Networks and Strategic Alliances in China*, Stewart Clegg, Karen Wang and Mike Berrell (eds). Cheltenham: Edward Elgar, 157–81.

Keister, L. A. (2009) 'Interfirm relations in China'. *American Behavioral Scientist*, 5212: 1709–30.

Keister, L. A. and Yanlong Zhang (2009) 'Organizations and management in China'. *Academy of Management Annals*, 31: 342–77.

Keith, M. (2007) 'Shanghai: capital of the 21st century'. *Street Signs*. Spring; 6–10.

Kelsen, H. (1997) *Introduction to the Problems of Legal Theory*. Oxford: Clarendon.

Kenworthy, J. and Laube, F. (2001) 'Millennium Cities Database for Sustainable Transport'. CD-ROM database. Brussels: International Union of Public Transport UITP.

Kenworthy, J. (2006) 'The eco-city: ten key transport and planning dimensions for sustainable city development'. *Environment and Urbanization*. 181: 67–85.

Khanna, T. (2008) 'Learning from economic experiments in China and India'. *Academy of Management Perspectives*. May: 36–43.

Khanna, T. and Palepu, K. (1997) 'Why focused strategies may be wrong for emerging markets'. *Harvard Business Review*. 75(4): 41–51.

Kipnis, A. (2002) 'Practices of Guanxi production and practices of ganqing avoidance'. In: *Social Connections in China*, T. Gold, D. Guthrie and D. Wank (eds). Cambridge: University of Cambridge Press.

Kipnis, A. (2007) 'Neoliberalism reified: *Suzhi* discourse and tropes of neoliberalism in the People's Republic of China'. *Journal of the Royal Anthropological Institute*. 13: 383–400.

Knight, F. (2009) *Risk, Uncertainty and Profit*. New York: Mineola.

Kristensen, P. H. (2005) 'Modelling national business systems and the civilizing process'. In: *Changing Capitalisms?*, G. Morgan, R. Whitley and E. Moen (eds). Oxford: Oxford University Press, 383–414.

Koolhaas, R. (1995) *S, M, L, XL*. New York: Monacelli Press.

Kraatz M. S. and J. H. (2002) 'Executive migration and institutional change'. *Academy of Management Journal*, 45(1): 120–43.

Kriz, A. and Kealing, B. (2010) 'Business relationships in China: lessons about deep trust'. *Asia Pacific Business Review*. 163: 299–318.

Krug, B. and Hendriscke, H. (2008) 'Framing China: transformation and institutional change through co-evolution'. *Management and Organization Review*. 41: 81–108.

Kung, J. (2002) 'Choice of land tenure in China: the case of a country with quasi-private property rights'. *Economic Development and Cultural Change*. 504: 793–817.

Kvale, S. (1996) *Interviews: An Introduction to Qualitative Research Interviewing*. London: Sage.

Kwinter, S. (2002) *Architectures of Time*, Cambridge, MA: MIT Press.

Lai, K. (2006) '"Imagineering" Asian emerging markets: financial knowledge networks in the fund management industry'. *Geoforum*. 374: 627–42.

Landry, C. (2000) *The Creative City: A Toolkit for Urban Innovators*. London: Earthscan Publications.

Lai, L. Wai-chung (1998) 'The leasehold system as a means of planning by contract: the case of Hong Kong'. *Town Planning Review*. 69(3): 249–75.

Lai, Sonia Wong Man and Yong Yang (2009) 'From scorned to loved? The political economy of the development of the stock market in China'. *Global Economic Review*. 38(4): 409–29.

Lash, S. (2010) *Intensive Culture*. London: Sage.

Latour, B. (2007) *Reassembling the Social*. Oxford: OUP.

Le Bail, H. (2009) *China's Large Cities as Places of Immigration: The Case of African Entrepreneurs.* Paris: Centre Asie Ifri.

Lee, Ching Kwan (1998) *Gender and the South China Miracle.* Berkeley, CA: University of California Press.

Lee, Ching Kwan (2007) 'The Unmaking of the Chinese Working Class in the Northeastern Rustbelt' In: *Working in China*, Ching Kwan Lee (ed.). New York: Routledge, 15–37.

Lee, J. and Ya-peng Zhu (2006) 'Urban Governance, Neoliberalism and Housing Reform in China'. *The Pacific Review.* 191: 39–61.

Lee, Leo Ou-Fan (2008) *City between Worlds: My Hong Kong.* Cambridge, MA: Belknap of Harvard University Press

Lee, Leo Ou-Fan (1999) *Shanghai Modern: The Flowering of a New Urban Culture in China.* Cambridge, MA: Harvard University Press.

LeGalés P. (2002) *European Cities.* Oxford: Oxford University Press.

Li, Cheng (2005) 'Coming home to teach: status and mobility of returnees in China's higher education'. In: *Bridging Minds across the Pacific: US–China Educational Exchanges, 1978–2003*, Cheng Li (ed.). Lanham: Lexington Books, 69–109.

Li, Haiyang and Zhang, Y. (2007) 'The role of managers' political networking and functional experience in new venture performance: evidence from China's transition economy'. *Strategic Management Journal*, 281: 791–804.

Li, H. (2008) 'A cost of less than 4 yuan for some stocks with expiring bans *Bufen jiejingu chengben buzu 4 yuan*'. *Information Times* [Xinxi Shibao], 16 May 2008, B1.

Li Ling (1997a) 'Privatization of the urban land market in Shanghai'. *Journal of Real Estate Literature*, 52: 161–8.

Li, Ling Hin (1997b) 'The political economy of the privatization of urban land market in Shanghai'. *Urban Studies*, 34(2): 321–35.

Li, Ling Hin (1999a) *Urban Land Reform in China.* London: Macmillan Press.

Li, Ling Hin (1999b) 'Impacts of land use rights reform on urban development in China' *RURDS.* I I(3)November 1999: 193–205.

Li, Hongbin, Lingsheng Meng, Qian Wang and Li-an Zhou (2008) 'Political connections, financing and firm performance: evidence from Chinese private firms'. *Journal of Development Economics.* 872: 283–99.

Li, Julie Juan, Laura Poppo and Kevin Zheng Zhou (2008) 'Do managerial ties in china always produce value? Competition, uncertainty, and domestic vs. foreign firms'. *Strategic Management Journal.* 29: 383–400.

Li, L. (2006) *Development and Operation of Real Estate.* Beijing: China People's University Press.

Li, L. (1997) 'Privatization of the urban land market in Shanghai'. *Journal of Real Estate Literature.* 52: 161–8.

Li, L. (2008) Guanxi *Intensive Market: A Study on the Micro-Social Dynamics of Real Estate Market in China.* Beijing: Social Sciences Academic Press.

Li, Meng 林蓉. (2009) 'Minhang building falls over: 6 are held, 7 bailed out, vice-district head is given administrative warning' 闵行倒楼：6人被拘 7人取保候审副区长遭行政警告 *Oriental Morning Post* 东方早报, July 29. A02.

Li, S. (2011) 'Beijing Urged to keep its foot on property brake'. *South China Morning Post*, 10 December, B2.

Li, Shiqiao (2007) 'City of Maximum Quantities', unpublished paper at Theory, Culture and City 'Megacities' Conference, Beijing 2008.

Liang, S. (2010) 'Property-driven urban change in post-socialist Shanghai: reading the television series *Woju*'. *Journal of Current Chinese Affairs.* 39(4): 3–28.

Liang, Zai and Zhongdong Ma (2004) 'China's floating population: new evidence from the 2000 census'. *Population and Development Review.* 30(3): 467–88.

Lin, Nan (2001) *Social Capital.* Cambridge: University of Cambridge Press.

Lin, Ping (2007) *Easy to Move, Hard to Settle Down: Taiwanese People in China.* Oxford: University of Oxford.

Lin, Yi-Chieh J. (2011) *Fake Stuff: China and the Rise of Counterfeit Goods.* London: Routledge.

Lin, G. and Ho, S. (2006) 'The state, land system, and land development processes in contemporary China'. *Annals of the Association of American Geographers.* 952: 411–36.

Lin, Ka and Hong Gao 林卡 高红. (2007) 'Analysis of the development power and system background of China's economical housing system' 中国经济适用房制度发展动力和制度背景分析, *Policy Research* 政策研究, 1: 23–32.

Liu, Ling (2008) 'Local government and big business in the People's Republic of China – case study evidence from Shandong province'. *Asia Pacific Business Review.* 144: 473–89.

Liu, K. (2007) *Chinese Economy.* 40(3): 12–92.

Liu, Qianchao 刘乾超 (2012) 'Happy housing centralized: municipality of Beijing people's representative examines changping's difficulties' 乐居聚焦：北京市人大代表关注昌平南行之困. Sina Real Estate 新浪地产. Available at: http://news.dichan.sina.com.cn/2012/02/13/ 441450.html (accessed 17 March 2012).

Liu, Sian Victoria (2007) '"Social positions": neighborhood transitions after danwei' In: *Working in China,* Ching Kwan Lee (ed.). New York: Routledge, 38–55.

Liu, Xiuhao 刘秀浩. (2009) 'The complex of the apartment building paid only 604 yuan per square meter for land, just 4.2% of housing price' 上海倒塌楼盘楼板价每平米604元 仅占房价4.2%, *Oriental Morning Post* 东方早报, June 29.

Liu, Xiuhao 刘秀浩. (2008) 'A 50-person wenzhou house-frying group re-appears in Shanghai' 50人温州炒房团重现上海. *Oriental Morning Post* 东方早报, December 1.

Lloyd, G. and Sivin, N. (2002) *The Way and the Word.* New Haven, CT: Yale University Press.

Logan, J. and Molotch, H. (1987) *Urban Fortunes: The Political Economy of Place.* Berkeley, CA: University of California Press.

Lovett, S., Simmons, L. C. and Kali, R. (1999) 'Guanxi versus the market: ethics and efficiency'. *Journal of International Business Studies.* 302: 231–47.

Lozada, E. (2000) 'Globalized childhood? Kentucky Fried Chicken in Beijing'. In: *Feeding China's Little Emperors,* Jing Jun (ed.). Stanford, CA: Stanford University Press, 114–34.

Lozada, E. (2006) 'Cosmopolitanism and Nationalism in Shanghai Sports'. *City and Society.* 182: 207–31.

Lu, F. (1998) [1989] 'The work unit: a unique form of social organization'. In: *Streetlife China,* Michael Dutton (ed.). Cambridge: Cambridge University Press, 53–8.

Lu, H. (2000) 'To be relatively comfortable in an egalitarian society'. In: *The Consumer Revolution in Urban China,* D. Davis (ed.). Berkeley, CA: University of California Press, 124–44.

Lu, J. W. and Xufei Ma (2008) 'The contingent value of local partners' business group affiliations'. *Academy of Management Journal.* 512: 295–314.

Lü, Xiaobo (1997) 'Minor public economy: the revolutionary origins of the Danwei'. In: *Danwei: The Changing Chinese Workplace in Historical and Comparative Perspective,* Xiaobo Lü and E. Perry (eds). Armonk, NY: M.E. Sharpe, 21–41.

Luhmann, N. (1987) *Soziale Systeme.* Frankfurt: Suhrkamp.

Luo K., Fei Guo and Huang Ping (2003) 'China: Government Policies and Emerging Trends of Reversal of the Brain Drain'. In: *Return Migration in the Asia Pacific,* R. Iredale, Fei Guo and S. Rozaria (eds). Cheltenham: Edward Elgar, 88–111.

Luo, Yadong (2005) 'Shifts of Chinese government policies on inbound foreign direct investment'. In: *International Business and Government Relations in the 21st Century*, R. Grosse (ed.). Cambridge: Cambridge University Press, 291–313.

Luo, Yadong and Min Chen (1997) 'Does guanxi influence firm performance?' *Asia Pacific Journal of Management*. 14: 1–16.

Luo, Yadong, Ying Huang and Lu Wang, S. (2012) 'Guanxi and organizational performance: a meta-analysis'. *Management and Organization Review*. 8(1): 139–72.

Luo, Shalin, Li Dongyuan and Xu Feng (2009) 'Thirty-six stratagems in the art of war: seeing through developers "wupan" hidden rules'. *Information Times*. 7 August 2009, D02.

Lyons, M., Brown, A. and Zhigang Li (2008) 'The "third tier" of globalization: African traders in Guangzhou'. *City*. 122: 196–206.

Lyotard, J. F. (2003) 'L'efficience du crabe'. In: *Dépayser la pensée*, T. Marchaise (ed.). Paris: Les Empêcheurs de penser en rond, 17–22.

Ma, Laurence and Fulong Wu (2005) *Restructuring the Chinese City*. London and New York: Routledge Curzon.

Ma, L. and Biao Xiang (1998) 'Native place, migration and the emergence of peasant enclaves in Beijing'. *China Quarterly*. 155: 546–81.

Ma, L. and Biao Xiang (1998) 'Native place, migration and the emergence of peasant enclaves in Beijing'. *China Quarterly*. 155: 68–103.

Mackenzie, A. (2010) *Wirelessness. Radical Empiricism in Network Cultures*. Cambridge, MA: MIT Press.

MacIntyre, A. (1984) *After Virtue, South Bend*: Notre Dame University Press.

MacKenzie, D. (2003) 'Long-term capital management and the sociology of arbitrage'. *Economy and Society*. 323: 349–80.

MacKenzie, D. (2004) 'The big, bad wolf and the rational markets: portfolio insurance, the 1987 crash and the performativity of economics'. *Economy and Society*. 333: 303–34.

MacKenzie, D. (2006) *An Engine, Not a Camera: How Financial Models Shape Markets*. Cambridge: MIT Press.

MacKenzie, D. (2008a) *China Capital Markets Development Report*. Beijing: China Finance Press.

MacKenzie, D. (2009) *Material Markets*. Oxford: Oxford University Press.

MacKenzie, D. and Yoval Millo (2003) 'Constructing a market, performing theory: the historical sociology of a financial derivatives exchange'. *American Journal of Sociology*. 1091: 107–45.

Marx, K. (1993) *Grundrisse*. Harmondsworth: Penguin

Marx, K. (2005) *Das Kapital. Erster Band*. Berlin: Dietz.

Mauss, M. (2011) *The Gift*. London: Routledge.

McCloskey, D. (1976) 'English open fields as behavior towards risk'. In: *Research in Economic History*, P. Uselding (ed.). Greenwich, CT: JAI Press, 1: 124–70.

McCloskey, D. (1991) 'The prudent peasant: new findings on open fields'. *Journal of Economic History*, 512: 343–55.

McCrummen, S. (2007) 'Struggling Chadians dream of a better life – in China'. *Washington Post*, 6 October: A17.

Mckinsey Global Institute (2009) 'Preparing for China's urban billion'. London and New York: McKinsey Global Institute.

Menger, C. (1950) *Principles of Economics*. New York: Free Press.

Meade, J. (1989) *Agathopia: The Economics of Partnership*. Aberdeen: The David Hume Institute.

Meipeng, Yang and Chen Zhongxiaolu (2008) 'Shanghai property puzzle of killed magnates'. *Caijing*. 26 December 2008.

Menger, C. (1963) *Über die Methode der Sozialwissenschaften und der Politischen Ökonomie insbesondere*. Champaign-Urbana, IL: University of Illinois Press.

Merchant, H. (2008) *Competing in Emerging Markets Cases and Readings*. New York: Routledge.

Meyer, J. (2009) 'Reflections: institutional theory and world society'. In: *World Society*, Georg Krücken and Gili S. Drori (eds). Oxford: Oxford University Press.

Meyer, J. W. and Rowan, B. (1991) 'Institutionalized organizations: formal structure as myth and ceremony'. In: *The New Institutionalism and Organizational Analysis*, Walter W. Powell and Paul J. Dimaggio (eds). Chicago, IL: University of Chicago Press, 41–62.

Meyer, M. W. and Xiaohui Lu (2004) 'Managing indefinite boundaries: the strategy and structure of a Chinese business firm'. *Management and Organization Review*, 11: 57–86.

Mihaljek, D. and Packer, F. (2010) 'Derivatives in emerging markets'. *BIS Quarterly Review*, December 2010. Available at: http://ssrn.com/abstract=1727412.

Minhang District Statisical Bureau (2008–2010, 2007–2009) 'Statistical bulletin of economic and social development Minhang district, city of Shanghai'. Available at: http://tj.shmh.gov.cn (accessed 13 May 2012).

Ministry of Land and Resources (2005) 'Rules for tender, auction and listing conveyance of state-owned land use rights' 招标拍卖挂牌出让国有土地使用权规定. Available at: www.mlr.gov.cn/zwgk/flfg/dfflfg/200504/t20050406_636761.htm (accessed 10 May 2012).

Ministry of Land and Resources (2007) 'MoLaR interprets "rules for tender, auction and listing conveyance of state-owned construction land use rights"' 国土资源部解读《招标拍卖挂牌出让国有建设用地使用权规定. Available at: www.law110.com/lawserve/beijing/law110com20068076.html (accessed 15 May 2012).

Mirowski, P. (1989) *More Heat than Light. Economics as Social Physics, Physics as Nature's Economics*. Cambridge: Cambridge University Press.

Mitchell, T. (2002) *Rule of Experts: Egypt, Techno-Politics, Modernity*. Berkeley, CA: California: University of California Press.

Mitchell, T. (2005) 'The work of economics: how a discipline makes its world'. *European Journal of Sociology*, 46(02): 297–320.

Moe, R. and Wilkie, C. (1997) *Changing Places: Rebuilding Community in the Age of Sprawl*. New York: Henry Holt and Company.

Monetary Policy Analysis Group of the People's Bank of China (2008) 'China monetary policy report quarter four, 2007'. Available at: www.pbc.gov.cn/showacc2.asp?id= 1201 (accessed 1 July 2008).

Moran, P. (2005) 'Structural vs. relational embeddedness: social capital and managerial performance'. *Strategic Management Review*. 26: 1129–51.

Mouffe, C. (ed.) (1999) *The Challenge of Carl Schmitt*. London: Verso.

Moulier B., Y. (2008) *Le Capitalisme Cognitive*. Paris: Editions Amsterdam.

Nara, Y. (2008) 'A cross-cultural study on attitudes toward risk, safety and security'. In: *KES*, I. Lovrek, R. J. Howlett and L. C. Jain. London: Springer, 734–41.

National Bureau of Statistics (NBS), Department of Population Science (2002) 'National floating population has hit 121.07 million' (全国流动人口 已达12107万人). National Bureau of Statistics website (accessed 6 May 2009).

National Bureau of Statistics of China (2008a) 'Gross domestic product quarters 1–4 2007'. Available at: http://219.235.129.54/cx/table/table_sc.jsp?bh=0000000000000702&dzm=000000000&bbzl=102 (accessed 1 July 2008).

National Bureau of Statistics of China (2008b) 'June national consumer price index increases 7.1% and city increases 6.8%, year-on-year'. July 18. Available at: www.stats.gov.cn/tjfx/jdfx/t20080718_402493167.htm (accessed 25 July 2008).

National Bureau of Statistics of China (2008c) 'June National Producer Price Index Increases 8.8%'. July 18. Available at: www.stats.gov.cn/tjfx/jdfx/t20080718_402493159.htm (accessed 2 July 2008).

National Statistics (2007) 'Foreign investors hold two-fifths of UK shares'. *News Release.* Available at: www.statistics.gov.uk/pdfdir/share0707.pdf (accessed 17 July 2008).

Naughton, B. (2002) 'The politics of the stock market', *China Leadership Monitor* 3: 1–12.

Naughton, B. (2003) 'The state asset commission: a powerful new government body'. *China Leadership Monitor* 8: 1–10.

Naughton, B. (2007a) *The Chinese Economy: Transitions and Growth.* Cambridge: MIT Press.

Naughton, B. (2007b) 'SASAC and rising corporate power in China'. *China Leadership Monitor* 24: 1–9.

Naughton, B. (2007c) 'The assertive center: Beijing moves against local government control of land'. *China Leadership Monitor.* 20: 1–11.

Naughton, B. (2008) 'A political economy of China's economic transition'. In: *China's Great Economic Transformation*, L. Brandt and T. G. Rawski (eds). Cambridge: Cambridge University Press, 91–135.

Nee, V. (1992) 'Organizational dynamics of market transition: hybrid forms, property rights, and mixed economy in China'. *Administrative Science Quarterly.* 37: 1–27.

Nee, V. (1996) 'The emergence of a market society: changing mechanisms of stratification in China'. *American Journal of Sociology.* 101: 908–49.

Nee, V. (2000) 'The role of the state in making a market economy'. *Journal of Institutional and Theoretical Economics.* 156: 64–88.

Nee, V. (2005) 'New institutionalism economic and sociological'. In: *Handbook for Economic Sociology,* Neil Smelser and Richard Swedberg (eds). New York: Princeton University Press

Nee, V. and Yang Cao (1999) 'Path dependent societal transformation: stratification in hybrid mixed economies'. *Theory and Society.* 28: 799–834.

Nee, V., Opper, S. and Wong, S. (2007) 'Development state and corporate governance in China'. *Management and Organization Review.* 31: 19–53.

Neftci, Salih N. and Yuan Ménager-Xu, M. (2007) *China's Financial Markets.* Amsterdam: Elsevier.

Negri A. (1992) *Marx Beyond Marx: Lessons on the Grundrisse.* London: Pluto Press.

Newman, P. and Kenworthy, J. (1999) *Sustainability and Cities: Overcoming Automobile Dependence.* Washington DC: Island Press.

New World (新世界). (1995) '1994 Annual Report for Shanghai New World Limited Company' (上海新世界股份有限公司1994年年度报告). 9 March 1995. Available at: http://JinKu.com (accessed 12 July 2012).

Ng, E. (2012) 'How 'Northern King' built his empire'. *South China Morning Post*, 15 August 2012.

Ng, S. (2004) 'Taiwanese gold rush to China'. *Asia Times* Online, June 30 2004.

Nonini, D. (2008) 'Is China becoming neoliberal?' *Critique of Anthropology.* 28(2): 145–76.

North, D. C. (1990) *Institutions, Institutional Change and Economic Performance.* Cambridge: Cambridge University Press.

North, D. (1981) *Structure and Change in Economic History.* New York: Norton.

North, D. and Thomas, R. (1973) *The Rise of the Western World: A New Economic History.* Cambridge: Cambridge University Press.

Nussbaum, M. (2003) 'Capabilities as fundamental entitlements: sen and social justice'. *Feminist Economics,* 9: 2–3, 33–59.

Observer, The (2006) 'Shanghai plans eco-metropolis on its mudflats'. 8 January 2006.

Ogilvie, S. (2007) 'Whatever is, is right? Economic institutions in pre-industrial Europe'. *Economic History Review.* 604: 649–684.

Oi, J. (1995) 'The role of the local state in China's transitional economy'. *China Quarterly.* 144: 1132–1111.

Oi, J. (1999) *Rural China Takes Off*. Berkeley, CA: University of California Press.

Oi, J. (2011) 'Politics in China's corporate restructuring'. In: *Going Private in China*, J. Oi (ed.). Stanford, CA: Walter H. Shorenstein Asia-Pacific Research Centre Books, 1–18.

Oi, J. and Chaohua, H. (2011) 'China's corporate restructuring'. *Going Private in China*, J. Oi (ed.). Stanford, CA: Walter H. Shorenstein Asia-Pacific Research Centre Books, 19–37.

Ong, A. (2006) *Neoliberalism as Exception*. Durham, NC: Duke University Press.

Ong, A. and Li Zhang (2008) 'Introduction: privatizing China'. In: *Privatizing China: Socialism from Afar*, Li Zhang and Aihwa Ong (eds). Ithaca, NY: Cornell University Press, 1–19.

Osnos, E. (2009) 'The promised land: Guangzhou's Canaan market and the rise of an African merchant class'. *The New Yorker*. 50–55.

Østbø Haugen, H. (2009) 'Chinese and African traders: different types of capital employed in transnational economic activity'. Paper presented at the Conference on 'Chinese in Africa/Africans in China', Johannesburg: Centre for Sociological Research, University of Johannesburg, 27–28 August 2009.

Otis, E. (2007) 'Virtual personalism in Beijing: learning deference and femininity at a global luxury hotel', In: *Working in China*, Ching Kwan Lee (ed.). London: Routledge, 101–23.

Otis, E. (2009) 'The labor of luxury: gender and generational inequality in a Beijing hotel' In: *Creating Wealth and Poverty in Postsocialist China*, Deborah Davis and Feng Wang (eds). Stanford, CA: Stanford University Press, 54–68.

Overman, H. (2004) 'Can we learn anything from economic geography proper?' *Journal of Economic Geography*, 4(5): 501–16.

Pan, Q. (2008) 'Southern air warrant encounters "doomsday theory", specialists warn investors not to "play with fire"' [*Nanhang quanzheng zaoyu "morilun", zhuanjia jingshi touzizhe qiewu "wan huo"*]. *Xinhua Net*. Available at: http://news.xinhuanet.com/fortune/2008-06/03/content_8307733.htm (accessed 1 July 2008).

Papademetriou, D. (2008) 'Reflections on the international migration system: introduction'. *Canadian Diversity*. 3: 3–6.

Park, Seung Ho and Yadong Luo (2001) 'Guanxi and organizational dynamics: organizational networking in Chinese firms'. *Strategic Management Journal*. 225: 455–77.

Parsons, T. (1967) *The Structure of Social Action*. New York: Free Press.

Peng, M. W and Luo, Y. (2000) 'Managerial ties and firm performance in a transition economy: The nature of a micro-macro link'. *Academy of Management Journal*. 433: 486–501.

Perera, Y. and Weisinger, J. Y. (2007) 'Social capital in organizations: emergent areas and key issues'. Paper presented at Decision Sciences Institute Western Region Meeting, San Diego, CA, 15–17 March 2007.

Perry, E. J. and Wong, C. P. W. (eds) (1985) *The Political Economy of Reform in Post-Mao China*. Cambridge, MA: Harvard University Press.

Pieke, F. (2007) 'Community and identity in the new Chinese migration order'. *Population, Space and Place*. 2: 81–94.

Pigou, A. (1912) *Wealth and Welfare*. London: Macmillan and Company.

Ping Hu and Qing Li (2000) 'The shady deals of funds [*Jijin heimu*]'. *Caijing Magazine*, 5 October. Available at: http://magazine.caijing.com.cn/20001005/2466.shtml (accessed 1 July 1 2008).

Plehwe, D. (2009) 'Introduction'. In: *The Road from Mont Pèlerin. The Making of the Neoliberal Thought Collective*, P. Mirowski and D. Plehwe (eds). Cambridge, MA: Harvard University Press, 1–44.

Podolny, J, M. (2001) 'Networks as the pipes and prisms of the market'. *American Journal of Sociology*. 1071: 33–60.

Powell, W. W. and Dimaggio, P. J. (1991) 'The iron cage revisited: institutional isomorphism and collective rationality in organizational fields'. In: *New Institutionalism in Organizational Analysis*, W.W. Powell and P.J. Dimaggio (eds). Chicago, IL: Chicago University Press, 63–82.

Pun, N. (2005) *Made in China*. Durham, NC: Duke University Press.

Pun, N. (2009) 'The making of a global dormitory labour regime'. In: *Labour Migration and Social Development in Contemporary China*, Rachel Murphy (ed.). London: Routledge, 154–70.

Pun, N. and Smith, C. (2007) 'Putting transnational labour process in its place'. *Work, Employment and Society* 21(1): 27–45.

Putnam, R. D. (2000) *Bowling Alone*. Simon & Schuster: New York.

Qi, D. W. W. and Hua Zhang (2000) 'Shareholding structure and corporate performance of partially privatized firms: evidence from listed Chinese companies'. *Pacific-Basin Finance Journal*. 8: 587–610.

Qin, Y. (2011) 'Rule, rules, and relations: towards a synthetic approach to governance'. *The Chinese Journal of International Politics*. 4(2): 117–45.

Qiu, J. (2009) *Working-Class Network Society*. Cambridge, MA: The MIT Press.

Qu, Z. and Wang Fuyou 曲振涛 王福友 (2004) *Economic Law* 经济法. Beijing: Higher Education Press.

Rabinowitch, S. (2011) 'Moody's warns on China's local debt'. *Financial Times*. 5 July 2011 (accessed 17 April 2012).

Rabinowitch, S. (2012) 'China extends loans to avoid mass default'. *Financial Times*. 12 February 2012 (accessed 17 April 2012).

Rajchman, J. (1994) 'Thinking Big: Dutch Architect Rem Koolhaas Interview'. *Art Forum*. December. Available at: http://findarticles.com/p/articles/mi_m0268/is_n4_v33/ai_16547724/pg_6/ (accessed April 2012).

Raju, P. (1985) *Structural depths of Indian thought*. New Delhi: South Asian Publishers.

Ramo, J. C. (2004) *The Beijing Consensus. Notes on the New Physics of Chinese Power*. London: Foreign Policy Centre.

Ramzy, A. (2010) 'Amid recovery, China's property market soars'. *Time Magazine*. 21 January. Available at: www.time.com/time/world/article/0,8599,1955424,00.html (accessed 2 January 2012).

Read, B. (2008) 'Property rights and homeowner activism in new neighborhoods'. In: *Privatizing China*, Li Zhang and Aihwa Ong (eds). Ithaca, NY: Cornell University Press, 41–56.

Read, B. (2003) 'Democratizing the neighborhood? New private housing and home-owner self-organization in urban China'. *China Journal*. 49: 31–59.

Redding, G. (2008) 'Separating culture from institutions: the use of semantic spaces as a conceptual domain and the case of China'. *Management and Organization Review*. 42: 257–89.

Redding, G. and Witt, M. (2007) *The Future of Chinese Capitalism*. Oxford: Oxford University Press.

Register, R. (2003) *Ecocities: Rebuilding Cities in Balance with Nature*. Berkeley, CA: Berkeley Hills Books.

Renaud, B., Pretorius, F. and Pasadilla, B. (1997) *Market at Work*. Hong Kong: Hong Kong University Press.

Richardson, G. (2005) 'The prudent village'. *Journal of Economic History*. 652: 386–413.

Ricoeur, P. (2003) 'Note sur Du "Temps", Eléments d'une philosophie du vivre'. In: *Dépayser la pensée*, T. Marchaise (ed.). Paris: Les Empêcheurs de penser en ronde, 211–23.

Rofel, L. (2007) *Desiring China: Experiments in Neoliberalism, Sexuality, and Public Culture*. Durham, NC: Duke University Press.

Rofel, L. (1999) *Other Modernities: Gendered Yearnings in China after Socialism*. Santa Cruz: University of California Press.

Rogers, R. (1998) *Cities for a Small Planet*. London: Icon Editions.

Rooker, T. (2006) *Zhongguancun: The Silicon Valley of China*. Ann Arbor: EMI Dissertations.

Rooker, T. (2011) 'Migrants making technology markets'. In: *The New Blackwell Companion to the City*, G. Bridge and S. Watson (eds). Oxford: Wiley-Blackwell, 193–209.

Rooker, T. (2008) '2008 stock markets and the race to the bottom: 'stuck' in China'. *World Economy and Finance Working Paper*, No. 40.

Rosen, S. and Zweig, D. (2005) 'Transnational capital: valuing academic returnees in a globalizing China'. In: Cheng Li (ed.). *Bridging Minds Across the Pacific: US–China Educational Exchanges, 1978–2003*. Lanham: Lexington, 111–32.

Ross, A. (2006) *Fast Boat to China*. New York: Pantheon Books.

Rost, K. (2010) 'The strength of strong ties in the creation of innovation'. *Research Policy*. 40(4): 588–604.

Rozelle, S. L. G., Shen, M., Hughart, A. and Giles, J. (1999) 'Leaving China's farms: survey results of new paths and remaining hurdles to rural migration'. *The China Quarterly*. 158: 367–93.

Roy, A. (2004) *Urban Informality: Transnational Perspectives from the Middle East, Latin America, and South Asia*. (Co-editor: Nezar Al-Sayyad). Oxford: Lexington Books.

Samuels, T. (1994) 'Traffic expands to fill the available road space: understanding North America's traffic congestion crisis'. The Better Transportation Coalition: Toronto, Ontario, November.

Sanyal, B. (ed.) (2005) *Comparative Planning Cultures*. London: Routledge.

Sassen, S. (1991) *The Global City*. Princeton, NJ: Princeton University Press.

Saunders, D. (2010) *Arrival City*. London: William Heinemann.

Saxenian, A. (2005) 'From brain drain to brain circulation: transnational communities and regional upgrading in India and China'. *Studies in Comparative International Development*. 402: 35–61.

Schmitt, C. (2005) *Political Theology: Four Chapters on the Concept of Sovereignty*. Chicago, IL: University of Chicago Press.

Schumpeter, J. (1994) *History of Economic Analysis*. London: Routledge.

Schumacher, P. (2011) *The Autopoeisis of Architecture*. New York: Wiley.

Schwartz, B. (1985) *World of Thought in Ancient China*. Cambridge, MA: Belknap Harvard.

Scott, R. W. (2008) *Institutions and Organizations*. Los Angeles, CA: Sage.

Sen, A. (1999) *Development as Freedom*. New York: Alfred Knopf.

Sen, A. (2009) *The Idea of Justice*. Harvard University Press; London: Penguin Books.

Sennett, R. (2003) *Flesh and Stone: The Body and the City in Western Civilisation*. London: Faber and Faber.

Shanghai County Statistical Yearbook 1993 (上海县年鉴) (1993) Shanghai: Internal Press (内部铅印本).

Shanghai Statistical Bureau (SSB) (2007–2010) *Shanghai Statistical Yearbook*. Beijing: China Statistical Press. Available at: www.stats-sh.gov.cn (accessed March 2012).

Shanghai Securities Exchange (2008) 'SSE Monthly Report, June 2008'. Available at: www.sse.com.cn/ps/zhs/yjcb/ybtj/sse_stat_monthly_200806.pdf (accessed 1 August 2008).

Shanghai New World Corporation Limited (上海新世界股份有限公司) (1994) '1993 Annual Report Summary for Shanghai New World Corporation' (上海新世界股份有限公司1993年年度报告摘要). Available at: http://share.jinku.com/affiche_article_600628_2601.html (accessed 15 September 2012).

Shanghai Securities Exchange (2008) *Shanghai Securities Exchange Statistical Yearbook (2008 Edition)*. Shanghai: Shanghai Securities Exchange. Available at: www.sse.com.cn/sseportal/ps/zhs/yjcb/yjycb_tjnj.shtml (accessed 1 August 2012).

Shanghai Securities Exchange (2009) *Shanghai Securities Exchange Statistical Yearbook (2009 Edition)*. Shanghai: Shanghai Securities Exchange. Available at: www.sse.com.cn/sseportal/ps/zhs/yjcb/yjycb_tjnj.shtml (accessed 1 August 2012).

Shen, Hsiu-Hua (2005) ' "The first Taiwanese wives" and "the Chinese mistresses": the international division of labour in familial and intimate relations across the Taiwan strait'. *Global Networks*. 4: 419–37.

Shenzhen Securities Exchange (2008a) 'Market statistics monthly report, June 2008'. Available at: www.szse.cn/main/images/2008/07/02/658165533294.html (accessed 1 August 2008).

Shenzhen Securities Exchange (2008b) 'Market statistics monthly report, June 2008'. Available at: www.szse.cn/main/images/2008/07/02/668192946817.html (accessed 1 August 2008).

Shenzhen Securities Exchange (2008c) *Shenzhen Securities Exchange Statistical Yearbook 2008*. Shenzhen: Shenzhen Securities Exchange. Available at: www.szse.cn/main/marketdata/wbw/marketstat/ (accessed 3 August 2012).

Shenzhen Securities Exchange (2009) *Shenzhen Securities Exchange Statistical Yearbook 2008*. Shenzhen: Shenzhen Securities Exchange. Available at: www.szse.cn/main/market data/wbw/marketstat/ (accessed 3 August 2012).

Shenzhen Labor Service (2008) 'Current situation analysis of Shenzhen labor service workers coming from outside' [深圳外来劳务工现状分析]. Available at: http://blog.szu.edu.cn/Attach/90E4303F 9E1D 4D32 808D (accessed August 2011).

Shi, Hanbing 时寒冰 (2006) 'State six articles face the danger of state eight articles' 国六条面临国八条危险. Shanghai Securities News, 15 June.

Shue, E. (1988) *The Reach of the State*. Stanford, CA: Stanford University Press.

Simone, A. (2004) *For the City Yet to Come*. Durham, NC: Duke University Press.

Silverman, D. (1993) *Interpreting Qualitative Data*. London: Sage.

Siu, H. (2007) 'Grounding displacement: uncivil urban spaces in post-reform south China'. *American Ethnologist*. 34(2)May 2007, 329–50.

Skeldon, R. (2008) 'Immigration futures'. *Canadian Diversity*. 3: 12–17.

Slovic, P. (1999) 'Trust, emotion, sex, politics, and science: surveying the risk assessment'. *Risk Analysis*. 191: 689–700.

Smart, A. (2000) 'The emergence of local capitalisms in China: overseas Chinese investment and patterns of development'. Si-ming Li and Wang-shing Tang (eds). Hong Kong: Chinese University Press, 65–95.

Smart, A. and Lin, G. (2007) 'Local capitalisms, local citizenship and translocality: rescaling from below in the pearl river delta region, China'. *International Journal of Urban and Regional Research*. 312: 280–302.

Smith, A. (2002) *The Theory of Moral Sentiments*. Cambridge: Cambridge University Press.

Smith, A. (2008) *The Wealth of Nations*. Radford, VA: Wilder Publications.

So, A. Y. (1988) 'Shenzhen special economic zone: China's struggle for independent development'. *Canadian Journal of Development Studies*, 9(2): 313–23.

Solinger, D. (1995) 'China's urban transients in the transition from socialism and the collapse of the communist "urban public goods regime"'. *Comparative Politics*. 27(2): 127–46.

Solinger, D. (1999) *Contesting Citizenship in Urban China: Peasant Migrations, the State, and the Logic of the Market*. Berkeley, CA: University of California Press.

Solinger, D. (2002) 'Labour market reform and the plight of the laid-off proletariat'. *China Quarterly*. 170: 304–26.

Song, Y.Y. Z. and Ding, C. (2008) 'Let's not throw the baby out with the bath water: the role of urban villages in housing rural migrants in China'. *Urban Studies*. 45(2): 313–30.

Sorel, G. (1999) *Reflections on Violence,* trans. T. E. Hulme. London: Allen and Unwin.

Stark, D. (2009) 'Recombinant property in east European capitalism'. *American Journal of Sociology.* 101(4): 993–1027.

State-Owned Assets Supervision and Administration Commission (2012) 'List of central enterprises' (央企名录). Available at: www.sasac.gov.cn/n1180/n1226/n2425/index. html (accessed 20 June 2012).

Strang, D. and Meyer, J. W. (1993) 'Institutional conditions for diffusion'. *Theory and Society.* 224: 487–511.

Strathern, M. (1992) *The Gender of the Gift.* Berkeley, CA: University of California Press.

Stieglitz, J. (2000) *Economics of the Public Sector.* New York: Norton.

Sudan Divestment Task Force (2007) 'PetroChina, CNPC, and Sudan: Perpetuating Genocide'. Available at: http://home.comcast.net/~berkshire_hathaway/reports/ PetroChina_CNPC_Sudan.pdf (accessed 3 May 2012).

Sun, Y. and Ke Wen (2007) 'Uncertainties, imitative behaviours and foreign R&D location: explaining the over-concentration of foreign R&D in Beijing and Shanghai within China'. *Asia Pacific Business Review.* 133: 405–24.

Sun Guangjing and Liu Xiaoyan (2008) 'Foreigners' employment environment must be improved and employment management strengthened – a survey of the employment situation of foreigners in Weihai'. *Shandong Laodong Baozhang,* 12.

Sustainability Radar (2006) *China Special Issue.* February.

Sun, W. (2009) *Maid in China.* London: Routledge.

Sundaram, R. (2005) *Pirate Modernity. Delhi's Media Urbanism.* London and Delhi: Routledge.

Sutherland, D., Ning, L. and Beatson, S. (2011) 'Productivity performance in Chinese Business groups: the positive and negative impacts of business group affiliation'. *Journal of Chinese Economic and Business Studies,* 9(2): 163–80.

Svetlova, E. and Arnoldi, J. (2011) 'Does performativity matter?' In: IX Conference of the International Network for Economic Methodology. Helsinki, Finland.

SWECO (2009) 'SWECO creates environmentally friendly city in China'. Available at: www.swecogroup.com/en/Sweco-group/Press/News/20091/Category1/Sweco-creates-environmentally-friendly-city-in-China/ (accessed 23 October 2009).

Tanabe, M. (2008) *Fashion Industry and Organisational Culture in Shanghai: The Case of a Taiwanese Multinational Enterprise.* Oxford: University of Oxford.

Tang, Bo-sin and Sing-cheong Liu (2005) 'Property developers and speculative development in China'. In: Chengri Ding and Yan Song (eds). *Emerging Land and Housing Markets in China.* Cambridge: Lincoln Institute of Land Policy.

Tang, Bo-sin and Sing-cheong Liu (2002) 'Property developers and speculative development in China'. Paper presented at Lincoln Institute of Land Policy Conference, Cambridge, March 2002.

Tang, Bo-sin, Siu-wai Wong and Sing-Cheong Liu (2006) 'Property agents, housing markets and housing services in transitional urban China'. *Housing Studies.* 21(6): 799–823.

Tang, W. (2002) 'Political and social trends in the post-deng urban China: crisis or stability?' *China Quarterly.* 168: 890–909.

Tang, W. and Parish, W. (1996) 'Social reaction to reform in urban China'. *Problems of Post-Communism,* 43(6): 35–47.

Tang, Wing-Shing (1994) 'Urban land development under socialism: China between 1949–1977'. *International Journal of Urban and Regional Research.* 18: 395–415.

Tang, Wing-Shing (1998) 'Inquiry into urban land system reforms in Shenzhen'. In: *Development in Asia: Restrospects and Prospects.* Y. M. Yeung (ed.). Hong Kong: Hong Kong Institute of Asia-Pacific Studies, The Chinese University of Hong Kong, 307–40.

Tang, Wing-Shing (2008a) 'China'. In: *Urban Science – Report on a Workshop Series,* A. Haila (ed.). Strasbourg: European Science Foundation, 30–1.

Tang, Wing-Shing (2008b) 'Hong Kong under Chinese sovereignty: social development and a land redevelopment regime'. *Eurasian Geography and Economics*. 49: 341–61.

Tang, Wing-Shing (2009) 'The spatiality of urban land development in China in Chinese'. *Journal of Urban and Regional Planning*. 2: 136–44.

Tang, Wing-Shing and Chung, H. (2002) 'Urban-rural transition in China: illegal land use and construction'. *Asia Pacific Viewpoint*. 431: 43–62.

Tang, W. and Parish, W. L. (1996) 'Social reaction to reform in urban China'. *Problems of Post-Communism*. 436: 35–47.

Taylor, C. (1971) 'Interpretation and the sciences of man'. *Review of Metaphysics*. 25: 3–51.

Thévenot, L. (2001a) 'Conventions of co-ordination and the framing of uncertainty'. In: *Intersubjectivity in Economics*, Edward Fulbrook (ed.). Florence: Routledge, 181–97.

Thévenot, L. (2000) 'Pragmatic regimes governing the engagement with the world'. In: *The Practice Turn in Contemporary Theory*, T. R. Schatzki, K. Knorr Cetina and E. von Savigny (eds). New York: Routledge, 64–83.

Thévenot, L. (2001b) 'Organized Complexity'. *European Journal of Social Theory*. 44: 405–25.

Thrift, N. (2005) *Knowing Capitalism*. London and New York: Sage.

Tian, C. and Hong, Y. (2007) 'Urban land reform and the development of land markets: evidence from Hangzhou'. The 12th Asian Real Estate Society AsRES Annual Conference and the 2007 AREUEA International Conference, July 9–12, Macau. Available at: www.asres2007.umac.mo/papers/182%20-%20PAPER.pdf (accessed 20 May 2012).

Tian, L. (2008) 'The Chengzhongcun land market in China: boon or bane? – a perspective on property rights'. *International Journal of Urban and Regional Research*. 32: 282–304

Tomba, L. (2010) 'Gating urban spaces in China: inclusion, exclusion and government'. In: *Gated Communities*, S. Bagaeen and O. Uduku (eds). London: Earthscan, 27–8.

Tomba, L. (2011) 'Remaking China's working class: *Gongren* and *Nongmingong*' In: *China's Changing Workplace*, Peter Sheldon, Sunghoon Kim, Yiqiong Li and Malcolm Warner (eds). London: Routledge, 144–59.

Townsend R. (1993) *The Medieval Village Economy*. Princeton, NJ: Princeton University Press.

Tribe, K. (1995) *Strategies of Economic Order. German Economic Discourse, 1750–1950*. Cambridge: Cambridge University Press.

Tsai, K. (2004) *Back-Alley Banking: Private Entrepeneurs in China*. Ithaca, NY: Cornell University Press.

Tseng, Y.-F. (2009) 'Emerging career maps in new times: migration patterns of skilled Taiwanese to China'. Paper presented at 'New Times? Economic Crisis, Geo-Political Transformation and the Emergent Migration Order', Centre on Migration, Policy and Society COMPAS annual conference, Oxford, 21–22 September 2009.

Tylor, E. (2010) *Primitive Culture*. Cambridge: Cambridge University Press.

Uehara, Y. (2006) *Casting Village Within City*. In: *Sarai Reader 2006: Turbulence*. 485–96.

Unger, J. and Chan, A. (1999) 'Inheritors of the boom: private enterprise and the role of local government in a rural south China township'. *The China Journal*. 42: 44–74.

Urry, J. (2002) *Global Complexity*. Cambridge: Polity.

Van Horn, R. and Mirowski, P. (2009) 'The rise of the Chicago School of Economics and the birth of neoliberalism'. In: *The Road from Mont Pèlerin: The Making of the Neoliberal Thought Collective,* P. Mirowski and D. Plehwe (eds). Cambridge, MA: Harvard University Press, 139–180.

Vandermeersch, L. (1989) 'Preface to Granet', *La Pensée Chinoise*, M. Granet (ed.). Paris: Albin Michel.

Venables, A. (2010) 'Productivity in cities: self selection and sorting'. Discussion Paper Series University of Oxford Department of Economics.

Virilio, P. (2009) *The Virilio Reader*. Der Derian, J. (ed.). Oxford: Blackwell.

Wakeman, F. (1993a) 'The civil society and public sphere debate: western reflections on Chinese political culture'. *Modern China.* 192: 108–38.

Wakeman, F. (1993b) 'Editor's Foreword'. *Modern China.* 192: 107

Walder, A. (1995) 'Local governments as industrial firms: an organizational analysis of China's transitional economy'. *The American Journal of Sociology.* 101(2): 263–301.

Walder, A. (2010) 'From control to ownership: China's managerial revolution'. *Management and Organization Review.* 71: 19–38.

Walder, A. G. (1993) 'Corporate organization and local government property rights in China'. In: *Changing Political Economies,* Vedat Milor (ed.). Boulder, CO: Lynne Rienner Publishers, 53–66.

Walder, A. (1986) *Communist Neo-Traditionalism: Work and Authority in Chinese Industry.* Berkeley, CA: University of California Press.

Walder, A. (1989) 'Factory and manager in an era of reform'. *China Quarterly.* 118(6): 242–64.

Walter, C. (2011) 'Stock markets and corporate reform: a pandora's box of unintended consequences'. In: *Going Private in China,* J. Oi (ed.). Stanford, CA: Walter H. Shorenstein APARC Centre Books, 203–39.

Wang, Fei-Ling (1998) 'Floaters, moonlighters, and the underemployed: a national labor market with Chinese characteristics'. *The Journal of Contemporary China.* 197: 459–76.

Wang, G. (2000) 'Cultivating Friendship through Bowling in Shenzhen'. In: *The Consumer Revolution in Urban China,* D. Davis (ed.). Berkeley, CA: University of California Press, 250–67.

Wang, H. (1997) 'Contemporary Chinese thought and the question of modernity'. *Social Text,* 55.

Wang, H. (2008) 现代中国思想的兴起。Xiandai zhongguo sixiang de xingqi, *The Rise of Modern Chinese Thought,* Beijing: Sanlian Shudian.

Wang, H. (2009) *The End of the Revolution.* London: Verso.

Wang, H. (2011) *The Politics of Imagining Asia.* Cambridge, MA: Harvard University Press.

Wang, H. (ed.) (2007) *Contemporary Chinese Returnees.* Beijing: Zhongguo Fazhan Chubanshe.

Wang, J. and Lau, S. (2008) 'Forming foreign enclaves in Shanghai: state action in globalization'. *Journal of Housing and the Built Environment.* 232: 103–18.

Wang, J. (2001) 'Culture as leisure culture as capital'. *Positions.* 91: 69–104.

Wang, J., Guthrie, D. and Zhixing Xiao (2012) 'The rise of SASAC: asset management, ownership concentration, and firm performance in China's capital markets'. *Management and Organization Review.* 8(2): 253–81.

Wang, K. (2007) 'Social capital within hierarchical relations in China'. In: *Business Networks and Strategic Alliances in China,* S. Clegg, K. Wang and M. Berrell (eds). Cheltenham: Edwin Elgar, 209–29.

Wang, Lu (2008) 'Only three days of trading remain for southern air JPT1', *Shanghai Securities Journal.* 11 June. Available at: www.cnstock.com/paper_new/html/2008-06/11/content_61940195.htm (accessed 1 July 2008).

Wang, Mark Yaolin and Xiaochen Meng (2004) 'Global-local initiatives in FDI: the experience of Shenzhen, China'. *Asia Pacific Viewpoint.* 452: 181–96.

Wang, X. (2003) 'A manifesto for cultural studies'. In: *One China, Many Paths,* Chaohua Wang (ed.). New York: Verso, 274–91.

Wang, Ya Ping and Murie, A. (1999) 'Commercial housing development in urban China'. *Urban Studies.* 369: 1475–94.

Wang, Ya Ping and Murie, A. (2000) 'Social and spatial implications of housing reform in China'. *International Journal of Urban and Regional Research.* 242: 397–417.

Wang, Yi. (2010) 'The mutual embrace of Yangpu, Shanghai and us'. *Yangpu Times,* January 8: 4-5.

Wank, D. (1999) *Commodifying Communism: Business, Trust, and Politics in a Chinese City.* New York: Cambridge University Press.

Wank, D. (2001) *Commodifying Communism: Business, Trust and Politics in a Chinese City.* Cambridge: Cambridge University Press.

Wank, D. (1996) 'The institutional process of market clientalism: Guanxi and private business in a south China city'. *China Quarterly.* 147: 820–38.

Wasserstrom, J. (2009) *Global Shanghai, 1850–2010.* New York: Routledge.

Watson, J. (2000) 'China's big mac attack'. *Foreign Affairs.* 793: 120–34.

Weber, Elke U. and K. Hsee, C. (1998a) 'Cross-cultural differences in risk perception, but cross-cultural similarities in attitudes towards perceived risk'. *Management Science.* 44(9): 1205–17.

Weber, Elke U. and K. Hsee, C. (1998b) 'What folklore tells us about risk and risk taking: cross-cultural comparisons of American, German, and Chinese proverbs'. *Organizational Behaviour and Human Decision Making.* 752: 170–86.

Weber, Elke U. and Hsee, C. (2000) 'Culture and individual judgment and decision making'. *Applied Psychology: An International Review.* 491: 32–61.

Weber, M. (1976) *Roscher and Knies.* New York: Free Press.

Weber, M. (2012) *Collected Methodological Writings,* H. Bruun and S. Whimster (eds). London: Routledge.

Weber, M. (1958) *The Religion of India.* New York: The Free Press.

Weber, M. (1964) *The Religion of China.* New York: The Free Press.

Weber, M. (1980) *Wirtschaft und Gesellschaft.* Tübingen: J.C.B. Mohr.

Weber, M. (1988) *Gesammelte Aufsätze zur Religionssoziologie I.* Tübingen: J.C.B. Mohr.

Weber, M. (1991) *Max Weber Gesamtausgabe. Studienausgabe: Die Wirtschaftsethik der Welt-religionen. Konfuzianismus und Taoismus: Schriften 1915–1920: Abt. I/19.* Tübingen: Mohr-Siebeck.

Weber, M. (2001) *The Protestant Ethic and the Spirit of Capitalism.* London: Routledge.

Wei Ran and Lin Yingying 蔚然 林颖颖 (2004) 'Shanghai: property brokers at over 100,000, 70% without certification' 上海：房产经纪人高达10万，七成无证. *Wenhui Daily* 文汇报, 1 September. Available at: http://edu.sina.com.cn/l/2004-09-01/82553.html (accessed 12 May 2012).

Weng Li (2006) 'Resident immigrants living peacefully and working happily is an important goal of the harmonious city – enlightenment from Yiwu city's public security work'. *Gong'an xuekan – Zhejiang Gong'an Gaodeng Zhuanke Xuexiao xuebao,* 53: 42–4.

Westphal, J. D. and Fredrickson, J. W. (2001) 'Who directs strategic change? Director experience, the selection of new CEOs, and change in corporate strategy'. *Strategic Management Journal,* 22(12): 1113–37.

White, H. C. (1981) 'Where do markets come from?'. *The American Journal of Sociology.* 873: 517–47.

White, H. C. (1988) 'Varieties of markets'. In: *Social structures: A Network Approach,* B. Wellman and S. D. Berkowitz (eds). New York: Cambridge University Press, 226–60.

White, H. C. (1992) *Identity and Control.* Princeton, NJ: Princeton University Press.

White, H. C. (2002) *Markets from Networks.* Princeton, NJ: Princeton University Press.

White, H. C. (2004) *Markets from Networks.* Princeton, NJ: Princeton University Press.

White, S. (2000) 'Competition, capabilities, and the make, buy, or ally decisions of Chinese state-owned firms'. *Academy of Management Journal.* 433: 324–41.

White, S. (2009) '"Revolutionary liberalism"? The philosophy and politics of ownership in the post-war Liberal party'. *British Politics,* 4(2): 164–87.

Whitehead, A. N. (2011) *Religion in the Making*. Cambridge: Cambridge University Press.

Whitley, R. (1994) *Business Systems in East Asia*. London: Sage.

Whitley, R. (1999) *Divergent Capitalism*. Oxford: Oxford University Press.

Whyte, M. and Parish, W. (1984) *Urban Life in Contemporary China*. Chicago, IL: University of Chicago Press.

Williamson, O. E. (1983) *Markets and Hierachies: Analysis and Antitrust Implications*. New York: Free Press.

Willis, K. and Yeoh, B. (2000) 'Gender and transnational household strategies: Singaporean migration to China'. *Regional Studies*. 343: 253–64.

Willis, K. and Yeoh, B. (2002) 'Gendering transnational communities: a comparison of Singaporean and British migrants in China'. *Geoforum*. 33: 553–65.

Wishnick, E. (2005) 'Migration and economic security: Chinese labour migrants in the Russian far east'. In: *Crossing National Borders: Human Migration Issues in Northeast Asia*, Tsuneo Akaha and Anna Vassilieva (eds). Tokyo: United Nations University Press, 68–92.

Witt, M. (2010) 'China: what variety of capitalism?' *INSEAD Faculty & Research Working Paper* No. 2010/88/EPS. Available at: www.insead.edu/facultyresearch/research/doc.cfm?did=46188 (accessed 20 July 2012).

Wittfogel, K. (1967) *Oriental Despotism*. New Haven, CN: Yale University.

Wittgenstein, L. (1958) *Philosophical Investigations*. Oxford: Blackwell.

Womack, B. (1991) 'Review essay: transfigured community: neo-traditionalism and work unit socialism in China'. *China Quarterly*. 126: 313–32.

Wong, P. P. W. (1991) 'Central-local relations in an era of fiscal decline: the paradox of fiscal decentralization in post-Mao China'. *The China Quarterly*. 128: 691–715.

Wong, S. H. W. (2010) 'Political connections and firm performance: the case of Hong Kong'. *Journal of East Asian Studies*. 102: 275–313.

Wong, S. and Yong Yang (2009) 'From scorned to loved? the political economy of the development of the stock market in China'. *Global Economic Review*. 384: 409–29.

Woodbridge, R. (2004) *The Next World War: Tribes, Cities, Nations and Ecological Decline*. Toronto: University of Toronto Press.

Wright, E. O. (2010) *Envisioning Real Utopias*. London: Verso.

Wu, F. (2002a) 'Real estate development and the transformation of urban space in China's transitional economy with special reference to Shanghai'. In: *The New Chinese City: Globalization and Market Reforms*, Logan, J. (ed.). Oxford: Blackwell.

Wu, F. (2002b) 'China's changing urban governance in the transition towards a more market oriented economy'. *Urban Studies*. 39(7): 1071–93.

Wu, F. (2010) 'How neoliberal is China's reform? The origins of change during transition'. *Eurasian Geography and Economics*. 515: 619–31.

Wu, F. (2005) 'Rediscovering the "gate" under market transition: form work-unit compounds to commodity housing enclaves'. *Housing Studies*. 202: 235–54.

Wu, F. and Webber, K. (2004) 'The rise of "foreign gated communities" in Beijing: between economic globalization and local institutions'. *Cities*. 213: 203–13.

Wu, F. and Yeh, A. G. O. (2007) *Urban Development in Post Reform China: State, Market and Space*. London: Routledge.

Wu, Yanrui (1999) *China's Consumer Revolution*. Cheltenham: Edward Elgar.

Xiang Biao (2000) *A Village Beyond Borders: The Life History of Beijing's Zhejiangcun*. Beijing: Sanlian Press.

Xiang Biao (2005) *Transcending Boundaries. Zhejiangcun: The Story of a Migrant Village in Beijing*. Leiden: Brill.

Xiang Biao (2008) 'A ritual economy of "talent": Chinese and overseas Chinese Professionals'. Centre on Migration, Policy and Society COMPAS Working Paper no. 2, 2008, Oxford.

Xie, Lei (2009) *Environmental Activism in China*. London: Routledge.

Xie Qingshu, Parsa, A.R. and Redding, B. (2002) 'The emergence of the urban land market in China: evolution, structure, constraints and perspectives'. *Urban Studies*. 398: 1375–98.

Xin, K. R. and Pearce, J. L. (1996) 'Guanxi: Connections as substitutes for formal institutional support'. *Academy of Management Journal*. 396: 1641–58.

Xinhua Net 新华网 (n.d.) 'The reform of China land system' 中国土地制度改革. *Party Knowledge* 党的知识. Available at: http://cpc.people.com.cn/GB/64156/64157/4512167.html (accessed 20 May 2012).

Xu, Dean and Shenkar, O. (2002) 'Institutional distance and the multinational enterprise'. *Academy of Management Review*. 274: 608–18.

Xu, Jiang, Yeh, A. and Wu, F. (2009) 'Land commodification: new land development and politics since the late 1990s'. *International Journal of Urban and Regional Research*. 334: 890–913.

Xu Jie and Wang Quanchun (2007) 'The current situation of house rental by foreigners in Beijing and suggestions for countermeasures to perfect the laws and regulations and strengthen management'. *Beijing Renmin Jingcha Xueyuan xuebao*, 48–50.

Yan, Yunxiang (2000) 'Of hamburger and social space: consuming McDonald's in Beijing', In: *The Consumer Revolution in Urban China*, Deborah Davis (ed.). Berkeley, CA: University of California Press, 201–25.

Yang, M. (1994) *Gifts, favors, and banquets: the art of social relationships in China*. Ithaca, NY: Cornell University Press.

Yang, X. (1993) 'Household registration, economic reform and migration'. *The International Migration Review*. 274: 796–818.

Yangcheng Wanbao 羊城晚报 (2001) 'Bo Xilai shocks: what does a mayor manage? Manage a city' 薄熙来一语惊人：市长经营什么？经营城市. 16 May 2001. Available at: http://news.sina.com.cn/c/254225.html (accessed 7 May 2012).

Yangpu District Gazette Editorial Committee (上海市杨浦区志编纂委员会) (1995) *Yangpu District Gazette* (杨浦区志). Shanghai: Shanghai Academy of Social Sciences Press (上海社会科学院出版社).

Yangpu District Statisical Bureau (2008–2010, 2007–2009) 'Statistical Bulletin of Economic and Social Development Yangpu District, City of Shanghai'. Available at: www.shyp.gov.cn (accessed 13 May 2012).

Yaqing, Q. (2011) 'Rule, rules, and relations: towards a synthetic approach to governance'. *Chinese Journal of International Politics*. 42: 117–45.

Yasheng, W. (2008) *The Writing on the Wall*. London: Abacus.

Yeh, A. (2000) 'Foreign investment and urban development in China'. In: *China's Regions, Polity and Economy. A Study of Spatial Transformation I the post-Reform era*, Li, S. and Wing, T. (eds). Hong Kong: The Chinese University of Hong Kong.

Yeh Anthony and Wu, F. (1996) 'The new land development process and urban development in Chinese cities'. *International Journal of Urban and Regional Research*. 202: 330–53.

Yeh, Wen-Hsin (2007) *Shanghai Splendor: Economic Sentiments and the Making of Modern China, 1843–1949*. Berkeley, CA: University of California Press.

Yuan, Victor and Xin Wong (1999) 'Migrant construction teams in Beijing'. In: *Internal and International Migration*, Hein Mallee and Frank Pieke (eds). Richmond, Surrey: Curzon Press, 103–18.

Yue, S. (2004) 'Laowai lai Shanghai zhao "ganjue" Foreigners are coming to Shanghai in search of "feelings"'. *Huaren shikan*. 12–13.

Zaheer, S. (1995) 'Overcoming the liability of foreignness'. *Academy of Management Journal*. 382: 341–63.

Zeng, J. and Kellee Tsai (2011) 'The local politics of restructuring state-owned enterprises in China'. In: *Going Private in China*, J. Oi (ed.). Stanford, CA: Walter H. Shorenstein Asia-Pacific Research Centre Books, 39–69.

Zhai, Guofang and Takeshi Suzuki (2009) 'Risk perception in northeast Asia'. *Environmental monitoring and assessment*. 1571–4: 151–67.

Zhang, Li (2001) *Strangers in the City: Reconfigurations of Space, Power, and Social Networks within National Bureau of Statistics Population*. Stanford, CA: Stanford University Press.

Zhang, Li (2008) 'Ethnic congregation in a globalizating city: the case of Guangzhou, China'. *Cities*. 256: 383–95.

Zhang, Li (2008) 'Private homes, distinct lifestyles: performing a new middle class' In: *Privatizing China*, Li Zhang and Aihwa Ong (eds). Ithaca, NY: Cornell University Press, 23–40.

Zhang, Li (2010) *In Search of Paradise*. Ithaca: Cornell University Press.

Zhang, T. (2000) 'Land market forces and government's role in sprawl'. *Cities*. 172: 123–35.

Zhang, L. (1992) *The Tao and the Logos*. Durham, NC: Duke University Press.

Zhang, Li and Aihwa Ong (eds) (2008) *Privatizing China: Socialism from Afar*. Ithaca, NY: Cornell University Press.

Zhang, T. (2002) 'Urban development and a socialist pro-growth coalition in Shanghai'. *Urban Affairs Review*. 37: 475–99.

Zhang, Z. (2006) '17 Years of China's stock markets [*Zhongguo gushi 17 nian*]', *Value Magazine*, September 2006.

Zhao, D. (2001) *The Power of Tiananmen: State-Society Relations and the 1989 Beijing Student Movement*. Chicago, IL: University of Chicago Press.

Zhao, J. (2012) 'Revealed! Salary threshold for living comfortably in big cities'. *Shanghai Dialy*, 23 October, A4.

Zhao Xiaohui and Tao Junjie (2008) 'The hyping of the "doomsday theory" for southern air warrant appears again, Guotai Jun'an restricts buying in *Nanhang quanzheng zaixian "morilun", Guotai junan xianzhi mairu*', *Xinhua Net*, 5 June 2008, Available at: http://ticket.cnfol.com/080605/165,1610,4249975,00.shtml (accessed 1 July 2008).

Zheng, Siqi Zheng, Fenjie Long, C. Cindy Fan and Yizhen Gu (2009) 'Urban villages in China: a survey of migrant settlements in Beijing'. *Eurasian Geography and Economics*. 50(4): 425–46.

Zheng, Tiantian (2007) 'From peasant women to bar hostesses: an ethnography of China's karaoke sex industry'. In: *Working in China*, Ching Kwan Lee (ed.). London: Routledge, 124–144.

Zhou Liquan (周立权) (2008) '"Big brother role model 777" sentences to 3 years imprisonment' ('带头大哥777'被判3年有期徒刑). *China Securities Journal*, 24 May.

Zhou, R. (2006) '"Urban villages" reminders of uneven growth'. *China Daily*. Available at: www.chinadaily.com.cn/opinion/2006-01/14/content_536996.htm (accessed 15 March 2011).

Zhou, Xueguang, Qiang Li, Wei Zhao and He Cai (2003) 'Embeddedness and contractual relationships in China's transitional economy'. *American Sociological Review*. 681: 75–102.

Zhu, J. (2002) 'Urban development under ambiguous property rights – a case of China's transition economy'. *International Journal of Urban and Regional Research*. 26(1): 41–57.

Zhu, J. (2000) 'Urban physical development in transition to market'. *Urban Affairs Review*. 362: 178–96.

Zhu, J. (2004) 'From land use right to land development right: institutional change in China's urban development'. *Urban Studies*. 417: 1249–67.

Zhu, J. (1999) 'Local growth coalition: the context and implications of Chinas gradualist urban land reforms'. *International Journal of Urban and Regional Research*. 233: 534–48.

Zhuang, H. (2007) 'Management of "three illegal" foreigners tests the government's capacity'. *Renmin gong'an*. 5: 28–9.

Zweig, D., Changgui Chen and Rosen, S. (2004) 'Globalization and transnational human capital: overseas and returnee scholars to China'. *China Quarterly*. 179: 735–57.

INDEX